D1083384

BACH'S
MUSICAL
UNIVERSE

Johann Sebastian Bach, oil portrait by E. G. Haußmann (1748).
Bach-Museum, Leipzig.

BACH'S MUSICAL UNIVERSE

The Composer and His Work

CHRISTOPH WOLFF

W. W. NORTON & COMPANY

Independent Publishers Since 1923

For information about permission to reproduce selections from
this book, write to Permissions, W. W. Norton & Company, Inc.,
500 Fifth Avenue, New York, NY 10110.

For information about special discounts for bulk purchases,
please contact W. W. Norton Special Sales at specialsales@wwnorton.com
or 800-233-4830

Manufacturing by LSC Communications, Harrisonburg
Book design by JAM Design
Production manager: Anna Oler

Library of Congress Cataloging-in-Publication Data

Names: Wolff, Christoph, author.
Title: Bach's musical universe : the composer and his work / Christoph Wolff. |
Includes bibliographical references and index.
Identifiers: LCCN 2019045952 | ISBN 9780393050714 (hardcover) |
ISBN 9780393651799 (epub)
Subjects: LCSH: Bach, Johann Sebastian, 1685–1750—Criticism and interpretation.
Classification: LCC ML410.B13 W63 2020 | DDC 780.92—dc23
LC record available at https://lccn.loc.gov/2019045952

W. W. Norton & Company, Inc., 500 Fifth Avenue, New York, N.Y. 10110
www.wwnorton.com

W. W. Norton & Company Ltd., 15 Carlisle Street, London W1D 3BS

1 2 3 4 5 6 7 8 9 0

CONTENTS

GENERAL ABBREVIATIONS

- BWV = *Bach-Werke-Verzeichnis* (see Bibliography).

- BWV 00/0 = BWV 00, movement 0 (e.g., BWV 38/6 = BWV 38, movement 6).

- BWV 00.0 = BWV 00, version 1, 2, etc. (e.g., BWV 782.2 = BWV 782, second version).

- Major keys are at times notated as capital letters, minor keys as lowercase (A = A major, b = B minor).

LIST OF ILLUSTRATIONS

PREFACE

The title "Bach's Musical Universe" is intended to signal that this book will pursue a path quite distinct from the conventional "composer and his work" approach. A critical examination of the entirety of Johann Sebastian Bach's musical output would only be a frustrating exercise in futility. The composer left such an astonishingly rich legacy of music that no single study could adequately address and cope with all of his works. Out of sheer necessity, then, I have decided to focus on a limited but highly significant array of works, a selection unlike any other made before. Studies of Bach's music are customarily organized around compositions of similar kinds, in the same or related genres, or from within the same time period. The selection made for this book, however, cuts across the conventional boundaries, and has in a sense been determined by the composer himself. Throughout his creative life, Bach methodically organized certain works of exemplary status, unique features, and innovative character in carefully designed collections, manuscript fair copies, and publications. These benchmark works, all of them without parallel or equivalent, introduced an extraordinary succession of highly original creations that were clearly meant to stand as paradigms of his musical art. They reveal an inquisitive and constantly searching musical mind that never lost the sense of discovery, and as such they present perhaps the most powerful and authentic musical autobiography imaginable.

Emerging from an extensive and highly complex oeuvre, a remarkable array of compositions—from the early set of six keyboard toccatas through the late *Art of Fugue* and *B-minor Mass*—metaphorically offer a vision of discernible planets within the greater firmament of Bach's music, distinctly organized units that illustrate the composer's sense of variety and the grasp for breadth and depth as his musical universe steadily unfolded. Largely independent of the external course of his life, Bach's universe resembles a grand cosmos wherein his boundless musical ideas all find their places. I will leave it at that and not push the metaphor any further into asteroids, black holes, and other regions of astronomy.

Another aspect of this book concerns its relationship to the long and abundant heritage of Bach studies. For all of the works and collections considered here, there are multiple dedicated monographs, book chapters, scholarly articles, and concise introductions available. Many of these have guided generations of Bach researchers and enthusiasts, with more recent publications continuing to inform and inspire up to the present moment. Yet all these various publications could not be listed in the bibliography at the end of this book, except for a few that specifically required mention. I am pursuing, in effect, an independent meta-study, whose primary intent is to focus on distinct overarching designs that are discernible within Bach's superabundant musical output. Such an essentially synoptic approach to Bach's oeuvre puts into sharper view the composer's inquisitive musical mind, which produced such a remarkably steady stream of transformational works.

For all the compositions under consideration, this volume considers aspects of genesis (with an emphasis on primary sources), salient musical features, and other essential facets of historical import and general consequence. I have also included concise illustrative tables for collections and individual pieces, designed for convenient reference and informative overview. Yet the chapters and sections of this book cannot fully live up to the music itself: they do not aspire to present detailed analyses, nor are they meant to supplant existing critical introductions to the works under consideration. Instead, they complement what is available in existing literature. In this book, I have drawn freely on my earlier writings, teachings, and research, but in conceiving its focus and thrust I primarily intended that it supplement and complete the picture offered in my biographical study, *Johann Sebastian Bach: The Learned Musician* (Norton, 2000).

Although the present study relates closely to the earlier book, my Bach biography is referenced only occasionally, vis-à-vis specific biographical information and other essentials. In general, any Bach biography can provide sufficient background. Important dates are presented in a brief synopsis at the end of this volume. Since Bach scores are readily available, musical examples have been kept to a minimum. Facsimiles of original sources provide much supplemental information regarding the chosen works, and draw the reader closer into their historical context. The facsimile pages reproduced in this book are extensively complemented by *Bach digital*, the comprehensive digital library of Bach manuscripts made available by the Leipzig Bach Archive, which provides navigation instructions in English (www.bach-digital.de). For searching secondary literature, readers might find useful the Bach Bibliography Online (www.bach-bibliographie.de), maintained by the Leipzig Bach Archive as well.

The pieces discussed here are identified by the numbers of the systematic-thematic catalog of Bach's works: the *Bach-Werke-Verzeichnis*, abbreviated BWV. These numbers readily facilitate searches for the pertinent scores and musical editions, as well as for the ample variety of recorded examples that exist for virtually every Bach composition. The most recent version of this indispensable reference manual, the thoroughly revised third edition of the BWV (issued under the auspices of the Leipzig Bach Archive), includes up-to-date information on every individual work, informed by the most recent scholarship.

The numerous illustrations and various tables in the book serve special purposes. Images of autograph fair copies and original prints document the weight the composer attached to his benchmark works, while autograph composing scores reflect the scrupulous care with which he approached his major projects. Other manuscript copies, which generally play a significant role in the transmission and preservation of Bach's music, offer further supportive evidence in this regard. The tables, on the other hand, provide basic outlines of contents and structures of the exemplary collections and the large-scale individual works, such as the Passion oratorios. In some cases, notably in Chapter 8, they are also meant to unburden the running text from more complex analytical or other details and issues, while being available for those who wish to delve more deeply into such aspects.

One of the most important and indeed pleasant functions of a preface consists in expressing gratitude to friends, colleagues, and institutions who have provided essential assistance at various stages in the preparation of this book. I place Michael Ochs, former Harvard music librarian and retired music editor at W. W. Norton, at the very top of the list. He commissioned the current project and its forerunner, my Bach biography. I am pleased that he continued to serve as a wise and encouraging editorial guide for this book. At the same time, I am sorry about having let him wait for the manuscript for many more years than I ever intended. I think, however, that the additional time invested has only had a positive influence on the conceptualization of the book's structure and contents.

Key experiences in an academic career include those special moments when a teacher realizes that he can learn from his doctoral students. There was a happy recurrence of this experience when I received the most welcome feedback on my manuscript from two former Harvard mentees, long since academics in their own right: Jay Panetta read every word, suggested adjustments of various sorts, and made sure that the arguments always remained on course; Peter Wollny came up with many a good point and made sure in particular that I did not miss the latest relevant wrinkle in current Bach scholarship. I am deeply indebted to both of them.

I gratefully benefitted from much general and technical support that I received from the Leipzig Bach Archive, which I had the privilege of presiding over part-time for more than a dozen years. Peter Wollny, its current director, generously made the institutional facilities available to me, and Christine Blanken, the good fairy of *Bach digital*, efficiently provided the digital files for the bulk of the illustrations in this book. Furthermore, I am most grateful to the various libraries that readily gave permission for reproductions from their holdings, above all to the Music Department of the Staatsbibliothek zu Berlin–Preußischer Kulturbesitz and its director, Martina Rebmann.

I also wish to thank the engaging staff of my New York publisher W. W. Norton, notably my editor, Quynh Do, and her capable team, for seeing this book through its production phase. Jodi Beder deserves special mention in this context; I gratefully acknowledge her expert, thoughtful, and constructive copyediting.

Finally, there is the one person who is already mentioned in the preface of my first book from more than fifty years ago: my dear wife Barbara, critical reader of all my writings. She merits a particular place of honor here, and once again I thank her deeply and profusely for her patience, support, and love.

C. W.

BACH'S
MUSICAL
UNIVERSE

On the Primacy and Pervasiveness of Polyphony

The Composer's Business Card

S eventeenth- and eighteenth-century composers and music theorists vig-
orously debated the general principles of musical composition, but they
rarely if ever recorded reflections on creative motivations, artistic aims,
and aesthetic priorities. We search in vain for discussions of individual compositional approaches, imaginative choices, and distinctive preferences—indeed,
for all the elements of artistic originality. How, then, can we determine the
essence of Johann Sebastian Bach's art of musical composition?

An inveterate practitioner of his art, Bach articulated his views as a composer almost exclusively through his works, that is, in purely musical terms
rather than in words. Despite his role as a devoted and inspiring teacher,
which made him one of the busiest and most influential musical educators
of all time, he was notoriously reluctant to write about his life and work. He
never followed up on a request from Johann Mattheson, made in 1717, for an
autobiographical note.[1] Likewise, in 1738 he left it to his friend Johann Abraham Birnbaum to answer Johann Adolph Scheibe's critical remarks about his
"turgid and confused style" resulting from "an excess of art."[2]

Bach's preference for letting the music itself speak for him is emphatically
evident in the only authentic likeness to have survived, the oil portrait painted

FIGURE P-1

Triple canon for six voices, BWV 1076: detail from oil portrait of J. S. Bach
by E. G. Haußmann (1748).

by Elias Gottlob Haußmann when the composer was in his early sixties (see
Frontispiece).[3] Painter of the Leipzig town council, Haußmann created many
portraits of various Leipzig officials, always showing them in more or less the
same standard pose. Bach's portrait does not differ substantially, except in one
detail: he is identified as a musician by a piece of music he holds in his hand
(see Fig. P-1). Bypassing the typical conventions for musicians' portraits, Bach
opted out of the traditional cantor and capellmeister posture, which depicts
the subject clasping a scroll of music for the purpose of conducting. He also
did not want to be shown as a performer with his instrument, though this
would have been particularly appropriate considering that throughout his lifetime Bach was most widely recognized and admired as a brilliant organist and
keyboard virtuoso.[4] Instead, he faces the viewer and presents a small sheet of
music, just as he might proffer a business card listing his name and profession.

If the analogy of a painted business card seems inappropriate or far-
fetched, we need only contemplate its paper version (see Fig. P-2). Engraved
on duodecimo-sized paper (imprint size 3.2" × 4") is the very same "Canon
triplex à 6 Voc:" (triple canon for six voices)—the only such individual print
ever published by Bach and the model for the painting's detail. Originally

FIGURE P-2

Triple canon for six voices, BWV 1076: original print (Leipzig, 1747).

composed neither for the portrait nor for the separate print, the canon was selected from the series of *Fourteen Canons*, BWV 1087,[5] on the ground bass of the aria of the *Clavier-Übung*, part IV ("Goldberg Variations") published in 1741 (see Chapter 8).

Bach had the single canon printed in 1747 for distribution among the members of the Corresponding Society of Musical Sciences, which he joined in the same year. He decided to introduce himself to the membership of this learned society, founded by his former student Lorenz Christoph Mizler, by placing copies of the canon in one of the Society's regular circulating parcels. As the members lived far apart from one another—for example, George Frideric Handel in London, Georg Philipp Telemann in Hamburg, and Meinrad Spieß in Irsee, Swabia—the organization functioned as a corresponding society. Its principal means of communication consisted, according to its statutes, in circulating parcels (*Zirkular-Pakete*) for the mutual exchange of papers and compositions, assembled by the secretary Mizler and shipped twice a year. The parcel was sent to the first member on the list, who then posted it along to the next, and so on.

Mizler reprinted Bach's canon at the end of the composer's obituary in the *Musikalische Bibliothek* (Leipzig, 1754), where he noted,

In the fifth parcel of the Society the late Capellmeister Bach presented a triple fugue [circular canon] for resolution.[6]

This very parcel is expressly mentioned in a letter of October 23, 1747, from Mizler to the composer-theorist Spieß, prior of the Benedictine abbey in Irsee:

The last parcel, however, which was posted already on May 29 of this year, has not come back yet, and I don't know where it rested so long. You will receive it from Mr. Bach.[7]

The copy eventually obtained by Father Spieß from the circular parcel happens to be one of only two surviving exemplars from the original print run.[8]

The seemingly unimposing little score of the canon, and its double exposure in painted and printed form, raise a question regarding its function as a deliberate projection of Bach's self-image. By combining the likeness of the composer with his creative work, the portrait painting makes a particularly strong statement. Mildly and quite benevolently smiling, Bach seems to declare, "This is who I am, and this is what I stand for: the art of contrapuntal polyphony." Quietly, proudly, and perhaps not devoid of a touch of arrogance, he challenges the viewer to figure out how this enigmatic three-line score can resolve in a perpetual triple canon for six voices.

The use of a canon for identifying a portrait sitter as musician is by no means unique. The space-saving notation in encrypted form permits a canon to represent a complete if short polyphonic setting, and as such canons can be found in various depictions, notably of seventeenth-century musicians.[9] In portraits, they are customarily placed either as labels or as emblematic inscriptions, usually detached physically from the sitter. The Haußmann painting, however, includes the canon as an integral element of an active gesture on the part of the musician portrayed.

The unusual canon specimen features a number of qualities, as indicated by its heading. The title "Canon triplex à 6 voc[ibus]" suggests both a triple canon and a six-part setting, yet neither entry points for the canonic voices nor any other specific clues for resolving the enigmatic notation are given. How can each of the three voices generate its canonic answer or counterpoint, such that the combination of three two-part canons may add up to a full score of six voices? The canon heading itself does not reveal that the little piece is not merely a simple triple canon, but is in fact an invertible or mirror canon as suggested by the two ways of looking at it, from the viewer's perspective and the presenter's, or Bach's, angle (see Diagram P-1 and Ex. P-1). In other words, the implied canonic counterpoints generated by each of the three notated voices in alto, tenor, and bass clefs (=1a–3a) must be derived from their individual melodic inversions and read in soprano, alto, and tenor clefs (=1b–3b). The canon as such has long been resolved,[10] but most often it is

DIAGRAM P-1

Canon triplex inversus, resolved.

VIEWER'S READING	PRESENTER'S READING	RESOLUTION
staff 1a. (A:) ccccc	staff 3b. (S:) ɔɔɔɔɔɔ	staff 3b. (S:) ɔɔɔɔɔɔ
staff 2a. (T:) ccccc	staff 2b. (A:) ɔɔɔɔɔɔ	staff 1a. (A:) ccccc
staff 3a. (B:) ccccc	staff 1b. (T:) ɔɔɔɔɔɔ	staff 2b. (A:) ɔɔɔɔɔɔ
		staff 2a. (T:) ccccc
		staff 1b. (T:) ɔɔɔɔɔɔ
		staff 3a. (B:) ccccc
S, A, T, B: parts read in soprano, alto, tenor, and bass clefs		

notated as a six-part score consisting of three canonic pairs without regard for its completely invertible design. Yet the full intended resolution is produced only through the simultaneous reading of the visible three-part score (1a–3a) and its imagined upside-down image (1b–3b), with the proper clefs (implied but not indicated): soprano (for the bottom part), alto (for the middle part), and tenor (for the top part). This results in an optimally spaced, melodically equalized, and musically effective presentation of the score:

* by reading score upside-down

EXAMPLE P-1

Triple canon, BWV 1076, resolved.

By emphasizing the clearly distinct functions of the three voices in their proper rhythmic-melodic balancing and harmonic spacing, the canon unmistakably defines the essence of a contrapuntal setting and thereby illuminates the nature of music. The canon's score repeats in musical notation what Bach had expressed in 1738 in the words of his friend and mouthpiece Johann Abraham Birnbaum regarding "the nature of music":

> This [i.e., the nature of music] consists of harmony. The harmony becomes far more perfect [*weit vollkommener*] if all voices collaborate. Accordingly, this is not a failing but rather a musical perfection.[11]

This statement was made in refutation of Johann Adolph Scheibe's critique of Bach's scores as lacking a "principal voice" [*Hauptstimme*] and "making all voices . . . collaborate with equal difficulty"[12]—a remark that prompted Bach's definition of musical perfection as the ultimate goal of his efforts. At the same time, he also placed himself in the time-honored tradition of contrapuntal polyphony when suggesting that one could

> look into the works of Praenestinus [Palestrina], among the old composers, or [Antonio] Lotti among the more modern ones, and he will find not only that all the voices are continuously at work but also that each one has a melody of its own that harmonizes quite well with the others.[13]

While Bach's canon in its notated three-part score points at the essence of simple counterpoint, in which each voice indeed has "a melody of its own," the six-part resolution then defines double counterpoint. Double or invertible counterpoint involves the principle of placing the lower voice above the higher and vice versa, with the new structure remaining harmonically correct. Since BWV 1076 involves the exchange of all three voices, the canon demonstrates simultaneously the categories of double, triple, and quadruple counterpoint. When all three notated voices and their respective mirrored versions are placed above one another other (see Diagram P-1 and Ex. P-1) they result in a perfectly harmonious setting in quadruple counterpoint, and thus provide a true sample of Bach's ideal of musical perfection.

In addition to its sophisticated multilayered polyphonic configuration, the miniature piece of two measures' length has an emblematic meaning as well. First of all, the open and unambiguous reference of the bass part to the monumental "Goldberg" variation cycle of the *Clavier-Übung* functions as a proud self-reference to the clavier virtuoso and the performer-composer, who had moved the art of the keyboard conceptually and technically to unprecedented and unparalleled heights. The middle part quotes the subject of Johann Caspar Ferdinand Fischer's Fugue in E from *Ariadne Musica* (1702), transposed to G—the same subject Bach used in slightly modified rhythmic form for the E-major Fugue, BWV 878/2, in part II of the *Well-Tempered Clavier*. This reference underscores the independence of the middle part's melody as counterpoint and, at the same time, its historic origin in seventeenth-century keyboard music[14] as well as its link to the revolutionary achievements of the *Well-Tempered Clavier*. The top voice of the three-part score, as the only freely invented and least melodious counterpoint, provides a crucial rhythmic spark and thereby gives the little setting its needed balance without any further implications. The eight "fundamental notes" of the Goldberg aria, on the other hand, represent a double reference because of its borrowing from Handel (Chapter 5, 185), who was in fact one of the recipients of the fifth circular packet of the Society of Musical Sciences, which included Bach's canon leaf. Thus, the canon may well be understood as including a friendly nod toward the London composer, perhaps combined with a subtle critique of the meek two-part canon at the conclusion of the latter's Chaconne in G major with 62 variations, HWV 442, constructed over the same notes. At any rate, the six-part canon shared with the Society's membership definitely conformed to the goals formulated in its statutes of 1746, among them "the renewal of the majesty of ancient music,"[15] even if that may not have been Bach's primary motivation.

What, then, is the primary message of Bach's portrait and business card? Above all, they both identify him as a composer. Despite its hints at the *Goldberg Variations* and the *Well-Tempered Clavier*, the canon *per se* clearly downplays the performer, as does the Haußmann portrait—by not showing the sitter holding a sheet of virtuoso keyboard music and by not placing him at an organ or harpsichord. It seems as if Bach sought to counter his predominant public image as a virtuoso performer, which was still echoed in the headline of his obituary with the placement of "world-famous organist" ahead of his court title.[16] Bach wished to be viewed primarily as a composer, and understood as an expert in the art of learned polyphony. The canon symbolizes and stands *pars pro toto* for the one area in music where, at the end of a long career, he believed himself to have made a difference: contrapuntal polyphony, in its primacy and its pervasiveness. The canon implies two further points. First, as a six-part composition and the only such setting from the set of *Fourteen Canons*, it emphasizes the author's expertise in all-embracing multi-voiced polyphony (*Vollstimmigkeit*), well beyond the standard four-part texture. Second, the canon's enigmatic notation symbolically refers to the "hidden secrets of harmony" to be discovered in the process of composition and brought to life in an artful manner.

Both points were specifically addressed in the first appraisal of the composer as it appeared in the abovementioned obituary.[17] Dating from the fall of 1750, shortly after the composer's death on July 28, it was written by Carl Philipp Emanuel Bach, second son of the deceased, in collaboration with his younger colleague and the future leader of the Berlin court capelle, Johann Friedrich Agricola, one of Bach's most eminent pupils. Agricola was responsible for the general evaluation of the composer's achievements that follows the biographical section of the obituary. Needless to say, eulogies require words of praise, and there is no lack of adulatory sentiments. Despite this tendency, Agricola's précis of Bach's art presents a remarkable summary, and it is safe to assume that its overall sentiments met with the approval of Bach's son. The first paragraph deals with compositional issues and reads (emphases added):

> If ever a composer showed **all-embracing polyphony** [*Vollstimmigkeit*] in its greatest strength, it was certainly our late lamented Bach. If ever a musician employed **the most hidden secrets of harmony** with the most skilled artistry, it was certainly our Bach. No one ever showed so many **ingenious and unusual ideas** as he **in elaborate pieces** such as ordinarily seem dry exercises in craftsmanship. He needed only to have heard any theme to be aware—in the first instant—of almost every intricacy that artistry could produce in its treatment. His **melodies** were **unusual** (*fremd*) to be sure, but always **varied, rich in invention,** and **resembling those of no other composer.** His serious temperament drew him by preference to music that was serious, elaborate, and profound, but he could also, when the occasion demanded, adjust himself, especially in playing, to a lighter and more humorous way of thought. His constant practice in the working out of polyphonic pieces [*vollstimmige Stücke*] had given his eye such facility that even in the largest scores he could take in all the simultaneously sounding parts at a glance.[18]

This passage is relevant for understanding what is unique about Bach's art and apparently coincides with the specific terminology, principles, and artistic prerogatives within the ultimate goals of his instructional practice as had been personally experienced by Agricola. Moreover, the first two sentences seem to represent a quasi-commentary on Bach's business card:

"all-embracing polyphony"

The German term *Vollstimmigkeit* is not identical with polyphony (*Mehrstimmigkeit*), and it has no proper English equivalent. *Vollstimmigkeit* describes a texture comprising simultaneous independent melodic lines, perhaps best rendered by the phrase "all-embracing polyphony"[19] purposefully applied "in its greatest strength." While an imaginative and ingenious combining, shaping, and weaving of voices constitutes Bach's style in general, this kind of polyphony implies two complementary types of setting. First, it alludes to a multi-voiced setting beyond the standard four-part texture, as the deliberate choice of a six-part canon for the composer's portrait and his business card demonstrates. Indeed, large polyphonic scores of five, six, seven, or more contrapuntal parts were a Bach specialty, the specific challenges of which he discussed in his later years with some advanced pupils, as we find documented by Agricola's notes (see page 286). Second, by extension, the concept of all-embracing polyphony includes the pervasive application of polyphonic techniques and textures as well as strains of contrapuntal material in typically non-polyphonic genres, so as to make one-, two-, or three-part scores sound complete and not lacking anything in the fullness of their sound. In other words, all-embracing polyphony encompasses even single-voice instrumental melodies or two-part scores as long as they establish perfect harmony.

"the most hidden secrets of harmony"

Bach's approach to composition entailed first and foremost the elaboration of musical ideas neither primarily nor exclusively as a free creative act, but rather as a process of imaginative research into the innate harmonic and contrapuntal potential of the chosen material. This veritable lifelong passion traces back to the formative years of the essentially self-taught Bach, for whom the engagement in musical composition by around 1714 had become an absorbing question to discover just what was possible. Hence, the contrapuntal elaboration of a theme presented from the outset the challenge of uncovering its latent harmonic qualities, such that in the final setting all parts would work "wonderfully in and about one another, but without the slightest confusion."[20] It would therefore genuinely represent unity in diversity, or what Bach considered "musical perfection," and also include a religious dimension. As Georg Venzky, a fellow member of the Society of Musical Sciences, put it:

> God is a harmonic being. All harmony originates from his wise order and organization. [. . .] Where there is no conformity, there is also no order, no beauty, and no perfection. For beauty and perfection consists in the conformity of diversity.[21]

Nevertheless, the "hidden secrets" as objects were of less interest to Bach the pragmatist than the vital and crucial aspiration of bringing them "into the most artful execution" and without making them sound like "dry exercises." Agricola may have remembered this point as a warning Bach issued to his students.

"unusual melodies" and "ingenious ideas"

The rich invention and design of Bach's "unusual melodies" and his "ingenious ideas" (*Gedanken*) were shaped by a conscious regard for their inherent potential for elaboration. The two points made by Agricola complement each other. Again, they connect with Bach the composition teacher's own view, and reinforce the testimony of Carl Philipp Emanuel Bach when he brings up "the invention of ideas" as a decisive criterion by which his father identified a promising composition student. "He required it from the very beginning, and anyone who had none he advised to stay away from composition altogether."[22]

The specific allusion to "unusual melodies resembling those of no other composer" is by all accounts Agricola's most uncommon and exceptional observation—indeed, it is a statement about artistic originality without precedent or parallel. Prior to 1750 no musical oeuvre had ever been thus described, and the allegation indicates that the authors of the obituary, with their broad knowledge of historical and contemporary musical repertoire, were intensely aware of the high degree of originality and individuality of Bach's music, which stood apart in so many ways from that of his contemporaries.

Bach was not only aware of these judgments himself, he actually underscored the difference when he described his church cantatas in a 1736 letter as "incomparably harder and more intricate."[23] He realized, of course, that no other composer had written anything like the *Well-Tempered Clavier*, the unaccompanied violin and cello solos, the double-choir *St. Matthew Passion*, or the concertos for one and more keyboards, to mention but a few. Even if the concept of originality and individuality—in contrast to the more general notions of amenity, beauty, artfulness, and the like—played no role in aesthetics during his lifetime, Bach self-consciously and without compromise cultivated this important facet of his personal style.

It remains astonishing how aptly Agricola's précis of 1750, written only months after the completion of Bach's lifework, captures some of the most essential components of his teacher's musical art. Having examined and copied many of Bach's works, he knew the music particularly well, but he was also aware of the often exceptional demands the composer made of his musicians. Agricola was referring to this problem when he wrote,

> His [Bach's] hearing was so fine that he was able to detect the slightest error even in musical pieces involving the largest ensembles [*vollstimmigsten Musiken*]. It is but a pity that it was only seldom that he had the good fortune of finding for his works enough such performers as could have spared him these grumpy remarks [*diese verdrießlichen Bemerkungen*].[24]

Bach himself, obviously aware of the difficulties the execution of his music presented to performers, considered it of absolutely crucial importance for understanding and judging the works that the written scores be studied:

> It is true, one does not judge a composition principally and predominantly by the impression of its performance. But if such judgment, which indeed may be deceiving, is not to be considered, I see no other way of judging than to view the work as it has been set down in notes.[25]

The performer-composer knew well that only the written score represented a reliable documentation of his ideas, and Bach's notorious inclination for corrections and revisions compounded the significance he attached to the written text. Yet what appears to be a phrase of self-evident truth was by no means customary in the discourse of eighteenth-century music criticism. The call "to view the work as it has been set down in notes" as the point of departure for the process of judging sounds like an echo from Bach's groundbreaking teaching studio: the composer instructing his pupils to analyze the music set before them.

The same echo actually embraces the beholder of the Haußmann portrait and the reader of Bach's business card. The perpetual triple canon, the music of which never ends unless deliberately stopped, is not offered for performance but instead invites serious contemplation about what the composer had in mind when, at the end of a long creative life, he chose to introduce himself to present and future friends with a little musical piece that symbolized what he stood for: the art of contrapuntal polyphony and its primacy and pervasiveness in his musical thinking. Ingeniously conceived and profoundly designed, the little canon does serve as an enlightening flash, but it can in no way adumbrate or epitomize, let alone adequately speak for, Bach's musical lifework.

CHAPTER 1

Revealing the Narrative of a Musical Universe

The First List of Works from 1750

The obituary for Johann Sebastian Bach was commissioned by Lorenz Christoph Mizler, editor of the *Musikalische Bibliothek*, from Bach's second-oldest son, Carl Philipp Emanuel, who shared the task with his Berlin colleague Johann Friedrich Agricola: the latter contributed at the end a general assessment of his much admired teacher's accomplishments, while Carl himself focused on the considerably more extensive opening biography.[1]

Ever since the obituary's publication, the biographical section, with its many unique details and also its numerous omissions, has played a crucial and significant role in the evolving narrative of the composer's life. A two-page catalog—enclosed between the story of the composer's professional and family life and Agricola's summary appraisal—provides an overview, and stands as the first public announcement of Johann Sebastian Bach's creative lifework. This is the least often utilized part of the obituary (Fig. 1-1). Yet it is not placed at the end as an appendix, but rather at the center of the obituary. Its opening phrase, "the works we owe to this great composer are the following," suggests that the Bach son felt the awe-inspiring weight of the inheritance—partly in its sheer quantity but more so in its diversity, substance, and exceptionality.

Whether or not the Bach family members realized that this centerpiece of

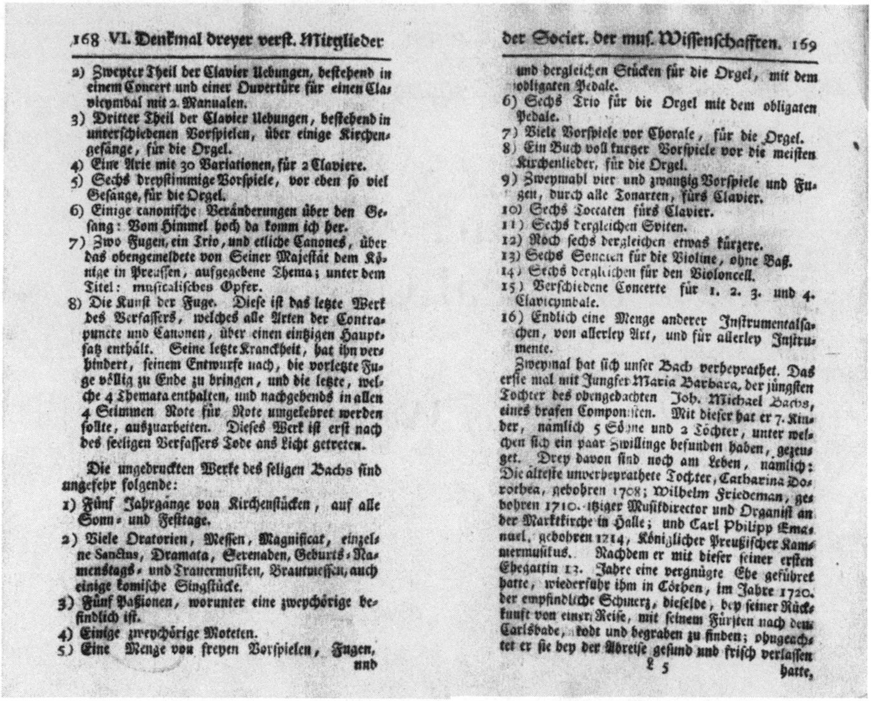

168 VI. Denkmal dreyer verst. Mitglieder

2) Zweyter Theil der Clavier Uebungen, bestehend in einem Concert und einer Ouverture für einen Clavicymbal mit 2. Manualen.
3) Dritter Theil der Clavier Uebungen, bestehend in unterschiedenen Vorspielen, über einige Kirchengesänge, für die Orgel.
4) Eine Arie mit 30 Variationen, für 2 Claviere.
5) Sechs dreystimmige Vorspiele, vor eben so viel Gesänge, für die Orgel.
6) Einige canonische Veränderungen über den Gesang: Vom Himmel hoch da komm ich her.
7) Zwo Fugen, ein Trio, und etliche Canones, über das obengemeldete von Seiner Majestät dem Könige in Preussen, aufgegebene Thema; unter dem Titel: musicalisches Opfer.
8) Die Kunst der Fuge. Diese ist das letzte Werk des Verfassers, welches alle Arten der Contrapuncte und Canonen, über einen einzigen Hauptsatz enthält. Seine letzte Krankheit, hat ihn verhindert, seinem Entwurfe nach, die vorletzte Fuge völlig zu Ende zu bringen, und die letzte, welche 4 Themata enthalten, und nachgehends in allen 4 Stimmen Note für Note umgekehret werden sollte, auszuarbeiten. Dieses Werk ist erst nach des seeligen Verfassers Tode ans Licht getreten.

Die ungedruckten Werke des seeligen Bachs sind ungefehr folgende:
1) Fünf Jahrgänge von Kirchenstücken, auf alle Sonn- und Festtage.
2) Viele Oratorien, Messen, Magnificat, einzelne Sanctus, Dramata, Serenaden, Geburts- Namenstags- und Trauermusiken, Brautmessen, auch einige komische Singstücke.
3) Fünf Passionen, worunter eine zweychörige befindlich ist.
4) Einige zweychörige Moteten.
5) Eine Menge von freyen Vorspielen, Fugen, und

der Societ. der musi. Wissenschafften. 169

und dergleichen Stücken für die Orgel, mit dem obligaten Pedale.
6) Sechs Trio für die Orgel mit dem obligaten Pedale.
7) Viele Vorspiele vor Chorale, für die Orgel.
8) Ein Buch voll kurzer Vorspiele vor die meisten Kirchenlieder, für die Orgel.
9) Zweymahl vier und zwanzig Vorspiele und Fugen, durch alle Tonarten, fürs Clavier.
10) Sechs Toccaten fürs Clavier.
11) Sechs dergleichen Suiten.
12) Noch sechs dergleichen etwas kürzere.
13) Sechs Sonaten für die Violine, ohne Baß.
14) Sechs dergleichen für den Violoncell.
15) Verschiedene Concerte für 1. 2. 3. und 4. Clavicymbale.
16) Endlich eine Menge anderer Instrumentalsachen, von allerley Art, und für allerley Instrumente.

Zweymal hat sich unser Bach verheyrathet. Das erste mal mit Jungfer Maria Barbara, der jüngsten Tochter des obengedachten Joh. Michael Bachs, eines braven Componisten. Mit dieser hat er 7. Kinder, nämlich 5 Söhne und 2 Töchter, unter welchen sich ein paar Zwillinge befunden haben, gezeuget. Drey davon sind noch am Leben, nämlich: Die älteste unverheyrathete Tochter, Catharina Dorothea, gebohren 1708; Wilhelm Friedeman, gebohren 1710, itziger Musikdirector und Organist an der Marktkirche in Halle; und Carl Philipp Emanuel, gebohren 1714, Königlicher Preußischer Kammermusikus. Nachdem er mit dieser seiner ersten Ehegattin 13. Jahre eine vergnügte Ehe geführet hatte, wiederfuhr ihm in Cöthen, im Jahre 1720, der empfindliche Schmerz, dieselbe, bey seiner Rückkunft von einer Reise, mit seinem Fürsten nach dem Carlsbade, todt und begraben zu finden; obgleich tet er sie bey der Abreise gesund und frisch verlassen hatte,
L 5   hatte,

FIGURE 1-1

First work listing in the obituary for J. S. Bach (Leipzig, 1750): detail from
Musikalische Bibliothek, vol. IV (Leipzig, 1754).

the obituary would tell its own extraordinary and lasting story, they definitely would have recognized its impact and meaning as a historic legacy. Bach himself had long endeavored to track down, gather, and make practical use of works by his seventeenth-century ancestors, notably the gifted brothers Johann Christoph Bach (1642–1703) and Johann Michael Bach (1648–1694). Some of these survived in a remarkable if smallish collection of 27 works later inherited by Bach's son Carl Philipp Emanuel as the "Old Bach Archive" (*Alt-Bachisches Archiv*). Now with the huge estate of the most productive family member to be added, the musical legacy of the Bach family had at one stroke grown to enormous proportions. At the same time, the family was definitely aware that under no circumstances could it all be kept together. As there was no question that the Thomascantor's estate would have to be divided among ten heirs (the widow and nine children), the situation of an uncertain future generated an additional reason for announcing an account of the composer's lifework in his obituary, while there was still some sense of Bach's output as an intact corpus.

Carl Philipp Emanuel Bach's summary catalog of his father's works provided the first—and for more than a century the only—published overview of his father's entire musical output (Table 1-1). Not an oeuvre catalog in the modern sense, this listing in a systematic order appears to have resulted from reading along the music shelves in Bach's office at the St. Thomas School, in preparation for dividing the large musical estate among the heirs. While an inventory was made of the household goods, no official papers were filed for documenting Bach's compositions and the holdings of his music library. Thus when commissioned to write the obituary, Bach's son had long since returned home to Berlin from Leipzig, and had no choice but to work from memory.[2] This may explain why he accidentally omitted a few items, including them later in his 1774 correspondence with Johann Nicolaus Forkel.[3]

The first part of the numbered list of works, comprising the published items, stands essentially complete, accounting for all titles in chronological order.[4] The second part, covering music in manuscript—by far the bulk of Bach's music library—separates vocal from instrumental music and lists the various work categories, apparently in the order they were kept on the shelves for practical use. First came the shelves for the largest single segment of Bach's musical output, the church cantatas, followed by sacred and secular works for special occasions, with Passions and motets kept separate. Then came organ music, with free and chorale-based works also separate, and followed by music for clavier (harpsichord and other stringed keyboard instruments), solo pieces for unaccompanied strings, chamber music, and orchestral works. In line with the catalog's summary function, no details were provided and no specific titles given, not even for major works such as the *St. Matthew Passion* or the *Well-Tempered Clavier*. They would have been meaningless for a largely uninformed readership, whereas mentioning the "double-choir" feature, "twice twenty-four preludes and fugues in all keys," and the indications "without bass" or "for one, two, three and four harpsichords" directly referred to the exceptional qualities of these works.

The manuscript music is numbered as well, and listed by category. The first four numbers comprise the vocal works described roughly by function. Number (1) embodies not only the largest unit by far of the vocal music, but also the repertoire most actively and regularly used Sunday for Sunday throughout the year. Number (2) essentially lumps together all the works for occasional use, and characteristically does not separate secular from sacred pieces. Instead of singling out any particular works, the listing accentuates the

TABLE 1-1. Carl Philipp Emanuel Bach: Summary catalog of his father's works (1750, amended 1774)*

PUBLISHED WORKS

(1) First Part of the *Clavier Uebungen*, consisting of six suites.

(2) Second Part of the *Clavier Uebungen*, consisting of a concerto and an overture for a harpsichord with 2 manuals.

(3) Third Part of the *Clavier Uebungen*, consisting of various preludes on several church hymns for the organ.

(4) [Fourth Part of the *Clavier Uebungen*,] An Aria with 30 Variations, for 2 manuals.

(5) Six three-part preludes on as many hymns, for the organ.

(6) Some Canonic Variations on the hymn *Vom Himmel hoch da komm ich her*.

(7) Two fugues, a trio and several canons, on the [. . .] theme given by His Majesty the King in Prussia; under the title *Musical Offering*.

(8) The *Art of Fugue*. This is the last work of the composer, which contains all sorts of counterpoints and canons, on a single principal subject. [. . .] This work saw the light of day only after the death of the late author.

UNPUBLISHED WORKS

(1) Five annual cycles of church pieces, for all the Sundays and holidays.

(2) Many oratorios, Masses, Magnificat, single Sanctus, dramas, serenades, music for birthdays, name days, and funerals, wedding Masses, and also a few comic vocal pieces.

(3) Five Passions, of which one is for double choir.

(4) Several double-choir motets.

(5) A lot of free preludes, fugues, and similar pieces for organ, with obbligato pedal.

(6) Six trios for the organ, with obbligato pedal.

(7) Many chorale preludes, for the organ.

(8) A book of short preludes on most of the church hymns, for the organ.

(9) Twice twenty-four preludes and fugues, in all keys, for the clavier.

(10) Six toccatas, for the clavier.

(11) Six suites for the same.

(12) Six more of the same, somewhat shorter.

[A] Fifteen two-part inventions and fifteen three-part sinfonias.

[B] Six short preludes for beginners.

(13) Six sonatas for the violin, without bass.

(14) Six of the same for the violoncello.

[C] Six sonatas for harpsichord and violin.

(15) Various concertos for one, two, three, and four harpsichords.

(16) Finally, a lot of other instrumental pieces, of all sorts, and for all kinds of instruments.

* Excerpt from the obituary; additions [A]–[C] from C. P. E. Bach, letters to J. N. Forkel (1774). *BD* IX, p. 106.

richness and breadth of the composer's reach, from Latin liturgical works to dramatic scenes and comic pieces on the other. Numbers (3) and (4) contain two distinct sacred genres for specific functions, with emphasis on double-choir structures.

Appropriately, the instrumental section contains many more subdivisions than the vocal section, beginning with the organ music—only proper for an obituary for "the world-famous organist"—and keeps the chorale-based works (7) and (8) separate from the free pieces (5) and (6), of which there are "a lot" besides the "six trios." Two particular specialties of the organ virtuoso Bach, obbligato pedal and trio texture, are expressly noted. The specifically cited "book" (8), identifiable as the *Little Organ Book* (*Orgel-Büchlein*), was perhaps the only bound book among the manuscript materials. Everything else, vocal and instrumental scores and parts, were for practical reasons kept unbound in wrappers and folders, respectively. The subsequent items (9) to (12) and [A] to [C] all represent collections of different sizes and kinds for stringed keyboard (clavier), and as such are individually identifiable. Numbers (11) and (12) make up the so-called English and French Suites, respectively, and [B] the short preludes BWV 933–938.

The last group continues to single out compositions of an unusual nature by putting at the top—(13) to (14)—the unaccompanied violin and cello solos, followed by concertos for one and more harpsichords (15), all groups of compositions without parallel. The same pertains also to the inserted item [C], described in 1774 as "6 Claviertrio." Other sonatas and chamber music for two and more instruments, as well as works for larger ensembles like the *Brandenburg Concertos* or the concertos for solo instruments other than keyboard, suites, sonatas, etc., are wrapped up as (16), "a lot" under the catch-all provision of "pieces of all sorts for all kinds of instruments"—in other words, ordinary pieces that most other composers would have written as well. By separating the special from the ordinary throughout, the summary catalog was meant primarily to present a forceful impression of the composer's unique musical legacy.

A comparison of Bach's obituary with the two other necrologies published in the same volume of the *Musikalische Bibliothek*—those of Georg Heinrich Bümler (1669–1745), capellmeister at the court of Brandenburg-Ansbach, and of Gottfried Heinrich Stölzel (1690–1749), capellmeister at the ducal court of Saxe-Gotha—reveals significant differences in the information provided about the musical output of each composer.[5] For the two latter figures, the respective works are enumerated within the biographical prose. For example, the relevant passage regarding Stölzel's thirty-year service to two dukes specifies that he composed during that time

> eight annual double cyles of cantatas, about fourteen Passion and Christmas oratorios, fourteen operettas, sixteen serenatas, more than eighty "Tafelmusiken," and nearly as many extraordinary church pieces for birthdays, plenary diets. . ., not to mention the lots of Masses, overtures, sinfonias, concertos, and the like.[6]

Carl Philipp Emanuel Bach's listing of his father's vocal works shows the same blanket approach, except for the highlighting of the double-choir feature where applicable; further distinguishing aspects seemed evidently dispensable for the purpose of an overview. However, the much more detailed listing of the published and unpublished instrumental works signifies an interest in emphasizing at least some salient characteristics in order to underscore what is special. Whether it concerns the requirement of "two manuals" for harpsichord works or the use of "obbligato pedal" in organ pieces, the reference to "all sorts of counterpoints and canons on a single principal subject," the mention of "in all keys" or "without bass," or the indication of concerto scorings "for one, two, three, and four harpsichords," the clear intention is to emphasize the unusual traits and singular qualities of the various respective compositions. In regard to such specifics, the catalog of 1750 is the first ever of this kind, and established an early model for the younger Bach's later systematic and thematic listings of his own works.[7]

By taking its overall summary character into account, a critical review of the catalog brings up a few further aspects that need to be addressed briefly, in particular the size of Bach's musical estate and the fate of the original materials.

SIZE OF THE ESTATE

Bach's altogether massive output originated over a time span of roughly half a century. In a number of areas, however, its full extent remains unknown. The reason for this unfortunate situation is that relatively few works were published during his lifetime, and the overwhelming majority existed in single manuscript copies. The overall losses of repertoire are considerable, yet the condensed summary catalog does not permit a comprehensive, let alone reliable, estimate of works lost before and after the composer's death. The losses include documented works such as the *St. Mark Passion* and numerous sacred and secular cantatas for which the published texts are extant but the scores have not survived. They also include pieces that are documented by archival references, such as the Latin Ode, BWV 1155 (formerly Anh. I/20), and works that survive in mutilated form like the Fantasia and (fragmentary) Fugue in C minor, BWV 562, or in an incomplete state like the unfinished last fugue from the *Art of Fugue*. Then there are instrumental ensemble works known only from their transcriptions, such as those in the organ sonatas BWV 525–530. Finally, there is the case of the bulk of Bach's chamber music: what the summary catalog in its entry (16) mentions as "a lot of other instrumental pieces of all sorts and for all kinds of instruments" is no way specific in terms of either the number of works or the variety of instrumental scorings.

Apart from works composed for the Weimar and Cöthen courts that Bach may have had to leave behind, most of the losses that diminished the size of the composer's known oeuvre resulted from the division of the estate in the fall of 1750. At an earlier point, however, he himself may well have destroyed an unknown quantity of mostly early compositions he considered immature, as well as other pieces he wanted to dispose of. The nearly total lack of autograph manuscripts from before around 1708 suggests some considerable house-cleaning activity. While Carl Philipp Emanuel Bach later in life engaged in just that, when he recognized that many of his early works were "too youthful" and no longer met his aesthetic standards, his father was likely even more cognizant of substandard work and mindful of his own musical legacy (see Chapter 7, page 250).

That portions of the estate are missing definitely inhibits more detailed insights into some crucial aspects of Bach's creative life, notably his upbringing, his first steps as a composer, and his deep and extensive involvement with chamber music as Weimar concertmaster and Cöthen capellmeister. On the other hand, the compromised integrity of the estate has limited impact on the big picture, in line with the traditional notion of "the whole is greater than the sum of its parts." The extant oeuvre most certainly exposes the general purpose and historical relevance of Bach's artistic contribution.

SURVIVAL OF ORIGINAL MANUSCRIPTS

The listing of unpublished works in the summary catalog is based exclusively on the manuscripts housed in the composer's office when his library was physically still intact. The vocal repertoire and the instrumental ensemble pieces invariably comprised autograph scores and sets of (mostly scribal) performing parts proofread and used by the composer. The keyboard music consisted mostly of autograph manuscripts and original prints. The catalog entries for the vocal works are too condensed to determine how many compositions have been lost altogether. But for the bulk of the vocal compositions known today—roughly two-thirds of what once existed—original sources have survived, often both scores and parts. Yet of the "several double-choir motets" in group (4), only the two autograph scores and some original parts for "Singet dem Herrn ein neues Lied" and "Der Geist hilft unsrer Schwachheit auf" are extant. The situation in the instrumental realm is much worse, because for many collections the autograph manuscripts are completely gone and their music is known solely from non-autograph sources, as is the case with the following items: (10) six toccatas, (11) six "English" suites, (14) six suites for cello solo, [B] six short preludes, and [C] six harpsichord-violin sonatas. Autograph manuscripts have remained for items (8), (9), (12), (13), (15), and [A] as well as an incomplete set of five *French Suites* in the *Clavier-Büchlein* for Anna Magdalena Bach of 1722.

Of the three larger lots in the category of unpublished instrumental works, as Table 1-2 illustrates, relatively few autograph manuscripts from the estate[8] have survived: for number (5) only four; for (7) only the partial autograph of the Great Eighteen Chorales; and for (16), no more than ten,[9] but some in fragmentary form. Were it not for the activities of Bach's students and their interest in securing copies for their own use, much less from these repertoires would have been transmitted.

BENCHMARK WORKS

When Bach made fair copies of his compositions, his practice generally reflects the importance he attached to them, and their status as paradigmatic works. The manuscripts usually show the high degree of care with which he

TABLE 1-2. Miscellaneous autograph manuscripts from the Bach estate

GROUP	WORK	BWV
5	Prelude and Fugue in G major	541
	Prelude and Fugue in B minor	544
	Prelude and Fugue in E minor (partial autograph)	548
	Fantasia and (fragmentary) Fugue in C minor	562
7	Great Eighteen Chorales (partial autograph)	651–688
16	Fantasia and Fugue in C minor for harpsichord	906
	Sonata in G major for harpsichord and viola da gamba	1027
	Sonata in B minor for harpsichord and flute	1030
	Sonata in A major for harpsichord and flute	1032
	Sonata in G major for flute, violin, and continuo	1038
	Sonata in G major for 2 flutes and continuo	1039
	Concerto in A minor for violin, strings, and continuo	1041
	Concerto in D minor for 2 violins, strings, and continuo	1043
	Concerto in D major for harpsichord, flute, and strings	1050
	Overture in B minor for flute, strings, and continuo	1067
	Overture in D major for 3 trumpets, timpani, 2 oboes, strings, and continuo	1068

prepared them, and they mirror the serious conceptual devotion he applied to their content. Most of the autograph copies cited in the previous section represent particularly special vocal and instrumental works, be they individual compositions or groups and planned collections. In terms of external criteria, the touchstone purpose seems no more strikingly reflected than in the three autograph scores of the six solos for unaccompanied violin, part I of the *Well-Tempered Clavier,* and the Inventions and Sinfonias, whose striking calligraphic layouts are without parallel among the composer's manuscripts.

Of the published and unpublished instrumental collections in which matching pieces of a certain kind or genre are gathered, a conspicuously large number have "opus character" and indicate that Bach prepared them with particular care. No fewer than eleven groups of works[10] follow the traditional scheme of opus collections introduced in seventeenth-century Italy, as used by Arcangelo Corelli, Antonio Vivaldi, and others for their instrumental publications made up of sonatas or concertos in standard sets of twelve or six. Although Bach himself used the term "opus" only once (in 1731 for the opening volume of the *Clavier-Übung*), he adhered to the well-established scheme in his manuscript collections of cognate works by designing most of them in sets of six matching pieces. Departing from this numerical scheme are opus-style collections that pursue a topical unifying theme, among them the *Orgel-Büchlein* (containing 44 organ chorales), the contrapuntal Inventions and Sinfonias (15 each), both books of the *Well-Tempered Clavier* (two sets of twenty-four preludes and fugues in all major and minor keys), parts II to IV of the *Clavier-Übung* (different collections of keyboard works), the *Musical Offering*, and the *Art of Fugue* (monothematic canonic and fugal settings).

The undeclared yet intended purpose of all these opus-style collections was Bach's interest in building thematically defined and well-rounded groups of different kinds, in both vocal and instrumental realms. Each one comprises exemplary works of a particular species, and at the same time establishes a benchmark index of his compositional range and achievements. He seems to have begun with such consciously designed benchmark projects around 1708, when he moved to Weimar as court organist and chamber musician. The post gave him more time than he had had before for pursuing ambitious compositional projects. The two oldest opus-style collections, the six toccatas (10) and the *Orgel-Büchlein* (8), both originate from around 1708 and subsequent years. Although the two differ significantly in nature and size, both clearly reveal their individual unifying concepts, a core principle that the composer consistently observed in his instrumental collections up to and including the *Art of Fugue*.

The large vocal repertoire does not follow these patterns because the kinds of sacred and secular cantatas Bach tended to write were not suited for publishable and marketable opus-style collections. Thus he never turned to the type of utilitarian cantata that Telemann published as an annual cycle of church pieces under the title *Harmonischer Gottes-Dienst* (Hamburg, 1725–26), nor to the type of chamber cantata for solo voice he issued under the title *6 moralische Kantaten* (Hamburg, 1736–37). Nevertheless, within the large corpus of Bach's church cantatas, there is a single body of pieces deliberately designed according to a unifying idea, the melodies and texts of the Lutheran hymnal. These several dozen chorale cantatas from the Leipzig annual cycle of 1724–25 not only involved extensive serial planning, but as a set of exemplary models they also embrace a genuine paradigmatic function within the cantata repertoire. Although he did not make fair copies of them as he did for the instrumental collections, Bach nevertheless showed a particular preference for these several dozen cognate cantatas by performing them more often than any others, and also by paying meticulous attention to the quality of their performance parts, some of which he expressly marked as "completely reviewed" (*völlig durchgesehen*). Only a few weeks after Bach's death, his widow Anna Magdalena offered the complete set of parts of these chorale cantatas to the St. Thomas School. Along with the motets, they were selectively used off and on in subsequent decades for performances at St. Nicholas's and St. Thomas's, the two Leipzig main churches, where they established a continuing Bach tradition.

Larger single vocal works such as oratorios do possess opus character by nature, inherent in their sizable structure and topical focus. Moreover, Bach's own particularly high esteem for them is again underscored by his interest in preserving them in fair-copy scores. Thus, he eventually replaced the working scores of the *St. Matthew* and *St. John Passions* and the *Easter Oratorio* in the 1730s with new autograph fair copies, while the *Christmas* and *Ascension Oratorios* were written from the outset as fair copies. Even though no score of the *St. Mark Passion* has survived, it is safe to assume that the entire group of six oratorio-style works formed a special entity of exemplary works within his sacred music oeuvre. In the same sense, the *B-minor Mass* also functioned as a paradigm. Unlike any other work in Bach's oeuvre, the Mass presented a large-scale rounded composition and concurrently serves as a topically defined collection of pieces for four different liturgical segments—individually numbered 1. *Missa*, 2. *Symbolum Nicenum*, 3. *Sanctus*, 4. *Osanna, Benedictus, Agnus Dei, et Dona nobis pacem*—as the late autograph score so aptly demonstrates.

The more or less systematic order of the materials kept in the composer's office—with the published works distinct from everything else in manuscript, and the latter divided into vocal, instrumental, and further subcategories—seems to have made it fairly easy for Carl Philipp Emanuel Bach to prepare a well-organized, useful, and informative survey. The specific library arrangement may also have facilitated the separation of paradigmatic pieces and collections from a large quantity of instrumental works in all categories that remained unrecorded. The latter included prominent individual pieces such as the Passacaglia in C minor, BWV 582, for organ, the *Fantasia chromatica*, BWV 903, for harpsichord, the Concerto in A minor, BWV 1044, for harpsichord, transverse flute, violin, and orchestra, and the *Overture* in C major, BWV 1066, for two oboes, bassoon, strings, and continuo, to mention only a few. However, the summary catalog focused on descriptive titles that would arouse the curiosity of readers who had no knowledge of the works as such, and who in this way might get a better idea about the unusual range of Bach's contributions to music. Therefore, the first work listing of 1750, in its selective approach and focus, provides much more than a summary overview of his musical oeuvre. It offers instead a narrative totally independent of the composer's biography, and a vision of Bach's musical universe in the sense of "a whole inclusive of all associated parts."[11]

Instrumental or vocal, the opus-style collections and the major works embody genuine landmarks, as it were, within the composer's total output, and reveal a process of expanding, broadening, and deepening aesthetic experiences. Moreover, these milestones reflect Bach's very own way of mapping an ever-expanding space that epitomizes a musical universe encompassing his entire oeuvre, but with quite a few momentous markers standing out. Their emergence within the context of Bach's various life stations, activities, and obligations is neither coincidental nor related to assignments or commissions. On the contrary, the benchmark works reveal, without exception, the independent mind of a composer who constantly and methodically makes new discoveries for himself, and deliberately explores a wide and deep musical landscape that is anything but predetermined. They deliver striking evidence of a continuously intensifying process of conquering new musical territory in terms of techniques, styles, genres, and means of performance. They document a composer who self-consciously charts, calibrates, shapes, and thereby defines and redefines his constantly evolving normative standards.

The narrative of the opus-style works in approximate chronological order reveals a musical biography that illustrates just how the composer evolves, steadily expands his reach, and continuously establishes new ambitions for himself. There is no hovering within any kind of musical routine. Hence he deals with the chapter of keyboard suite by basically taking three decisive steps, from the six *English* to the six *French Suites* to the six Partitas, and leaves it at that without ever returning. He approaches and concludes the chapter of the Passion oratorio in three similarly distinctive steps, from the St. *John* to the St. *Matthew* to the St. *Mark Passion*, without conceptually repeating himself.

This bird's-eye view, encouraged by the work listing of 1750, is not meant to gloss over the reality that in its own way, every single composition happens to be an integral part of the composer's overall creative accomplishments. And as the losses of works are both considerable and unmeasurable, the full dimensions of Bach's total output will never be known.

The focus on benchmark works also sheds light on how later generations understood and dealt with Bach's musical legacy. Unlike his close friend and colleague Georg Philipp Telemann, whom he admired and considered among his equals, Bach at no time acted as a protagonist of new stylistic trends and progressive aesthetics, or as a contributor to the musical marketplace of his day. He was well aware of the music that was in vogue, and could easily have composed according to prevailing fashionable trends—as he did in Pan's comic aria "Zu Tanze, zu Sprunge, so wackelt das Herz" (To dance, to leap, thus the heart wiggles) in the *dramma per musica* BWV 201. Yet Bach instead hewed to altogether different preferences and priorities. Agricola's summary appraisal from 1750, which highlights the phenomenon of all-encompassing polyphony, captures the composer's foundational orientation well. Bach offered path-breaking examples of modern counterpoint, advanced harmonic tonality, formal discipline, and distinct originality. These culminated in sophisticated fugues, but also ranged down as far as the four-part chorale, influencing nearly everything in between. And these decidedly powerful models exerted a lasting influence on later generations.

CHAPTER 2

Transformative Approaches to Composition and Performance

Three Unique Keyboard Workbooks

When taking a bird's-eye view of Johann Sebastian Bach's total musical output, what stands out above all is its transformative nature and distinctly original character. The genuinely metamorphic approach that shapes this composer's evolving creativity, from early on through his late works, is what has given his art such strength and endurance, and has provided to the subsequent history of musical composition both a sense of orientation and also many a new direction. If indeed Bach set the stage, as it were, for rethinking basic principles of musical composition, well beyond the conventional categories of instrumental and vocal styles and genres, the question arises as to where, when, and how this formative line of musical thinking crystallized in his own works.

Bach's reflective attitude and his deep contemplation of compositional issues that had not previously been addressed, at least not in such bold ways, is strikingly represented in three keyboard collections that originated one after another in the 1710s. Only by the turn of 1722, and for very specific reasons soon to be discussed, were they given the titles under which they became known: the *Orgel-Büchlein* (Little Organ Book), with some forty short chorale preludes on Lutheran hymns, *Das Wohltemperierte Clavier*

(The Well-Tempered Clavier), with 24 preludes and 24 fugues in all keys, and the *Aufrichtige Anleitung* (Faithful Guide), with 15 two-part inventions and 15 three-part sinfonias. The genesis of the three works suggests that the composer worked on each one of them over several years, but initially without express definition of their dual function: as appealing performing pieces on the one hand and as working materials for study and learning on the other. For Bach, who started out early on as a brilliant organ and keyboard virtuoso, the complementary aspects of performing and composing became ever more essential to his art. All three musical workbooks address both aspects, but clearly give priority to fundamental compositional precepts: establishing and maintaining the internal logic of a musical setting as well as forging a musical language of highly flexible expression. Even though Bach's incomparable intellectual command over the art of composition prevails, all three collections also provide vivid evidence of the deliberate advancement of performing techniques.

REVEALING AFTERTHOUGHTS: THREE UNIQUE TITLE PAGES

In the fall of 1722, the Cöthen capellmeister Bach seriously contemplated a major career move, and decided to apply for the distinguished position of cantor and music director at St. Thomas's in Leipzig. It appears that he was at first happy at the court of Anhalt-Cöthen, where in Prince Leopold he had a most supportive patron. Yet after five years there, things were looking quite different. An assessment of new taxes levied by the neighboring kingdom of Prussia severely affected the budget of the court, notably at the expense of music. Moreover, the attractions of the Leipzig post included the long-established reputation of the St. Thomas cantorate and its related manifold activities, the general appeal of life in a major city, and above all, much better educational opportunities for the growing children in the Bach household. In short, after the death of his first wife Maria Barbara in 1720, and his recent remarriage to Anna Magdalena, he apparently felt ready for a fresh start.

Bach was not an unknown musician in Leipzig: he had examined the new large organ for the University Church in 1717, and had probably stayed in the city and made guest appearances from nearby Cöthen thereafter.[1] He could take it for granted that his capellmeister experience and reputation in

Cöthen and his background as organist and concertmaster in Weimar would all count in his favor. At the same time, he must have realized that in his lack of a university education, he fell short in one important category as a candidate for the job: the cantorate was primarily a school position that required teaching qualifications, and from the sixteenth century on, all previous cantors at the prestigious St. Thomas School had attended a university—and some had even held advanced degrees. Two principal applicants for the post, Georg Philipp Telemann and Christoph Graupner, had both studied at the University of Leipzig in the early 1700s. By comparison, Bach had received a sound and enlightened humanistic education, and had graduated from the renowned Latin school of St. Michael's in Lüneburg. Yet he had not attended an institution of higher learning. He would therefore have to demonstrate his academic standing and teaching qualifications to the authorities at St. Thomas's. Although he could report that from about 1705 he had taught more than a dozen private students,[2] most of whom had subsequently ended up in respectable professional positions, this background might not have been deemed sufficient. Hence, he needed to submit hard evidence of his commitment to scholarship and experience in teaching—especially given that the school's long-time rector, Johann Heinrich Ernesti, was a distinguished and widely published classicist, philosopher, theologian, and professor of poetry at the University of Leipzig.

Anticipating this situation, Bach seems to have undertaken a critical review of his existing compositions, with a view toward identifying works already completed that demonstrated his learning, interests, didactic skills, and teaching methods. He filed his application for the Leipzig cantorate in November 1722, after receiving the news of Telemann's rejection of the post, and he became a serious candidate for the position following his successful audition on February 8, 1723. Yet he still needed to submit further materials attesting to his expertise, within just a few weeks. That gave him an extremely tight time frame, during which he expeditiously prepared the three keyboard collections in presentable form. The collection of chorale preludes was already in a satisfactory state, but fair copies had to be made of the other two working manuscripts. Also, he needed to furnish descriptive titles for all three sets that would explain their instructional utility and impress the Leipzig authorities—a step that eventually helped him to win the prestigious appointment.[3]

St. Thomas's was not just a highly selective Latin school. It was also at the time—and had been for more than a century—in all but name a conservatory, indeed the preeminent breeding ground for musicians in the German lands.[4] Mindful of the numerous scholarly publications of his potential colleagues at St. Thomas's, Bach settled on three special keyboard sets that were unrelated to his princely duties in Weimar and Cöthen, and that stood apart from both traditional performing repertoires and conventional teaching manuals. All three certainly displayed a distinct profile of imaginative musical instruction and as such would qualify, in terms of both pedagogical suitability and didactic variety, for the edification of students at the St. Thomas School. Of the three, one was an incomplete book, the other two were working manuscripts. All three still lacked descriptive titles classifying them as pedagogical works.

(1) A manuscript book with forty-plus short chorale preludes for organ, begun between 1708 and 1710, was only partially filled, but its contents seemed sufficiently representative. Its front page was still blank and had been left so for many years, perhaps because the composer wanted to wait until the project was completed. Bach now inscribed it with a rather neutral main title: *Orgel-Büchlein*. The subsequent lines, however, expanded on the collection's concept and function, and culminated in a rhymed and devout dedicatory couplet. (Fig. 2-1). At the very end, the composer referred to himself remarkably and for the first time as "author," and thereby placed himself proudly in the academic company of originators of written work.[5]

The two later collections, somewhat less ready for presentation than the *Little Organ Book*, existed only in hard-to-read working manuscripts. Hence, during the winter months of 1722/23, Bach prepared fair copies of them, notable showpieces of his calligraphic music hand and virtually free of corrections.

(2) The working manuscript comprising 24 preludes and 24 fugues in all major and minor keys and originating from well before 1720 was replaced by an autograph fair copy that was given the imaginative main title *Das Wohltemperirte Clavier*, followed by the subtitle *Praeludia und Fugen durch alle Tone und Semitonia* (preludes and fugues through all the tones and semitones; Fig. 2-2).

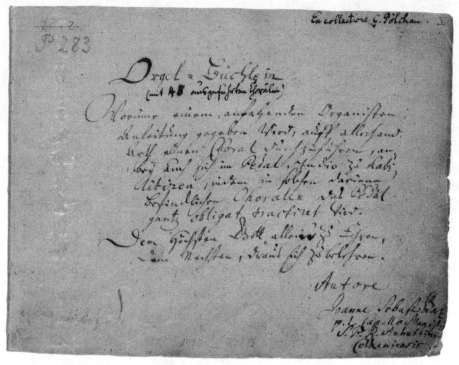

FIGURE 2-1

Orgel-Büchlein, BWV 599–644: autograph title (1723); line 2 "mit 48 ausgeführten Chorälen" (with 48 executed chorales) added by J. C. F. Bach (1750).

(3) Working manuscripts from around 1721/22, mainly composing scores of thirty compact contrapuntal pieces, 15 two-part preambles and 15 three-part fantasias in the *Little Clavier Book for Wilhelm Friedemann Bach*, were replaced by an autograph fair copy with an elaborate title under the main heading *Auffrichtige Anleitung* (Faithful Guide) followed by a description of its instructional function (Fig. 2-3). Additionally, in this new copy Bach relabeled the pieces from "Praeambulum" to "Inventio" and from "Fantasia" to "Sinfonia."

All three keyboard collections remained unique among the composer's autograph music manuscripts in their coordinated and elaborate title pages, written in the final months of his employment at the princely court of Anhalt-Cöthen. (For the painstakingly crafted wording of the complete titles, see Table 2-1).

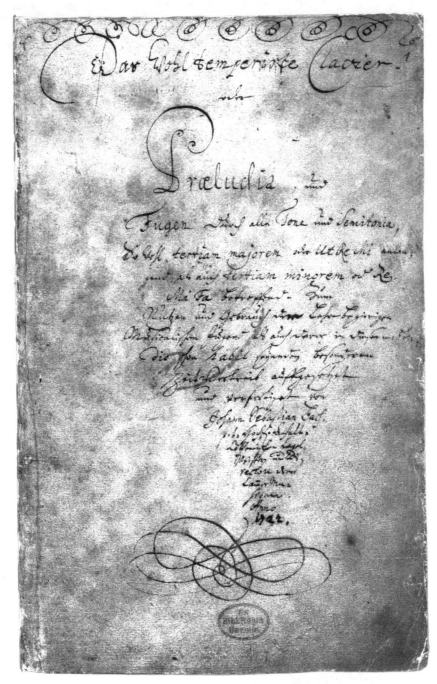

FIGURE 2-2

Das Wohltemperirte Clavier, BWV 846–869: autograph title (1722).

FIGURE 2-3

Auffrichtige Anleitung (Inventions and Sinfonias), BWV 772–801:
autograph title (1723).

TABLE 2-1. Three keyboard works turned into texts: New titles, 1722/23

1. ORGEL-BÜCHLEIN / LITTLE ORGAN BOOK

Orgel-Büchlein,
Worinne einem anfahenden Organisten Anleitung gegeben wird, auff allerhand Arth
einen Choral durchzuführen, anbey auch sich im Pedal studio zu habilitiren, indem
in solchen darinne befindlichen Choralen das Pedal gantz obligat tractiret wird.
    Dem Höchsten Gott allein zu Ehren,
    Dem Nechsten, draus sich zu belehren.
Autore Joanne Sebast: Bach p[ro]. t[empore]. Capellae Magistri S[erenissimi]. P[rin-
cipis]. R[egnantis]. Anhaltini-Cotheniensis.

Little Organ Book,
in which a beginning organist is given guidance to realize a chorale in all sorts of
ways and, in passing, also to qualify in pedal studies, since in the chorales contained therein the pedal is treated as wholly obbligato.
    To the glory of the Highest God alone
    and for the neighbor to be learning from.
By the author, Johann Sebast: Bach, for the time being Capellmeister of the Most
Serene Governing Prince of Anhalt-Cöthen.

2. DAS WOHLTEMPERIERTE CLAVIER / THE WELL-TEMPERED CLAVIER

Das Wohltemperirte Clavier.
oder Praeludia und Fugen durch alle Tone und Semitonia, So wohl tertiam majorem
oder Ut Re Mi anlangend, als auch tertiam minorem oder Re Mi Fa betreffend.
Zum Nutzen und Gebrauch der Lehr-begierigen Musicalischen Jugend, als auch
derer in diesem studio schon habil seyenden besonderem ZeitVertreib – auffgesetzet
und verfertiget von Johann Sebastian Bach. p[ro]. t[empore]: HochFürstlich Anhalt-
Cöthenischen Capel-Meistern und Directore derer CammerMusiquen. Anno 1722.

The Well-Tempered Clavier.
or preludes and fugues passing through all the tones and semitones, both as
regards the *tertia major* or *Ut Re Mi*, and as concerns the *tertia minor* or *Re Mi Fa*.
For the benefit and use of the musical youth that is eager to learn as well as for
the special pastimes of those already qualified in this study, drawn up and produced by Johann Sebastian Bach, for the time being Princely Anhalt-Cöthen
Capellmeister and Director of chamber music there. In the year 1722.

3. AUFRICHTIGE ANLEITUNG / *FAITHFUL GUIDE*

Auffrichtige Anleitung,
Wormit denen Liebhabern des Clavires, besonders aber denen Lehrbegierigen, eine
deütliche Art gezeiget wird, nicht alleine (1) mit 2 Stimmen reine spielen zu lernen,
sondern auch bey weiteren progreßen (2) mit dreyen obligaten Partien richtig und
wohl zu verfahren, anbey auch zugleich gute inventiones nicht alleine zu bekom-
men, sondern auch selbige wohl durchzuführen, am allermeisten aber ein cantable
Art im Spielen zu erlangen, und darneben einen starcken Vorschmack von der
Composition zu überkommen. Verfertiget von Joh: Seb: Bach. Hochfürstlich Anhalt-
Cöthenischer Capellmeister. Anno Christi 1723.

Faithful Guide,
Wherein the lovers of the clavier, and especially those eager to learn, are shown
in a clear way not only (1) to learn to play cleanly with two voices but also, after
further progress, (2) to deal correctly and well with three *obbligato* parts; further
in passing not only to obtain at once good ideas, also to develop the same well but,
above all, to arrive at a singing style in playing and beside it to acquire a strong
foretaste of composition. Produced by Joh: Seb: Bach, Princely Anhalt-Cöthen
Capellmeister. In the year of Christ 1723.

The typically Baroque long-winded wordings were formulated in such a
way that they complemented one another as summaries of the didactic texts.
Thus, the term "Anleitung" (guide) is prominently featured in titles 1 and 3;

titles 2 and 3 specifically address the "lehr-begierige" (those eager to learn) while 1 and 2 refer to "anfahende Organisten" (beginning organists) and the "musicalische Jugend" (musical youth), but also to more advanced musicians, that is, "derer in diesem studio schon habil seyenden." All three titles emphasize variety in genres and keys (chorale settings of various sorts; preludes and fugues; pieces with two and three contrapuntal lines of music) and also stress aspects of performance and progress therein—including playing cleanly and in a singing (cantabile) manner and applying the obligatory (obbligato) organ pedal. Furthermore, the wordings accentuate the dual purpose of all three works: supplying materials for performance, but also providing study materials for general compositional principles, treatments of chorale settings, specimens of writing in free and strict styles, and models for obtaining and developing good musical ideas.

The three substantially different keyboard collections, as they were fashioned and refashioned in 1722/23, shared a common goal in displaying exemplary musical designs for which there existed no equivalents. Their methodical outlook portrayed Bach as he wished to introduce himself: as an experienced teacher and an author of innovative, imaginative, practical, and versatile keyboard texts for performance and composition. Nevertheless, the elaborate titles and their explicit didactic focus—without parallel in Bach's oeuvre—were genuine afterthoughts and were, in their specific wording, unrelated to the conceptual origin of the works. At the same time, the added-on titles reveal much about the original motivation for the various compositions, reflecting Bach's natural disposition as a teacher who devised no dry exercise material, but instead provided authentic and demanding compositions, not in the least for the inherent purpose of his own learning process.

ORGEL-BÜCHLEIN: A COLLECTION OF SHORT CHORALE PRELUDES

Despite its small oblong-quarto format (6" × 7.5"), the *Orgel-Büchlein* counts among the largest collection of extant autographs of Bach's organ music. It contains 45 chorale preludes (BWV 599–644) and the beginning of a forty-sixth (BWV 1167).[6] Yet although its 182 pages contain headings for 164 chorales, two-thirds of the book remains otherwise empty except for pre-ruled music staves (Fig. 2-4). The large number of chorale headings indicates that the initially unnamed collection was planned as an extensive project that would eventually have gathered together the most comprehensive extant group of organ chorale settings on the classic Lutheran hymn tunes from the sixteenth and seventeenth centuries. Such an ambitious compilation of short chorale preludes, apart from their sophisticated and innovative compositional concept, had never before been undertaken—nor was it thereafter. As such, the collection stands as a statement that proclaims the aplomb and "can-do" attitude of the self-assured Weimar court organist Bach.

The *Orgel-Büchlein* project originated near the beginning of the composer's appointment as organist and chamber musician at the ducal court in Weimar, effective July 1, 1708.[7] Handwriting and stylistic evidence suggest that Bach must have embarked on the collection soon after settling into his Weimar post. From the outset he must have considered that writing 164 chorale preludes of the kind he had in mind was not a matter of weeks or even months, but would be a long-term undertaking. Indeed, the manuscript evidence demonstrates that the organ chorales were entered in irregular sequence over a period of several years in Weimar, most likely up to 1714/15. There is no evidence of entries made much beyond 1715, but later in Leipzig, Bach added two pieces (BWV 613 and the fragment BWV 1167) and revised two settings (BWV 620 and BWV 631) entered earlier.[8]

The headline of the title page, "Orgel-Büchlein" (Table 2-1; Fig. 2-1), or for that matter "Orgel-Buch," does not represent a customary German title for collections of organ music. On the contrary, this particular title stands apart from the names of other organ collections, and was chosen by Bach in obvious reference to the French tradition of the "Livre d'orgue." He owned copies of at least three such *livres d'orgue*—by André Raison (1688), Nicolas de Grigny (1699), and Pierre du Mage (1708)—and most likely knew a few more. All of them contain predominantly short and diverse liturgical pieces, mainly settings of Latin hymns and movements from organ masses. That Bach opted for the German diminutive version "Büchlein" related not only to the pocket-sized book but also to the diminutive format of the chorale settings projected for the entire collection, most of them even shorter than the typical French pieces.

The basic idea of the *Little Organ Book* as an assemblage of "short organ preludes" is specifically referred to only in the summary catalog of Bach's obituary (Table 1-1). The autograph title page curiously mentions the "guidance to realize a chorale in all sorts of ways" but not the deliberately small-scale format.

However, in preparing the manuscript and before setting down a single note, Bach spaced the headings of the 164 hymns throughout the manuscript in such a way that the compact format of each single piece was actually predetermined by the length of the chorale tune. For the vast majority of the chorale preludes he allowed a single page ruled with six staves. Only sixteen longer melodies were spread over two pages: one that varied in all three strophes received three pages (BWV 627), and a single very short melody was confined to two-thirds of a page, leaving extra room for the following longer chorale tune (Fig. 2-4). This scheme indicates how Bach plotted the entire collection largely in advance, and thereby obliged himself to design each setting to fit and fill the space provided. This rigorous discipline failed him in only a few instances, where he had to add a measure or two at the very end of the piece in space-saving tablature notation. In general, however, Bach met his predetermined goal with remarkable consistency, an outcome that would hardly have been possible had he merely prepared the manuscript mechanically, without considering each individual chorale tune and premeditating its setting.

FIGURE 2-4a

"Christus, der ist mein Leben" and "Herzlich lieb hab ich dich, o Herr":
autograph titles with calculated spaces for projected chorales (page 152).

The fundamental unifying idea for the ambitious collection of short chorale preludes is an imaginative exploration of the generative potential offered by each chorale melody and text. Bach could not have chosen a better project for demonstrating the principle of variety ("all sorts of ways"), drawing upon 164 very different tunes and related poetic texts. They bespeak a wide range of functions and a variety of distinctive themes, including chorales for the various seasons of the ecclesiastical year, catechism hymns for the teaching of dogmatics, and songs for praising the Lord and loving Jesus. Many of them reflect a wide variety of human expression, from the joyful to the sad, and also project the manifold experiences of a Christian life. The idea of involving text-inspired imagery and articulating specific expressions in purely instrumental settings also had direct implications for vocal composition, in which the relationship between words and music is of crucial importance. Therefore, unlike the two later workbooks, the *Orgel-Büchlein* functioned as a general guidebook for text-bound composition, with emphasis on concrete word-tone relationships and content-specific musical expression.

FIGURE 2-4b

Space reserved for "Herzlich lieb hab ich dich, o Herr" (page 153).

Chorale settings of various kinds traditionally belong in the toolbox of every organist. Bach grew up with chorale preludes, variations, and fantasias of many kinds, and early on showed particular interest in the large-scale types. His earliest extant autograph music manuscript testifies to the Ohrdruf schoolboy, thirteen–fourteen years old, copying down Dietrich Buxtehude's longest, most complex, and technically very demanding chorale fantasia, "Nun freut euch, lieben Christen g'mein," BuxWV 210.[9] Some very early Bach settings of short chorale preludes, particularly from the so-called Neumeister Collection,[10] show certain trends in uniform construction and motivic control. Yet they fall short of the compact designs, sophisticated polyphonic textures, expressive devices, and in particular the obbligato pedal requirements of the pieces in the *Little Organ Book*. So while this collection is not entirely without a prehistory, no real precedent in the organ literature existed for such an extensive production of exemplary musical material pursuing a unifying idea. Bach had entered uncharted territory—and proceeded to produce a consummate masterpiece in this very first attempt.

In each chorale prelude, the hymn serves as a stimulus for effectively determining the compositional design of the compact setting—whether through a motif derived or extracted from the given chorale tune, through an accompanying motif illustrating or interpreting the topical content of the sacred song, or both when possible. In short, Bach intended "to realize a chorale in all sorts of ways" by taking the tune and text of each individual chorale as a point of departure, and by developing and individualizing each instrumental setting to enhance the sacred poetry and intensify its hermeneutic message. Four representative examples from the first section of the collection may illustrate Bach's aims and the procedures he used to achieve them.

"Gott, durch deine Güte oder: Gottes Sohn ist kommen" (God, by your goodness or: The son of God is come), BWV 600 (Fig. 2-5)

The 1544 hymn tune that forms the basis of this prelude, the second in the book, serves two different texts, as the double heading indicates. Both are Advent hymns. Realizing the tune's contrapuntal suitability for a canon at the octave, Bach notates the F-major melody in whole and half notes, then begins the same melody one measure later and an octave lower. Thus, the soprano line and the tenor (to be played on the organ pedal) establish the canonic frame for the setting. The alto and bass voices complete the texture

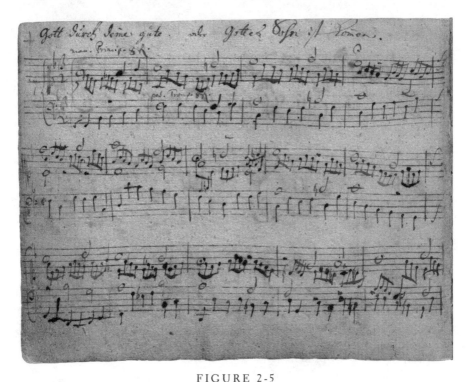

FIGURE 2-5

"Gott durch deine Güte" or "Gottes Sohn ist kommen," BWV 600: autograph composing score.

as independent counterpoints in eighth- and quarter-note motion—that is, in contrasting speeds to the slow motion of the chorale canon. Since the setting is serving two different hymn texts, the relations between words and music cannot be specific. However, the intricate three-layered rhythmic structure gives rise to an openly cheerful piece that defines the general character of both chorales as hymns of praise for the season of Advent.

"Herr Christ, der ein'ge Gottes Sohn oder: Herr Gott, nun sei gepreiset" (Lord Christ, the only Son of God or: Lord God, now be praised), BWV 601 (Fig. 2-6)

Another chorale prelude with two different texts for the Advent season, this setting also projects the general character of a hymn of praise. Unlike the entry for BWV 600, which shows a number of corrections, this entry is a fair copy, suggesting that the piece existed before the book was begun. The melody of

FIGURE 2-6

"Herr Christ, der ein'ge Gottes Sohn" or "Herr Gott, nun sei gepreiset," BWV 601:
autograph fair copy.

1524, one of the oldest Lutheran chorale tunes, is constructed in the standard
bar form (AAB) consisting of two shorter repeated *Stollen* (A), collectively
called *Aufgesang*, followed by a longer *Abgesang* (B). However, Bach arbitrarily
changed the design to an AABB form, so that the setting resembles a movement from a dance suite with two unequal repeated halves. While it does not
reach the dominant at the first double bar, in other ways it follows the dance
model, with a dominating melody and a consistent motivic accompaniment.
Additionally, Bach gives the chorale tune a rhythmic twist by emphasizing
the downbeat of most chorale line incipits by way of a dotted rhythm. The
original tune actually begins with the interval of a third (a'–$c\sharp''$, which the
composer turns into a motivic pattern that penetrates the entire three-part
accompaniment. The organ pedal actively participates in the same pattern,
thereby helping to create a sense of vibrancy and briskness—in appropriate
support of a song of praise.

FIGURE 2-7

"Das alte Jahr vergangen ist," BWV 614: autograph score.

"Das alte Jahr vergangen ist" (The old year has passed), BWV 614 (Fig. 2-7)

This piece, based on a 1588 New Year's hymn, gives special emphasis to the melody by embellishing it in a nuanced and elegant manner. The tune itself is assigned to a separate manual of the organ with a combination of expressive stops, its timbre differentiated from that of the lower accompanying lines. These, however, because of the work's contrapuntal design, still play a vital role in the musical interpretation of the text. The quatrain of the first strophe, which usually defines the hymn's focus, reads as follows:

Das alte Jahr vergangen ist,	The old year has passed,
wir danken dir, Herr Jesu Christ,	we thank you, Lord Jesus Christ,
dass du uns in so groß'r Gefahr	that in such great danger
behütet hast lang Zeit und Jahr.	you have protected us this year.

As in BWV 601, Bach modifies the quatrain structure, in this case by repeating the first and last lines, thus lengthening the song and its setting. He does this not only to fill the page in the autograph manuscript, but also to emphasize the crucial third line of the verse. There the words "such great danger" are set to a rising chromatic tetrachord in the melody, the traditional "lament" figure *a–b♭–b♮–c–c♯–d*. This musico-rhetorical figure inspires the slow tempo of the piece, and shapes the entire three-part texture of the accompaniment in sophisticated polyphony, with both the chromatically ascending motif and its descending inversion employed from the very first measure. The composer thus transforms the chorale prelude into an expressive setting that proclaims gratitude for the deliverance from all the dangers of the old year.

"In dir ist Freude" (In you, there is joy), BWV 615 (Fig. 2-8)

A strikingly different New Year's hymn immediately follows BWV 614 in the book. The hymn speaks of the love of Jesus and ends with jubilation, triumph, and Alleluja in a positive and confident outlook on the New Year. Bach enhances the rejoicing triple-meter tune—based on a 1588 German sacred parody of a secular Italian madrigal by Giovanni Gastoldi—through a particularly spirited, indeed snappy setting in vivid motion. The melody runs primarily in the upper voice but is broken up in various ways, from short snippets and chordal insertions to various up-and-down running figures, which are also picked up in the refined and varied accompanying texture. Short phrases of the tune also occur elsewhere in the largely four-part polyphonic score. One particular element, however, leaves a distinct mark on the entire setting: a prominent single-measure ostinato motif in the pedal bass, introduced at the very beginning and repeated throughout the setting, which functions as a contrasting but compatible counterpart to the chorale melody and underscores its joyous tone.

This sort of imaginative motivic invention—replete with affective, figurative, metaphorical, or symbolic implications that communicate Bach's untexted musical message—prompted Albert Schweitzer's highly perceptive description of the *Orgel-Büchlein* as "the dictionary of [Bach's] musical language, the key to the understanding of his music as a whole."[11] The term "dictionary," while characterizing the collection too narrowly as a quasi-directory of illustrative musical motifs, nevertheless emphasizes its central function as a guidebook "to realize a chorale in all sorts of ways." Bach achieves this by

FIGURE 2-8

"In dir ist Freude," BWV 615: autograph fair copy.

varying the compositional approach from piece to piece, in order to enhance the singular melodic qualities of each chorale tune and the meaning of the sacred poem, or a principal poetic phrase. These instrumental chorale preludes indeed represent a decisive milestone in the advancement, expansion, and concentration of Bach's art of composition, with immediate repercussions in the realm of vocal composition.

The highly condensed and focused textures of the chorale preludes are designed to integrate fully an obbligato pedal part, a feature not found as consistently elsewhere, including Bach's own earlier organ works. Hence, the secondary function of the chorale preludes as pedal studies is expressly noted in the added title page. Yet the carefully penned repertoire of the *Little Organ Book* indicates that it was not specifically or primarily meant for liturgical use. The Weimar court organist Bach, an experienced improviser, would hardly have needed to write down such pieces for service playing, so his motivation for committing these elaborate settings to paper went well beyond such needs. Clearly, he was focused on compiling a workbook for inspiring and testing musical imagination, in the form of compact compositions that are not based on free thematic invention. Rather, they draw on a broad range of preexisting modal, major, and minor chorale melodies, with associated texts that invite a wide spectrum of musical expression. Moreover, by the self-imposed compositional challenge of fitting everything into miniature-sized format, Bach specifically focused on original solutions—not only in creating the texturally varied, tightly constructed, and mostly four-part contrapuntal scores, but also in making innovative organ pedal technique a signature element of every single piece.

In this regard, the *Little Organ Book* offers truly transformative perspectives, first and foremost for Bach's self-study and use as performer-composer. His method of designing short pieces with maximum musical content was as brilliant as it was unique. This process was, in addition, absolutely consequential for his progress as a composer. No other set of virtually all-inclusive compositional exercises had such a direct and lasting impact on Bach, stimulating the composer's musical intellect and sharpening his imagination, such that devoting serious attention to detail in smaller or larger scores eventually became a matter of routine. This circumstance might also explain why he did not complete the ambitious *Orgel-Büchlein* project, leaving the staves for more than one hundred chorale preludes empty. After writing forty-five exemplary works and filling just about a quarter of the book's pages, Bach may well have felt that he had achieved his goal, and was eager to move on. Yet even in its incomplete state, the *Orgel-Büchlein* could more than fulfill its intended purpose—and then readily assume its newly assigned function as a model text for teaching both performance and composition.

DAS WOHLTEMPERIERTE CLAVIER: PRELUDES AND FUGUES IN ALL KEYS

Around 1717, Bach began a new workbook project that involved a major experiment. It put to the test the heretofore unproven idea that substantial pieces in free and strict styles could be composed and built on two emerging musical systems long before they became accepted norms: (1) the modern harmonic tonality based on twelve major and twelve minor keys; (2) a new approach to temperament, replacing the traditional meantone temperament and enabling keyboard instruments to accommodate all twenty-four major and minor keys.

In the 1680s, the German organist, mathematician, and music theorist Andreas Werckmeister proposed various new schemes for tuning, called "well-tempered," that were meant to replace the old and highly restrictive meantone temperament, which provides pure major thirds in the common keys, but leaves the more remote triads unplayable. Late-seventeenth-century keyboard composers eager to explore and experiment with the expanded major-minor tonality included Buxtehude in particular, a close friend of Werckmeister's. The young Bach followed suit early on when, beginning in 1703, he had a well-tempered organ at his disposal in Arnstadt. However, the concept of the circle of fifths—which defined the relationships in tonal harmony among the twelve steps of the chromatic scale, their keys in the major and minor modes, and their related key signatures—was not fully developed until around 1710, and was first written up the following year by Johann David Heinichen (Fig. 2-9).[12]

As some of his early keyboard works demonstrate, Bach had already started experimenting with and testing the limits of tonal harmony in his Arnstadt years. Yet it was not until 1722 that he dealt with the issue systematically, when he pursued the concept of what he named *Das Wohltemperierte Clavier.* His autograph from that year is a fair copy[13] that does not cast any light on the extended genesis of the work, whose date of origin is unclear because the composing manuscripts do not survive. The earliest extant sources—in the *Clavier-Büchlein vor Wilhelm Friedemann Bach,* begun in 1720—transmit only eleven preludes (without fugues), mostly in Friedemann's hand and dating from around 1721.[14] Deviating considerably from their counterparts in the later autograph fair copy, these pieces obviously derive from an earlier version of the work. Further evidence of the compositional history of *The Well-Tempered Clavier* is provided by certain other manuscripts,[15] notably the earliest extant complete copy of the work in the hand of Bernhard Christian Kayser, a Bach pupil from Cöthen who eventually moved with his teacher to Leipzig.[16] Around 1722/23, Kayser apparently copied directly from Bach's composing score, which was heavily corrected after Friedemann had taken copies. Therefore Kayser's manuscript resembles an intermediate stage of the work on the way to the autograph fair copy.

Additional and rather specific information about the collection's history is found in the Bach article of Ernst Ludwig Gerber's *Historisch-Biographisches Lexicon der Tonkünstler* (Leipzig, 1790). His father, Heinrich Nicolaus Gerber, had studied with Bach for two years, beginning in 1724. The younger Gerber related that "according to a certain tradition" Bach wrote his *Well-*

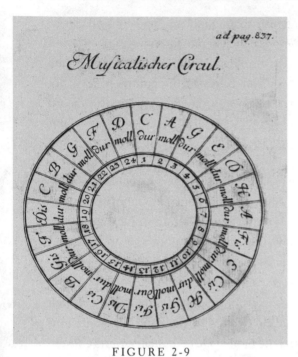

FIGURE 2-9

"Musical Circle": J. D. Heinichen, *Der General-Bass in der Composition* (Dresden, 1728).

Tempered Clavier "in a place where discontent, boredom and the lack of musical instruments of any kind forced him to this pastime."[17] While the exact place and circumstances remain unidentified, the story has long been associated with Bach's four-week arrest by the Weimar duke "because of his stubborn behavior and forced dismissal"[18] immediately prior to taking up the capellmeister post in Cöthen. If the reported "tradition" is taken literally, the *Well-Tempered Clavier* was essentially composed between November 6 and December 2 of 1717, during Bach's confinement to a detention cell without a keyboard instrument, but apparently not without paper and writing utensils. During these twenty-six days, Bach would have drafted roughly one prelude and fugue per day—not an unrealistic pace for this composer. Moreover, the absence of a keyboard instrument does not speak against the story because Gerber mentions the work as an example in the context of reporting that Bach "was never accustomed to consulting his clavier for advice during composing." Carl Philipp Emanuel Bach corroborates this statement when he later explains that with the exception of pieces derived from improvisation, his father "composed everything else without instrument, but later tried it out on one."[19] The twenty-four preludes and fugues were perhaps in a conceptual planning stage prior to Bach's confinement, but there may not have been sufficient scope for pursuing the plans until the imposed downtime of the arrest period. The work's compositional history definitely continued beyond December 1717, with the composer steadily making improvements to the composing scores. These scores became dispensable after the 1722 fair copy, and have not survived.

The issue of composing in all twenty-four keys was obviously in the air, as shown in Johann Mattheson's *Organisten-Probe* (Hamburg, 1719), which published for the first time two sets of twenty-four short figured-bass exercises ("Prob-Stücke") in all keys.[20] An earlier attempt at exploring the expanded tonal system, Johann Caspar Ferdinand Fischer's widely disseminated *Ariadne musica neo-organoedum* (Schlackenwerth/Ostrov, 1702; reprinted Vienna, 1713 and 1715), had presented a modest and serviceable collection of twenty simple preludes and fugues ("Viginti Praeludia, todidem Fugas") in as many keys and in ascending order, but lacking examples in E-flat minor, F-sharp major, G-sharp minor, and B-flat minor. Therefore, the task of demonstrating that indeed all twenty-four major and minor keys could be used for truly elaborate and serious compositions and for more demanding performances on keyboard instruments fell to Bach. Though following the prototype of Fischer, whom he regarded highly,[21] Bach chose to prove to an unprecedented extent the validity and necessity of this gradual evolution toward equal temperament, as well as the indisputable efficacy and potential of the full-blown major-minor tonal system for musical composition.

The ornamental layout of the calligraphic title page for *Das Wohltemperirte Clavier* (Fig. 2-2) makes it clear that the top heading identifies the main idea of the collection, namely its relationship to a central innovation in the history of keyboard instruments. Until far into the eighteenth century, meantone temperament prevailed as the standard tuning method for organs and stringed keyboard instruments like harpsichord and clavichord. This tuning, introduced for keyboard instruments in the sixteenth century, was suitable for the traditional system of the church modes, and provided both radiant major triads and the possibility for strikingly dissonant but still usable sonorities. Yet it could no longer keep pace with the steadily advancing expansion of major-minor tonality, as well as the demands for more far-ranging modulations within an increasingly complex harmonic language that called for usable major within minor triads in every position.

Bach's use of the term "well-tempered," borrowed from Werckmeister, refers to a tuning distinct from equal temperament that nevertheless enabled playing in all keys. But exactly which of the several variants of well-tempered tunings he preferred, and which modifications over the decades he may have made, remains unknown. Relevant statements by Bach have been transmitted only indirectly, without specific details, and only from his later years. The obituary states, for example, that "in the tuning of harpsichords, he achieved so correct and pure a temperament that all the keys sounded beautiful and agreeable. He knew of no keys that, because of impure tuning, one must avoid."[22] Complementing this testimony, Carl Philipp Emanuel related in a letter of 1774 that "no one could tune his instrument to his liking. He did everything himself."[23] Thus, his father did not follow any of the published, scientifically derived tuning systems, including equal temperament,[24] but rather followed his own tuning method. This seems to be in keeping with Johann Philipp Kirnberger's report that his teacher Bach "expressly demanded of him that all major thirds should be sharpened."[25] It is not possible to deduce a precise temperament from such information, but through the early 1740s Bach apparently still preferred the compromise solution of a mildly unequal temperament in which the various keys retained at least some individual (if weakened) character.

Immediately below the headline of the *Well-Tempered Clavier*, Bach's fair copy introduces the subtitle "preludes and fugues passing through all the tones and semitones" (Table 2-1). The whole phrase mentions not only the two constituent genres that make up the collection but also their chromatic sequence through the octave as well as the organization by modes, major before minor. The principle of an ascending key order was not new and can be found in Johann Caspar Kerll's *Modulatio organica super Magnificat octo ecclesiasticis tonis* (Munich, 1686) and Johann Pachelbel's slightly later Magnificat fugues, both organized according to church modes. A more modern equivalent in terms of major and minor modes occurs in the suites of Johann Kuhnau's *Neue Clavier-Übung*, with seven partitas rising from C major via D–E–F–G–A to B-flat major in part I (Leipzig, 1689) and from C minor via D–E–F–G–A to B minor in part II (Leipzig, 1692). With its twenty short preludes and fugues, Fischer's *Ariadne Musica* (referred to above) displayed an even wider range of keys, and probably influenced Bach's choice of a special title. However, while Fischer chose his emblematic title to associate the mythology of Ariadne's thread with a labyrinth of keys, Bach more prosaically but no less effectively chose the concrete imagery of a virtual keyboard instrument named "Wohltemperierte Clavier."

Again emulating Fischer, Bach organized his preludes and fugues in rising key order beginning with C major but, as the autograph fair copy shows, in a strictly chromatic sequence and with the major mode always preceding the minor. This appears not to have been the case from the beginning, however, because in the *Clavier-Büchlein* for Friedemann Bach the key order of the eleven preludes is C major–C minor–D minor–D major–E minor–E major–F major–C-sharp major–C-sharp minor–E-flat minor–F minor. In other words, triads with their natural thirds on the ascending white-note scale from C to F took precedence in determining the key order. Similarly, the aforementioned complete copy of the work by Kayser displays a similar key order, with the natural thirds taking precedence: that is, D minor before D major, E minor before E major, etcetera. In some cases, Kayser's copy also uses the so-called Dorian notation for minor keys with flats, meaning the modern key signature minus one flat. In contrast, Bach's fair copy of late 1722 reflects a thorough reworking of these details in organization and notation. Regarding key signatures, Bach went his own way, even in comparison to Mattheson's *Organisten-Probe*, by consistently using signatures from zero to six sharps and flats. In so doing, he thereby established a notational standard that remains the norm to the present day.

Besides the issues of temperament and tonality, the *Well-Tempered Clavier* explored in depth the ramifications of two fundamentally different kinds of free and strict musical composition in juxtaposition: the improvisatory prelude and the contrapuntal fugue. Even though the collection of twenty-four has each prelude followed by a fugue in the corresponding key, the two contrasting types are not necessarily understood as a single unit. This is so despite the many indications of "verte, sequitur fuga" (turn [page], fugue follows) in Bach's fair copy, which suggests that the prelude be played as a free introduction to the strict fugue. At the same time, the autograph fair copy unmistakably and consistently numbers both the preludes and fugues individually, not by heading them "Prelude and Fugue" (as in most modern editions)[26] but with separate captions, such as "Praeludium 1." and "Fuga 1. à 4" (Fig. 2-10). In other words, Bach deliberately stresses the strong contrast in the makeup and governing principles of the two types of composition. Although placed and performed next to each other, they constitute individual entities throughout, with their different keys identified merely by key signatures. The inclusion of preludes entirely without fugues in the *Clavier-Büchlein vor Wilhelm Friede-mann Bach*, as discussed above, supports the point that in the *Well-Tempered Clavier* each prelude and each fugue should be understood as a composition in its own right, and also as a demonstration that all keys can accommodate free and strict styles of composition and performance.

Prior to conceiving the collection, Bach the organist and keyboard virtuoso had performed, improvised, and composed many samples of both preludes and fugues. Thoroughly familiar with the two complementary genres, he intended much more for this ambitious new collection than merely proving

FIGURE 2-10

Prelude in C♯ major, BWV 848/1: autograph fair copy.

the viability of the new major-minor modes in all chromatic keys. Thus he presented a varied collection of exemplary models that departed from the more typical longer or shorter formats then current. As he did with the chorales in the *Orgel-Büchlein*, Bach devised an unparalleled and concise design that would underscore the nature and model character of the individual pieces within the collection. Hence, the standard length in the autograph manuscript for each prelude and each fugue averages about two pages. Sixteen preludes with their corresponding fugues fit the scheme of nearly equal length for both. In five instances, the fugues (nos. 3, 4, 8, 12, and 20) are about twice the length of the preludes in the same keys, whereas two of the preludes (nos. 7 and 10) are about twice the length of the corresponding fugues. At the very end of the collection, both prelude 24 and fugue 24 are the most expansive in either category. Regardless of the differing formats, however, each single item represents a model case in compact and well-focused musical structure and character that sets it apart from the ways in which Bach had previously composed such pieces—as, for example, in the toccatas or the opening movements of the *English Suites* (Chapter 3).

The most obvious technical design feature of the preludes is their uniform motivic construction, reminiscent of the construction principle in the *Little Organ Book* yet on a larger scale. In most instances a single short and distinctive motivic idea—not merely a melodic phrase but always a pattern that involves both hands of the player—establishes the key and defines the makeup of the prelude from the very beginning—as, for instance, in BWV 848/1 (Fig. 2-10). At times, some free passagework leads into the final cadence, giving the piece a virtuosic touch. Fundamental improvisatory ideas such as arpeggio figures and other triadic patterns play a major role in helping to underscore the prelude's function of establishing and confirming the key. Such textures are present in astonishing variety in preludes 1–3, 5, 6, 11, 15, and 21. Yet as preludes 7, 19, and 24 demonstrate, even occasional imitative counterpoint can occur. Tempo, rhythmic patterns, metric devices, and other features all contribute to compositional diversity. While most of the preludes are written in common time, Bach employed an almost complete array of metric schemes: cut time (alla breve), $\frac{3}{2}$, $\frac{3}{4}$, $\frac{3}{8}$, $\frac{6}{4}$, $\frac{6}{8}$, $\frac{9}{8}$, $\frac{12}{8}$, $\frac{12}{16}$ and $\frac{24}{16}$. As examples of imaginative improvisatory and free-style composition, with highly differentiated and con-centrated amalgamations of diverse components, these works stand as novel, innovative, and extremely inventive kinds of preludes, which in some ways foreshadowed the expressive character pieces of a later generation.

As for the fugues, their focus is directed first and foremost on the proce-dural approach inherent in fugal composition, as opposed to the capricious improvisatory fancy that shapes the preludes. As a whole they establish the genre of fugue in a systematic manner not seen before, embracing all the theoretical and practical aspects of fugal composition. Traditionally, fugue as a special case of imitative counterpoint requires strict maintenance of num-ber of voices. In the first exposition, the subject statement is answered in the dominant and, depending on the subject, the answer is either real (exact) or tonal (with certain melodic intervals modified). Statement and answer alter-nate throughout, expositions and episodes or interludes alternate, contrapuntal techniques such as thematic inversion or stretto (overlapping statements) may be applied, and countersubjects or multiple themes may be used. All of this is standard in the *Well-Tempered Clavier*, but the preexisting conventions are elevated to an unparalleled level of compositional sophistication and musical variety. These traits are largely defined by Bach's highly individual subjects of varying length, melodic character, and rhythmic contour, and by non-thematic episodes filled with motivically linked or contrasting material. The two-, three-, four-, and five-voiced fugues of the *Well-Tempered Clavier* repre-sent the first crowning achievement of the composer, who reportedly "through his own study and reflection alone . . . became even in his youth a pure and strong fugue writer."[27] By thoroughly exploring all the possibilities for writing fugues, Bach presented a definitive survey of fugal composition, and thereby established the standard for the genre.

The fugues, even more than the preludes, allowed Bach to display his exceptional strength in the threefold combination of imaginative fecundity, intellectual penetration of the compositional task, and performing ability. Nevertheless, the collection, in its thoroughly revised 1722 autograph fair copy, does ample justice to both compositional types. Minor improvements made from time to time in subsequent years, however, indicate his subtle sense of musical detail, as two examples of different character reveal (Fig. 2-10):

- In Prelude 3 (C-sharp major) the revision concerns a localized primarily technical matter and mainly concerns contrapuntal logic, voice-leading, and texture: Bach merely reversed the first three notes in the top part from g#'–c#"–e#" to e#"–c#"–g#' (parallel corrections in mm. 17 and 55), and altered the transition to the initial motif in the bottom part of m. 8 from three eighths c#'–b#–a# to c#'–b#–a#–g#–a# (parallels in mm. 16, 24, and 54). With clean erasures and overwriting the composer achieved a more elegant voice-leading. The reason behind this intervention was obviously to adopt the reading that had always been present in m. 9, bottom part, and thereby to gain belatedly a unification of all parallel passages.
- In Fugue 1 (C major) the revision pertains to the rhetorical process of setting music, and includes a formal rationale, variegated expressive diction, and pointed harmonic moves: Bach changed notes 4–6 of the fugal subject in m. 1 and in all later entries by dotting the eighth note and squeezing the even sixteenths into two thirty-second notes:

later rhythmic correction:

EXAMPLE 2-1

Fugue in C, BWV 870/2: subject with rhythmic-melodic improvement.

He thus sharpened the rhythmic profile of the subject—a correction made only in the mid-1730s (earlier copies made from the autograph all show the original reading).

Bach may have introduced further minor changes, and surely additional ornamentation—without altering the actual autograph score—when performing for his pupils, who then entered what they had heard in their copies. Such performance is reported by the aforementioned Heinrich Nicolaus Gerber, who recalled that his teacher had played the entire collection "altogether three times through for him with his unmatchable art." He counted "among his happiest hours, when Bach, under the pretext of not feeling in the mood to teach, sat himself at one of his fine instruments and thus turned these hours into minutes."[28]

The *Well-Tempered Clavier* represents the composer's first truly significant work. Its prominent ornamental title page, without counterpart in Bach's output, underscores the importance he himself attached to it. At the time of its conception, the performer-composer, then well into his thirties, had become keenly aware of where the art of keyboard composition stood and what more could be done. Thus he taught himself the lessons that prepared him for the momentous project, and finally nurtured his ambition to tackle and integrate with one stroke several transformative ideas for which the time was ripe: acceptance of major-minor tonality, new norms for free and strict composition, and unrestricted utilization of the four-octave chromatic scale, and a fully developed range of keyboard idioms and textures—to be seen as corresponding to the intellectual spirit of an era that delighted in systematic, encyclopedic endeavors.

AUFRICHTIGE ANLEITUNG: INVENTIONS AND SINFONIAS

In comparison with the *Little Organ Book* and the *Well-Tempered Clavier*, the genesis and chronology of the two-part inventions and three-part sinfonias, under the heading *Aufrichtige Anleitung*, leaves little room for speculation. The earliest manuscript source for the twice fifteen pieces is again the *Little Clavier Book for Wilhelm Friedemann Bach* of 1720, and the autograph fair copy determines the work's completion date of no later than April 13, 1723—insofar as Bach could no longer put his Cöthen court title next to his name after his dismissal on that date (Table 2-1; Fig. 2-3). The inventions and sinfonias happen to be the only major instrumental works by Bach for which two sets of originals, composing scores and fair copies, have survived—a situation that reveals certain important facts:

- First of all, the older manuscript source provides evidence of the collections' direct relationship with a concrete program of instruction. Its first intended beneficiary was the composer's oldest son: the 144-page bound book was begun on January 22, 1720, exactly two months after Friedemann's ninth birthday.

- The various entries by both father and son throughout Friedemann's *Little Clavier Book* were not made in strict chronological sequence. The two-part inventions, each headed "Praeambulum" and numbered 1–15, occupy pages 71–103; the three-part pieces, each named "Fantasia" and likewise numbered 1–15, follow as a separate block on pages 118–44. Nevertheless, the thirty pieces were entered one after another within a relatively short period of time, and were paced in relation to the rapid progress the young boy was making during the course of 1721 and perhaps early 1722.

- The father's entries represent composing scores throughout (Fig. 2-11), but contain surprisingly few formative changes: the C-major Fantasia, BWV 787, for example, looks almost like a fair copy. The cleanliness of the notation demonstrates Bach's ability to conceive and quickly write down complex two- and three-part contrapuntal settings. Friedemann's entries within these two blocks of pieces are limited to preambles 4–7. These four only were copied from their autograph composing scores, not notated in the book but apparently written on separate sheets, and they indicate that copying music was an important part of Friedemann's education.[29]

- The autograph fair copy of early 1723 combined for the first time both sets of two- and three-part pieces in a separate single manuscript as a unified collection, under the title *Aufrichtige Anleitung*, "Faithful Guide."

The overall compositional history of the work covers a time span of less than two years between the first drafts in Friedemann's *Little Clavier Book* and the autograph fair copy. There are relatively few differences between the musical texts of the two manuscripts: the fair copy merely touches up a few spots in some pieces, changes a few notes here and there for improved voice-leading, and specifies articulation in certain places. Some more noticeable but still localized changes occur in the four-measure expansion of Invention 8, BWV 779, and the modifications at the end of several individual compositions, notably Invention 11, BWV 782 (mm. 21–23), Invention 14, BWV 785 (m. 19), and Sinfonia 10, BWV 796 (m. 32):

Praeambulum B♭ / Inventio 14 (BWV 785)

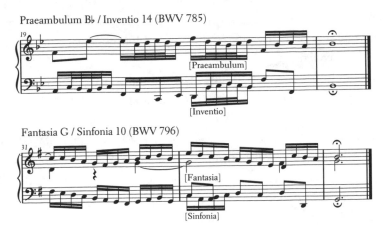

EXAMPLE 2-2

BWV 785 and BWV 796: corrections, to extend motivic continuity.

They primarily increase emphasis on the final cadences, and reflect Bach's subtle sense for the rhetorical effect of a proper conclusion.[30] The last three measures of both Praeambulum 10, BWV 782.1 (Fig. 2-11), and its polished final version, Invention 11, BWV 782.2 (Fig. 2-12), illustrate how the compos-

FIGURE 2-11

Preamble in G minor, BWV 782.1: autograph composing score (m. 11b to end).

er's removal of the two octave leaps in the penultimate measure of the early version creates greater rhythmic, melodic, and harmonic tension toward the delayed final cadence.

Yet, of much greater consequence for the work as a whole is the complete reorganization of the tonal configuration as it had been originally designed for Friedemann's *Little Clavier Book*. Unlike the *Well-Tempered Clavier*, with its ascending chromatic organization, the overall tonal plan stayed within the conventional framework of fifteen keys not exceeding four sharps or flats, a decision that preserved more strongly each key's distinct character. Bach obviously chose to honor and to teach his son initially the older practice of major-minor tonal harmony, as well as the related tuning method. Thus, each fifteen-piece set was arranged in a kind of circular fashion, beginning with the ascending diatonic scale from C to A with the natural root triads (C major, D minor, etc., up to A minor) and, after passing the pivotal keys (and triads) of B-flat major and B minor, concluding with the descending diatonic scale from A to C with the altered triads (A major, G minor, etc., down to C minor).

This key organization relates in some way to the earlier key order of the *Well-Tempered Clavier*, with the initial sequence C major, C minor, D minor,

FIGURE 2-12

Invention in G minor, BWV 782.2: autograph fair copy (with revised ending).

D major, E minor, E major and the tonic triad of the C major scale preceding the altered triad (as recorded in the *Clavier-Büchlein*). The fair copy of 1722 then changed the sequence to a scheme that consistently puts the major before the minor modes on a single ascending chromatic scale. Since Bach prepared the fair copies of the two collections one shortly after the other, he made corresponding adjustments so that the inventions and sinfonias would resemble more closely the one-directional ascending scheme of the *Well-Tempered Clavier*. As a result, both the numbering and tonal plans in the *Faithful Guide* departed from the earlier order scheme of the preambles and fantasias (capital letters = major mode keys; lower case letters = minor mode keys):

1721 (Preambles/Fantasias, 1–15):   C–d–e–F–G–a–b–B♭–A–g–f–E–E♭–D–c

1723 (Inventions/Sinfonias, 1–15):   C–c–D–d–E♭–E–e–F–f–G–g–A–a–B♭–b

The other, no less important change made at the same time involved the terminology. Not one of the four terms (praeambulum, fantasia, inventio, and sinfonia) has a specific genre connotation, and there was no precedent for naming the kinds of two- and three-part contrapuntal keyboard compositions as they first appeared in Friedemann's *Little Clavier Book*. The latter, however, also contained some earlier entries of separate preambles and preludes, including eleven pieces under the heading "Praeludium" that would find a place in what would become the *Well-Tempered Clavier*. Hence Bach differentiated between the two conceptually different kinds of preludes in the same book by giving the two-part contrapuntal variety the heading "Praeambulum." When he later reconsidered the essentially neutral designations of "praeambulum" and "fantasia" initially chosen for such original and anomalous contrapuntal keyboard pieces, Bach came up with the clever and original terms of "Inventio" and "Sinfonia" (see below) that relate them to the elaborate wording of the title page for the 1723 fair copy.

The title "Aufrichtige Anleitung" has little meaning without an explanation of what the "Faithful Guide" was supposed to provide (Table 2-1). There Bach carefully described the various objectives to be achieved by performing and studying the practical musical examples offered by this multipurpose pedagogical collection. As in the case of the *Well-Tempered Clavier*, its contents deliberately differ from dry exercises, and are designated for "lovers of the clavier, and especially those eager to learn." And just as with the *Little*

Organ Book and the *Well-Tempered Clavier*, the external format of the pieces in the *Faithful Guide* is predetermined, only more tightly so because each single composition is confined to exactly two pages of one manuscript opening, which obviates page turns.[31] Maintaining such a strict limitation governs a disciplined process of compositional logic and requires, from the outset of every single piece, a viable musical idea capable of driving the course of concentrated contrapuntal writing. Hence, at the center of each work stands the rhetorical concept of invention, that is, of inventing "good ideas" in the form of distinct musical subjects: melodic or composite themes that serve as points of origin for the work. Bach underlined this crucial inceptive moment of the creative process by renaming the two-part preambles "inventions," at the time a not at all common designation for musical pieces.

The Latin term "inventio" relates to the origination process of an oration in classical rhetoric, but it plays a role in music theory as well. Notably, in Italian usage it also refers to an unusual *soggetto* or subject, as in the *Invenzioni da camera* (Bologna, 1712) for violin and basso continuo by Antonio Bonporti, a collection Bach had taken note of prior to 1723.[32] Though a work of a completely different kind, its title probably intrigued Bach and prompted the renaming. At any rate, the choice of the term "invention" related directly to those users of the *Faithful Guide* who wanted "to acquire a strong foretaste of composition" and learn how "to obtain . . . good ideas" and "to develop the same well." These phrases clearly emphasize Bach's most important prerequisites for the study of composition, as related later by Carl Philipp Emanuel Bach: "As for the invention of ideas [*Erfindung der Gedanken*], he required this from the very beginning, and anyone who had none he advised to stay away from composition altogether."[33] Conceptually, the fantasias as objects for compositional studies could be subsumed under the title "inventions" as well, since they served essentially the same purpose. However, as Bach named the two- and three-part pieces differently in the *Little Clavier Book for Friedemann*, he intended not only to preserve the terminological distinction between the preambles and fantasias, but also to improve it. By relabeling the latter "sinfonias," again an uncommon designation within the keyboard repertory, he in fact drew attention to their distinctive contrapuntal makeup, based on the configuration of three separate parts that constituted triadic harmony. Hence, their new name (from the Greek *symphonia*, concord of sound) specifically underscored the sounding together of three voices. While the inventions demonstrate that *Vollstimmigkeit* can be successfully achieved even in a two-voice texture, the sinfonias explore the additional melodic and harmonic possibilities afforded by a third part.

The newly chosen headings "Inventio" and "Sinfonia" match, in their originality, the innovative designs of the pieces themselves. Bach certainly realized that with both the two- and three-part contrapuntal settings, he had entered completely uncharted territory. *The Little Organ Book* and *The Well-Tempered Clavier* were in a way linked to general if unspecific precursors in the realm of organ chorales, preludes, and fugues. Yet the pieces of the *Faithful Guide* represented a paradigmatic demonstration of the development of freely invented, concise, and distinct ideas, employed within strongly unified but contrapuntal settings—in which the two and three independent voices are equally essential, all derived from the material outlined in the first few measures. Each single piece highlights Bach's premise that only a good musical thought is worth developing, that only a clearly defined original idea—often shaped by the interplay of a concise subject with its countersubject—is worth carrying forward. The pieces are meant to demonstrate the endless possibilities of contrapuntal instrumental polyphony beyond the classic realm of fugue, with its obligatory thematic statement-and-answer principle.

The demonstrations include smooth and stylish applications of complex invertible or double counterpoint as, for example, in the three-part Sinfonia 9 in F minor (= Fantasia 11), BWV 795 (Fig. 2-13). The threefold exchange

FIGURE 2-13

Sinfonia in F minor, BWV 795.2: autograph fair copy.

of voices in the sinfonia evolves over the course of the composition, which introduces three distinct contrapuntal motifs in the opening four measures: **a**, the sigh motif (*suspiratio*) in the middle part, accompanied by **b**, the chromatic tetrachord, followed by motif **c**, with its pointed and sharp-edged rhythm, immediately used in combination with motifs **a** and **b** (Table 2-2). All three motifs occur regularly throughout the piece (and simultaneously eight more times), in a remarkable variability of combinations and inversions, as well as key areas.

TABLE 2-2. Sinfonia 9 (Fantasia 11), BWV 795: Invertible counterpoint passages using three motifs (**a–c**)

MEASURES	1–2	3–4	7–8	11–12	13–14	18–19	24–25	26–27	31–32	33–34
Part 1	–	a	b	c	a	b	b	a	a	c
Part 2	a	b	c	a	b	a	c	b	b	a
Part 3	b	c	a	b	c	c	a	c	c	b
KEYS	f	C	f	A♭	E♭	c	f	A♭	f	f

Sinfonia 9 offers but one of numerous examples of transformative approaches to applying contrapuntal techniques and artifices in a freely conceived new type of strict two- and three-voiced keyboard music. Individually and collectively, the inventions and sinfonias exhibit the art of counterpoint in its full range of thematic and motivic imitation, with variation, inversion, canon, stretto, and other features which, more often than not, are almost imperceptibly embedded in the two- and three-voiced compositional structures of unparalleled instrumental polyphony.

Never again would Bach compose any instrumental settings like those in this collection. Yet the general principles of contrapuntal writing exhibited here became an ever more essential aspect of the fabric of his instrumental and vocal scores. The two-part and then the three-part settings emerged one after another as lessons for his oldest son, and also reflected the end result of the composer's own learning process. Their creation also motivated him to illustrate the experience he had gained over time in the musico-rhetorical art of invention (*ars inveniendi*), and to present his expertise in exemplary models of varied and attractive contrapuntal settings through a systematic series of original pieces.[34]

Bach's references to the compositional approach applied in the settings of the *Faithful Guide* are actually preceded by the more specific performance instructions in the wording of the title, which serves as a reminder of Bach's lifelong commitment to integrating performance and the study of composition. The contrapuntal scores of the two sets of pieces are designed to mirror directly the two technical learning modes of performance, that is, "to play cleanly in two voices but also, after further progress, to deal correctly and well with three obbligato parts." The upper and lower parts of the inventions require the absolute physical independence and equal facility of the player's left and right hands, supported by a new method of fingering that involves the thumb as the indispensable fifth finger of both hands. Traditional fingering practice limited the use of the thumb to chordal playing and did not normally employ it in linear writing, this being so in both virtuosic passagework and polyphonic keyboard pieces.[35] Although there exist various examples of seventeenth-century keyboard pieces that require use of the thumb, pedagogical works continue to uphold the traditional four-finger method. Hence and in quasi-programmatic fashion, the head motif of Invention 1 is devised to fit exactly the advanced fingering pattern relying on the equal use of all five fingers.

right-hand fingering:	1–2–3–4–2–3–1–5
melodic line:	c–d–e–f–d–e–c–g
left-hand fingering:	5–4–3–2–4–3–5–1

Invention 1 is also remarkable in that Bach demonstrates throughout, with greatest resourcefulness, the manifold ways in which material can be generated from a given head motif via inversion, augmentation, fragmentation, recombination, and the like. Furthermore, the piece exemplifies a very great deal about how to achieve a satisfactory musical composition. It offers a compact yet highly illustrative example in terms of the handling of form: the first six-measure segment is capped by an arrival at the dominant, followed by a deftly calibrated modulation to the relative minor. The move to that key is accompanied by an intensification of activity in both parts and an extension of range. Thus the peak of the piece is located about two-thirds of the way through (m. 14)—an approach that would become a pervasive archetype in terms of formal procedure through the later eighteenth century and beyond.

The particular challenge of the three-voiced pieces essentially relates to the same physiological aspect of properly playing polyphonic music on the organ that Bach emphasized when requiring the systematic use of the pedal in the *Orgel-Büchlein* for the bass voice. Additionally, the three-voiced sinfonias focused on the management of independent voices in which each hand might play two voices and voices can move between hands. Having all five fingers of both hands take a share in playing middle voices is a technique not taught before, one that also provided training for manual performance of polyphonic keyboard music for more than three parts on all keyboard instruments. Yet Bach's stated goal was not merely "to play cleanly" and "to deal correctly and well" with the musical text but "above all, to arrive at a singing style in playing," that is, to perform in a style that would imitate a duo or trio of human voices, each presenting its assigned lines in a well-articulated and expressive manner. This notion brought into play an entirely new and critical aesthetic category that became of vital importance to the performance of keyboard music, an aspect not expressly mentioned in the formulation of the titles of the *Little Organ Book* and the *Well-Tempered Clavier*, let alone in performance instructions by other composers. Moreover, it anticipated the performing style advocated and described a generation later by Carl Philipp Emanuel Bach in his keyboard treatise, *Versuch über die wahre Art das Clavier zu spielen* (Berlin, 1753).[36]

When in 1722/23 Bach prepared the fair copies of the three special musical workbooks in order to substantiate his didactic expertise, given the prospect of the Leipzig appointment as Thomascantor, the *Faithful Guide* was taken up last, no doubt because the inventions and sinfonias needed little additional work or further editing. When he actually started teaching in Leipzig, however, he used the guide as fundamental material for the pre-professional musicians among the St. Thomas School students and his many private pupils. Heinrich Nicolaus Gerber remembered the basic and essential function of the *Faithful Guide* in what apparently became a typical course of study with Bach: "At the first lesson he set his [two- and three-part] inventions before him. When he had studied these through to Bach's satisfaction, there followed a series of suites [the French followed by the English], then the Well-Tempered Clavier."[37] Gerber discussed only his harpsichord lessons and his composition lessons on the harpsichord, and therefore the *Little Organ Book* remained unmentioned. However, as he later became court organist in Sondershausen, he surely took organ lessons too, at which time the *Little Organ Book* would have played a major role.

When initially conceiving the three workbooks, Bach could hardly have imagined their eventual impact on the integration of composition and performance, their transformational function, and their complementary value as sources of musical recreation and intellectual nutrition for future generations of students. However, as keyboard virtuoso and performer-composer, the acts of composing and performing were inseparable for him. Thus Bach's innovative approaches in composing organ chorales, for example, advanced the means of both musical expression and the techniques of pedal playing. Likewise, the unparalleled collection of preludes and fugues in all keys rationalized and ratified not only the essence of modern tonal harmony, exemplified in free and strict styles, but also the gradual if incomplete shift toward equal temperament and the freedom of a new fingering that made systematic use of the thumb and permitted passing through all the chromatic keys of the keyboard with equal ease. Finally, his ingenious idea of devising tightly controlled two- and three-voiced contrapuntal pieces furthered the intertwined purposes of compositional and analytical study, while introducing the play of polyphonic music in a distinctly transparent way and in an aesthetically pleasing cantabile manner.

The three keyboard workbooks are distinct from conventional anthologies. They are instead individually designed collections, each with a particular purpose and coherent focus, and without a direct parallel elsewhere. Moreover, all three established new standards for both composition and performance, and in different areas. They established principles that Bach would continue to pursue in further benchmark works within the various instrumental and vocal genres, relating principles and genres to one another and to the image of an expanding musical universe, with keyboard art functioning as a quasi-gravitational force. The disposition, nature, and talent of a full-blooded instrumentalist shaped and penetrated the quintessential performer-composer's mind-set and general musical outlook, in which the dynamic interrelationship of performance and composition was a basic condition. Hence, Bach's ever-increasing and deepening devotion to composition remained decisively influenced by his keyboard authority in every respect, and especially in the continuous advancement of ingenious and forceful originality, technical mastery, and intellectual control. All these were constituent elements of Bach's musical language—with its ultimate goal of moving the heart.

CHAPTER 3

In Search of the Autonomous Instrumental Design

Toccata, Suite, Sonata, Concerto

I n determining the conceptual elements of musical design for the three expository workbooks discussed in the previous chapter, Bach paid little attention to related keyboard genres of the day, and drew only limited inspiration from them. The kinds of organ chorale, prelude and fugue, and invention and sinfonia he composed had few precedents or parallels. Yet he was nevertheless also deeply interested in, and vitally engaged with, the prevailing repertoires that had long preoccupied keyboard performers and composers alike. Initially and in particular, this meant the large toccatas in the manner of his admired North German idols, Dietrich Buxtehude and Johann Adam Reincken. He was also drawn to the increasingly popular genres of suites, sonatas, and concertos, which dominated European instrumental music during the first half of the eighteenth century. In their formal and structural designs, all of Bach's pertinent contributions in these categories essentially followed extant formal models, without effecting wholesale changes or redefining the fundamental premises. With a mind-set quite different from the manner in which he approached the *Orgel-Büchlein*, the *Well-Tempered Clavier*, and the *Faithful Guide*, the composer clearly maintained the well-established external parameters of the prevailing forms. At the same time, however, the several opus-like collections that feature carefully selected additions to these various existing genres emphatically stress the idioms of his distinct musical language as it emerged in the early 1700s. In this regard, the early set of six toccatas, BWV 910–915, provides a striking testimonial, the first such demonstration in a gradually emerging series of pathbreaking follow-ups. In all these works, Bach weighed and reassessed the existing conventions of instrumental music, all as part of a genuine and determined quest for original and autonomous language—that is, sounding outcomes that would be readily identifiable as his own musical creations.

The way in which this series of benchmark collections materialized—first bolstering the keyboard core with two different sets of suites, then branching out into two books of unaccompanied solos for violin and violoncello, and eventually embracing orchestral concertos—appears to reflect a carefully chosen path. There is, of course, no shred of evidence for any such methodical plan, laid out in advance and in anticipation of an unfolding professional life with unpredictable turns. In retrospect, however, the series and its overall context presents itself as a development with compelling logic, one that chronicles critical steps in the composer's steady quest to broaden and deepen his experience. The successive deposition of each opus stands as a deliberate and methodical summary of Bach's achievements in each given category.

The posthumous catalog recorded by Carl Philipp Emanuel Bach (Table 1-1) lists all the instrumental works that his father placed together in opus-style manuscript collections. The few exceptions include the harpsichord concertos for one and more solo instruments, which are lumped together as a single group, and also the so-called *Brandenburg Concertos*, which are completely missing from the list. Regarding the former, the keyboard concerto as such was considered a particular Bach specialty, and thus the single reference citing concertos for one to four solo instruments makes an even stronger point. As for the latter, these six concertos for various instruments existed as a special set only in the dedication score given to Margrave Christian of Brandenburg and hence did not constitute a tangible opus, since they were kept as individual pieces on Bach's music shelves.[1] It is doubtful, however, that more such dedicatory or similar collections existed at any one time, because a complete set of pieces was far less likely to get lost without a trace. Still, the known manuscript collections surely represent a mere fraction of the composer's total instrumental output, as the many surviving individual works indicate—a situation only compounded by the many unspecified losses resulting from the division of Bach's estate in 1750. In this respect, the blanket reference at the end of the posthumous list of works—to "a lot of . . . instrumental pieces, of all sorts, and for all kinds of instruments"—unfortunately proves useless for any sort of numerical estimate. On the other hand, a proper accounting for the numerous and presumably priceless single works was hardly possible as the family dealt with a vast musical estate. Even so, the clearly recognizable separation of itemized opus collections from the unspecified bulk of pieces very likely reflects a distinction made by the composer himself, one well known within the Bach household.

As implied by the work listing of 1750, Bach apparently intended to set his assembled groups of exemplary pieces apart from related but scattered individual works. This arrangement does not necessarily suggest any discrimination based upon musical quality. But the opus-style collections were not only internally organized but also—as extant autograph scores show—compiled in separate physical entities, suggesting the composer's aim to make a particular statement in each case. By designing a homogeneous collection of exemplary works, Bach intended to summarize proudly his accomplishment, and to showcase a distinctive approach to the respective category of composition. He clearly considered his instrumental opus collections a more or less final word in every category, and he decided each time to move on rather than add another comparable opus. Only part II of the *Well-Tempered Clavier* represents an exception: about twenty years after finishing part I, Bach the teacher apparently felt a strong need—for his students' sake as well as his own—to update and modernize his premier keyboard textbook by offering new solutions to the challenging task of composing in all twenty-four keys.

Bach the composer competed with himself constantly, and in many ways he himself was his most important critic—as his regular practice of judicious revisions to his own works demonstrates. His generally competitive attitude also inspired him to assess most attentively and carefully the work of other composers, contemporary and earlier masters alike: for the purpose of learning new music, for viewing alternative compositional approaches, and ultimately for establishing a clearer definition of his very own pathway. Primarily through examining with greatest care what others had done, he was subsequently able to pursue his consistent goal of making his music decidedly original, discernibly different from everyone else's. Unlike such contemporaries as Telemann, Vivaldi, and François Couperin, he never recast the conceptual and formal patterns of suites, sonatas, and concertos in order to suit his own distinctive resolve.[2] Rather, he preferred to stay within the confines of the given parameters. Yet what he added to the various instrumental categories over time consisted in effect of rejoinders to existing repertoires, which patently demonstrate his ambition to eclipse and outclass his models in terms of internal refinement, textural riches, and depth of expressive character. He thereby played a truly seminal role in the arena of autonomous and original compositional design, in a manner that proved to be of profound influence well beyond his own time.

AT HOME ON KEYBOARDS AND OTHER INSTRUMENTS

Even a cursory survey of Bach's overall instrumental output shows shifting stages of engagement, related for the most part to changing official duties and self-chosen priorities. Key turning points are marked by Bach's appointments: as town organist in Arnstadt (1703) and Mühlhausen (1707), as court organist and chamber musician in Weimar (1708) with promotion to concertmaster in 1714, followed by the post as princely capellmeister in Cöthen (1717), and finally the position of cantor and music director in Leipzig (1723). There he also served for more than a decade as director of the preeminent Leipzig Collegium Musicum, forerunner of the Gewandhaus Orchestra.[3] These positions affected the overall balance in his production of instrumental ensemble compositions and vocal works, but they never impinged on the output of keyboard works, the most consistent (yet constantly evolving) activity in Bach's musical life. The performer-composer was truly obsessed with the organ and other keyboard instruments, such that they never drifted away from the center of his interests—and were, in fact, a nearly exclusive absorption until about 1714.

From very early on, Bach also played the violin and viola, and probably the violoncello as well. As the youngest member of the household of the director of the Eisenach town music company (a professional ensemble employed by the town council), born into the third generation of professional musicians and growing up with different instruments around the house, Bach learned the basics of their handling and playing from childhood on. Since his father Johann Ambrosius Bach (1645–1695) was an accomplished violinist and leader of the instrumental ensemble at St. George's Church, Johann Sebastian must have picked up the violin before age ten and trained under his father's guidance; the valuable Jacobus Stainer violin he owned was likely the instrument he inherited from his father.[4] Ambrosius Bach also regularly played at the court of Saxe-Eisenach under its capellmeister, the distinguished violinist Daniel Eberlin (later Telemann's father-in-law), and he surely knew about (and may perhaps even have met) the famous Italian-trained virtuoso Johann Paul von Westhoff (1656–1705) from the neighboring court of Saxe-Weimar. One of the foremost violinists of the day, Westhoff was still active at the Weimar capelle in 1703, during Johann Sebastian's initial six-month tenure there. Later, notably as Weimar concertmaster and Cöthen capellmeister, but also in his various Leipzig functions, Bach led his ensembles often if not primarily from the violin, and he regularly played the viola as well. As Carl Philipp Emanuel Bach related in 1774,

> As the greatest expert and judge of harmony, he liked best to play the viola, with appropriate loudness and softness. In his youth, and until the approach of old age, he played the violin clearly and penetratingly, and thus kept the orchestra in better order than he could have done with the harpsichord.[5]

There are no specific references to Bach's cello playing, but his expert and idiomatic treatment of the instrument as a composer strongly suggests his thorough familiarity with the cello as well.

Throughout his life a passionate instrumentalist, Bach earned his reputation first and foremost as a superlative performer on the organ and harpsichord. The ducal court in Weimar recognized his celebrity status early on, and rewarded him periodically with generous salary increases. His achievements as a virtuoso were also well recognized beyond his professional posts: he traveled frequently as a guest artist, largely within Thuringia and Saxony but occasionally also to places as far off as Kassel, Hamburg, and Berlin. He certainly had made a serious name for himself by 1717, when Johann Mattheson published a reference to "the famous organist of Weimar."[6] The same year also saw the harpsichord duel that wasn't. The man who was to be Bach's opponent, famous French virtuoso Louis Marchand, fled the Dresden competition venue in the dead of night, perhaps fearing that his skills were not in fact sufficient for this sort of competition. Bach thus performed alone the next day, to the applause of a distinguished court audience. Only a fraction of Bach's frequent keyboard recitals and concerts, often related to his numerous organ examinations, were reported in detail. They range from the well-attended organ recital in 1720 at St. Catherine's Church in Hamburg, to at least three public organ recitals in Dresden (1725, 1731, and 1736), to Bach's famous appearance before King Friedrich II of Prussia in 1747. All these performances received the sort of unanimous praise typified by an adulatory poem published in a Dresden newspaper, the last line of which proclaims, "as soon as he plays, he amazes everyone."[7] Exploring pathbreaking approaches to expanding the uses of the harpsichord, organ, and, later, the fortepiano as well remained a lifelong constant in Bach's artistic life. Finally, and surely for reasons of general perception beyond Leipzig, the headline of his published obituary does not refer to him as "The Composer," but terms him instead "The World-Famous Organist."[8]

Bach's very early and quite remarkable progress as a keyboard player is anecdotally reported in the well-known story about "a book of clavier pieces by the most famous masters of the day—Froberger, Kerl[l], Pachelbel" that the little boy borrowed without permission from his brother-teacher. The young Johann Sebastian "would fetch the book out at night, . . . and copy it by moon-light. . . . Secretly and with extraordinary eagerness he was trying to put it to use."[9] If the ten- or eleven-year-old played intricate toccatas and contrapuntal works by Johann Jakob Froberger, and the thirteen-year-old overcame the challenges of Dietrich Buxtehude's most demanding chorale fantasia, "Nun freut euch, lieben Christen g'mein" (BuxWV 210), then a promising virtuoso career was already well in the making—even during the Ohrdruf years prior to 1700. It comes as no surprise that shortly after graduating from the Lüneburg Latin School in 1702, the seventeen-year-old lad was elected town organist in Sangerhausen. The job soon slipped away, as the reigning duke overruled the town council's vote and installed his own protégé. Yet in 1703 Bach landed an even more desirable post in Arnstadt, where he had at his disposal a brand-new, top-quality organ at the New Church. In 1705, he visited for three months with his idol Buxtehude, composer of the most technically advanced and musically sophisticated organ repertoire of the day. Bach proceeded to assimilate the Lübeck composer's style, and then began writing similar pieces—in Buxtehude's spirit but now to his own credit.

THE INAUGURAL OPUS: SIX KEYBOARD TOCCATAS

Considering the self-confidence and ambitions of the young keyboard virtuoso, it seems entirely plausible that in choosing to make a debut of sorts within the substantial and impressive format of the North German toccata, Bach had determined to announce his powers to the world with a compelling gesture. In assembling six large-scale virtuosic pieces, he would establish himself as the true heir of his North German idols, as a directly comparable performer-composer of fanciful, musically varied, and technically demanding keyboard works. The relevant models, provided notably by Buxtehude, Johann Adam Reincken, and Nicolaus Bruhns, had been well known to Bach since his time in Lüneburg (in the immediate and inspiring vicinity of Georg Böhm), his side trips to visit Reincken in Hamburg, and his 1705 sojourn with Buxtehude in Lübeck. The North German keyboard toccata achieved its magnificent culmination in the organ toccata or prelude, whose particularly imposing effects derived primarily from the exceptional sonic resources of the Hanseatic organ, the largest and most powerful musical instrument of the era and one that profoundly influenced the structure and content of contemporary keyboard repertoire.

In his various early organ works, most typically in the Toccata in E major, BWV 566, and the Prelude in A minor, BWV 551, Bach consciously emulated the North German model, even though the central German organ landscape did not offer instruments of a scale comparable to contemporary Hanseatic examples. As a consequence, when Bach elected to fashion an imaginative realization of the keyboard toccata as the epitome of the seventeenth-century *stylus fantasticus,* he deliberately focused on the manualiter toccata for harpsichord as the medium of choice. This decision allowed him to concentrate on compositional and structural details, quite independently of the varied sonic effects provided by a large organ. His toccata headings in the early sources contain, without exception, the reference "manualiter," thereby clarifying their explicit destination for keyboard instruments without pedal—that is, harpsichords in particular—although they could certainly be played on the organ.

As Bach's organ works of the "pedaliter" variety ordinarily required the obbligato pedal, a compilation of manualiter toccatas was a prudent choice that supported the overall paradigmatic qualities of the collection, including the advanced harmonic design that required well-tempered tuning. Yet even as he was investing his creative efforts in this uniquely attractive type of large-scale keyboard music, Bach did not quite realize that he was engaging in a genre without a future: that these works would represent not only the culmination of this type of toccata, but also the end point of a venerable tradition. Apparently he soon recognized this circumstance, as the hampered transmission and survival of the toccatas and their sources indicate. The works did not remain in his performing and teaching portfolio for long, and were soon replaced by more current repertoire.

Bach's toccatas have not survived in an autograph score nor in any complete scribal manuscript. The only reference to the collection as it once existed is found in the entry "Six toccatas, for the clavier" among the unpublished compositions enumerated in the 1750 work catalog. This listing, however, does not square with the total count of seven transmitted harpsichord toccatas, each in a different key (Table 3-1). The first six works, BWV 910–915, strictly follow

TABLE 3-1. Six keyboard toccatas, BWV 910–915, and BWV 916

Toccata in F♯ minor BWV 910	Toccata in C minor BWV 911	Toccata in D major BWV 912	Toccata in D minor BWV 913	Toccata in E minor BWV 914	Toccata in G minor BWV 915
passaggio **C**: mm. 1–18	*passaggio* **C**: mm. 1–12	*passaggio* **C**: mm.1–10	*passaggio* **C**: mm.1–15	*passaggio Allegro* 3/2: mm. 1–13	*passaggio* 24/16: mm. 1–4
[*adagio*] 3/2: mm. 19–48	*adagio* **C**: mm. 12–33	*allegro* **C**: mm. 11–67	[*adagio*]—*presto* **C**: mm. 15–32		*adagio* 3/2: mm. 5–17
fugue—presto e staccato **C**: mm. 49–107	*fugue—allegro* **C**: mm. 34–83	*adagio* **C**: mm. 68–79	*fugue* **C**: mm. 33–120	*fugato—un poco allegro* **C**: mm. 14–41	*fugato—allegro* **C**: mm. 18–67
[*adagio*] **C**: 108–35	*adagio* **C**: mm. 84–86	*fugue* **C**: mm. 80–111	*adagio—presto* **C**: mm. 121–45	*adagio* **C**: mm. 42–70	*adagio* 3/2: mm. 68–78
fugue 6/8: mm. 135–88	*fugue—allegro* **C**: 86–170	*con discrezione* **C**: 111–26	*fugue allegro* 3/4: mm. 146–294	*Fuga* **C**: mm. 71–138	*Fuga* **C**: mm. 79–189
finale 6/8: mm. 191–99	*finale—adagio-presto* **C**: mm. 171–75	*fugue* 6/16: mm.127–275		*finale* **C**: mm. 138–142	*finale* 24/16: mm. 189–94
		finale **C**: mm. 276–77			

Toccata in G major, BWV 916:

[1.] **C**: mm. 1–56; [2.] *adagio* (E Minor)—**C**: 57–89; [3.] *presto* [fugue]—6/8: mm. 81–177

the typical multi-sectional layout of the North German toccata. But the form of BWV 916 differs substantially from the others: influenced stylistically by the Italian concerto model, it consists of three clearly delineated movements with a slow middle movement. In their stylistic and structural affinity, then, BWV 910–915 form a homogeneous and closed group of six toccatas—corroborating the entry in the list of works—and suggest that the supernumerary toccata BWV 916 originated independently, and was added to the group of six as a later supplement.

The lost autograph—most likely a portfolio holding six scores in separate fascicles or a book with a title reference to the number six (as reflected in the 1750 list of works)—shared its fate with quite a few other items that disappeared after the division of the composer's estate. Therefore no information on its exact content and organization is available. Yet some noteworthy details are nonetheless provided by the early, though scattered, manuscript transmission within the inner Bach circle, including copies made by Bach's older brother Johann Christoph of Ohrdruf in two manuscript anthologies known as the "Möller Manuscript"[10] and "Andreas Bach Book."[11] These copies include both older versions of BWV 912 and BWV 913, from around 1704, as well as thoroughly revised versions from about 1708, and seem to represent the earliest layer of the toccatas, both chronologically and stylistically. Moreover, the Latinized heading for the early version, "Toccata Prima. ex Clave D.^{b}. manualiter per J. S. Bachium"[12]—a typical feature of the earliest Bach sources—suggests that this piece in the traditional *modus primus* (the Dorian "D" mode notated without a flat in the key signature) may have been the first one composed. Extending to almost 300 measures, it is by far the longest of Bach's toccatas, and as such may well have functioned as the opening piece of the set. Since its revised version shares with the sources of four other toccatas the Italianized author's name "Giov[anni]. Bast[iano]. Bach"—a later preference of the composer—the compilation of an opus of six toccatas in revised and edited versions most likely stems from around 1707–8, with BWV 916 added or inserted around or after 1710. The schematic structural details given in Table 3-1 relate to the final versions of the toccatas.[13]

The North German toccata, especially its prototype for large organ with pedal, represents the most impressive genre of large-scale keyboard music from around 1700. The category encompasses a great variety of compositional ideas, techniques, textures, and virtuoso features as well as varied tempos and diverse modes of expression, all to be underscored with colorful registrations—in the overall manner that Johann Mattheson described as the "fantastic style" ("fantastische Styl").[14] The Lübeck master Buxtehude had put his unmistakable stamp on this genre, one so closely tied to the unique northern European landscape of large three- and four-manual church organs with fifty-plus stops. His Hamburg colleague and friend Johann Adam Reincken, and Buxtehude's pupil Nicolaus Bruhns, also contributed significantly to the evolution of the multi-sectional toccata. The young Bach took up their works as inspirational models, then experimented extensively with his own approach to composing organ works in this extroverted musical manner, one so suited to virtuoso players of the highest rank. That Bach's opus of toccatas was chiefly designated for harpsichord is made particularly clear by the D-major Toccata, BWV 912 (Fig. 3-1a), whose opening section derives from the stunning pedal-solo scale of the organ prelude BWV 532 in the same key (Fig. 3-1b). In their divergent elaborations, the two works demonstrate Bach's intent to differentiate between organ and harpsichord, or "pedaliter" and "manualiter," idioms—that is, between works specifically designed for keyboard instruments with pedal and those without pedal.

Among the North German repertoire of manualiter toccatas readily accessible to Bach, only Reincken's Toccata in G, with its two embedded fugues, serves as a true model, even though it is of a smaller scale. After his return

FIGURE 3 1a

Toccata in D major, BWV 912: copy J. C. Bach (c. 1710), detail.

FIGURE 3-1b

Prelude in D major, BWV 532/1: copy L. Sichart (c. 1740), detail.

from Lüneburg, Bach seems to have brought the work to the attention of his brother Johann Christoph, who then copied it along with BWV 910–911 into one of his keyboard anthologies.[15] Two smaller manualiter toccatas by Buxtehude, BuxWV 164–165, each with only one fugue, went through Bach's hands as well,[16] but the Lübeck composer's large pedaliter organ preludes, most of which contain two fugal sections, influenced Bach to a far greater degree. As shown in the schematic outlines of Table 3-1, Bach's six toccatas loosely adopt the conceptual framework of their collective models, but also exceed them in every respect: in sheer technical virtuosity, significantly expanded format, number of contrasting sections, overall contrapuntal density, and in particular, the complexity of the fugues—some of which feature thematic inversion and combine subjects with countersubjects. Although they resemble Buxtehude's related pedaliter organ pieces, Bach's manualiter rejoinders follow no single pattern of multi-sectional organization, with the result that they represent six emphatically dissimilar musical solutions.

Differences from their presumptive North German models already turn up at the very beginning of each toccata. In his more drawn-out *passaggio* (passagework) openings, Bach offers an uncommonly wide range of melodically and rhythmically differentiated devices: runs, scales, arpeggios, and figurative patterns. Especially effective are the adagio sections, which are filled with adventurous harmonic moves, daring chromaticism, and surprising rhetorical devices. In this regard the Toccata in F-sharp minor, BWV 910, reached an unprecedented level (Fig. 3-2). Its extended fugal sections dominate the formal outlines, and each single section unfolds in an experimental balancing act that combines stretched-out fanciful themes and contrasting countersubjects with strict contrapuntal developments. The imaginative interplay of free figuration and discrete sequential patterns toward the end of the second fugue points toward the flamboyant finale.

Bach's set of six toccatas exhibits, above all, a special fascination with large-scale form—single pieces reaching a length of more than ten minutes of playing time—as well as an ambition to exceed the venerable benchmarks established by his various models. This goal is not without parallel elsewhere in his instrumental output, and echoes do appear quite prominently in some of his pedaliter organ works from about the same time. A special case in this respect is the Passacaglia in C minor, BWV 582, a work of more than 12 minutes' duration (the average for the toccatas as well). It represents another characteristic example of Bach having learned from and then attempting to surpass Buxtehude,[17] in

FIGURE 3-2

Toccata in F♯ minor, BWV 910: copy J. C. Bach (c. 1710),
detail.

the process raising the performance threshold and establishing a new compositional paradigm.

OPUS COLLECTIONS FROM WEIMAR AND CÖTHEN

If a set of formidable toccatas was an obvious choice for a first opus by the young keyboard virtuoso, Bach's subsequent opus collections seem at first completely disconnected from such an old-fashioned starting point. Yet, still concerned about the challenge of dealing with and mastering large-scale extended instrumental works but not eager to move in the direction of the exceptional three-movement Toccata in G major, BWV 916, he turned away completely from the soon-to-be-outmoded toccata in favor of the ever more trendy suites, sonatas, and concertos, with their modern structure of three or more distinct movements. The suite or partita consisted from the very beginning of a chain of dances and as such formed a sequence of self-contained movements, while it was only after 1700 that the sonata and concerto moved in the direction of a sequence of three or four movements each in the form of a closed, self-contained musical unit.

Two sets of six suites for harpsichord, with and without preludes

Ever curious about what was musically in vogue, the young Bach also played and composed suites at around the same time that he wrote the toccatas. This link is confirmed by the "Möller" and "Andreas Bach" anthologies compiled by his older brother Johann Christoph, largely drawn from materials received from Johann Sebastian, mostly prior to 1710. They contain not only four toccatas but also three suites: Ouverture in F major, BWV 820 (Ouverture–Entrée–Menuet/Trio–Bourrée–Gigue), Suite in A major, BWV 832 (Allemande–Air–Sarabande–Bourrée–Gigue), and Praeludium and Partita in F major, BWV 833 (Praeludium–Allemande-Corrente–Sarabande/ Double–Air).[18] These pieces represent the two different types of suites as they emerged within the French repertoire: the suite "avec prélude" and "sans prélude"—that is, with and without a free introduction in the form of an overture or prelude. However, the movement schemes of BWV 820, 832, and 833 show no consistent pattern of formal organization; the same holds true for their irregular compositional makeup. On the other hand, these works do reveal a combination of experimental daring with a highly developed understanding of rhythmic-metric declamation, diversified texture, and pointed musical characterization. The three early suites are placed in the two manuscripts side by side with a substantial number of suites by Reincken, Böhm, and others, which invariably present a uniform four-movement scheme of allemande–courante–sarabande–gigue. Although this movement order was standard in North Germany, Bach initially intended to steer an independent course—probably inspired by the great variety of suite types found in genuine French suite collections such as the *Pièces de clavecin* (Paris, 1677) by Nicholas Lebègue. The particularly influential works of Lebègue were widely disseminated in Germany, and can also be found in the two Ohrdruf keyboard anthologies. Bach is known to have had access to other genuine French collections as well, including Jean-Henri d'Anglebert's *Pièces de clavecin* (Paris, 1689), from which he excerpted the ornament table for Wilhelm Friedemann Bach's *Clavier-Büchlein*, and the *Six Suites de Clavecin* by Charles François Dieupart (Amsterdam, 1701), from which he made copies between 1709 and 1715.[19]

Recognizing the significance of courtly dance music, its influence within the growing *galant* culture outside the courts, and the resulting demand for keyboard suites by an increasing number of accomplished amateur players, Bach eventually turned his full attention to this popular instrumental genre in the 1710s and early 1720s. He put out three exemplary sets of six suites each, but by around 1725 he determined that he was essentially finished with the genre. The last opus represents a special case, as it became the opener for his *Clavier-Übung* series, but the earlier two opus-style suite collections already demonstrate the composer's transformational musical goals. Later known under the names *English* and *French Suites*, the two collections exemplify the two principal types of suite—the earlier set consisting of overture suites (that is, suites of dances with opening preludes), the later one of suites without such openings.

Dates for the first collection are difficult to ascertain, as no autograph manuscript for the *English Suites* survives. A copy of the first Suite in A major, BWV 806, with the heading "Prélude avec les Svites composeé par Giov: Bast: Bach," in the hand of Bach's Weimar friend and colleague Johann Gottfried Walther,[20] clearly establishes an origin prior to 1717. The mixed French-Italian title not only points to the relatively early Weimar years, but in particular emphasizes the importance of the opening movement (prélude avec . . .) within the individual suite. For the *French Suites*, Cöthen origin is verified definitively by the composing scores of Suites I–V in the *Clavier-Büchlein* for Anna Magdalena Bach of 1722.[21] However, since this little book has been transmitted in mutilated form, many of the autograph entries, including pages from the first three suites, are unfortunately lost. Student copies indicate that Bach put some finishing editorial touches on the two sets in Leipzig around 1724,[22] most likely in the context of reviewing both in preparation for his final statement in this voguish genre, the partitas of *Clavier-Übung* I.

The original collective title for the *English Suites* cannot be determined, but the most authoritative scribal copies, which transmit wordings like "Six Svittes avec leurs Préludes pour le Clavecin composées par Jean Sebast: Bach," may come close to the original. The later nickname appears first in Berlin manuscripts from the mid-1750s, with headings like "Sechs Suiten für das

Clavier . . . , die Englischen Suiten genannt."[23] The English reference derived from a copy owned by the young Johann Christian Bach,[24] which remained with his half-brother Carl in Berlin when the former left for Italy in 1755. There, the head title "Suite I. avec Prelude pour le Clavecin" is supplemented by the remark "Fait pour les Anglois" (made for the English).[25] The reference as such is unspecific, ambiguous, and insufficient to corroborate the later explanation given by Johann Nicolaus Forkel, namely that the collection was titled "English Suites because the composer made them for a noble English-man."[26] As no connections to this effect are documented, the nickname may be explained quite differently by the makeup of the suites and their close relationship to François Dieupart's *Six Suittes De Clavecin Divisés en Ouver-tures, Allemandes, Courantes, Sarabandes, Gavottes, Menuetts, Rondeaux & Gigues* (Amsterdam, 1701), from which Bach took (indirect) copies in Weimar after 1709.[27] Dieupart was London-based from about 1702/3, and was much appreciated by his English clientele.[28]

The *French Suites*, on the other hand, also received their nickname in Berlin after 1750, apparently by analogy with the *English Suites* and for the sole purpose of distinguishing the two from one another—though clearly without any stylistic implications. The earliest reference to the name "French Suites" shows up in a copy written in the mid-1750s by Carl Friedrich Chris-tian Fasch,[29] a member of the Berlin circle of Carl Philipp Emanuel Bach. Another member of that same circle, Friedrich Wilhelm Marpurg, speaks in 1762 also of "VI French Suites of the late Capellmeister Bach."[30] At any rate, both nicknames definitely improve on the neutral listing of the two collections as "Six suites" and "Six more of the same, somewhat shorter" in the first work listing of 1750 (Table 1-1).

It may not be coincidental that the earlier set of *English Suites* includes prominent preludes. Although these introductory movements do not represent a direct carryover from the previous collection of toccatas, they nevertheless provide a link to, and a recollection of, the toccatas' improvisatory manners and polyphonic styles (Fig. 3-3). Moreover, with as many as 213 measures, they resemble the toccatas in length. Yet they forego the multi-sectional struc-ture of the toccatas and establish a more focused approach, with emphasis on imitative motivic and thematic textures that foreshadow the polyphonic principles of the Inventions and Sinfonias, BWV 772–801. The Prelude to Suite 6 actually comes closest to the model of an extended toccata, albeit one governed by a consistent $\frac{9}{8}$ meter and made up of only two sections: an impro-

FIGURE 3-3

Prelude of *English Suite* in A minor, BWV 807/1: copy J. G. Walther (c. 1720).

visational opening section that concludes with an adagio cadential measure, and an extended fugal section with interspersed free figuration, a fractionated approach that Bach later on completely abandoned in the *Well-Tempered Clavier*. The Prelude to Suite 3 on the other hand, with its ritornello-and-episode structure, represents a modern and elaborate concerto movement, while the Prelude to Suite 1 takes as its point of departure the French prototype of the *prélude non mesuré* (unmeasured prelude), in which the duration of note values is largely left to the performer. In general, the preludes establish a clearly individual profile for each suite.

The sequences of dances that follow each prelude throughout the entire collection of English Suites establish a consistent formal plan, based on the firm framework of allemande–courante–sarabande–gigue, with a pair of additional dances inserted between the sarabandes and gigues, to be played in da capo manner as, for instance, Bourrée I–II–I (Table 3-2). Here Bach followed the basic model of Dieupart's suites, with the movement order Ouverture–

Allemande–Courante–Sarabande–Gavotte, Menuet, or Passepied–Gigue,[31] though he departs slightly from this pattern by adding bourrées to the list of possible dances (here, always paired) between the sarabande and gigue: bourrées (Suites 1 and 2), gavottes (Suites 3 and 6), minuets (Suite 4), and passepieds (Suite 5).

TABLE 3-2. *Six English Suites*

Suite 1 in A major BWV 806	Suite 2 in A minor BWV 807	Suite 3 in G minor BWV 808	Suite 4 in F major BWV 809	Suite 5 in E minor BWV 810	Suite 6 in D minor BWV 811
Prélude $\frac{12}{8}$	$\frac{3}{4}$	$\frac{3}{8}$	¢	$\frac{6}{8}$	$\frac{9}{8}$
Allemande C	C	C	C	C	C
Courante I $\frac{3}{2}$	$\frac{3}{2}$	$\frac{3}{2}$	$\frac{3}{2}$	$\frac{3}{2}$	$\frac{3}{2}$
Courante II[1] $\frac{3}{2}$	–	–	–	–	–
Sarabande $\frac{3}{4}$	$\frac{3}{4}$	$\frac{3}{4}$	$\frac{3}{4}$	$\frac{3}{4}$	$\frac{3}{2}$[5]
	$\frac{3}{4}$[2]	$\frac{3}{4}$[2]			
Bourrée I 2	Bourrée I 2	Gavotte I 2	Menuet I 3	Passepied I[4] $\frac{3}{8}$	Gavotte I 2
Bourrée II 2	Bourrée II 2 (A major)	Gavotte II[3] 2 (G major)	Menuet II 3	Passepied II $\frac{3}{8}$	Gavotte II 2
Gigue $\frac{6}{8}$	$\frac{6}{8}$	$\frac{12}{8}$	$\frac{12}{8}$	$\frac{3}{8}$	$\frac{12}{16}$

[1] avec deux Doubles
[2] Les agréments de la même Sarabande
[3] ou la Musette
[4] en Rondeau
[5] avec Double

Compared to the *English Suites*, with ordinarily seven movements per piece, the formats and structures of the *French Suites* are not only more compact but also both more varied and more irregular (Table 3-3). Keeping the same basic scheme of four core movements (allemande–courante–sarabande–gigue), the supplementary dances inserted after the sarabande range from a *da capo* pair to two or three independent dances, including not only minuet, gavotte, and bourrée, but also three new and more fashionable types: air, loure, and polonaise. Similar in both sets is the treatment of the gigue as a prominent, lengthy, and elaborate conclusion. With the sole exception of the gigue in the second *English Suite*, all the gigues include imitative fugato textures, which invariably feature melodic inversion of the theme after the double bar for the second half of each piece.

The origin of the *French Suites* is inextricably connected with Bach's second wife, Anna Magdalena, whom he married on December 12, 1721, following the death of Maria Barbara Bach in the summer of 1720. At an unspecified occasion and date in 1722, the composer presented his young wife with a beautiful little album three-quarters bound in leather, its green cover engraved with floral patterns. Inside it is inscribed "Clavier-Büchlein vor Anna Magdalena Bachin ANNO 1722." The *French Suites* opened the book (which, as indicated above, has been only partially preserved), and the fact that for the most part the movements were directly composed onto its pages (Fig. 3-4) suggests that these particularly elegant works were written for and dedicated to Anna Magdalena. Assuming that her husband not only wrote but also played them for her, she would have enjoyed and understood the novel character and intimacy of the various dance pieces and their wide range of nuanced musical expression—from serious, sorrowful, dolorous, and melancholic to consoling, flattering, buoyant, and overtly cheerful.

The suites as they were notated in the *Clavier-Büchlein* primarily served the performer-composer himself, who, playing them for his family, would

FIGURE 3-4

Sarabande of *French Suite* in C minor, BWV 813: autograph composing score in the *Clavier-Büchlein* for A. M. Bach of 1722.

hardly have needed indications for embellishments. For teaching purposes Bach prepared a new master copy with carefully embellished versions, including some further improvements in the texts of the suites, and he also added minuets to BWV 813, BWV 814, and BWV 815. Bach's master copy is unfortunately lost, but everything was carefully recorded in a manuscript written by Bernhard Christian Kayser, who was Bach's pupil in Cöthen and continued studying with him in Leipzig[32] (Table 3-3 reflects the revised versions). Anna Magdalena later copied the first two of "her" suites (in their revised versions) into her second *Clavier-Büchlein* (1725),[33] but only after 1735, by which time she had probably learned to play them.

TABLE 3-3. *Six French Suites*

Suite 1 in D minor BWV 812	Suite 2 in C minor BWV 813	Suite 3 in B minor BWV 814	Suite 4 in E♭ major BWV 815	Suite 5 in G major BWV 816	Suite 6 in E major BWV 817
Allemande C	C	C	C	C	C
Courante $\frac{3}{2}$	$\frac{3}{4}$	$\frac{6}{4}$	$\frac{3}{4}$	$\frac{3}{4}$	$\frac{3}{4}$
Sarabande $\frac{3}{4}$	$\frac{3}{4}$	$\frac{3}{4}$	$\frac{3}{4}$	$\frac{3}{4}$	$\frac{3}{4}$
	Air C	Gavotte $\frac{2}{[2]}$	Gavotte $\frac{2}{[2]}$	Gavotte C	Gavotte C
Menuet I $\frac{3}{4}$	Menuet I $\frac{3}{4}$	Menuet I $\frac{3}{[4]}$	Air ¢	Bourrée ¢	Polonaise $\frac{3}{[4]}$
Menuet II $\frac{3}{4}$	Menuet II $\frac{3}{4}$	Menuet II $\frac{3}{[4]}$	Menuet $\frac{3}{4}$	Loure $\frac{6}{4}$	Menuet $\frac{3}{[4]}$
					Bourrée $\frac{2}{[2]}$
Gigue C	$\frac{3}{8}$	$\frac{3}{8}$	$\frac{6}{8}$	$\frac{12}{16}$	$\frac{6}{8}$

Despite the gap of perhaps a decade between the two opus collections, the *English* and *French Suites* reveal comparable musical goals, which moved well beyond the achievements of the toccata opus. Still addressing the issue of mastering large-scale instrumental form, Bach now focused on dealing with a sequence of clearly defined smaller units, each in the same major or minor key and with the same binary formal pattern ‖: —— :‖: —— :‖ with the second part equal to or longer than the first. However, each dance movement establishes its own distinct character, defined by the rhythmic-metric structure of a melody designed to underscore and enhance the specific choreographic pattern of steps of each individual dance type.

Melody and its rhythmic-metric makeup are the driving force behind the dance. Dancing masters working at the aristocratic courts throughout Europe taught the various dance types to their students, usually to the tune of a small fiddle or "Tanzmeister-Geige," as the most important contemporary dance manual indicates.[34] The name of the Weimar dancing master during Bach's time is not known, but in Cöthen it was the Frenchman Jean François Monjou. In all his suites, Bach pays close attention to this crucial melodic aspect of the dance tunes, and to their distinct repetitive step patterns and their phrases of mostly two or four measures. Much differently than in his earlier dance suites, like BWV 820 and others mentioned above, in the *English Suites* he followed the Dieupart model, in which the bass part is activated as a contrapuntal voice to match the top melody[35] at least in some respects, and with intermittent harmonic fillings in inner voices (Fig. 3-5).

Yet Bach went far beyond Dieupart, not only in his much more extensive and elaborate preludes for the *English Suites* but also, especially, in his strong focus on creating a singular melody for the top voice of every dance type, clearly articulated in subphrases and proper period structures. An accompaniment of the prevailing melody line in strict three- or four-part texture would, of course, run against the "style brisé" or "style luthé" (broken or lute

FIGURE 3-5

François Dieupart, Suite in F major: copy J. S. Bach (c. 1708).

style) native to the texture of French dances. Yet Bach managed to put his own stamp on the style of accompaniment by repeatedly integrating strains of counterpoint. These are most frequently short motifs derived from the dance melody, often deployed in contrary motion. Bach set forth the harmonies with regular motoric beats, and at times introduced surprising harmonic twists. In this way, he created a sophisticated and very personal approach to a highly dynamic and instantly recognizable movement texture. This general procedure became a hallmark, comparably applied later on in sonata and concerto scores. Benefitting from the earlier opus, the *French Suites* generally went a step further in the direction of rhythmic-contrapuntal animation of the dance types, in order to sharpen their individual characters and make them more compelling. A case in point is found in the Sarabande of the Suite in D minor, BWV 812, where in the second section (mm. 9–13) Bach introduced double counterpoint by making the bass line identical to the top melody of the first section.

The metric designs that govern the spectrum of dances provided Bach with the opportunity to explore a maximum variety of options. He consciously observed the difference between the moderately paced allemande and the fast courante, both with their elemental short pickups. Similarly, he abided by the downbeat start of the expressive sarabande in slow triple meter, with an emphatically prolonged second beat and many different ways of accentuating it. He also employed various kinds of compound time in the gigues, creating sparkling finale movements in quick ternary meter or in fast duple meter with triplets, typically with a short pickup. In some of the gigue movements Bach turned to the North German tradition of organ toccatas and preludes with concluding fugues in gigue manner.[36] Each set of suites features three gigue movements in strict fugato style (BWV 808, 810, and 811; BWV 812, 815, and 816), with extended virtuoso subjects that are melodically inverted after the double bar. The remaining gigue movements display imitative textures as well, including contrapuntal inversion.

While most composers did not go beyond the regular metric schemes of $\mathbf{C}$, $\frac{3}{2}$, $\frac{3}{4}$, and $\frac{6}{8}$ time for the various dance types, Bach broadened the variety significantly in both the *English* and *French Suites*, making use of $\mathbf{\mathbb{C}}$, $\frac{6}{4}$, $\frac{9}{8}$, $\frac{12}{8}$, and $\frac{12}{16}$ time signatures (Tables 3-2 and 3-3). Beyond that, the works also incorporate cross-rhythms and other unexpected departures from metric norms. Overall, there is an infinite variety of realizations, not only in the core suite movements but also in the additional dances.

The keyboard suites also fed directly into enriched designs that became prominent in an increasing number of Bach's vocal compositions, in the Weimar years after 1714 and subsequently in Cöthen as well. In this sense, Bach's learning experience with a great variety of dance movements proved to be a decisive resource for the technical design and expressive character-building of arias and choruses. It logically followed that he urged his students to begin their exercises in composition with minuets and other simple dances, in order that they would come to understand how to organize melodies by means of regular meters, phrases, and periods, and how to enhance the melodic line with appropriate accompanimental support. The two *Clavier-Büchlein* volumes for Anna Magdalena Bach include a number of illuminating and charming examples of marches, minuets, and polonaises, through which we can watch the teenage Bach sons[37] taking their first steps in formulating musical ideas and writing down small compositions.

Two books of unaccompanied solos, for violin and for violoncello

The widely circulating solo and trio sonatas with basso continuo by Arcangelo Corelli, published as opp. 1–5 during the last two decades of the seventeenth century and frequently reprinted, laid the foundation for chamber repertoire as it developed throughout Europe for the next several decades. Although thoroughly familiar with the chamber works of Corelli and his followers, Bach in his first non-keyboard opus did not elect to emulate their works for one or more stringed instruments and basso continuo. Instead, he made the unusual decision to create unaccompanied solos for violin and for violoncello. By 1720, he had completed the first book of six violin solos, which were soon joined by a companion book of six cello solos. It is difficult to imagine that in his dual role as Weimar court organist and chamber musician, he would not have composed solos and trios with basso continuo. His Weimar cantatas, with their highly imaginative instrumental scoring, in fact strongly point in that direction. Yet from whatever chamber music he may have composed by that time, only a single remnant has survived in the Fugue in G minor, BWV 1026, for violin and continuo. It is a one-movement piece whose violin part features, from the first of its 181 measures, extensive and highly demanding polyphonic figures. This work demonstrates that the composer was primarily interested in exploring and experimenting with the treatment of the violin part as such, rather than its accompaniment.

Not surprisingly, the keyboard virtuoso and composer had turned the organ console at church and the harpsichord at home into experimental laboratories. He was inspired to arrange concertos for violin and orchestra by Vivaldi and others for organ or harpsichord, and to transform trio sonatas designed for several players into one-man shows for the organ. He did so not for the sake of physical acrobatics, but instead in order to test the limits of what was possible within the framework of autonomous instrumental design, free of support by any kind of accompaniment. With apparently the same determination, he treated the violin and the cello as study objects in musical independence, focusing on these dominant string instruments of the Baroque orchestra—with their differing sizes, playing techniques, and timbres, as well as their distinct functions as the outer layers of a musical score. This inquisitive, eagerly innovative, and highly resourceful musician worked things out for himself, in the solitary company of the pertinent instrument, as he searched for performing solutions that would at the same time advance his compositional goals.

Bach's engagement with music for unaccompanied violin very possibly came from the Weimar violinist Paul von Westhoff, whose name and music he very likely was familiar with even before coming to Weimar. Westhoff had published a collection of suites under the title *Erstes Dutzend Allemanden, Couranten, Sarabanden und Giguen Violino Solo sonder Passo Continuo* (Dresden, 1682), which was later supplemented by a second set of six partitas (Dresden, 1696).[38] His choice of dance suites made perfect sense, since there was a long tradition of dancing masters in the service of nobility, improvising on a kit violin or pochette (a small violin to fit in a pocket) when teaching dance lessons. Westhoff elevated such unaccompanied improvisatory practices to a new and truly artful level. He spent the final years of his career at the ducal court of Weimar, where in 1703 Bach received his very first (if only temporary) employment, from January through June. Considering this circumstance, and the young musician's eagerness to meet and learn from his most talented contemporaries, direct personal contact with the acclaimed violinist is more or less a given. Two and a half years later, Bach traveled to Lübeck for a three-month encounter with Dietrich Buxtehude. It would appear that the young Bach took the torch directly from Westhoff and Buxtehude—the preeminent German masters of the violin and the organ.

If Westhoff provided the principal impulse for the idea of violin solos, no model Bach would have known existed for the violoncello suites. In any case, with respect to the technical and stylistic makeup of both sets, Bach was completely on his own. He most likely improvised and experimented for some time before reaching a satisfactory level of attainment that left him ready to commit music to paper. No drafts or composing scores have survived for either set. Yet the autograph fair copy of the "Sei solo. a Violino senza Basso accompagnato. Libro primo," a manuscript of extraordinary tidiness and calligraphic beauty, clearly implies that the composer was not writing the pieces down for the first time, but working instead from drafts. He did not adopt Westhoff's clever if peculiar multi-clef and eight-line staff notation (Fig. 3-6), but instead used the standard five-line staff notation with which he was perfectly content and comfortable, despite his call for complex polyphonic textures (Fig. 3-7). The autograph with the original date of 1720 falls into the middle of the Cöthen period—an interval during which, considering the light duties of his capellmeister post, Bach enjoyed more time and flexibility than he ever had before or would after. Tellingly, manuscripts of comparable calligraphic quality are known only from this very period. Even though no drafts for these solo violin works have survived, the challenges of the project suggest a fairly long gestation time, of perhaps a decade or so. Stylistic evidence indicates that the actual composition of the unaccompanied violin

FIGURE 3-6

Johann Paul von Westhoff, Partita in A minor for unaccompanied violin:
Allemande (Dresden, 1696).

sonatas and partitas could hardly have started before 1718/19: the Siciliana of the G-minor sonata (BWV 1001), for instance, happens to be the earliest occurrence of this movement type in Bach's music. Finally, the reference to "Libro Primo" (first book) on the title page of the violin solos implies that the second book—of cello solos—was, if not yet completed, then at least in the works.

In the absence of an autograph score, the dating of the cello suites must remain open. Yet their composition was surely completed after 1720, but before Bach's move to Leipzig in the spring of 1723. The only extant copy of the lost autograph is in the hand of Anna Magdalena Bach.[39] It was prepared at the request of Georg Heinrich

FIGURE 3-7

Fuga of Sonata in G minor for unaccompanied violin, BWV 1001/2: autograph fair copy (1720).

Ludwig Schwanenberger (1696–1774), a chamber musician at the ducal court of Brunswick-Wolfenbüttel, who in 1727/28 spent several months studying with Bach in Leipzig. Mrs. Bach prepared copies of both violin and cello solos in a single two-part manuscript,[40] with "Pars 2" bearing the title in Schwanenberger's hand: "6 Suites a Violoncello Solo senza Basso composes par S.ʳ J. S. Bach. Maitre de Chapelle." The use of the composer's Cöthen court title, and no other, confirms that the work was indeed completed there rather than later in Leipzig. Anna Magdalena's copy of the cello suites and other early manuscript copies show a number of internal inconsistences, indicating that the lost autograph may not have been a calligraphic fair copy comparable to the one that transmits the violin solos. This in turn suggests that Bach did not have time to prepare a fair copy before leaving Cöthen, and that he never got around to doing it in Leipzig. Off and on, he probably made small additions and minor changes, as implied by secondary copies. Yet the fate of the autograph score remains completely uncertain. It was probably identical with a lost manuscript once in the possession of Carl Philipp Emanuel Bach.[41] That particular manuscript must have been the model for the copy made sometime after 1757 by Johann Nicolaus Schober, scribe of the Berlin court capelle, who copied much from Bach's library before he left for Hamburg in 1768. Schober's copy also formed the basis for the manuscript transmission—most likely via Jean-Pierre Duport (1741–1818), from 1773 a Prussian court cellist—that eventually led to the first edition, published in Paris about 1824.[42]

Considering Bach's primary reputation as an organist and keyboard authority, it is highly notable that his violin and cello solos were already widely disseminated before 1800, notwithstanding the relatively small number of twenty-plus surviving manuscript copies. The violin solos appeared in print in 1801/2, at almost the same time as the first edition of the *Well-Tempered Clavier*. Both collections were published simultaneously by Simrock in Bonn and his distributor in Paris; the cello suites followed two decades later.

At the time, proof of Bach's competence with and expertise in string instruments rested primarily upon the two collections of unaccompanied solos. Carl Philipp Emanuel Bach's testimony of 1774 illuminates the background:

> He understood to perfection the possibilities of all stringed instruments. This
> is evidenced by his solos for the violin and for the violoncello without bass.
> One of the greatest violinists told me once that he had seen nothing more
> perfect for learning to be a good violinist, and could suggest nothing more
> perfect to anyone eager to learn, than the said violin solos without bass.[43]

While the Bach son specifically mentions his father's playing of both the violin and viola, the cello is not referred to explicitly. But Bach's intensive and long-time involvement with various four- and five-string instruments, held and played in various positions, is clearly reflected in the two books of unaccompanied solos. Moreover, the phrase "he understood to perfection the possibilities of all stringed instruments" emphasizes in particular his deep knowledge of these instruments and their most effective uses. Carl Philipp Emanuel's declaration is in fact a considerable understatement, given that the two books of unaccompanied solos established technical and aesthetic thresholds that have never been surpassed.

Carl did not identify the witness referred to in the quote above as "one of the greatest violinists," but there are only three plausible candidates. One is the Berlin concertmaster Johann Gottlieb Graun (1703–1771), with whom Carl entered the Prussian court capelle in 1740. Johann Sebastian also knew Graun, a distinguished pupil of both Johann Georg Pisendel in Dresden and Giuseppe Tartini in Padua, and he sent his son Wilhelm Friedemann to take lessons with him. It is nearly inconceivable that Graun was not familiar with the violin solos. Another possibility may be the Berlin court musician Franz Benda (1709–1786), a pupil of Graun's and a distinguished violinist in his own right, and a friend of Carl's. The third candidate is the brilliant violin virtuoso Johann Peter Salomon of Bonn (1745–1815), who was hired by Prince Heinrich of Prussia in 1765 as concertmaster for his ensembles in Rheinsberg and Berlin. Emanuel Bach knew him well from that time, and kept in touch with him even after his own move to Hamburg.[44] Regardless of whom Carl had in mind, the emphatic characterization of the violin solos—and by analogy, those for cello—as "nothing more perfect for learning" refers to their unrivaled instructional value. It may not be a coincidence that the title pages of the abovementioned first editions of the solos for violin and for cello, both based on eighteenth-century manuscripts from the Berlin Bach circle, alluded to "studio" and "études" respectively, and thus reaffirmed the use of the works for study purposes. The two earliest copies of the violin solos in fact already point in exactly that direction. One was made in 1720 or shortly thereafter by a Cöthen copyist, for use of the princely capelle there, and the other was copied 1723 by the St. Thomas student Johann Andreas Kuhnau, for Bach's Leipzig ensembles.[45] The performer-composer seems to have held these uncompromisingly demanding solos before the string players with whom he worked, regardless of their proficiency, in very much the same way that he provided his keyboard students with highly challenging instructional materials. These were no mere exercises for building technical skills. They were also exquisite creations suited to engage mind and soul, peerless exemplars that demonstrated just how craft and art could merge and become one.

The paucity of documented performances of these solo works must not lead to mistaken conclusions. There were plenty of possible performance occasions at the princely court in Cöthen, or within the Leipzig Collegium Musicum. Surely Bach's Cöthen concertmaster, the distinguished violinist

Joseph Spieß, or his Dresden violinist friend Johann Georg Pisendel—not to mention the composer himself—might have presented an unaccompanied solo at one time or another. And we are also certain that the virtuoso Salomon regularly played the violin solos at concerts in Berlin and elsewhere, over a period of decades. The Prussian capellmeister Johann Friedrich Reichardt recalled in his memoirs an event from the 1774 Carnival season in Berlin:

> For me, the most interesting artist acquaintance was that of the excellent violinist Salomon. Through him I first learned the splendid violin solos without accompaniment by Seb. Bach, in which the setting is often developed in two or three parts, but also in one voice delightfully invented, so that any further accompaniment seems superfluous. The great vigor and security with which Salomon presented these masterpieces was a new impetus to me to perfect polyphonic playing on the violin, which I had long practiced with fondness.[46]

In 1781 Salomon relocated via Paris to London, where he spent the rest of his life. But he continued to play the Bach solos, as Ernst Ludwig Gerber reported in 1790:

> Germany and England unanimously boast of this great master on the violin. He knows how to perform the Adagio and the Allegro with the same art. He is said even to play fugues by Johann Sesbastian Bach on the violin with precision and expression.[47]

Noteworthy here is the reference to the expressive playing of fugues, indicative of Salomon's enchanting manner of performance. In 1819, four years after his death, a report on music in England relates that he "was still one of the few who could and would play Sebastian Bach's famous solos"[48]—suggesting that there had been others beside him, and thus that these works were indeed played throughout the entire first century after Bach's completion of the score. Most unfortunately, no comparable information is available regarding the early performance tradition of the cello suites.

In their formal makeup, the two collections show equally original approaches. Book I (Table 3-4) stresses the contrasting juxtaposition of two distinct genres, alternating between four-movement sonatas and very irregularly structured suites in the Italian guise of a partita,[49] containing movements like Preludio, Allemanda, Corrente, Sarabanda, Borea, and Giga. The sonatas and partitas of Book I do not form separate groups of three each; they instead alternate, as underscored by their original numbering, and thus give the two prevailing instrumental genres equal rights, as it were. For the sonatas, Bach preferred the Corellian type having four movements (slow–fast–slow–fast), with the first three movements of all sonatas polyphonically conceived and the fourth being a monophonic rapid finale movement. The second movements are written as fugues, and the warmly lyrical third movements are placed in a related key. Within each four-movement sonata cycle, every single movement displays a highly individual profile. The fugal movements function in their particular role as exemplary settings of imitative polyphony, even though much of the part-writing—executed with double-stop, triple-stop, and arpeggiated chords—is not sustainable and can only create the illusion of strict three- and four-part polyphony. Expositions of clearly articulated thematic entries, the spinning forth of motifs mainly derived from the fugal subjects, and free figurative interludes all alternate, establishing the formal structures of genuine fugues.

TABLE 3-4. Six Sonatas and Partitas for Unaccompanied Violin

Sonata 1 in G minor BWV 1001	Partita 1 in B minor BWV 1002	Sonata 2 in A minor BWV 1003	Partita 2 in D minor BWV 1004	Sonata 3 in C major BWV 1005	Partita 3 in E major BWV 1006
Adagio C	Allemanda C	Grave C	Allemanda C	Adagio $\frac{3}{4}$	Preludio $\frac{3}{4}$
Fuga ¢	Double ¢	Fuga $\frac{2}{4}$	Corrente $\frac{3}{4}$	Fuga ¢	Loure $\frac{6}{4}$
Siciliana $\frac{12}{8}$	Corrente $\frac{3}{4}$	Andante $\frac{3}{4}$	Sarabanda $\frac{3}{4}$	Largo C	Gavotte en
(B♭ major)	Double $\frac{3}{4}$	(C major)	Giga $\frac{12}{8}$	(F major)	Rondeau ¢
Presto $\frac{3}{8}$	Sarabande $\frac{3}{4}$	Allegro ¢	Ciaccona $\frac{3}{4}$	Allegro assai $\frac{3}{4}$	Menuet I $\frac{3}{4}$
	Double $\frac{9}{8}$				Menuet II $\frac{3}{4}$
	Tempo di Borea ¢				Bourrée 2
	Double ¢				Gigue $\frac{6}{8}$

In contrast to the sonatas, the three partitas do not share the same movement sequence, nor do any of them follow a conventional pattern. In this regard the violin partitas, in their freedom of movement choices, also differ substantially from Bach's keyboard suites. In his desire to seek unique solutions and avoid the appearance of any uniformity, Bach gave each partita a different makeup and number of movements. Partita 1 features four dance types, each with a variation movement. Partita 2 alone presents the typical allemande–courante–sarabande–gigue core sequence, but without inserted dances after the sarabande, and instead with an outsized concluding ciaccona. Finally, Partita 3 commences with a prelude of considerable proportions, followed by a sequence of five dances without parallel elsewhere. In contrast to the procedure followed in the sonatas, chordal textures generated here by double- and triple-stops do not serve the purpose of implying contrapuntal polyphony. Instead they present a great variety of harmonic accentuations and inflections, serving the needs of distinct rhythmic patterns characteristic of the various dance types and intensifying their expressive reach.

Within the partitas, the sole Ciaccona stands out in every respect, not just as a movement without equivalent within Bach's instrumental oeuvre, but also in its sheer length of 257 measures—and most especially in its unparalleled aspect of extreme virtuosity.[50] This enormous structure consists of 64 variations on an ostinato ground of eight notes. It is a consummate exercise in combining formal discipline with imaginative fantasy, and in juxtaposing extroverted effects with eloquent moments of introspection. Not merely the pinnacle of the set but also representative of the entire collection, the Ciaccona is the ideal example for the seemingly impossible task that Johann Friedrich Reichardt perceptively described in 1805—with his felicitous metaphor of the great master being able "to move in chains with freedom and assurance."[51]

Book II contains six solos for violoncello, with an exclusive focus on suites (Table 3-5). It closely follows the organization of the *English Suites*, not merely in the typological choice "avec prélude," and in the consistent use of highly distinct opening movements and prominent gigue finales, but also in Bach's systematic placement of paired minuets, bourrées, and gavottes between the sarabande and gigue in all the suites. The collection as a whole displays the most regular and consistent movement organization among Bach's sets of instrumental suites. Yet the makeup and appeal of the individual movements reflect the remarkable results of the composer's search for solutions to a problem never tackled before: namely that of enabling a single violoncello to produce in idiomatic fashion the distinct characteristics of a variety of setting types, all while avoiding the impression that anything is missing. In this sense, the *arpeggiando* Prelude of Suite 1 in G major, BWV 1007, may be understood as a congenial cello response to the opening prelude in C of the *Well-Tempered Clavier*, and the opening gesture of the Prelude to the C-major Suite, BWV

1009—with its sweeping two-octave scale from c' to C—as a statement that the cello can readily accommodate the entire gamut of musical notes.

TABLE 3-5. Six Suites for Unaccompanied Violoncello

	Suite 1 in G major BWV 1007	Suite 2 in D minor BWV 1008	Suite 3 in C major BWV 1009	Suite 4 in E♭ major BWV 1010	Suite 5 in C minor BWV 1011 *discordable*	Suite 6 in D major BWV 1012 *a cinque cordes*
Prélude	C	3/4	3/4	¢	¢–3/8	12/8
Allemande	¢	C	C	¢	¢	C
Courante	3/4	3/4	3	3/4	3/2	3/4
Sarabande	3/4	3/4	3/4	3/4	3/4	3/2
Menuet I	3/4	Menuet I 3/4	Bourrée I ¢	Bourrée I ¢	Gavotte I ¢	Gavotte I ¢
Menuet II	3/4	Menuet II 3	Bourrée II ¢	Bourrée II C	Gavotte II ¢	Gavotte II 2
Gigue	6/8	3/8	3/8	12/8	3/8	6/8

In recognition of the parameters of cello technique, Bach used double- and triple-stop textures more sparingly than in the violin solos. For instance, the fugue section of the Prelude to Suite 5 (the only fugue within the cello suites) consists of a monophonic line with the subject clearly articulated in standard fugal manner: that is, in the exposition, the statement is in the tonic and the follower in the dominant. Yet, the subject never connects with a counterpoint, as it always does in the multiple-stop treatment of the violin fugues. Instead, Bach ingeniously and artfully transformed the vertical score into a linear score. On the other hand, he very effectively applied double-stop textures in a number of dance movements, notably in the sarabandes of five of the six suites. By contrast, the exceptional Sarabande of Suite 5 in C minor, framed by the chordal textures of the Courante and Gavotte movements, offers an unusually intimate and melancholic melody—resulting in the most abstract and compelling rendition of this grave solo dance that Bach ever conceived (Fig. 3-8). The melodic line veils the omnipresent rhythmic pattern of the sarabande, with its accent on the second beat. It persistently obfuscates beat 2, the typical sarabande step, by the seemingly displaced quarter note at the end of the first two measures in both sections of the piece. Beat 2 in fact appears to be smoothed over throughout the entire movement. But it is clearly meant to be mildly emphasized in the manner of equalized appoggiaturas from

FIGURE 3-8a

Sarabande of Suite in C minor for unaccompanied cello, BWV 1011/4:
copy A. M. Bach (c. 1728), detail.

FIGURE 3-8b

Sarabande of Suite in C minor for unaccompanied cello, BWV 1011/4:
copy of a Berlin scribe working with J. N. Schober (after 1759), detail.

below and above. The symmetric arrangement of beat 2 with the half steps
B–c, e–f, e–f, B–c in the first four measures illustrates an extraordinarily subtle and cogent rhythmic-melodic strategy. The cello suites as a whole present
notably imaginative and sensitive elucidations of the various dance types, with
their wide-ranging and distinctive emotional characters—all within a musical
idiom that neither a keyboard instrument nor a violin could emulate.

A further aspect of Book II pertains to the special requirements called for
in the last two suites, "discordable" and "à cinque cordes," respectively. For the
Suite in C minor, the instrument must be tuned *discordable* or in *scordatura*—
a technique more frequently applied to the violin and signifying an alteration
of the normal tuning. In this case, the "accord" indicates a change from the

normal C-G-d-a cello tuning to C–G–d–g. Such deliberate "mistuning" was intended to facilitate the playing of particular passages, and contributed to the production of special sonic effects.

The D-major Suite, according to the instruction "à cinque cordes," involves the use of a five-string instrument with an additional e'-string above the regular a-string. The frequent use of the alto and even soprano clefs indicates that Bach had in mind a different instrument from the one to be used for the other five suites. This was most likely a smaller-sized cello known under three names: violoncello piccolo, viola da basso,[52] and viola pomposa; Bach was specifically credited with the "invention" of the last of these.[53] The cello, unlike the violin, was present in multiple sizes and configurations and would not be standardized until later in the eighteenth century. The various mid- to large-sized bass-range string instruments also at times required particular performing positions, as with the arm-held viola da braccio, or the viola da spalla, braced with a strap against the shoulder. The vertically positioned instruments were played with either an overhand or underhand bow grip. Bach's own instrument collection included three violas, a "Bassetgen" (violoncello piccolo or viola pomposa), and two vio- loncellos[54]—information that does not provide an answer to the question of which instrument he had in mind for the last two suites, but does reflect the contemporary variety of lower register strings. The score of the cello suites suggests that Bach intended to accommodate a fluid situation without being prescriptive. Hence, in light of Carl Philipp Emanuel Bach's remark that "he understood to perfection the possibilities of all stringed instruments," the two special suites at the end of Book II broaden the versatility of the collec- tion, such that Books I and II taken together indeed address players of "all stringed instruments." In many ways, this adaptable string project effectively required the same sort of flexibility that Bach had known from his keyboard experience—namely the need for mastering organs, harpsichords, and clavi- chords alike, not to mention the "Lautenclavier" (a harpsichord variant with gut rather than metal strings).

In the category of pieces for unaccompanied instruments, Bach wrote only one other work, the "Solo pour la flûte traversière" in A minor, BWV 1013 (Allemande–Corrente–Sarabande–Bourrée Anglaise). Curiously, its one and only source forms an appendix to the Cöthen manuscript of the violin solos mentioned above.[55] The time frame suggests that by composing a piece for solo transverse flute, the composer intended to inform himself—as well as the musicians working with him—of the possibilities of a new instrument that had just entered their orbit. In Bach's output, the transverse flute first appears in *Brandenburg Concerto 5* and in the Cöthen congratulatory cantatas "Durchlauchtster Leopold," BWV 173.1, and "Erwünschtes Freudenlicht," BWV 184.1. Bach's regular use of the transverse flute does not actually commence, however, until the spring of 1724. By then it seems that he had neither time for nor interest in complementing the two books for violin and cello with further works for solo winds. He left this task to his friend and colleague Georg Philipp Telemann, who eventually published three successful sets of twelve multi-movement "Fantasies . . . sans Basse" for transverse flute (1733), violin (1735), and viola da gamba (1736).

In contrast to Telemann's creative mixing and matching of sonata- and suite-style movements in his solo fantasies, Bach made no crossover attempts. He strictly adhered to the format and conventions of the traditional genres, but instilled in them where appropriate his pervasive stylistic signature of contrapuntal polyphony. Bach's prodigious keyboard empiricism had clearly shaped a sense of *Vollstimmigkeit* ("all-embracing polyphony"; Prologue, page 8). This overall enrichment of texture and sound, well beyond what was common in fugues and the strict contrapuntal forms, greatly affected his approach to reshaping and expanding the possibilities for string writing. Well aware of the given instrumental limitations of four or five strings and a bow, Bach forged an unprecedented idiomatic style of polyphonic play. In this context, some later arrangements of the unaccompanied string solos—the Harpsichord Sonata, BWV 964, based on BWV 1003, the Lute Suite, BWV 995, on BWV 1011, and the Cantata Sinfonia, BWV 29/1, on BWV 1006/1—provide instructive samples that illuminate the internal links between different realizations of the same piece of music. Bach's former student Johann Friedrich Agricola addressed this very point, and the general principle of *Vollstimmigkeit*, when remarking in 1775 on the unaccompanied solos that

> their author often played them on the clavichord himself and added as much harmony to them as he deemed necessary. In doing so he recognized the necessity of resonant harmony which in this kind of composition he could not otherwise attain.[56]

In the solo sets for strings, the pursuit of all-embracing polyphony—summoned by means of omission and through the effects of illusion—not only implied chordal and polyphonic textures, but also involved extended single lines designed to suggest vertical harmonics, concordant and discordant alike. Bach pupil Johann Philipp Kirnberger pointed out in 1771 some of the technical difficulties that came with this particular challenge:

> To write a plain melody without the slightest accompaniment in such a way, with regard to harmony, that it is impossible to add another voice without committing errors, quite apart from the fact that the added voice would be clumsy and utterly unsingable. From J. S. Bach we have, in this style, six sonatas for the violin and six [suites] for the violoncello, all without any accompaniment.[57]

The two books of violin and cello solos elevate the levels for both composition and performance to unparalleled heights. In line with their singular designs, multipurpose potentiality, and variety of expressive characters, the two collections benefit conceptually from the collective experience gained from *The Little Organ Book*, *The Well-Tempered Clavier*, *The Faithful Guide*, and the two sets of keyboard suites. With their singular focus on violin and cello, these sets establish a remarkably complete framework for instrumental polyphony—in terms of their idiomatic compositional handling of the upper and lower registers, their broad range of timbral colors, and their highly varied modes of expression.

Six concertos for several instruments

As remarkable as the concerto opus known as the *Brandenburg Concertos* was, it remained without any echo or impact for a very long time. The set of six existed only in the single score that Bach prepared for and dedicated to Margrave Christian Ludwig of Brandenburg-Schwedt (1677–1734), brother of the first king in Prussia. Following the margrave's death in 1734, the compositions slumbered for generations on various library shelves, until their first publication on the occasion of the Bach centennial in 1850.[58] Bach had of course saved performing materials for all six works for his own use. Yet it seems that he did not keep them apart as a separate set, so that they eventually ended up being lumped together with numerous other works in the 1750 obituary catalog under the rubric "a lot of other instrumental pieces, of all sorts and for all kinds of instruments" (Table 1-1).

The six works Bach selected for the margrave in 1721 as "Six Concerts avec plusieurs instruments" (six concertos for diverse instruments), which sit outside the standard types of concertos and concerti grossi, were combined as a set of concertos with various combinations of solo instruments (Table 3-6). They apparently belonged to a larger body of individual concertos of various kinds from the Weimar and Cöthen years, a repertoire that no longer exists as such, thus precluding a more detailed description.[59] Moreover, since no composing scores of the *Brandenburgs* have survived, their composition dates cannot be firmly established. Chronological clues are available for two of them, BWV 1046 and BWV 1050. The first concerto exists in a slightly shorter three-movement version (Allegro–Adagio–Menuet with two Trios) that originally functioned as an overture suite (BWV 1046.1) for the *Hunt Cantata*, BWV 208. The latter work was commissioned by the court of Saxe-Weißenfels and performed as a serenade on the birthday of Duke Christian at his hunting lodge in February 1713 (and performed again in Weimar in 1716). For the fifth concerto, autograph performing parts from around 1720 have survived, and were used through the 1740s. The earlier date suggests a likely origin related to Bach's visit to Berlin in the spring of 1719, when he picked up a new harpsichord made by the Berlin instrument maker Michael Mietke. That trip may also have provided an occasion for a meeting with the margrave and his private capelle, a conceivable precondition for the 1721 dedication.

Losses from the Weimar-Cöthen sources make it impossible to estimate the size, let alone the nature, of the concerto repertoire of which the *Brandenburg Concertos* represent a core element. Each of the *Brandenburgs* requires a uniquely configured ensemble of solo instruments, combining strings, brass, woodwinds, and harpsichord in differing and distinctive ways. There is no ready equivalent of such combinatorial fancy, although Bach's friend and colleague Georg Philipp Telemann had, by 1721, composed concertos for mixed solo groups of strings and woodwinds. These were produced during Telemann's Eisenach and Frankfurt periods, and the two composers were certainly familiar with the general outlines of each other's output.

Well aware of the typology and general range of contemporary concertos and published collections, Bach pursued a novel and largely original strategy by selecting from an extant repertoire six different and essentially unparalleled concertos, placing them together to form an opus. These works were not initially created with any intention of forming a set, but were instead purposefully gathered together at a later point. Yet the presentation set for the Margrave of

Brandenburg nevertheless resembles in its singularity the Cöthen sister collections of the two books of violin and cello solos, the *Well-Tempered Clavier*, and the Inventions and Sinfonias.

A contributing factor regarding the colorful instrumental combinations of the *Brandenburg Concertos* was surely Bach's background and experience as organist with a predilection for pulling and mixing stops in order to make use of the organ's rich and varied potential for expressive purposes, notably in chorale preludes. The trend in this direction became noticeable in the flexible and unusual scoring of some of his Weimar cantatas. A case in point is Cantata BWV 18, with its low-register sinfonia for four violas and basso continuo, comparable to a similar effect in *Brandenburg* 6, and Cantata BWV 152, with its colorful sinfonia combining recorder, oboe, viola d'amore, viola

TABLE 3-6. *Six Concerts avec plusieurs instruments*
(Brandenburg Concertos)

Concerto 1 in F major BWV 1046	Concerto 2 in F major BWV 1047	Concerto 3 in G major BWV 1048	Concerto 4 in G major BWV 1049	Concerto 5 in D major BWV 1050	Concerto 6 in B♭ major BWV 1051
cor da caccia,* ob I–III, bsn, vn picc; vn I–II, va, bc	tpt, fl, ob, vn princ; vn I–II, va, bc	vn I–III, va I–III, vc I–III, bc	rec I–II, vn princ; vn I–II, va, bc	fl, vn princ, cemb conc; vn I–II, va, bc	va I–II, vc, va da gamba I–II, vne/vc, bc
[Allegro] ¢ Adagio $\frac{3}{4}$ (D minor^V)† Allegro $\frac{6}{8}$ Menuet $\frac{3}{4}$ –Trio $\frac{3}{4}$ (D minor) Polonaise $\frac{3}{8}$ (F major) –Trio $\frac{2}{4}$ (F major)	[Allegro] ¢ Andante $\frac{3}{4}$ (D minor) Allegro assai $\frac{2}{4}$	[Allegro] ¢ Adagio ¢ (E minor^V) Allegro $\frac{12}{8}$	Allegro $\frac{3}{8}$ Andante $\frac{3}{4}$ (E minor^V) Presto ¢	Allegro ¢ Affetuoso ¢ (B minor) Allegro $\frac{2}{4}$	[Allegro] ¢ Adagio ma non tanto $\frac{3}{2}$ (E♭ major^V) Allegro $\frac{12}{8}$

* Instrument key: bc = basso continuo; bsn = bassoon; cemb conc = concertato harpsichord; cor da caccia = corno da caccia (French horn); fl = flute; rec = recorder; ob = oboe; tpt = trumpet; va = viola; vc = violoncello; vn = violin; vn picc = piccolo violin (tuned a minor third higher than a violin); vn princ = violino principale (solo violin); vne = violone.
† Superscript V designates cadences ending on the dominant. Four middle movements end with Phrygian cadences to V. In Concerto 2, only the cadence is given for the movement. In Concerto 6, the movement is in E-flat major, but the Phrygian cadence is on D (V of G).

da gamba, and continuo, comparable to the four different solo instruments in *Brandenburg* 2. If the collection for the margrave was supposed to live up to its title of "plusieurs instruments," Bach could not have created a more variegated array of solo instruments in addition to the essential standard complement of ripieno strings: piccolo violin, violin, viola, violoncello, and viola da gamba; corno da caccia and trumpet; recorder, flute, and oboe; and harpsichord. How the margrave's residential ensemble could have met Bach's requirements is another story.

The sheer number of different instruments is only a part of the picture. The different instrument combinations within each concerto—sometimes varying for individual movements—are used to help define formal design. For example, two concertos with pure string ensembles feature significantly different solo groups: the ten-part score of *Brandenburg* 3 puts three groups of three violins, three violas, and three cellos side by side over a basso continuo, resulting in the concertizing relationship of three trio groups of different registers. On the other hand, the six-part score of *Brandenburg* 6 juxtaposes two concertino groups of contrasting sounds of string instrument families, two violas and cello ("modern" strings) and two viole da gamba and violone (old-line viols). Similarly, Concerto 4 combines two solo principles within a single work by juxtaposing the idea of concerto grosso with that of a solo concerto in alternating episodes: the three-part concertino of two recorders or "flauti d'echo" (4' instruments)[60] and violin (8' instrument) as "bassetto" (high bass) fundament contrasts with the extensive solo role of the violin, now playing a dominant and demanding virtuoso part that has no equivalent in any other violin concerto by Bach.

The innovative use of the concertizing harpsichord in *Brandenburg* 5, the first example of its kind in history, results in a similarly hybrid form combining a concertino of transverse flute, violin, and harpsichord, with the solo harpsichord predominating. The middle movement presents the concertino (without ripieno accompaniment) in perfect balance with one another, whereas the extended cadenza in the opening movement definitely tips the balance in favor of the harpsichord. However, it is only the concerto version in the Margrave's score where the sense of proportion is negatively affected. In the dedication score of 1721, Bach replaced the original seventeen-measure cadenza from the earlier concerto version[61] with a new 78-measure cadenza in order to impress the dedicatee and to accentuate the composer's virtuosic prowess; since the cadenza takes up one-third of the entire movement, he added it clearly at the expense of balance, perhaps misjudging the aesthetic impact of the outcome.

Brandenburg 2 features the unusual combination of four treble instruments representing the four orchestral families of brass, labial woodwinds, reed woodwinds, and strings. But it is *Brandenburg 1* that features the largest ensemble: it pits the three contrasting instrumental choirs against one another (an effect that also plays a role in the cantata BWV 208), calling for two corni da caccia, three oboes, and bassoon, as well as a full complement of strings crowned with a piccolo violin. The multipartite minuet suite of the concerto at the end effectively sums up the options by differentiating the three trio sections, scoring them respectively with two oboes and bassoon, three strings, and two horns with a "bass" part of unison oboes. The concerto demonstrates Bach's highly refined and forward-looking sense of instrumentation, a phenomenon—again related to his experience as organist—particularly effective in the four concluding measures of the second movement, which ends with a half cadence in the movement's key of D minor. The descending cadential bass steps (*d–c–Bb–A*) gradually unfold in *piano* dynamics and in three chords per measure, presented with contrasting shades of alternating instrumental colors; the instruments decisively rejoin *forte* in the final A-major chord:

EXAMPLE 3-1

Adagio, BWV 1046/2: contrasting sounds and complementary harmonies.

The fanciful scoring of the final cadence of this Adagio movement provides but one example of the composer's magisterial command of orchestral effects, an assertion of mastery that places the entire opus into a category of its own within the vast Baroque concerto repertory. *Brandenburg 1* signals the degree of innovation right at its beginning, when in measures 2–3 of the opening movement the two hunting horns present cross-rhythms (three triplet eighth notes) against the regular four sixteenth notes of all the other instruments—a witty and ear-catching device of disjunctive horn calls that immediately commands attention. And Bach, perhaps accustomed to performing before partly distracted and bored audiences, had much more in store for galvanizing the attention of listeners. To cite only one example, in the fast third movement the virtuoso piccolo violin engages in dialogues successively with first horn, first oboe, and first violin, and then suddenly leads the allegro movement to a surprise halt on an unexpected fermata chord. This head-turning and whimsical moment abruptly interrupts the flow of the music, which unexpectedly resumes with a brief and lyrical adagio cadenza before picking up the allegro once again and completing the final third of the movement.

Bach admittedly adhered in all of his concerto compositions to the fairly standardized concerto style of the Vivaldi generation, notably its tonality-driven principles. Yet the *Brandenburg Concertos*, as a group of diverse pieces with a chronology roughly fitting into the years 1713–20, offer a unique perspective on one of the most formative periods of the composer. The time frame coincides with Bach's choice to delve deeper into musical composition. He determined that he would no longer focus primarily on keyboard performance and genres, but would begin to study and experiment with the new type of concerto, and to explore systematically the possibilities and potential of the orchestra. It was a period of challenges to his musical imagination, and of considerable effort toward winning compositional control over the musical substance at hand—as well as its theoretical underpinnings. The essential parameters of his personal style were formed by a process of learning "how to think musically," as Forkel's 1802 biography related it. The idea of musical thinking[62] revolves first and foremost around issues of order (*Ordnung*) in terms of organizing musical material; coherence (*Zusammenhang*), in the sense of connectivity and continuity of musical thoughts; and proportion (*Verhältnis*), meaning the relation and correlation of musical elements. For Bach, musical thinking was in fact nothing less than the conscious application of generative and formative procedures—the meticulous rationalization of the creative act. More than any other type of musical setting, concerto composition concretized these seemingly abstract principles, and for Bach it proved to be the ideal vehicle for considering and developing compelling modes of musical thinking. Those approaches quickly permeated other instrumental and vocal forms and genres as well, including fugue and aria.

FIGURE 3-9

Allegro of *Brandenburg Concerto* in G major, BWV 1048/1:
autograph fair copy (1721).

The ritornello theme of the opening movement of *Brandenburg Concerto* 3 presents a case in point (Fig. 3-9). In its melodic-rhythmic profile, it reveals the interplay of order, coherence, and proportion that essentially defines the developmental process growing out of this initial material: first setting it forth, then breaking it down into smaller units, then moving it into other key areas. Thus the initial theme imparts its musical identity to the entire movement, including the building blocks for a well-rounded tonal plan (G major–E minor–B minor–D major–G major) that nonetheless embraces many further moments of harmonic variety.

The six *Brandenburg Concertos* provide great insight into Bach's refined application of concerto composition patterns, made particularly attractive and diverse through the unique scoring of each work. In addition to his habitual incorporation of contrapuntal strains to enrich the textures of the scores, he regularly inserted more prominent contrapuntal features, such as imitative treatment of the embellished principal melody in the Adagio of *Brandenburg* 1. Further examples include the dense points of imitation in the rather polyphonic Andante of *Brandenburg* 2, the sequential patterns of double counterpoint between basso continuo and the solo violin in the Andante of

Brandenburg 4, and the fugal design of the main sections in the finale move-ment of the same piece.

Oddly enough, after composing the *Brandenburg* set, with its manifold exemplary qualities, Bach never returned to this type of concerto for several instruments, at least not in fully original compositions. After 1730 and defi-nitely in review mode, he produced the Concerto in A minor, BWV 1044, scored like *Brandenburg* 5 for a threefold concertino group of transverse flute, violin, and harpsichord—but with a four-part rather than three-part string rip-ieno. To a certain extent, BWV 1044 exceeds its older sister work in composi-tional refinement, especially in its even more formidable harpsichord solo part. Yet all three of its movements are based on or make use of earlier music: the Prelude and Fugue BWV 894 for keyboard (for movements 1 and 3), and the Adagio of the Sonata BWV 527 for organ (for movement 2). In a similar way and toward the end of the 1730s, Bach also rearranged *Brandenburg Concerto* 4 for solo harpsichord, replacing the solo violin (see Table 7-3).

EARLY LEIPZIG REVERBERATIONS

When Bach took up the post of cantor and music director in Leipzig, the parameters of his responsibilities and activities changed drastically. No longer would he enjoy the comparatively relaxed working conditions he had known in Cöthen, where his post had provided him with much latitude for pursuing musical projects separate from his immediate capellmeister duties. Neverthe-less, despite an excruciating schedule in Leipzig, he somehow managed to continue pursuing independent projects. Moreover, the commercial atmo-sphere of this city—long established as a hub of printing, publishing, and book trading—inspired Bach to consider the publication of selected works. No later than 1726, he launched a trial balloon in the market with the first installment of his *Clavier-Übung* (see Chapter 5).

The move to Leipzig, with its imperative focus on vocal music, did not, however, lead Bach to cease his composition of instrumental ensemble works. On the contrary, most of his extant ensemble and orchestral works actually originate from the Leipzig years, and were written primarily for use at the Collegium Musicum concerts he directed from 1729 to 1741. These include, among others, the four orchestral suites, BWV 1066–1069, the Violin Concerto in A minor, BWV 1041, the Double Violin Concerto in D minor, BWV 1043, the Triple Concerto in A minor, BWV 1044, and several sonatas with obbligato harpsichord or basso continuo, for violin, flute, and viola da gamba. Yet although they represent some of the finest works in their respective categories, none of these show any evidence of having been part of an opus collection. Their manuscript transmission shows no grouping pattern—the only exception being the set of six Sonatas for Obbligato Harpsichord and Violin, BWV 1014–1019, which precede the Collegium Musicum repertoire proper.

It is worth noting, however, that Bach's Leipzig production of instrumental ensemble pieces in no way compares with the expansive projects of his Hamburg colleague Telemann, whose rich and varied output of chamber and orchestral works in all conceivable categories remains unmatched—culminating in major published collections like the three-volume *Musique de Table* of 1731 and the *Nouveaux Quatuors* (the so-called Paris Quartets) of 1738. Bach, who frequently performed Telemann's works in Leipzig, generally trailed his friend in virtually every category of solo and ensemble sonatas and concertos, not just in quantity but notably in the variety of formal design and trendy stylistic approaches. In only three instances after 1723 did Bach truly invest in creating exceptional opus collections within the traditional sonata and concerto genres. These three innovative sets were all created with a special focus on the keyboard, the arena in which Bach easily surpassed Telemann and in fact could claim supremacy. The harpsichord-violin sonatas and the trio sonatas for organ originated in the earlier Leipzig years, while the harpsichord concertos came from the late 1730s (see Chapter 7). All these compositions relate directly to the core of Bach's instrumental expertise, and reflect an unabated zeal for experimenting in composition and advancing the standards of performance.

Six sonatas for harpsichord and violin

Like the *Brandenburg Concertos*, the set of six sonatas for harpsichord and violin are missing from the obituary work listing of 1750 and appear only in a later amendment by Carl Philipp Emanuel Bach. An autograph manuscript has not survived, nor has an authentic title of the collection been transmitted, and it is not known whether a manuscript exemplar of the set was sitting on Bach's music shelves at the time of his death. The earliest extant copy, from around 1725 and primarily in the hand of Bach's nephew and pupil Johann

Heinrich Bach (with autograph additions), bears the heading "Sei Sounate â Cembalo certato è Violino Solo."[63] A copy dating from the late 1740s in the hand of Bach's student and later son-in-law Johann Christoph Altnickol plays an important role in tracing the history of these sonatas, as it reflects certain careful revisions the composer made to the text, affecting all of the pieces.[64] This copy also indicates not only that the collection, dating back some twenty years, continued to be performed, but also that the composer persisted in making further improvements, even during the later stages of his life. This fact happens to be corroborated by a curious notation that Bach's second-youngest son, Johann Christoph Friedrich, entered on the title cover of the Altnickol manuscript: "NB. Diese Trio hat er vor seinem Ende componiret" (He composed these trios prior to his end; for the usage of "trio," see quote below). The inscription by the Bach son, who left the parental home in late 1749, was made in conjunction with organizing his father's estate (see also Fig. 2-1). It clearly implies that Johann Christoph Friedrich remembered seeing his father at work on these pieces around 1748/49, and erroneously assumed that he was writing them anew at that time. Johann Sebastian himself must have realized that these works, while absolutely novel in the mid-1720s, were still at the cutting edge in the 1740s—or else he would not have returned to them with such care. Even three decades later, Carl Philipp Emanuel felt the same way, as he testified in a letter of 1774:

> The six clavier trios . . . still sound very good now, and give me much pleasure, despite the fact that they are over fifty years old. There are a few Adagios in them that to this day are unexcelled in their cantabile qualities.[65]

The slow movements of these sonatas, with their particularly distinct, sensitive, and affettuoso melodious features, were from the outset the most modern settings within the group, and since every sonata contains two slow movements, they figure prominently within each individual work (Table 3-7). While stylistically less forward-looking, the fast movements excel in their discursive thematic-motivic development. All are contrapuntally conceived, and make liberal use of virtuoso effects for both the harpsichord and the violin. In five of the six sonatas, Bach adhered to the traditional four-movement (slow–fast–slow–fast) format, departing from it only in the final sonata, BWV 1019. Further manuscripts from the Bach circle indicate that this sixth piece underwent major changes to its movement structure around 1730, and then again in the late 1730s.[66] Bach initially had a hybrid form in mind that combined sonata and suite movements—much like the *Brandenburg Concerto 1*, sharing with it the same determination to avoid uniformity and predictability. In the second version of BWV 1019, Bach restored the unalloyed sonata character and decided to repeat the opening movement at the end—only to reintroduce in the third and final version the distinctly unconventional element of a harpsichord solo, in a newly composed movement placed at the center.

TABLE 3-7. Six sonatas for harpsichord and violin

Sonata 1 in B minor BWV 1014	Sonata 2 in A major BWV 1015	Sonata 3 in E major BWV 1016	Sonata 4 in C minor BWV 1017	Sonata 5 in F minor BWV 1018	Sonata 6 in G major BWV 1019*
Adagio $\frac{6}{4}$	Dolce $\frac{6}{8}$	Adagio **C**	Largo† $\frac{6}{8}$	Lamento‡ **3**	Allegro **C**
Allegro ¢	Allegro assai $\frac{3}{4}$	Allegro **2**	Allegro **C**	Allegro **C**	Largo $\frac{3}{4}$ (E minor)
Andante **C**	Andante un poco	Adagio ma non tanto	Adagio $\frac{3}{4}$	Adagio **C**	Allegro (*Cembalo*
(D major)	**C** (F♯ minor)	$\frac{3}{4}$ (C♯ minor)	(E♭ major)	(A♭ major)	*solo*) **C** (E minor)
Allegro	Presto **2**	Allegro $\frac{3}{4}$	Allegro $\frac{2}{4}$	Vivace $\frac{3}{8}$	Adagio **C**
					Allegro $\frac{6}{8}$

*Three versions of Sonata 6 (movements 3–5):
  Version I (c. 1725): 3. Courante $\frac{3}{8}$ (E minor) = BWV 830/3; 4. Adagio **C** (B minor); 5. Gavotte (Violin solo) **2** (G minor) = BWV 830/6; 6. Movement 1 repeated.
  Version II (c. 1730): 3. Cantabile, ma un poco Adagio $\frac{6}{8}$ = BWV 120/4; 4. Adagio (as in version III); 5. Movement 1 repeated.
  Version III (before 1739/40): as in Table 3-7.
†Headed *Siciliano* (version I, 1725).   ‡Headed *Adagio* (version I); *Lamento* (version II).

   Of primary importance in these harpsichord-violin works is their departure from the conventional design of sonatas for a solo instrument with basso continuo—that is, with accompaniment by a continuo group, ordinarily consisting of keyboard or lute with a violoncello or similar instrument reinforcing the bass part. Bach not only limited the accompaniment of the violin to a single harpsichord, but also assigned the harpsichord a new partnership function by having it join the violin in the treble register, in addition to having it present the bass line. This essentially provided the sonatas with a basic trio structure—and, in fact, handed the lead role to the harpsichord, which is appropriately reflected in the formulation of the title. The point of departure for this new structural design consisted of a simple performance arrangement, one in which the right-hand part of the harpsichord effectively took the second-violin part in a trio for two violins and continuo. The trio texture (two treble parts and bass fundament)—"the greatest masterpiece of harmony" according Johann Mattheson[67]—was the prevailing and ideal mode of composition for instrumental and vocal chamber music throughout the first half of the eighteenth century. Indeed, all the fast and several of the slow movements of the harpsichord-violin sonatas are constructed this way. The right-hand harpsichord and violin parts form a treble duo, while the left hand of the harpsichord provides the basso continuo, at some movement openings even in the manner of figured bass when the right hand does not have an obbligato function.

The title of the oldest manuscript from 1725, referenced above, includes in the hand of Bach's nephew Johann Heinrich the performance instruction "col Basso per Viola da Gamba accompagnato se piace"—suggesting that use of a reinforcing string instrument, joining the left hand of the harpsichord, is permitted as an *ad libitum* choice. At the same time, the instruction suggests the close association between this new kind of "duo" sonata and the traditional trio with basso continuo. That relationship is also preserved in the term "clavier trio," as it became customary by mid-century—notably in the Bach school—for harpsichord/fortepiano sonatas with the participation of violin or flute, but not necessarily with the participation of an additional bass instrument doubling the left-hand keyboard part. Moreover, the title formulation "Sei Sonate a Cembalo concertato e Violino solo" in later manuscripts of BWV 1014–1019[68] clarifies that the use of an additional string bass was no longer considered an option. The execution of these sonatas solely by harpsichord and violin had indeed become the new norm by the later 1720s, and that formula began to serve as a model for related compositions by Bach's pupils, notably his son Carl Philipp Emanuel.[69]

In the most pioneering of the slow movements, the free-style and mixed textures of the harpsichord parts go well beyond typical trio conventions by introducing polyphonic devices, this in order to confer upon the keyboard part a relatively independent function. This free treatment enabled Bach to capitalize on the contrasting sound qualities of harpsichord and violin, and also to pitch the short-lived sounds of the harpsichord against the sustained tone of the violin—so as to achieve clearly differentiated and idiomatic writing styles for the two instruments. This contrast is featured conspicuously at the very beginning of Sonata 1 in B minor, and even more prominently throughout the first movement of Sonata 5 (see Fig. 3-10). On the other hand, a movement like the C-sharp-minor Adagio of Sonata 2 demonstrates the compatibility and mutually supportive potential of both instruments, when they exchange the functions of rhythmically driven melodic lines and accompanying harmonies

FIGURE 3-10

Lamento of Sonata in F minor for obbligato harpsichord and violin, BWV 1018/1:
copy J. C. Altnickol (1747 or later), detail.

(see Fig. 3-11). This kind of truly autonomous handling of the two partnering instruments represents the point of departure for a new type of duo sonata with an elaborate keyboard part—a clavier trio, in the terminology of the Bach school. His consummate artistry having placed this category on a promising path, Bach apparently considered the potential to be fulfilled, as it were, and added no further such violin pieces. Nonetheless, unspecified contacts with proficient instrumentalists prompted him in the 1730s and '40s to compose three sonatas with flute, BWV 1030–1032, and three with viola da gamba, BWV 1027–1029, all standing as individual pieces and not constituting two closed groups of works.

Six trio sonatas for organ

While the sonatas for harpsichord and violin generally belong in the category of the instrumental trio, they do not exemplify it in its pure form. On the other hand, the organ sonatas—properly listed in the first work listing of 1750 as "Six trios for the organ, with obbligato pedal"—do fulfill the pertinent expectations as Mattheson described them: "all three voices, each by itself, must maintain a fine melody, and yet, as much as possible, form triadic harmony as if it had come about by accident."[70] Nearly two decades before Mattheson's account, Bach's three-part sinfonias had met the demands of trio texture in its purest

FIGURE 3-11

Adagio of Sonata in E major for obbligato harpsichord and violin, BWV 1016/3:
copy J. C. Altnickol (1747 or later), detail.

mode by strictly observing both its linear-contrapuntal and vertical-harmonic
aspects. Yet the parameters of a conventional trio, with paired treble parts
over a figured continuo bass, were fundamentally different from the absolute
contrapuntal ideals realized in the three-part sinfonias of the *Faithful Guide*.
Besides exemplifying a regular multi-movement trio format, the organ sonatas (Table 3-8) were meant to demonstrate the possibility of a single-player
trio. Whereas regular chamber trios required at least three players, one per
individual part, the two treble parts in an organ trio were to be executed by
the player's left and right hands on two separate manuals, and the bass part
by both feet on the organ pedals—the same acrobatic if less risky technique
that Bach had perfected in Weimar for the organ performance of orchestral
concertos, BWV 592–596.

TABLE 3-8. Six trio sonatas for organ

Sonata 1 in E♭ major BWV 525	Sonata 2 in C minor BWV 526	Sonata 3 in D minor BWV 527	Sonata 4 in E minor BWV 528	Sonata 5 in C major BWV 529	Sonata 6 in G major BWV 530
[Allegro] ¢	Vivace ¢	Andante $\frac{2}{4}$	Adagio–Vivace **C** – $\frac{3}{4}$	Allegro $\frac{3}{4}$	Vivace $\frac{2}{4}$
Adagio $\frac{12}{8}$ (C minor)	Largo $\frac{3}{4}$ (E♭ major)	Adagio $\frac{6}{8}$ (F major)	Andante **C** (B minor)	Largo $\frac{6}{8}$ (A minor)	Lente $\frac{6}{8}$ (E minor)
Allegro $\frac{3}{4}$	Allegro **2**	Vivace $\frac{3}{8}$	Un poc' Allegro $\frac{3}{8}$	Allegro $\frac{2}{4}$	Allegro ¢

The extant autograph fair copy of the six consecutively numbered trios entitled "Sonata 1[–6]. à 2 Clav: et Pedal" permits the dating of the collection to
around 1730 (Fig. 3-12);[71] a second manuscript was copied from it around 1732
by Wilhelm Friedemann and Anna Magdalena Bach, with additional autograph
entries.[72] Whether or not "Bach composed them for his eldest son, Wilhelm
Friedemann, who by practicing them would prepare himself to become the
great performer on the organ that he afterwards was,"[73] they clearly served Bach
the organ instructor as a touchstone collection for his pupils—as later student
copies confirm. Yet it remains the case that these organ sonatas may well have
originated as concert pieces for recitals given by the composer. Trio settings of
various kinds—including transcriptions of sonatas for two treble instruments and
basso continuo, freely composed sonatas, and chorale preludes in trio format—
constituted the signature genre of Bach the organist. Early in his career he had
refined his specialty, the technique of exercising two hands and two feet in
order to achieve absolute independence and equal facility for the three voices
represented on the two manuals and the pedalboard of the organ. Only a single
sonata movement, the Largo of Sonata 5, can be traced back to the Weimar
years, through an early copy of an inserted middle movement for Prelude and
Fugue in C major, BWV 545, transmitted under the heading "Preludio con
Fuga e Trio."[74] Beyond that, a good number of early chorale trios from before
1714, contained in the revised collection of Eighteen Chorales (Table 7-1), provide relevant substantiation of early organ trios.

   Whereas the chorale-based trios usually distribute the three obbligato parts
relatively evenly as upper (right hand), middle range (left hand), and bass
(feet), the organ sonatas typically feature two treble lines of comparable range.
Following the model of chamber trios, they typically combine two treble parts
functioning like a thematic duo with an accompanying bass (pedal) part,
which occasionally incorporates material from the upper parts. The organ

sonatas generally adhere to this scoring principle, which is most clearly demonstrated by the unison theme in the two upper voices of the opening movement of Sonata 6. Yet in the interest of a balanced sound and anatomically comfortable hand positions, the left-hand part is generally treated as the lower one. This example also indicates Bach's striving for distinct treatment of the three parts whenever possible. Furthermore, the use of different organ stops for the several lines of the trios serves to underscore their individuality. The technical demands of these sonatas in both manualiter and pedaliter performance were without precedent— and the composer was surely aware that they established a new threshold in the art of organ playing.

FIGURE 3-12

Allegro of Sonata in G major for organ, BWV 530/1:
autograph fair copy (c. 1730).

The conceptual derivation from ensemble trios had practical implications, for at least some of the organ sonatas seem to have consisted of or incorporated actual transcriptions of sonatas for two solo instruments and basso continuo. Of the total of eighteen movements, only one can actually be traced back to an earlier version: the sinfonia of the cantata BWV 76 (1723), an E-minor instrumental introduction to part 2 of the cantata, for oboe, viola da gamba, and basso continuo, was reworked by Bach as the opening Adagio–Vivace of Sonata 4, in the same key. As the cantata sinfonia may itself have been borrowed from a complete chamber sonata, the entire Sonata 4 in E minor may possibly be based on that same piece. But there is no evidence that all movements stemmed from the same sonata: compilations from various disparate works are entirely possible as well, and this surmise extends to the entire set of organ trios. In sum, it could be reasonably conjectured that some subset of movements from sonatas 1–5 represent quality selections from suitable preexisting chamber works—selections with adjustments made not only in order to accommodate the compass of the upper parts for the convenience of two hands, but also in order that the lines would not resemble typical violin or woodwind parts. There is no question that the entire autograph manuscript of the organ sonatas signifies three layers of history: (1) the practice of Bach's organ recitals; (2) his fascination with performing ensemble pieces like concertos and sonatas on a single instrument; and (3) editing and polishing unfigured scores, resulting in the endpoint of a novel opus.

Since no composing scores are available, the actual genesis of the organ sonatas remains in doubt. Yet Sonata 6 in its entirety seems to have been originally composed for organ (along with the outer movements of Sonatas 2 and 5). This is suggested by the unusual unison main subject of its first movement (see Fig. 3-12), as well as the distinctly idiomatic keyboard figuration employed throughout. Additionally, this sonata's manifestly modern $\frac{2}{4}$ meter and concertato character imply an origin around 1730 rather than earlier. The work's first page perfectly exemplifies the concept of an ideal trio by demonstrating, after the initial eight measures, just how two independent but motivically related parts can grow out of a unison theme and respond to one another. After the tonic cadence in m. 20, the two upper parts conduct a dialogue using the subsidiary motif, supported by a bass line that features its own motivic profile. From m. 37, all three parts move in differing yet complementary rhythmic realms, in steady sixteenth-, eighth-, and quarter-note motion.

In general, the outer movements of the sonatas are more polyphonically conceived than the slow middle movements, with their sensitive and embellished melodic lines. These outer movements consistently juxtapose principal subjects (frequently introduced in fugal manner) and subsidiary thematic ideas, which often lead to a development-like area in the middle sections. The formal design results in an aria-like rounded ABA structure, which for the first and last movements of Sonata 3 and the opening Allegro of Sonata 5 is not written out in Bach's autograph, but is instead marked by a simple *da capo* instruction. Contrapuntal devices like thematic inversion (featured in the second half of the finale movement of Sonata 1) or invertible counterpoint (particularly obvious at the very end of Sonata 4) are pervasive throughout. The pedal parts in the organ sonatas show clear structural differences from their manualiter treble parts, since Bach designed the bass parts as usually more active and more densely involved with the two upper voices than a normal continuo bass. Moreover, since the organ trio scores—in contrast to those of the ensemble sonatas—lack a figured bass, the three voices must relate to one another in a way that would make any harmonic filling superfluous. In this way, the organ trios present an autonomous alternative to conventional sonatas with traditional figured bass. In some sense, the exclusion of figured bass in the scoring of Bach's organ trios in fact anticipated the development of the unfigured (chordless) bass part in the later history of musical composition—as it is manifested, for example, in the string quartet, where Haydn and his followers dropped the keyboard accompaniment altogether.

The organ sonatas stand out from the rest of Bach's sonata compositions in their movement structure of fast–slow–fast. Bach's preferred sequence of sonata movements is the four-movement cycle, slow–fast–slow–fast, a type that prevails throughout his repertoire of sonatas for violin, flute, and viola da gamba (except for BWV 1029)[75] and in the trio sonatas as well. He still favored it when writing his last work in this category, the trio sonata in the *Musical Offering* (1747), even though the more fashionable sonata type then favored at the Prussian court consisted of three movements: fast–slow–fast. Since the three-movement type relates closely to the standard concerto form, Johann Adolph Scheibe dubbed it "Sonate auf Concertenart" (sonata in concerto style) in 1740.[76] This new kind of sonata, with largely homophonic opening movements, became popular around that time. Telemann and others composed such works, but Bach's approach in the organ sonatas—except for their three-movement structure—shows no resemblance to this type. When he conceived his opus of six organ trios in the middle to late 1720s, he adopted no established patterns, and deliberately followed his own devices in each of the altogether eighteen sonata movements. Hence, the collective result emerged just as fully innovative as was the entire idea of a trio sonata for organ. Bach surely realized that there was no precedent for this flexible sonata style, which in many ways paralleled the variety of approaches reflected in the set for harpsichord and violin—and thereby made the two related though contrasting sonata collections quite distinctive in both composition and performance. Moreover, the fact that the chronology of the organ trios overlapped with the closing phase of the publication of *Clavier-Übung* I suggests that Bach may at one point have considered including this new paradigm for the art of organ music within his projected multivolume *Clavier-Übung*.

In retrospect, the two sonata collections completed during the early Leipzig years—which are, in fact, Bach's only opus-style groups of sonatas— combine to evoke the composer's past as chamber musician in Weimar and director of chamber music in Cöthen. Indeed, he may well have begun with the harpsichord-violin opus while still in Cöthen; he completed it in Leipzig around 1725. In similar fashion, some movements of the organ sonatas may actually go back to Weimar models, even though the opus as such definitely originated in Leipzig. At any rate, the five instrumental collections of the 1720s, starting with the violin and cello solos and followed by the *Brandenburg Concertos*, the harpsichord-violin sonatas, and the organ sonatas, form a magisterial series of related groups of instrumental works. Yet these chamber genres remain without any further representations, with the exception of a single and eventually abandoned project to assemble a collection of harpsichord concertos (see Chapter 7). From the later 1720s, and particularly during his Collegium Musicum period, Bach composed an instrumental ensemble work from time to time, but the available evidence clearly points to a general lack of creative engagement in the area of chamber and orchestral music. Nevertheless, this did not keep Bach from occasionally producing individual compositions of exceptional quality and stylistic refinement, from the double violin concerto, BWV 1043, and the orchestral overtures, BWV 1067–1068, to the trio sonata of the *Musical Offering*, BWV 1079/3. None of these, however, exhibit the sorts of highly innovative strategies that Bach continued to pursue in the realm of vocal composition, and on his perpetual home turf of keyboard music.

CHAPTER 4

The Most Ambitious of All Projects

Chorale Cantatas throughout the Year

To characterize the chorale cantata cycle of 1724/25[1] as Bach's most ambitious of all compositional projects might at first glance seem hyperbolic. Yet a quick overview of the series fully supports this characterization. In terms of mere statistics, this second cantata cycle, with its several dozen cognate works, comprises by far the largest unit within Bach's copious musical output. It presents a chain of complex and highly impressive works that are focused on the recurring themes of selected Lutheran hymns,[2] and it originated within a period of only about ten months. At no other time did he turn out cantatas at the pace of at least one per week. And neither before nor afterward did he pursue an annual cantata cycle predicated around a single organizing principle, one that would serve as the foundational basis for an "opus" production. This was in fact a model that Bach had adopted primarily from his composer friend Georg Philipp Telemann.

By the end of his first year in Leipzig, Bach had already created a substantial repertoire of sacred and secular vocal music. Even though he had begun his career as an organist and instrumental virtuoso, he had already composed some vocal music in Arnstadt and Mühlhausen, mainly in the form of church cantatas—at the time a new genre that had quickly become fashionable in Protestant churches. He continued to compose such pieces on a more regular basis for the ducal court in Weimar, notably after the 1714 promotion to concertmaster that afforded him the opportunity of presenting a cantata monthly. As Cöthen capellmeister serving a Calvinist court from 1717 to 1723, Bach wrote virtually no church cantatas, but instead turned primarily to secular chamber cantatas. Yet never before had he engaged in vocal composition to the extent that he would during his first several years in Leipzig.

As an essential part of his duties, Bach was expected to mount some sixty cantata performances for the Sundays and feast days of the ecclesiastical year—excepting the three Sundays following the first Sunday in Advent and the seven-week period in Lent, following Estomihi Sunday. Although the regularly presented cantatas did not necessarily have to be of his own composition, he decided at the outset to establish a considerable repertoire of his own music during his early years in office, such that he would be able to perform these works again in subsequent years. He did not consider and treat these cantatas as mere utility music, but instead wholeheartedly invested himself in creating works of compositional excellence, overall musical quality, and spiritual depth. He also did not compromise in demanding the utmost in technical proficiency and professional finesse from both vocal and instrumental performers.

Between completing his service at the princely court in Cöthen and his new start in Leipzig, Bach had very little time to prepare for carrying out the ambitious plans he had in mind for church music in his new city. Since his first year in office in fact coincided with the academic year at the St. Thomas School, he was immediately placed under certain pressures, however congenial, as he put together a heterogeneous series of newly composed cantatas on texts by various authors, and availed himself of preexisting material that included both cantatas from the Weimar years and newly fashioned sacred parodies of secular Cöthen cantatas. The entirely new works in particular demonstrated his commitment to elevating the genre of sacred cantata to a new plane of compositional refinement, well beyond the level he had attained in Weimar. Already in the second set of new cantatas, for the seventh, eighth, and ninth Sundays after Trinity—"Erforsche mich Gott" (BWV 136), "Herr, gehe nicht ins Gericht" (BWV 105), and "Schauet doch und sehet" (BWV 46), with their intricate and sumptuous opening choruses—he pursued new aspirations for compelling musical expression. In addition, Bach's output during the first year included two large-scale works: the Magnificat, BWV 243 (prepared in a standard version for major holidays and an expanded one specifically for Christmas), and the *St. John Passion*, BWV 245, for Good Friday of 1724.

Anticipating his second year in office, Bach shifted plans for the Leipzig church music program toward the model successfully used by Telemann, which involved adopting an overall organizing principle for the projected annual cycle (*Jahrgang*) of cantatas. As capellmeister in Eisenach, a ducal court neighboring Weimar, Telemann had composed *Geistliches Singen und Spielen* in 1710/11, which set to music a full year's cycle of published cantata lyrics by a single poet, the theologian Erdmann Neumeister. Subsequently, as music director in Frankfurt, Telemann wrote additional cantata cycles on texts by Neumeister and others, furthermore incorporating purposeful adaptations of French, mixed, and Italian musical styles—in the collections *Französischer Jahrgang* (1714/15), *Concertenjahrgang* (1716/17), and *Sicilianischer Jahrgang* (1718/19).[3]

For his second year in Leipzig, Bach embarked on a cantata project that focused on the rich stockpile of traditional chorale texts and melodies in the Lutheran hymnbook. As an organist, he had both improvised and composed numerous and often highly elaborate organ chorales based on these melodies, and had used the hymnbook and his own *Orgel-Büchlein* as central teaching materials. The Lutheran chorale, notably its melodies, held a lifelong fascination for Bach. Yet his idea of building a cantata cycle on the melodies and texts of these chorales, given that he had never before done anything remotely similar, represented a notable inflection point within his constantly evolving musical universe. In an overall scheme that went well beyond Telemann's models, Bach's conception of cyclical chorale cantatas was a major step forward. It not only influenced the overall cohesion of the cantata series, with its sequence of changing melodies, but also helped to determine the inner musical coherence of the cantatas themselves, each of which derives its unmistakable musical identity from its individual chorale melody. In other words, each cantata is both a unit in itself and also a part of the grand scheme of the annual cycle.

BACKGROUND, CONCEPT, AND SCHEDULE

The history of vocal-instrumental chorale settings essentially begins with the chorale-based sacred concertos of the influential cantor Johann Hermann Schein, one of Bach's Leipzig predecessors; these works were published in two volumes as *Opella Nova*, 1618 and 1626. Later in the century, Dietrich Buxtehude and Johann Pachelbel were notable among those Protestant German composers who wrote chorale-based and cantata-like works *per omnes versus* (through all strophes) of the hymn. These were multi-movement pieces comprising a sequence of varied chorale elaborations, each devoted to one strophe of a complete hymn. Bach's Easter cantata "Christ lag in Todesbanden," BWV 4, his audition piece of 1707 for the organist post in Mühlhausen, represents this older type of pure chorale-text cantata. This work resembles, in many structural and musical details, an identically named cantata by Johann Pachelbel.[4] Bach did not revisit this cantata type until he performed BWV 4 seventeen years later in Leipzig, on Easter Sunday 1724, and again in 1725 at the very end of the chorale cantata cycle.

The guiding concept that Bach developed for the chorale cantatas of his second annual cycle differed significantly from the *per omnes versus* approach. In order to meet the formal criteria of the modern church cantata, the strophes of the chosen chorale were divided in such a way that the first and last were kept verbatim (Table 4-1). They formed a highly effective framing device, in which the chosen chorale melody provided the musical basis for the cantata's opening movement, in the form of an elaborate setting, and then also for the concluding movement, in the form of a straightforward four-part chorale harmonization—with both outer movements performed by the entire vocal-instrumental ensemble. The texts of the inner chorale strophes, greatly varying in number (from two or three up to a dozen or more), were recast into the typical madrigalian poetry of cantata librettos—that is, as recitatives and arias, with their varying metric patterns and rhyme orders. These solo movements, typically four or five, could contain direct quotations from the hymn—with or without its related melody—or even a full-scale solo chorale elaboration of a single strophe. Moreover, the reworked poetic texts regularly included references to the liturgically prescribed gospel lessons for the day. The resulting madrigalian format for the chorale cantatas of the 1724/25 cycle typically evolved according to the scheme shown in Table 4-1.

TABLE 4-1. Schematic format of the chorale cantatas of 1724/25

HYMN STROPHES	CANTATA MOVEMENTS		
First strophe: melody and text →	Figural Chorale (elaborate polyphonic setting)		
Inner strophes: text recast into madrigalian poetry, with references to gospel lesson and → occasional quotes from hymn verses and/or melodic lines	{ Aria		Recitative
	Recitative		Aria
	Aria	or	Recitative
	Recitative		Aria
	Aria		Recitative
Last strophe: melody and text →	Final Chorale (four-part chorale harmonization)		

This flexible scheme allowed for variation, but generally limited to the number and order of the solo movements. In some cases, the model resulted in a longer two-part cantata to be performed before and after the sermon—as, for instance, in the inaugural piece of Bach's 1724/25 cycle, "O Ewigkeit, du Donnerwort," BWV 20, with altogether eleven movements. Its first part contains Figural Chorale–Recitative–Aria–Recitative–Aria–Aria–Final Chorale; its second part, Aria–Recitative–Aria–Final Chorale.

Around 1690, Bach's Leipzig pre-predecessor Johann Schelle reportedly collaborated with Johann Benedict Carpzov, pastor at St. Thomas's, by presenting chorale settings to match the Sunday sermons, based on Lutheran hymn texts.[5] There is no evidence of any such collaborative efforts some thirty years later, but a particular tradition of elaborate chorale settings had prevailed in Leipzig church music ever since the time of Schein in the 1620s. Bach's familiarity with specific vocal chorale concertos (concerted chorale motets with instruments) and other vocal chorale elaborations from a rich seventeenth-century repertoire can be presupposed, because he had grown up in this tradition from his earliest experiences as a choirboy. The closest traceable link lies in the remarkable musical parallels that occur, as mentioned above, between "Christ lag in Todesbanden," BWV 4, the only pre-Leipzig chorale cantata, and the setting by Pachelbel, the teacher of Bach's older brother, Johann Christoph. That BWV 4 originated as Bach's audition piece for the organist post in Mühlhausen speaks of its close link to the repertoire of Lutheran hymns, the musical staples of the church and the daily bread of an organist. Bach's fascination—and indeed love—for devising multiple ways of dealing repeatedly with a single hymn tune, exploring its polyphonic potential and harmonic implications in many and varied organ works, relates directly to general context of the chorale cantata project. This captivation likewise was the driving force behind his decision to settle on chorale tunes and texts as the special focus for the second cantata cycle. His extensive experience as an organist—more than his awareness of vocal models and his familiarity with them—inspired him to realize and capitalize upon the opulent and abundant possibilities within the great melodic treasure chest of Lutheran hymns.[6]

It is no surprise, then, that even Bach's first Leipzig cantata cycle of 1723/24 included some works that open with prominent and elaborate chorale choruses. In fact, the idea of an entire cantata cycle with a focus on chorales appears to have emerged in conjunction with a group of five works performed between late August and early October 1723. These particular five (Table 4-2) are based either on chorale texts and melodies (group a) or on biblical texts in combination with instrumental chorale tunes without words (group b). Such general parameters would eventually play a role in the creation of the 1724/25 cycle.

TABLE 4-2. Nucleus of cantatas with emphasis on chorales, from first Leipzig cycle (fall 1723)

(a) Based on chorale texts and melodies
"Warum betrübst du dich, mein Herz," BWV 138 (15th Sunday after Trinity):
   Opening chorale chorus with intermittent recitative; final chorale based on the same melody.
"Christus, der ist mein Leben," BWV 95 (16th Sunday after Trinity):
   Opening chorale chorus with intermittent recitative and combined with second chorale, "Mit Fried und Freud ich fahr dahin"; two additional chorales, "Valet will ich dir geben" and "Wenn mein Stündlein vorhanden ist," appear in movements 2, 3, and 7.

(b) Based on biblical texts in combination with instrumental chorale tunes without words
"Du sollt Gott, deinen Herren lieben," BWV 77 (13th Sunday after Trinity):
   Opening biblical chorus with instrumental chorale "Dies sind die heilgen zehn Gebot."
"Es ist nichts Gesundes an meinem Leibe," BWV 25 (14th Sunday after Trinity):
   Opening biblical chorus with instrumental ensemble chorale "Ach Herr, mich armen Sünder."
"Ich elender Mensch, wer wird mich erlösen," BWV 48 (19th Sunday after Trinity):
   Opening biblical chorus with instrumental chorale "Herr Jesu Christ, du höchstes Gut"; final chorale based on same melody.

Curiously, four of these five cantatas were composed in a gap-free sequence, for the thirteenth to the sixteenth Sundays after Trinity, from August 22 through September 12, 1723. BWV 138 and 95 begin with very similar compound structures of alternating chorale strophes and interpolated recitatives, both unique in Bach's cantata repertoire. Cantata BWV 138 in particular appears to be of pivotal significance in terms of Bach's evolving ideas for the treatment and formal design of a madrigalian chorale cantata. To begin with, this cantata uses a single chorale melody as a musical focus for the entire composition. Furthermore, it combines the strophic text of the hymn with typical madrigalian poetry. And finally, it establishes a framing device by using the intact first and last chorale strophes as opening and concluding movements. Such clear constituent elements were not precisely duplicated in the other four cantatas, yet their specific features and general context nevertheless point to a germinal cell for a cantata type with an emphasis on chorale melodies, one that eventually defined the essence of Bach's compositional activity from June 1724 through March 1725.

The librettists for these five interrelated cantatas are unknown, and none of their texts were taken from identifiable published collections. The texts of BWV 138 and 95, however, are structurally so similar that they were most likely written by the same author, possibly the one who would also contribute to the libretto format and the anonymous texts of the chorale cantata cycle. Since Leipzig had no shortage of poetically active literati, Bach may well have benefitted from that rich pool of academic poets. This is suggested by the case of the divinity student Christoph Birkmann, who wrote texts for Bach in 1725–26.[7] However, the instrumental chorales in cantatas BWV 77, 25, and 48 (Table 4-2, group b) were not dictated by the librettos, but are instead Bach's own contributions to the interpretive content of these works. They indicate his predilection for the kinds of emblematic references that would become so prominent in the 1724/25 cycle.

If it was indeed during the process of composing cantata BWV 138 that the idea of the madrigalian chorale cantata was born—that is, the notion of writing music that combined the hymn with free poetic verses—this would likely have happened during Bach's busy scramble to maintain a steady stream of performances for the Sundays and feast days of his first year in the cantor's office. He would hardly have had much time for any sort of gestation period, or any real opportunity for extended reflection on just how to construct a logically conceived and coherent second annual cantata cycle. This would follow a highly productive, remarkably diversified and rich first year of church music—if also one that had been rather erratic and fortuitous. Thus it came to pass that at the beginning of the new school year on June 11, 1724, the first Sunday after Trinity, Bach quietly began with a cantata performance that initiated the most extensive and ambitious compositional endeavor he would ever undertake, a project that eventually added up to more than fifteen hours of chorale-based musical polyphony.

The extraordinarily demanding project schedule shown in Table 4-3 has no precedent or equivalent in the composer's creative life. The stressful experience of the first annual cantata cycle had certainly served as preparation, but the composer had still allowed himself to sidestep a deadline on various occasions, via performance of a work from the Weimar repertoire. The second cycle required him to compose one new work after another in relentless succession. That meant composing entirely fresh multi-movement scores, preparing all performing materials, and then rehearsing and performing, week after week. Additional cantatas had to be prepared and performed in a given week for the Apostle Days, Marian Feasts, and Reformation Festival. Such an instance first occurred when two new cantatas were due on consecutive days, June 24 and 25, 1724. Particularly crowded was the Christmas season, when no fewer than six new works were required within less than two weeks. The two periods without figural church music, three weeks in Advent and seven weeks in Lent, hardly offered any relief, because these blocks of time were essential periods of preparation for the subsequent holiday seasons. How Bach managed to maintain such a grueling schedule, in addition to all the other activities of his day-to-day personal and professional lives, remains difficult to imagine.

TABLE 4-3. The annual cycle of chorale cantatas, 1724/25: Performance calendar

BWV	CANTATA TITLE	LITURGICAL DATE (Academic Year)	FIRST PERFORMANCE
	(1) The original cycle of 1724/25: 42 cantatas		
20	O Ewigkeit, du Donnerwort	1st Sunday after Trinity	June 11, 1724
2	Ach Gott, vom Himmel sieh darein	2nd Sunday after Trinity	June 18
7	Christ unser Herr zum Jordan kam	St. John's Day	June 24
135	Ach Herr, mich armen Sünder	3rd Sunday after Trinity	June 25
10	Meine Seel erhebt den Herren	Feast of the Visitation	July 2
93	Wer nur lieben Gott läßt walten	5th Sunday after Trinity	July 9
—		6th Sunday after Trinity	July 16
107	Was willst du dich betrüben*	7th Sunday after Trinity	July 23
178	Wo Gott der Herr nicht bei uns hält	8th Sunday after Trinity	July 30
94	Was frag ich nach der Welt	9th Sunday after Trinity	Aug. 6
101	Nimm von uns, Herr, du treuer Gott	10th Sunday after Trinity	Aug. 13
113	Herr Jesu Christ, du höchstes Gut	11th Sunday after Trinity	Aug. 20
—		12th Sunday after Trinity	Aug. 27
33	Allein zu dir, Herr Jesu Christ	13th Sunday after Trinity	Sep. 3
78	Jesu, der du meine Seele	14th Sunday after Trinity	Sep. 10
99	Was Gott tut, das ist wohlgetan	15th Sunday after Trinity	Sep. 17

8	Liebster Gott, wenn werd ich sterben?	16th Sunday after Trinity	Sep. 24
130	Herr Gott, dich loben alle wir	St. Michael's Day	Sep. 29
114	Ach lieben Christen, seid getrost	17th Sunday after Trinity	Oct. 1
96	Herr Christ, der einge Gottessohn	18th Sunday after Trinity	Oct. 8
5	Wo soll ich fliehen hin	19th Sunday after Trinity	Oct. 15
180	Schmücke dich, o liebe Seele	20th Sunday after Trinity	Oct. 22
38	Aus tiefer Not schrei ich zu dir	21th Sunday after Trinity	Oct. 29
—		Reformation Festival	Oct. 31
115	Mache dich, mein Geist, bereit	22th Sunday after Trinity	Nov. 5
139	Wohl dem, der sich auf seinen Gott	23th Sunday after Trinity	Nov. 12
26	Ach wie flüchtig, ach wie nichtig	24th Sunday after Trinity	Nov. 19
116	Du Friedefürst, Herr Jesu Christ	25th Sunday after Trinity	Nov. 26
62	Nun komm der Heiden Heiland	1st Sunday in Advent	Dec. 3
91	Gelobet seist du, Jesu Christ	1st Day of Christmas	Dec. 25
121	Christum wir sollen loben schon	2nd Day of Christmas	Dec. 26
133	Ich freue mich in dir	3rd Day of Christmas	Dec. 27
122	Das neugeborne Kindelein	Sunday after Christmas	Dec. 1
41	Jesu, nun sei gepreiset	New Year's Day	Jan. 1, 1725
58	Ach Gott, wie manches Herzeleid	Sunday after New Year's Day	Jan. 5
123	Liebster Immanuel, Herzog der Frommen	Epiphany	Jan. 6
124	Meinen Jesum laß ich nicht	1st Sunday after Epiphany	Jan. 7
3	Ach Gott, wie manches Herzeleid	2nd Sunday after Epiphany	Jan. 14
111	Was mein Gott will, das g'scheh allzeit	3rd Sunday after Epiphany	Jan. 21
92	Ich hab in Gottes Herz und Sinn	Septuagesimae Sunday	Jan. 28
125	Mit Fried und Freud ich fahr dahin	Fest of the Purification	Feb. 2
126	Erhalt uns, Herr, bei deinem Wort	Sexagesimae Sunday	Feb. 4
127	Herr Jesu Christ, wahr' Mensch und Gott	Estomihi Sunday	Feb. 11
1	Wie schön leuchtet der Morgenstern	Feast of the Annunciation	Mar. 25
[245.2	St. John Passion, "O Mensch bewein"†	Good Friday	Mar. 30]
4	Christ lag in Todesbanden* (1707)‡	Easter Sunday	Apr. 1

(2) Later supplements: 8 cantatas to fill liturgical gaps

177	Ich ruf zu dir, Herr Jesu Christ*	4th Sunday after Trinity	Jul. 6, 1732
9	Es ist das Heil uns kommen her	6th Sunday after Trinity	Aug. 1, 1734
137	Lobe den Herren, den mächtigen König*	12th Sunday after Trinity	Aug. 19, 1725
80	Ein feste Burg ist unser Gott	Reformation Festival	1728–31 & Oct. 31, 1739
140	Wachet auf, ruft uns die Stimme	27th (last) Sunday after Trinity	Nov. 25, 1731
14	Wär Gott nicht mit uns diese Zeit	4th Sunday after Epiphany	Jan. 30, 1735
112	Der Herr ist mein getreuer Hirt*	Misericordias Domini	Apr. 8, 1731
129	Gelobet sei der Herr, mein Gott*	Trinitatis	June 8, 1727

(3) Later supplements: 4 chorale-text-only cantatas without liturgical designation

117	Sei Lob und Ehr dem höchsten Gut*	——	1728–31
192	Nun danket alle Gott*	——	c. 1730
100	Was Gott tut, das ist wohlgetan*	——	c. 1734
97	In allen meinen Taten*	——	1734 (autogr. date)

* Chorale text only; no madrigalian poetry.
† St. John Passion, second version of 1725 (to fit the chorale cantata cycle).
‡ Composed 1707, revised 1724; repeated in 1725 and integrated into chorale cantata cycle.

Utterly puzzling is the fact that Bach brought the chorale cantata series to a halt in the spring of 1725. The cantata BWV 1, composed for the Marian Feast of the Annunciation and performed on that March 25, concluded a homogeneous series of altogether 41 works composed in a single sweep of 37 weeks. This was followed only a few days later, on Good Friday, March 30, by the second version of the *St. John Passion* (Chapter 6, page 210)—with adjustments made to that work, which had been premiered a year earlier, such that it would fit it into the ongoing series of chorale cantatas. At that point the series came to a premature end, and the main work for Easter Sunday, April 1, 1725, was an Easter cantata, BWV 249, a work parodied from a secular piece that had been performed only six weeks before at the court of Weißenfels (Chapter 6, page 241). For the sake of preserving continuity in the chorale cantata project (though it was clearly a makeshift solution), Bach added a second cantata for this high holiday. He chose for this purpose the older cantata BWV 4, which had been performed the year before and happened to be a chorale cantata, albeit of the chorale-text-only type. It seems that some time in early 1725, after preparing the cantata text booklet for the Sundays after Epiphany through Annunciation, the composer had run out of chorale cantata texts. The reasons for this are completely unknown, but beginning on Easter Monday of 1725, with the cantata "Bleib bei uns, denn es will Abend werden" (BWV 6), Bach returned for the remaining two months of the school year to regular madrigalian cantatas. All of those had to be newly composed, most of them on texts by Mariane von Ziegler, so the apparently forced and abrupt shift had absolutely no effect on the weekly production schedule. In other words, the circumstantial change brought absolutely no relief to the composer.

When the chorale cantata cycle of 1724/25 was initially in progress, Bach skipped only two Sundays, the sixth and twelfth Sundays after Trinity, apparently for commitments outside Leipzig (Table 4-3, section 1).[8] Additionally, he did not compose cantatas for the fourth Sunday after Trinity, because the Feast of Visitation took precedence on that date. Nor are there cantatas for the twenty-sixth and twenty-seventh Sundays after Trinity and the fourth Sunday after Epiphany, because these liturgical dates were absent from the church year 1724/25. Intending to fill in these holes by adding pertinent supplements, Bach began doing so in 1725 with cantata BWV 137 for the twelfth Sunday after Trinity, after which he returned only intermittently to the project of the proper (*de tempore*) cycle of the liturgical year (Table 4-3, section 2). By 1734/35, Bach had essentially completed the cycle from Trinity Sunday (BWV

129) through Annunciation.[9] Yet with the sole exception of BWV 112 for the Misericordias Domini Sunday, he seems not to have turned to the segment from Easter through Pentecost. On the other hand, in the early 1730s he added four chorale-text-only cantatas, following the model of BWV 137 but without specific liturgical destination (Table 4-3, section 3). Since the four chosen hymns were liturgically neutral, these were cantatas that could be performed at any time outside the major holidays of the ecclesiastical year, and could also be used for wedding masses. They served as a pragmatic extension of the chorale cantata cycle proper, but owing to their multifunctionality, they were kept separate from the *de tempore* cantatas.[10]

A SERIAL OPUS

What distinguishes the incomplete chorale cantata cycle of 1724/25 from a more regular musical opus, like the *Well-Tempered Clavier* or the *Brandenburg Concertos*, is not merely the sheer scale of the project, but also its gradual, week-by-week progression over a ten-month period. Formal continuity throughout the entire opus was guaranteed by Bach's strict adherence to a standard cantata format, ordinarily of six or seven movements as outlined in Table 4-1. Moreover, each cantata, in its function within the Lutheran worship service, enhanced the gospel reading of the day, which immediately preceded it in the liturgy. It thus represented a musical sermon, with the goal of communicating and reinforcing the spiritual message of the sacred poetry. Finally, the specific chorale tunes that served as musical themes for each work in its entirety, and as core devices for its outer movements, formed a prominent defining element in terms of focus and continuity. Hence each cantata could draw its particular identity from the referential value of its chorale melody.

Regarding the planning of the annual cycle as a serial opus, Bach himself apparently determined its content and overall shape by selecting the chorales for the various Sundays and feast days before commissioning the texts from one or more poetic collaborators. Considering his intimate familiarity with the Lutheran hymnal, this selection process would have been an easy task. The process also enabled him to make some crucial musical decisions from the outset, starting with the choice of melodies that had sufficient generative musical capacity. He also seems to have gravitated to his own favorite tunes, and those he deemed particularly suitable for the intended purpose, while at the same time avoiding unwanted duplication—given that very many melodies of the vast Lutheran hymn repertory are used for more than one text. Finally, he attempted to establish sufficient variety among the chosen chorale melodies, in terms of their musical character and their compositional potential within the extended cyclical opus.

It is noteworthy that Bach made his selection of tunes almost exclusively from the classic stockpile of chorale melodies from the Reformation period through the mid-seventeenth century, an emphasis that matched his personal preferences in setting organ chorales. In the case of the cantata cycle, it was probably also a unifying strategy. Within this repertoire of melodies (Table 4-4), more than half of the sixteenth-century tunes are derived from medieval songs based on the church modes; out of a total of forty-seven tunes, only two date from the early eighteenth century, those for cantatas BWV 8 and BWV 133. He also aimed at maximum diversification by avoiding repeats of melodies. Within the original cycle of 1724/25, only two melodies are used in two different cantatas (in BWV 178 and BWV 114, and in BWV 111 and BWV 92); out of the total of 54 chorale cantatas, just five tunes are set twice (Table 4-5). Moreover, when setting a tune for the second time, Bach differentiated its pivotal opening movement from the earlier setting in terms of meter, key, and scoring. Additional structural and compositional elements throughout the cantatas with "repeat" settings further established a strong sense of contrast.

TABLE 4-4. Tunes (cantus firmi) of the chorale cantatas and their origins

CANTATA/TUNE (BWV)	HYMNAL OR COMPOSER (Primary Text for Tune)
(1) 16th century	
Ach Gott, vom Himmel sieh darein (BWV 2)	Erfurt 1524*
Christum wir sollen loben schon (BWV 121)	Erfurt 1524*
Herr Christ, der einge Gottessohn (BWV 96)	Erfurt 1524*
Aus tiefer Not schrei ich zu dir (BWV 38)	Erfurt 1524*
Nun komm der Heiden Heiland (BWV 62)	Erfurt 1524*
Gelobet seist du, Jesu Christ (BWV 91)	J. Walter, 1524*
Wär Gott nicht mit uns diese Zeit (BWV 14)	J. Walter, 1524*
Christ lag in Todesbanden (BWV 4)	J. Walter, 1524*
Mit Fried und Freud ich fahr dahin (BWV 125)	J. Walter, 1524*
Christ unser Herr zum Jordan kam (BWV 7)	Wittenberg 1524* (Es woll uns Gott genädig sein)
Es ist das Heil uns kommen her (BWV 9)	Nuremberg 1524*
Sei Lob und Ehr dem höchsten Gutt (BWV 117)	

Ich ruf zu dir, Herr Jesu Christ (BWV 177)	Wittenberg 1526*
Wo Gott der Herr nicht bei uns hält (BWV 178)	Wittenberg 1529*
Ach lieben Christen, seid getrost† (BWV 114)	
Ein feste Burg ist unser Gott (BWV 80)	Wittenberg 1529
Meine Seel erhebt den Herren (BWV 10)	Wittenberg 1529 (Tonus peregrinus)*
Nimm von uns, Herr, du treuer Gott (BWV 101)	Leipzig 1539 (Vater unser im Himmelreich)
Der Herr ist mein getreuer Hirt (BWV 112)	Leipzig 1539* (Allein Gott in der Höh sei Ehr)
In allen meinen Taten (BWV 97)	H. Isaac, 1539 (O Welt, ich muss dich lassen)
Erhalt uns, Herr, bei deinem Wort (BWV 126)	Wittenberg 1543
Allein zu dir, Herr Jesu Christ (BWV 33)	Leipzig 1545*
Herr Gott, dich loben alle wir (BWV 130)	Geneva 1551 (Ihr Knecht des Herren allzugleich)
Was mein Gott will, das g'scheh allzeit (BWV 111)	J. Magdeburg, 1572
Ich hab in Gottes Herz und Sinn† (BWV 92)	
Was willst du dich betrüben (BWV 107)	J. Magdeburg, 1572 (Von Gott will ich nicht lassen)
Jesu, nun sei gepreiset (BWV 41)	Wittenberg 1591
Herr Jesu Christ, du höchstes Gut (BWV 113)	Dresden 1593 (Wenn mein Stündlein vorhanden ist)
Herr Jesu Christ, wahr' Mensch und Gott (BWV 127)	J. Eccard, 1597
Wachet auf, ruft uns die Stimme (BWV 140)	P. Nicolai, 1599
Wie schön leuchtet der Morgenstern (BWV 1)	P. Nicolai, 1599

(2) 17th century

Ach Herr, mich armen Sünder (BWV 135)	H. L Hassler, 1601 (Herzlich tut mich verlangen)
Du Friedefürst, Herr Jesu Christ (BWV 116)	B. Gesius, 1601
Das neugeborne Kindelein (BWV 122)	M. Vulpius, 1609
Ach Gott, wie manches Herzeleid (BWV 3)	Leipzig, 1625 (Herr J. Christ, meins Lebens Licht)
Wo soll ich fliehen hin (BWV 5)	J. H. Schein, 1627 (Auf meinen lieben Gott)
Wohl dem, der sich auf seinen Gott (BWV 139)	J. H. Schein, 1628 (Machs mit mir, Gott, nach deiner Güt)
Nun danket alle Gott (BWV 192)	J. Crüger, 1647
Schmücke dich, o liebe Seele (BWV 180)	J. Crüger, 1649
O Ewigkeit, du Donnerwort (BWV 20)	J. Crüger, 1653
Wer nur den lieben Gott läßt walten (BWV 93)	G. Neumark, 1657
Meinen Jesum laß ich nicht (BWV 124)	Zittau 1658
Ach wie flüchtig, ach wie nichtig (BWV 26)	J. Crüger, 1661
Jesu, der du meine Seele (BWV 78)	Frankfurt/M 1662 (Wachet doch, erwacht ihr Schläfer)
Lobe den Herren, den mächtigen König (BWV 137)	Stralsund 1665 (Hast du denn, Jesu, dein Angesicht)
Was Gott tut, das ist wohlgetan (BWV 99)	Nuremberg 1690
Was Gott tut, das ist wohlgetan† (BWV 100)	
Was frag ich nach der Welt (BWV 94)	Meiningen 1693 (O Gott, du frommer Gott)
Gelobet sei der Herr, mein Gott† (BWV 129)	
Mache dich, mein Geist, bereit (BWV 115)	Dresden 1694 (Straf mich nicht in deinem Zorn)
Liebster Immanuel, Herzog der Frommen (BWV 123)	Darmstadt 1698

(3) 18th century

Liebster Gott, wenn werd ich sterben? (BWV 8)	D. Vetter, 1713
Ich freue mich in dir (BWV 133)	J. B. König, c. 1714

* Medieval origin.   † Cantata based on same melody.

TABLE 4-5. Different settings of the same chorale tune
(opening movements)

CHORALE TUNE	FIRST SETTING*	SECOND SETTING*
Wo Gott der Herr nicht bei uns hält	BWV 178: **C**, A minor; hn, 2 ob, 2 ob d'amore	BWV 114: $\frac{6}{4}$, G minor; hn, fl, 2 ob
Was mein Gott will, das g'scheh allzeit	BWV 111: **¢**, A minor; 2 ob	BWV 92: $\frac{6}{8}$, B minor; 2 ob d'amore
O Gott, du frommer Gott	BWV 94: **C**, D major; fl, 2 ob d'amore	BWV 129: **C**, D major; 3 tpt+timp, fl, 2 ob
Es ist das Heil uns kommen her	BWV 9: $\frac{3}{4}$, E major; fl, 2 ob d'amore	BWV 117: $\frac{6}{8}$, G major; 2 fl, 2 ob
Was Gott tut, das ist wohlgetan	BWV 99: **C**, G major; hn, fl, ob d'amore	BWV 100: **¢**, G major; 2 hn+ti, fl, ob d'amore

* Scoring: only wind instruments indicated, regular strings and basso continuo assumed.

Like all annual cycles of church cantatas, Bach's chorale cantata cycle had to fulfill its primary function of providing moving musical sermons, thus enhancing the religious message associated with the liturgical character of each Sunday and feast day within the ecclesiastical year. Yet apart from Bach's manifest commitment to emphasizing the devotional character of each cantata, the true driving force for the opus of chorale cantatas was of a musical nature—just as were the artistic aims of the *Orgel-Büchlein*, although the latter's quasi-miniaturist approach to chorale elaboration differed significantly from the scale of a multi-movement vocal-instrumental score. The guiding principle for both opus series consisted of a logically conceived plan for varied settings of well-known tunes, carried out with an exploratory and experimental orientation that afforded scope for the widest possible range of solutions. Furthermore, the compositions of both sets consistently remained truthful to their religious functions, underscored and highlighted the meaning of the sacred poetry's text. In this connection, it may not be at all far-fetched to view Bach's dedicated and sophisticated compositional efforts as his own deeply informed response to the professorial sermons delivered by his theological colleagues from the pulpits of Leipzig's two main churches, St. Thomas's and St. Nicholas's. Yet whereas the preachers had a full hour for presenting their homiletic interpretations of the biblical scriptures, the cantor's time allocation was ordinarily less than half that. More than three centuries later, the preachers' words have faded away completely, while their cantor's music is still being heard and studied—though sadly, this cannot bring the composer any posthumous satisfaction.

On June 11, 1724, the official beginning of the school year, Bach launched his second annual cantata cycle with an unprecedented gesture, although in all likelihood, few if any in the captive audience of some two thousand worshipers would have grasped the extraordinary implications of what he had initiated—from the opening measures of the overture to "O Ewigkeit, du Donnerwort" (BWV 20) through the movements that followed. He apparently had devoted much thought to the project's start, and his exhaustive planning efforts can be readily perceived in the scores themselves. The first unusual detail consisted in the special prayer formula that Bach placed at the beginning of the first cantata's composing score, entered before he wrote down the first note. The customary two-letter invocation "J. J." (Latin *Jesu juva*, "Jesus help") was the one that many other composers normally inscribed at the tops of their scores. Yet this time Bach, surely conscious of the prodigious dimensions of his new undertaking, instead turned to a more ceremonial formula, the six-letter phrase "I. N. D. N. J. C." (*In Nomine Domini Nostri Jesu Christi*, "In the name of our Lord Jesus Christ")—the only time this formula appears in any of Bach's autographs (Fig. 4-1). Bach used it here to cover not only the first cantata but the entire annual cycle; in the second score of the series, that of cantata BWV 2 for June 18, he then reverted to "J. J." (Fig.4-2).

The prayer formula in the autograph score of BWV 20 is, to be sure, of a very private nature, but the overall musical design of the opening cantata movement clearly amounted to a stunning and highly meaningful public statement. Bach decided to start the new cycle with the momentous gesture of a French overture, an idiom borrowed from the Baroque opera tradition. He had employed this idea on a more modest scale ten years earlier in Weimar, for the cantata "Nun komm, der Heiden Heiland," BWV 61, composed to open the ecclesiastical year on the first Sunday in Advent, December 2, 1714. The first movement of BWV 20, with its tripartite form characteristic of a French overture, opens with pointed downbeats and energetic dotted rhythms (Fig. 4-1), then moves into a fast section of imitative polyphony, and finally returns in the concluding slow section to the initial dotted rhythms. The majestic and measured forward drive of the opening measures prepares for the introduction of the chorale tune and its first strophe, "O Ewigkeit, du Donnerwort" (O

FIGURE 4-1

"O Ewigkeit, du Donnerwort," BWV 20/1:
autograph composing score (1724), page 1.

FIGURE 4-2

"Ach Gott, vom Himmel sieh darein,"
BWV 2/1: autograph composing score (1724

eternity, you word of thunder), which is presented line by line in the soprano
part and in prolonged note values throughout all three sections.

The symbolic gesture of the opening overture is enhanced by further
musical imagery evident in the orchestral score, such as Bach's juxtaposition
of the two key words of the first chorale line, "Ewigkeit" and "Donnerwort."
Prolonged and slowly moving chords in the wind section (three oboes) depict
and symbolize the tranquil aura of everlasting eternity, whereas the harsh and
emphatic accents in the strings invoke the frightening sounds of thunderous
words. The rewriting of the vocal bass within the first chorale line provides
evidence for Bach's deliberate intent to associate the imagery of lightning and
thunder with the prominent rhythmic patterns in the strings (Fig. 4-3a: m. 5
in the top brace). The hymn's allusion to death and eternity corresponds to

FIGURE 4-3a&b

"O Ewigkeit, du Donnerwort," BWV 20/1: autograph composing score (1724), pages 2–3.

that Sunday's gospel lesson of Luke 16:19—the parable of the rich man and Lazarus, one facing death and hell and the other paradise. This sets the tone for the cantata as a whole, and by extension for the entire annual cycle, one created with the objective of delivering striking chorale-based musical sermons.

Opening movements

The carefully planned design of the first cantata of the cycle carried implications for the subsequent works, particularly regarding the construction of their opening movements and their distinctive profiles. The variable placement of the chorale melody within the four-part vocal score, a special feature of the initial four cantatas, allowed for a logical scheme that involved moving the tune as cantus firmus (c.f.) systematically through all four vocal registers:

"O Ewigkeit, du Donnerwort," BWV 20:	S̲ATB
	trpt (c.f.), 3 ob, str, bc
"Ach Gott, vom Himmel sieh darein," BWV 2:	SA̲TB
	4 tromb, 2 ob, str (colla parte), bc
"Christ unser Herr zum Jordan kam," BWV 7:	SAT̲B
	solo vn, 2 ob d'amore, str, bc
"Ach Herr, mich armen Sünder," BWV 135:	SATB̲
	tromb (c.f.), 2 ob, str, bc

At the same time, the variously applied contrapuntal techniques were amalgamated with different stylistic models and orchestral scorings. The open dissimilarity of the first two cantatas, BWV 20 and 2, is particularly notable, as their scores immediately reveal (see Figs. 4-1 and 4-2). These starkly contrasting passages exhibit the wide range of possibilities at the composer's disposal. The prevailing "white notation" of BWV 2 indicates that the piece is set in the manner of sixteenth-century vocal polyphony, which makes little use of blackheaded note values smaller than half notes. In effect it represents a four-part chorale motet with basso continuo on a medieval tune in the Phrygian church mode, with the plain cantus firmus placed in the alto voice. The orchestral instruments are not independent, as they are in BWV 20 and the subsequent cantatas, but instead are set *colla parte*—that is, they double the vocal lines. In addition, four sackbuts (Renaissance trombones) lend to the overall sound a decidedly retrospective character.

The first movement of BWV 7, the third cantata, combines the idea of an instrumental concerto, featuring a solo violin with orchestral accompaniment, with that of a free polyphonic chorale elaboration, in which the melody is placed in the tenor voice. For the periodic vocal entries, the orchestral score is reduced to a transparent texture in piano dynamic, with the solo violin swirling around the chorale tune in the tenor voice. Finally, BWV 135 offers an opening movement in ternary meter and places the chorale melody in the bass voice. The latter decision directly influences the scoring of the entire orchestral setting, with the regular continuo bass replaced by a "bassetto" (high bass) part for viola. The bassetto repeatedly quotes the first line of the chorale tune, and supports a configuration of chorale-based motifs in diminished note values. This unusual orchestral score effectively delays and then accentuates the actual entry of the choir bass, which, along with the full continuo complement, carries the chorale tune.

After the chorale melodies in the four opening cantatas of the cycle have traveled through the four voices from the soprano down to the bass, it seems nearly inevitable that for the fifth cantata, BWV 10, Bach would seek a new solution, which involved placing the tune not in a single voice but rather in two different registers.

"Meine Seel erhebt den Herren," BWV 10:   S̲A̲TB

trpt (c.f.), 2 ob, str, bc

The first verse of the liturgical Magnificat melody in the ninth psalm tone is presented by the soprano, and the second verse by the alto, both parts reinforced by a trumpet. Such exceptional dual staging of the chorale melody does not recur elsewhere. In fact, beginning with BWV 93, the sixth work of the cycle, it becomes more or less standard for the soprano to carry the chorale tune in the opening chorus, though the practice frequently varies between presentation in augmented and regular note values. Only two other opening movements in the cycle have the tune in a voice other than the soprano: BWV 96 (alto) and BWV 3 (bass).

The first movements of Bach's cantatas ordinarily define the character of the entire work to follow, and the openings of cantatas BWV 20, 2, 7, 135, and 10 collectively outline a vision for the annual project and its overall scope. Taken together, they herald a broad variety of chorale treatments employing highly diverse polyphonic techniques, stylistic traits, and vocal-orchestral scorings. From the composer's original planning perspective as it emerged in the spring and early summer of 1724, the first five cantatas would naturally have represented only a declaration of intent (meant principally for himself, of course), an establishment of the general frame for the annual cycle. Even though Bach may well have sketched out in advance certain governing ideas for the project as a whole, he would hardly have preplanned all the details of an anticipated opus of several dozen multi-movement pieces.

Bach escaped the danger of repeating the structural designs of opening choruses (and for that matter, of all other movement types), primarily by choosing a different chorale tune for each cantata. Hence, each movement is defined first and foremost by the constantly changing formal and musical qualities and characteristics of each individual melody. This makes even the two motet-like choruses of "Aus tiefer Not schrei ich zu dir" BWV 38 and "Christum wir sollen loben schon" BWV 121, which closely follow the retrospective model (*stile antico*) of BWV 2, appear quite different on account of their common modality, Dorian and Phrygian, respectively[11] (on Bach's treatment of modes, see also page 178). The same is true of the various concerto-style settings resembling BWV 7, such as BWV 96 (solo transverse flute), BWV 177 (solo violin), BWV 1 (two solo violins), and BWV 124 (solo oboe d'amore)—not to mention the works for the high feasts with larger orchestra and a full brass complement of three trumpets or two horns, like BWV 130, 41, and 129. Additional means of variety are introduced via Bach's ever-resourceful and imaginative treatment of his instrumental ensemble. The works in the long cycle feature a colorful and constantly changing orchestra with a broad range of instruments, particularly within the various categories of winds: trumpet, *tromba da tirarsi* (slide trumpet), horn, cornetto, trombone, recorder, *flauto piccolo* (piccolo recorder), flute, oboe, oboe d'amore, oboe da caccia, and bassoon. Even the regular strings are several times supplemented by a piccolo violin (BWV 96, 140) and a violoncello piccolo (BWV 41, 115, and 180).

Structural diversity is created by compositional means. Bach varies considerably his handling of the four-part vocal setting within each cantata score, through the use of different kinds of homophonic and imitative-polyphonic textures. The treatments of the chorale melodies include straightforward, rhythmically augmented, or slightly embellished presentations of the predominant tune-carrying voice (most often the soprano). The opening movement of BWV 78 differs from all others in its construction in the form of a chaconne: in this case, a set of variations based on a chromatically descending melodic pattern of four measures, occurring mostly in the basso continuo but here and there in the upper vocal and instrumental parts as well. The slow dance character of the chaconne, the triple meter of the minor-mode tune, and the *lamento* ground (the chromatically descending six-note pattern), along with the many chromatic inflections in the accompanying contrapuntal voices, unite in a movement of particularly deep-felt expression, one that dramatically and forcefully represents the chorale strophe's reference to the "bitter death" of Jesus.

The penultimate work of the cycle, the cantata "Herr Jesu Christ, wahr' Mensch und Gott" (BWV 127), represents another special case. It was performed on February 11, 1725, the last Sunday preceding the quiet, music-free Lenten period.[12] Its first movement features the chorale melody of the same name, but adds to it the tune of "Christe, du Lamm Gottes," the German Agnus Dei—not sung but played by violins and recorders. Moreover, the first line of a third tune, "Herzlich tut mich verlangen" (the same melody as Paul

Gerhardt's classic Passion hymn "O Haupt voll Blut und Wunden"), resounds prominently and repeatedly in the basso continuo, emphatically articulated in the manner of a sigh motif, the musico-rhetorical figure of *suspiratio*. This unusual combination of a sung principal melody and two complementary chorale tunes in the instrumental texture reflects the composer's determination to enhance the movement's emotional weight, and also to provide a theologically meaningful preview of the forthcoming liturgical period commemorating the suffering and death of Christ. On that February Sunday, however, only Bach himself knew that several weeks later, on Good Friday (March 30, 1725), the projected performance of the *St. John Passion* in its second version (BWV 245.2) would end with a new finale movement, an extended chorale elaboration of the traditional Agnus Dei hymn "Christe, du Lamm Gottes." In a remarkable example of deliberate cyclical planning, the first movement of the Estomihi cantata and the last movement of the Passion aligned, if only in the composer's mind, as a musical bridge across the seven-week Passiontide.

Arias, recitatives, and final chorales

Arias

For the most part, the aria types that occur in the chorale cantata cycle of 1724/25 are fundamentally no different from those that appear throughout Bach's Leipzig cantatas. More often than not the melodic profiles of the instrumental aria introductions and interludes (ritornellos), as well as the shapes of the vocal solo parts, are largely independent from the principal chorale tune of the cantata. As in most cantatas, the musical makeup of the 1724/25 arias is usually derived from the text, whether defined by a distinctive opening line, suggestive individual words, or the general scope of the poem. There are, however, quite a few instances where the tune of the chorale cantata is woven in by various means, from subtle allusion to outright quotation.

The most distinctive chorale arias, which as compositional types have their origins in the cantata cycle of 1724/25, are the ones that present the principal tune in its entirety and in plain fashion as the focal point, very much as Bach had done previously in organ chorales. Hence it is no surprise that some twenty years later, Bach transcribed a few of the chorale arias for organ. These transcriptions, which became known as the Schübler Chorales, BWV 645–650, were published around 1746 (Chapter 7, page 259). The first two of the arias that were later thus transcribed were from early in the cycle, one directly following the other in July 1724: BWV 10/5, a duet for alto and tenor with instrumental cantus firmus for two oboes or trumpet and basso continuo (= BWV 648), and BWV 93/3, a duet for soprano and alto with instrumental cantus firmus for violins and violas in unison, and continuo (= BWV 647). Two more such chorale arias from later supplementary cantatas were also transcribed: BWV 137/2 for vocal cantus firmus (soprano), solo violin, and continuo (= BWV 650), and BWV 140/4 for vocal cantus firmus (tenor), violins and violas in unison, and continuo (= BWV 645). Curiously, BWV 6 for Easter Monday 1725, coming close to the end of the chorale cantata series, contains a chorale aria (movement 3) of exactly the same model, for vocal cantus firmus (soprano), solo violoncello piccolo, and continuo (= BWV 649; see concluding section below). This in turn suggests the possibility that the only "Schübler" Chorale for which there exists no model, "Wo soll ich fliehen hin" (BWV 646), may have its origin in the draft score of a lost chorale aria, if not the lost score of an entire chorale cantata. It cannot be an accident that similar chorale arias that fit the organ chorale type are found in the chorale cantata movements BWV 178/4, BWV 113/2, and BWV 92/4.

More common within the cycle are arias of the modified da capo or ritornello type, in which thematic or other motivic materials echo recognizable elements from the chorale tune in the vocal or instrumental parts. Partial quotations from chorale melodies also appear in some arias, and there are solo movements where the text and melodic portions of internal strophes of the chorale are combined with free poetry and aria structures. These are in many ways the most original movements, created by Bach as always with the conscious goal of enhancing and interpreting the text. A representative example is the aria BWV 101/4, "Warum willst du so zornig sein," for bass accompanied by three oboes and continuo. The aria text begins with the opening line of strophe 4 from Martin Moller's hymn (1584), which is followed by five lines of free madrigalian poetry:

A	**Warum willst du so zornig sein?**	**Why do you wish to be so angry?**
	Es schlagen deines Eifers Flammen	The flames of your vengeance
	Schon über unserm Haupt zusammen.	Strike down already upon our heads.
B	Ach stelle doch die Strafen ein	Oh, put punishment aside
	Und trag aus väterlicher Huld	And with fatherly indulgence
	Mit unserm schwachen Fleisch Geduld!	Harbor mercy for our weak flesh!

The music of the A section alternates between two musical ideas: a fast and aggressively animated ritornello for two oboes, taille, and continuo that offers a vivid musical depiction of rage and the imagery of flames of vengeance (*vivace, forte*), and a pacifying bass voice, twice pleadingly expressing the question of the initial chorale line "Why do you wish . . . ?" (*andante, piano*), all in an abruptly slower tempo with subdued instrumental accompaniment. The vocal and instrumental roles are subsequently reversed in the slow B section (*andante* and *piano* throughout), in which the suddenly gentle sound of three oboes presents all six phrases of the chorale tune. The oboes now act as a harmonic accompaniment to the solo bass and offer wordless affirmation of God's mercy, which is explicitly enunciated by the bass voice.

This aria offers merely one illustration of the many and diverse ways in which Bach used the chorale texts and melodies to fulfill the function of the cantata as a musical sermon—and, from a musical design perspective, to link the outer frame of the work with the inner movements. The cantata "Nimm von uns Herr, du treuer Gott" (BWV 101) happens to be one of the most elaborate and artful examples from the entire cycle, and it can serve as a concrete illustration of the scheme outlined in Table 4-1, with the chorale tune employed in six out of seven movements:

(1) Figural chorale: Fugal elaboration of chorale tune in the vocal score, with intermittent citations of the tune in the orchestra.
(2) Aria: No references to the chorale tune.
(3) Chorale–Recitative: In the soprano solo, embellished line-by-line citation of the chorale tune, alternating with recitative sections in free declamatory prosody.
(4) Aria: In the first part, solo bass cites interpolated first line of the chorale twice; in the second half, woodwind setting of the complete chorale tune (see discussion above).
(5) Chorale–Recitative: In the tenor solo, line-by-line citation of the chorale tune, alternating with recitative sections in strict time and prosody.
(6) Aria (duet): The six lines of the chorale tune penetrate all solo parts: both the soprano-alto duet and the flute–oboe da caccia duet.
(7) Chorale: Four-part chorale harmonization

A special phenomenon within the 1724/25 cycle is the unique clustering of arias with solo parts for transverse flute during the Trinity season. This instrument happens to be completely absent from the woodwind category in Bach's Leipzig church music throughout 1723 and the early months of 1724, whereas recorders and various types of oboes are consistently present. The sudden, prominent, and frequent occurrences of solo arias with transverse flute from mid-July through late November therefore come as a surprise. No fewer than thirteen cantatas (BWV 107, 94, 101, 113, 78, 99, 8, 130, 114, 96, 180, 115, and 26; see Table 4-3) feature flute parts of considerable technical and musical demands, implying perhaps that the composer wrote them for an accomplished player previously not available to him, possibly a musician on a temporary visit. The situation suggests that the composer was quick to take advantage of special opportunities when they arose. Another part for solo flute appeared three months later in BWV 125, and from then on the transverse flute gradually became an integral part of Bach's orchestra—as it seems he could regularly count on able players. Nevertheless, the sudden flowering of flute solos from 1724 remains exceptional in every respect. It certainly had an important impact on Bach's later employment of the instrument, and made him more intimately familiar with the idiomatic treatment of the flute as well as its coloristic and expressive possibilities—notably in delicate duo combinations with oboe d'amore (BWV 9, 99, and 125), oboe da caccia (BWV 101), or violoncello piccolo (BWV 115).

Recitatives

Free declamatory recitative style does not naturally lend itself to the integration of evenly measured chorale melodies and segments thereof. At the same time, Bach's adventurous experimentation with his chorale cantata concept inspired him to break with conventions and enter uncharted territory. Inserting individual chorale lines and longer tune segments, or making melodic allusions to them in measured time—a requirement for the proper declamation of cantus firmi or portions thereof—are the most frequent ways by which Bach has the voice or instruments quote from chorales within recitatives. However, already in the second cantata of the annual series, in the secco recitative BWV 2/2, he involves the continuo accompaniment as well, accentuating the two chorale quotations (mm. 1–2 and 6–8) by introducing a canon between the tenor voice and its accompanying continuo, and by further enhancing the passages by adagio declamation.

A more complex application can be found in the recitative BWV 178/5, which combines solo recitative with a complete chorale strophe in a four-part setting. In order to make this merger work, Bach settled on a strict rhythm (*a tempo giusto*) for the entire movement. It is metrically and harmonically defined by a short repetitive motif consisting of an ascending triad, suggesting the open jaw to which the first chorale line refers: "Auf sperren sie den Rachen weit . . ." (They stretch their jaws wide open):

EXAMPLE 4-1

BWV 178/5: musical imagery of a lion's stretching jaws.

The movement unfolds in an unusual format of alternating texts and vocal styles:

> four-part chorale, line 1
> free recitative (bass)
> chorale, lines 2–3
> free recitative (tenor)
> chorale, line 4
> free recitative (alto)
> chorale, lines 5–6
> free recitative (bass)
> chorale line 7

In cases where the chorale tune is integrated in its entirety, the recitative can be performed only in strict time, or *a tempo*, as Bach specifically indicates in BWV 5/4, "Mein treuer Heiland tröstet mich" (My loving savior comforts me). Here the principal melody of the cantata is carried from the beginning to the end of the movement by the first oboe, which offers an ardent wordless commentary on the alto recitative. At the same time, the recitative invokes the text of chorale strophe 5, which refers to consolation and redemption. BWV 38/4, "Ach! daß mein Glaube noch so schwach" (Alas! that my faith is yet so weak), represents a similar case of a complete strophe firmly embedded in a recitative. Yet what makes this example extraordinary and unparalleled is that Bach dares to place the entire ancient tune of "Aus tiefer Not" with its AAB form in the continuo part: A (mm. 1–5) transposed A-Phrygian; AB (mm. 5–16) transposed D-Phrygian. The chorale thus provides the harmonic bass

FIGURE 4-4

"Aus tiefer Not schrei ich zu dir," BWV 38/4: original continuo part,
copy J. A. Kuhnau (1724).

for the setting (Fig. 4-4). The composer's strategy is amply clear, since the
chorale strophe implied here complements the words of the recitative that
speak of placing trust in God's worthy word ("sein wertes Wort").

Final chorales

The formal concept of the chorale cantata, with its deliberate return at the
end to the unaltered text of the hymn's closing strophe, is in line with the prevailing general format of Bach's cantatas overall, in which a four-part chorale
setting represents the standard closure. The chorale cantatas thus provide little
flexibility for formal modifications of the final chorale, including the addition
of obbligato instruments, a practice that can frequently be found outside the
chorale cantata cycle. Ritornello-like instrumental inserts between the chorale lines, as in BWV 107/7, or instrumental extensions of chorale lines, as in
BWV 130/6, are therefore not unusual. However, at the end of the cantata
"Jesu nun sei gepreiset" (BWV 41, for New Year's Day), Bach introduced the
idea of instrumental cross-referencing. In the chorale BWV 41/6, after every
line of the tune, he introduced a short interlude for the brass instruments
with a fanfare motif derived from the trumpet parts in the cantata's opening
movement. The idea was prompted by textual correspondences between the
first and last chorale strophes, and it creates a strong musical return. This sort
of symmetric reminiscence is a first in Bach's cantatas, but he came back to

the idea ten years later in part II of the *Christmas Oratorio* with literal motivic correspondences between the opening sinfonia and the concluding chorale.

The presentation of the plain chorale as a conclusion in effect inverts a customary dynamic. In instrumental variation sets such as chorale partitas for organ, the plain setting is stated at the outset, followed by the elaborations. The chorale cantatas in effect do the opposite. The result is exceptionally powerful and striking: after the various wanderings of the earlier movements, the conclusion affords a highly vivid, resonant, and radiant presentation of the elemental aspects of both chorale melody and text—an affirmation of the fact that, in the Lutheran realm, the hymnal was second only to the Bible itself as a symbol of religious authority.

In this chorale cantata cycle, Bach made use of a large number of sixteenth-century tunes, almost all of them in the old church modes (Table 4-4: section 1). These choices in turn influenced his harmonic experiments, including the use of plagal cadences (subdominant chords resolving directly to the tonic) and modal tonalities. Thus the composer's distinctive and highly inventive applications of chord progressions emerge as a major feature of these pieces. For example, "Aus tiefer Not schrei ich zu dir" (BWV 38) concludes with a chorale strophe audaciously beginning on a dissonant chord (third inversion of the dominant seventh chord), fitting well within the overall context of unconventional harmonization:

EXAMPLE 4-2

BWV 38, final chorale: emphatic dissonance at opening of plain harmonization.

Yet Bach did not come up with such an idea merely for variety's sake. As ever, he wished for the harmony to serve the text of the opening line, "Ob bei uns ist der Sünden viel," which translates, "Although the sins among us are many"—hence the "offensive" chord.

Bach treats the very few contemporaneous chorale melodies included in the cycle (Table 4-4) in a notably different way: "Straf mich nicht" (1694 Dresden hymnal, used in "Mache dich, mein Geist, bereit," BWV 115/1 and 6); "Liebster Immanuel, Herzog der Frommen" (1698 Darmstadt hymnal, in

BWV 123/1 and 6); "Liebster Gott, wenn werd ich sterben" (Daniel Vetter, 1713, in BWV 8/1 and 6); and "Ich freue mich in dir" (Balthasar König, c. 1714; in BWV 133/1 and 6). Their treatments in the respective cantatas illustrate the composer's clear intention to match their more fashionable melodic styles. In all instances he applied particularly subtle wind scorings, for example the rare combination of transverse flutes and oboi d'amore in BWV 8, BWV 115, and BWV 123. Moreover, the translucent polyphonic textures of the opening choruses inform the treatment of the final chorales as well, as is particularly noticeable in the texturally transparent and rhythmically vibrant setting of BWV 8/6:

EXAMPLE 4-3

BWV 8, final chorale: polyphonically loosened harmonization.

Even with certain older melodies, Bach did not shy away from such unambiguously modern handling of four-part chorales, as one of the supplementary chorale cantatas demonstrates. In the cantata "Ich ruf zu dir, Herr Jesu Christ" of 1732 (BWV 177) he ingeniously converted the venerable Dorian-mode tune into an elegantly embellished aria-like melody, the rhythmic-melodic contours of which resemble closely the sacred songs BWV 511–514 he composed at around the same time for his wife Anna Magdalena, which are included in her second *Clavier-Büchlein*:

EXAMPLE 4-4

BWV 177, final chorale: embellished melody and more intricate setting.

The latest among the supplements to the 1724/25 cycle, the cantata "Wär Gott nicht mit uns diese Zeit" of 1735 (BWV 14), on a tune from 1524, also demonstrates a comparable aria-style approach, not so much in its concluding chorale as in the shaping of the melodic profile of the chorale within the polyphonic texture of the opening movement.

INCOMPLETE AND YET MONUMENTAL

In the 1724/25 chorale cantata opus as a whole, Bach most definitely fulfilled and even surpassed the initial promise implied by the first five cantatas: he sustained over a long span of time a systematic and exhaustive exploration of the Lutheran chorale repertory for the purposes of cantata composition. The suggestive and program-like design of the opening cantata sequence BWV 20, 2, 7, 135, and 10 exemplifies the degree of planning and deliberation that Bach invested in the entire project from its very beginning, a level of focus that he maintained for more than forty weeks without interruption. The tangible results were dozens of superlative musical scores, which speak most eloquently for themselves. Never again would Bach place himself in such a stressful and demanding situation of composing such an extensive series of new works over such a lengthy period. Yet the self-inflicted stress can hardly be seen as responsible for the resulting serial opus and its exceptional overall quality, which would never have materialized had the project not been driven first and foremost by decidedly positive factors, including Bach's continuing fascination with making familiar chorale tunes sound entirely new, as well as his experience of sharing with singers, players, and a large audience his innermost feelings about what these hymns mean to him. Above all, the project afforded him an opportunity for achieving joy—and serving the Lord—through the act of conceiving and writing such a singularly expressive and evocative body of music.

As to the incomplete state of the cantata cycle, there may well have been specific obstacles that forced Bach to depart from the original plan that he had so painstakingly pursued with, one assumes, the original goal of finishing an entire annual cycle. The change of plans was most likely related to an unexpected problem in the delivery of commissioned cantata texts. Yet the music-free seven-week Lenten period left Bach with sufficient time to achieve an uninterrupted production of new cantatas up to the end of the school year, from the Easter holidays through Trinity Sunday. After the performance of BWV 1 on March 25, the chorale cantata project began to taper off, though elegantly. This process began on Good Friday (March 30) with the second version of the *St. John Passion*, which opens and concludes with two prominent chorale movements. Genuine change began on Easter Sunday, when two cantatas were performed, one before and one after the sermon. The first cantata embodied a sacred parody of the secular birthday serenade, BWV 249.1, composed for Duke Christian of Saxe-Weißenfels and performed in Weißenfels less than six weeks earlier, on February 23, 1725; this Easter cantata, "Kommt, fliehet und eilet," BWV 249.2, was later reworked into the *Easter Oratorio* (Chapter 6, page 242). The second cantata for that same day happened to be the only extant pre-Leipzig chorale cantata, namely BWV 4 from 1707—a work of the traditional chorale-text-only variety and a piece that had already been performed on the same Sunday in 1724. Thus Bach ended the cycle of chorale cantatas on Easter, though only in a technical sense and not with a newly created work.

Further echoes of the discontinued cycle persisted over the following weeks. On Easter Monday and the two subsequent Sundays, Quasimodogeniti and Misericordias Domini (April 8 and 15, 1725), Bach performed the madrigalian cantatas BWV 6, BWV 42, and BWV 85. All three of these are based on a six-number libretto form, typically beginning with a biblical verse and ending with a hymn strophe, and include among the middle movements a strophe from a hymn different from the concluding chorale. But instead of setting these strophes as simple four-part chorales, as he frequently did in the first Leipzig cycle, he (apparently still in chorale cantata mode) opted for typical chorale arias: BWV 6/3, for soprano, violoncello piccolo, and continuo, with text and melody of "Ach bleib bei uns, Herr Jesu Christ" (later transcribed as one of the "Schübler" Chorales for organ, BWV 649, see page 259); BWV 42/4, a chorale duet for soprano, tenor, bassoon and cello, and continuo, with text and melody of "Verzage nicht, du Häuflein klein"; and BWV 85/3, for soprano, two oboes, and continuo, with the melody of "Allein Gott in der Höh sei Ehr." Neither of the latter two tunes had been set within the chorale cantata cycle.

On Jubilate Sunday, April 22 of 1725, and through Trinity Sunday, Bach turned to a short subseries of nine cantatas in order to conclude the running cycle. He had commissioned the madrigalian librettos from the Leipzig poetess Christiane Mariane von Ziegler, who at the time was commencing a notable career under the encouragement of Johann Christoph Gottsched, whose literary circle she had joined.[13] It may not be a coincidence that two

of the Ziegler cantatas feature rather elaborate figural chorales as first movements. The Ascension Day cantata "Auf Christi Himmelfahrt allein" (BWV
128) opens with a festive concertante setting of the eponymous hymn to the
tune of "Allein Gott in der Höh sei Ehr," used a few weeks earlier for BWV
85/3. The other cantata, "Also hat Gott die Welt geliebt" (BWV 68), for the
less significant holiday of Whitmonday, presents a buoyant chorale elaboration in siciliano manner on the identically named tune, again a melody
not used in the chorale cantata cycle.[14] Ziegler deviated radically from the
libretto format of the chorale cantatas, but it seems possible that Bach (when
commissioning the texts) initially expressed a preference for chorale-based
librettos without insisting that it be observed. It is possible also that Ziegler
herself—an amateur musician, regular church attendant, and hearer of the
chorale cantatas—simply liked at least the idea of this sort of opening and
applied it to two of her texts.

It hardly comes as a surprise that following the academic year 1724/25,
by far the busiest and most productive twelve months in his life to that point,
Bach began to slow the pace of newly composed cantatas. After Trinity Sunday
(May 27, 1725), he gave himself a break of nine weeks by returning to older
works and scheduling pieces by other composers. He did not perform a new
cantata until "Tue Rechnung! Donnerwort" (BWV 168), for the ninth Sunday after Trinity, on a text by his former Weimar librettist Salomon Franck.
However, on the twelfth Sunday after Trinity, he filled a gap for a Sunday
he had skipped the previous year and composed the chorale cantata "Lobe
den Herren" (BWV 137), a chorale-text-only work that needed no librettist.
Following this, it would be almost two years until he filled another gap in the
earlier cycle with "Gelobet sei der Herr" (BWV 129), for Trinity Sunday. He
apparently decided to extend his third annual cantata cycle over more than a
single year (it eventually stretched across three years, 1725–27), and he elected
not to give it a unifying theme. Nevertheless, even within the generously paced
plan for the third cycle, the composer gravitated toward special musical ideas
in a serial manner, though without realizing them in the form of *Jahrgang*
themes. These tendencies led to cantata types that Bach had not explored in
the two previous cycles, including works with extended instrumental sinfonias
(notably some with obbligato organ) as well as solo and dialogue cantatas.

When Bach eventually returned to chorale cantatas in order to fill gaps in
the 1724/25 cycle, he managed to complete the extended pre-Easter section by
adding BWV 177, BWV 9, BWV 80, BWV 140, and BWV 14, all for the Trinity

and Epiphany seasons. With BWV 112 and BWV 129 he even ventured into the post-Easter season. Yet he never made the cycle whole, though only eight additional cantatas would have been needed to accomplish that. In general, it remains difficult to understand why Bach reduced cantata composition so noticeably between 1725 and 1729, only rather sporadically turned out new works thereafter, and lacked any impetus to write additional cantatas after 1735. However, the obvious finality in the incomplete state of the chorale cantata cycle recalls the hundred-plus projected yet unwritten chorales of the *Orgel-Büchlein* (see Chapter 2, page 44). Either case represents an unfinished opus. Both were private projects, unannounced to the public, and at the time only the composer himself was aware of the voids—and was presumably able to live with them. This same situation pertains to other instances in which a major project was left unfinished, the most prominent example being the revision of the *St. John Passion* from the late 1730s (see Chapter 6, page 210). While Bach no doubt had many external or technical reasons for temporary interruptions, he could certainly have overcome them had he wished to do so. It is therefore plausible to assume that changes in his own priorities are the explanation for his departure from a previously significant but no longer imperative goal.

On the other hand, the concept of the chorale cantata quite obviously remained an attractive idea, and one that Bach kept alive long after 1725, primarily owing to the multifarious and highly suggestive qualities of the chorale tunes themselves. In his later supplements (see Table 4-3, sections 2 and 3), Bach focused more frequently on chorale-text-only works, since they mandated particular emphasis on the Lutheran melodies and texts. He surely also realized that the classic hymns possessed notable aesthetic value, and that they appealed greatly to his audiences—who knew them intimately and were thus in a position to appreciate even his most musically sophisticated realizations. Traces of use in the original performing materials of the chorale cantatas document more frequent repeat performances of these works in the 1730s and 1740s than for any other body of cantatas. Moreover, their extant sources demonstrate that the perfectionist composer never stopped investing in this outsize and treasured opus—for Bach in fact reviewed and amended the performing parts for each later performance.

Whatever he later entered in the manuscripts rarely touched on the compositional substance—although it occasionally did, as in the painstaking revisions of movements 5 and 6 of BWV 91, or in the scoring adjustment, transposition,

FIGURE 4-5

"Nimm von uns Herr, du treuer Gott," BWV 101/1: original alto part,
copy J. A. Kuhnau (1724), with late additions by Bach.

and detailed reworkings in BWV 8, both around 1746/47.[15] The composer
often aimed at audible improvements by adding or replacing instruments, or
by altering the text underlay to arrive at better and more natural declamation
in the vocal parts. While additional performing instructions mostly pertain
to enhanced text declamation (Fig. 4-5), as well as more refined articulation
and dynamics, they also include some essential modifications to the quality
and character of the sound. Such instances demonstrate that Bach aimed at
adjusting his works in response to contemporary developments in performance
practice, which various protagonists described in terms of "a most accurate and
refined execution" and hailed as initiating "a new period" in the art of music.[16]
One relevant example, again from Bach's final years, is the more differentiated
bass line prescribed by the "divisi" instruction for the violoncello and violone
parts in the duet "Wir eilen mit schwachen, doch eifrigen Schritten" (We
hasten with weak, yet eager steps), BWV 78/3—a nuanced refinement that
underscores the imagery of "weak, yet eager steps." A related example occurs
in the aria "Wie furchtsam wanken meine Schritte" (How fearfully my steps
wavered), BWV 33/3, for alto, strings, and continuo. There the composer, in
the thick pen strokes of his late hand, added specific directions to the parts,
asking the first violins to play "col s[o]urdino" (muted; Fig. 4-6a), the second
violins, violas, and cellos "pizzicato" (plucked; Fig. 4-6b), and the continuo
organ "staccato" (detached; Fig. 4-6c). By cleverly manipulating the instru-

FIGURES 4-6a–c

"Allein zu dir, Herr Jesu Christ," BWV 33/3, original performing parts: (a) violin I,
copy J. A. Kuhnau (1724); (b) violin II, copy J. A. Kuhnau (1724); (c) organ,
copy C. G. Meißner (1724); all with late additions by Bach.

mental interplay in this aria, the performer-composer thereby created a more colorful yet at the same time softer and more focused sound, one that would eloquently highlight the poetic image of fearfully wavering steps.

There is no question that Bach rated his chorale cantatas most highly. He performed them more frequently than any other cantatas, and continued to review them to the end of his life, with particular editorial care and in a consistent quest for perfection. After his death in 1750, the physical entity of the chorale cantata cycle—perhaps considered the most valuable single portion of the estate—was divided between the widow and the eldest and most favored son, likely according to specific instructions left by the composer himself: Anna Magdalena received the performing parts and Wilhelm Friedemann inherited the scores. The majority of the scores, like much else from Friedemann's inheritance, were most unfortunately lost, while the parts were saved and survived. Only a few weeks after the composer's death, in August 1750, Anna Magdalena contacted the city council "wegen derer Kirchen-Lieder" (concerning those church songs),[17] and made financial arrangements for the permanent transfer of the performing parts to the St. Thomas School.[18] She may have hoped, if not assumed, that they would not be forgotten there. Yet she surely could not have anticipated that Bach's successors at the school, without exception and well into the nineteenth century, would continue to perform selected cantatas from Bach's most ambitious of all cyclical projects. They thereby established these works, along with the motets, as a living memorial to the composer.

CHAPTER 5

Proclaiming the State of the Art in Keyboard Music

The Clavier-Übung *Series*

T he title that Bach chose for his multivolume keyboard music series could hardly have been plainer, duller, or more innocuous. Yet behind the bland heading *Clavier-Übung* (Keyboard Practice, or Keyboard Exercise) is conceptually the most innovative, stylistically the most varied, technically the most advanced, and in sum the most ambitious and demanding published collection of keyboard music from the first half of the eighteenth century. It stands as a superlative achievement in harpsichord and organ art, offering as it does a balanced cross-section of keyboard repertory quite representative of its period, compositions that exhibit the very highest level of mastery and originality within each of the genres included. Bach would have been well aware that the music market knew of no equivalent to his projected *Clavier-Übung* series. Beyond that, he could hardly have anticipated that his all-encompassing keyboard project would in fact remain without a real successor, for beginning in the second half of the eighteenth century, collections uniting clavier and organ music became increasingly uncommon, with instrument-specific compilations becoming the norm.

Bach published his four-part series within a span of about fifteen years, a time frame that coincides with the genesis of the works themselves; no preexisting compositions were included. Taken together, the four volumes reveal themselves as a logical sequence that explores the most important genres and styles of keyboard music for various types of instruments:

Part I (1726–30, single issues; 1731, complete edition): Six partitas for single-manual harpsichord

Part II (1735): French- and Italian-style works for double-manual harpsichord

Part III (1739): Chorale preludes and other pieces for organ (large organ with pedals and smaller instruments without)

Part IV (1741): *Aria with 30 Variations* (*Goldberg Variations*) for double-manual harpsichord

Each volume by itself represents a coherent and discrete unit, while the parts taken together form a decidedly impressive larger whole, one that offers up a series of exemplary state-of-the-art works in various genres. From the time of their appearance, these four collections served and encouraged the general advancement of keyboard music, establishing new and formidable standards for playing technique and compositional sophistication. They presented a melding of qualities that insured a popularity that has extended to the present day, in that they combined highly attractive musical aspects and profound intellectual content.

Considering Bach's multitude of activities during the later 1720s and throughout the 1730s, it might seem surprising that he could and would undertake such a large-scale instrumental project in addition to his rigorous schedule of ongoing musical endeavors. During the same period, he completed numerous major compositions, including the *St. Matthew* and *St. Mark Passions*, the five Kyrie-Gloria Masses (including one that would become the *B-minor Mass*), and the *Christmas*, *Easter*, and *Ascension Oratorios*. He also composed an abundance of large-scale secular congratulatory works for the Dresden court and other patrons, as well as chamber works, concertos, and orchestral suites for his Collegium Musicum concerts. Yet even in light of all these undertakings, it must be remembered that throughout his life Bach remained first and foremost a proud keyboard virtuoso, one who continually performed in private and public venues and composed far more music for the keyboard than can ever be accounted for. Even though he had not held an organist post since 1717, the improvising, composing, and playing of music for organ, harpsichord, and clavichord was second nature to him, and very likely a near-daily activity. Thus his writing for keyboard did not represent an extra burden or additional workload, but instead took its place as an enduring priority, an utterly essential aspect of his life as a musician. Bach was always driven by an interest in maintaining and promoting his reputation as an incomparable keyboard composer and soloist—one whose public appearances, whenever reported, inspired consistent admiration for his remarkable artistry. As one more element in Bach's proud and lifelong self-promotion among the wider public of keyboard amateurs and professionals, the *Clavier-Übung* series was surely intended to enhance and further elevate the composer's already lofty status.

Virtually all of Bach's earlier keyboard collections are organized according to explicit cyclical plans, and they thereby form a part of the conceptual pre-history of the *Clavier-Übung*. The six toccatas, *Orgel-Büchlein, Well-Tempered Clavier, Faithful Guide,* and in particular the sets of *English* and *French Suites* all played a role in the genesis and development of the *Clavier-Übung*, though none of them in the sense of a specific model. On the contrary, Bach clearly wished to open new pathways, meaning that he did not choose to reapply certain organizational principles like key order (as in the *Well-Tempered Clavier* and the *Faithful Guide*) or fixed dance sequences (as in the *English* and *French Suites*). Furthermore, since the *Clavier-Übung* series was a publishing project, entirely novel considerations—including financing, engraving and printing, marketing, and distribution—entered the picture as well.

There is no evidence that Bach had specific plans early on for the eventual extent, serial organization, or overall content of his keyboard publishing initiative. In other words, at the commencement of part I he did not anticipate when and how the series would continue, let alone end. It was most likely this uncertainty, and also the possibility of keeping his options open, that inspired him to choose the neutral and flexible title *Clavier-Übung*. At the same time, the title happened to be a meaningful remembrance of—if not an outright homage to—his Leipzig predecessor Johann Kuhnau, whom Bach had come to know during a 1716 joint organ examination in Erfurt and whose keyboard works he had encountered in his youth. Kuhnau, prior to his appointment as Thomascantor in 1703, he had been organist at St. Thomas's, and had published two volumes of keyboard suites: *Neuer Clavier-Übung Erster Theil* (Leipzig, 1689) and *Neuer Clavier-Übung Anderer Theil* (Leipzig, 1692). Kuhnau was the first to use the term "Clavier-Übung" in a keyboard publication, employing the German equivalent (*Übung*) to the Latin *exercitium*, the standard educational term for a lesson.[1] Given that the regular music lessons and rehearsals at the

St. Thomas School and other Latin schools were generally designated *Exercitium Musicum*, the term "Übung" had academic implications, which were entirely in line with Bach's intention to create works that would establish newly advanced artistic standards.

A further important factor influenced not merely Bach's choice of title, but in fact the entire notion of putting keyboard works into print, namely the faculty environment at the Schola Thomana. There Bach was surrounded by professorial colleagues who were quite active in scholarly and didactic publishing, especially the rector Johann Heinrich Ernesti. To demonstrate his own commitment to advanced musical instruction, Bach was able to present upon arrival in Leipzig his three existing manuscript teaching collections: the *Well-Tempered Clavier*, the *Faithful Guide*, and the *Orgel-Büchlein* (see Chapter 2). Yet unlike his predecessor Kuhnau, or his co-applicant Christoph Graupner—who had produced two smaller collections of keyboard suites for beginners, the *Partien auf das Clavier* (Frankfurt, 1718) and the *Monatliche Clavir Früchte* (Darmstadt, 1722)—Bach still had no publications to his credit.[2] With the examples of his peers well in mind, Bach was certainly under appreciable pressure to catch up in his own fashion.

CLAVIER-ÜBUNG, PART I: SIX PARTITAS

On November 1, 1726, the Leipzig newspaper issued the following announcement:

> As the Capellmeister of Anhalt-Cöthen and Director Chori Musici Lipsiensis, Herr Johann Sebastian Bach, intends to issue an opus of clavier suites, of which he has made the beginning with the first partita, and which he means to continue, step by step, until the opus is complete; such will be made known to amateurs of the clavier. This also serves as a message that the author of this work is himself the publisher.[3]

Without citing the actual title *Clavier-Übung*, this first reference to the projected opus of keyboard suites signaled the composer's plan to publish the work in installments. The reasons for this process were probably twofold: a step-by-step financial arrangement for the self-publisher would spread out the required capital investments, and the piecemeal issuing of single suites would allow him to test the market. The trial balloon launched in the fall of 1726 was apparently a success, for one year later, on September 19, 1727, the second and third installments were announced. At that point, additional information was presented regarding a clever distribution system, according to which the prints could be

> obtained not only from the author, but also from (1) Herr [Christian] Petzoldt, the Royal Polish and Electoral Saxon Chamber Organist in Dresden; (2) Herr [Johann Gotthilf] Ziegler, Music Director and Organist at St. Ulrich's in Halle; (3) Herr [Georg] Böhm, Organist at St. John's in Lüneburg; (4) Herr [Georg Heinrich Ludwig] Schwanenberger, Chamber Musician to the Prince of Brunswick in Wolfenbüttel; (5) Herr [Gabriel] Fischer, Town and Council Musician in Nuremberg; and (6) Herr [Johann Michael] Roth, Town and Council Musician in Augsburg.[4]

This promising scheme, which cast a net in all geographic directions, involved six close and well-connected colleagues in different strategic locations of northern, central, and southern Germany, who would all assist in promoting the publication. The results must have been satisfactory, because after the various installments had appeared in sequence, the collected edition was published in 1731 (Fig. 5-1).

FIGURE 5-1

Clavier-Übung, part I: title page (Leipzig, 1731).

Sales were sufficiently promising so that a certain quantity of the edition was taken on commission and distributed by the Leipzig publishing house Boëtius. Its proprietor, Rosine Dorothee Krügner (née Boëtius), was married to the owner of the engraving shop involved in producing the publication. The details of Bach's business arrangements with Krügner for the self-publishing project remain unknown. However, the first two single issues, Partitas 1 and 2, were engraved by Balthasar Schmid of Nuremberg, apparently a temporary contributor to the Krügner shop during his study period of 18 months at the University of Leipzig, beginning in March 1726; Partitas 3–6 were executed by other Krügner engravers.[5] In consideration of the fact that Schmid maintained lifelong connections with Bach, and also with his son Carl Philipp Emanuel and several Bach pupils, it seems plausible that Bach made a kind of special deal with the young Schmid, perhaps having him engrave the copperplates (probably purchased from Krügner) in exchange for music lessons. At any rate, Schmid returned to his home town in 1728 and opened his own publishing business there. He eventually returned to the *Clavier-Übung* project, producing parts III and IV, and was later involved with yet another publication venture.

Although Bach may well have been wishing for some time to publish a major keyboard work, the German market happened to be notoriously unfavorable for music publications. His friend Georg Philipp Telemann, who since 1715 had managed to get some chamber music into print, most likely supplied the model for self-publishing. Yet the figure who truly stoked Bach's ambition, triggering in due course the *Clavier-Übung* project, was likely none other than George Frideric Handel. Bach had long been curious about his same-aged compatriot, whom he had tried without success to meet in Handel's birthplace of Halle in 1719. In 1720, the London composer's first keyboard volume appeared in print: the *Suites de Pièces pour le Clavecin* (known as the *Eight Great Suites*, HWV 426–433). This publication must have suggested forcefully to Bach that he could no longer delay in offering his own contribution to the field. It is not known when Handel's suites reached Bach, but the collection soon became a best seller, and was reprinted in 1722. Unfortunately, no copies of Handel's keyboard output survive from Bach's music library, only copies of vocal works.[6] Yet there is no question that Bach was familiar with the major keyboard publications of his most renowned contemporary. A direct relationship between the *Eight Great Suites* and part I of the *Clavier-Übung* is in fact insinuated by a plausible case of borrowing from Handel's D-minor Allemande, HWV 428, in the C-minor Allemande, BWV 826.[7] A connection is even more strongly implied by the deliberate formal and musical contrasts that Bach chose to set forth in his debut published opus (Tables 5-1 and 5-2).

In the early decades of the eighteenth century, suites of dances were by far the dominant genre of keyboard music, sought out by both professional and amateur players and widely favored by the music-loving audience. Both composers accordingly aimed their collections of suites at essentially the same target group, whom the title page of the *Clavier-Übung* specifically addresses in its dedicatory phrase "denen Liebhabern zur Gemüths-Ergötzung" (for music lovers, to refresh their spirits). A comparison of the overall designs of each collection and the arrangement and content of their respective suites reveals significant differences. Both composers chose the type of suite with prelude, and included extended fugues and fugal sections in their preludes. Handel, however, departed freely from any standard movement order, while Bach, for his part, basically preserved the traditional German dance sequence of allemande–courante–sarabande–gigue (with insertions before the gigue) as a structural backbone, in nearly the same manner as he had in the *English* and *French Suites* (see Tables 3-2 and 3-3). Within the conventional dance types, Bach alternated between the Italian *corrente* and the French *courante*, while Handel kept the French variety, even adding a *passacaille*. Bach also, as indicated on his title page, included various *gallanterie* pieces with names like *capriccio*, *burlesca*, and *scherzo*—movement titles he had never used in suites before—thereby lending to his collection a trendier and more modish character.

TABLE 5-1. Handel, *Suites de Pièces pour le Clavecin*, vol. 1 (London, 1720)

Suite 1 in A HWV 426	Suite 2 in D HWV 427	Suite 3 in d HWV 428	Suite 4 in e HWV 429	Suite 5 in E HWV 430	Suite 6 in f♯ HWV 431	Suite 7 in G HWV 432	Suite 8 in f HWV 433
1. Prelude	1. Adagio	1. Prelude	1. Allegro*	1. Prelude	1. Prelude	1. Ouverture	1. Prelude
2. Allemande	2. Allegro	2. Allegro*	2. Allemande	2. Allemande	2. Largo	2. Andante	2. Allegro*
3. Courante	3. Adagio	3. Allemande	3. Courante	3. Courante	3. Allegro	3. Allegro	3. Allemande
4. Gigue	4. Allegro	4. Courante	4. Sarabande	4. Air**	4. Gigue	4. Sarabande	4. Courante
			5. Air**	5. Gigue		5. Gigue	5. Gigue
			6. Presto			6. Passacaille	

* Fugue.   ** With 5 Doubles.

TABLE 5-2. *Clavier-Übung* I (Leipzig, 1731)

Partita 1 in B♭ major BWV 825	Partita 2 in C minor BWV 826	Partita 3 in A minor* BWV 827	Partita 4 in D major BWV 828	Partita 5 in G major BWV 829	Partita 6 in E minor* BWV 830
. Praeludium	1. Sinfonia†	1. Fantasia	1. Ouverture†	1. Praeambulum	1. Toccata†
. Allemande	2. Allemande	2. Allemande	2. Allemande	2. Allemande	2. Allemande
. Corrente	3. Courante	3. Corrente	3. Courante	3. Corrente	3. Corrente
. Sarabande	4. Sarabande	4. Sarabande	4. Aria	4. Sarabande	4. Air
. Menuet I	5. Rondeaux	5. Burlesca	5. Sarabande	5. Tempo di Minuetta	5. Sarabande
. Menuet II	6. Capriccio	6. Scherzo	6. Menuet	6. Passepied	6. Tempo di Gavotta
. Giga		7. Gigue	7. Gigue	7. Gigue	7. Gigue

* Early versions in the *Clavier-Büchlein* for Anna Magdalena Bach of 1725:
  BWV 827 (in A minor): 1. Prelude–2. Allemande–3. Corrente–4. Sarabande–5. Menuet [= Burlesca]–6. Gigue.
  BWV 830 (in E minor): 1. Prelude–2. Allemande–3. Corrente–4. Sarabande–5. Tempo di Gavotta–6. Gigue. (Corrente and Gavotta
  movements borrowed from earliest version of Sonata in G for harpsichord and violin, BWV 1019—see Table 3-7.)
† Includes fugue.

Bach clearly admired the London composer, as his various Leipzig performances of vocal—and likely other works by Handel suggest. (There is
no evidence that Handel reciprocated such interest.) For Bach's competitive
disposition, the *Eight Great Suites* proved to be a highly stimulating challenge,
and in part I of the *Clavier-Übung* he responded to them in the manner of a
quiet rivalry. The two collections certainly served as a platform for the meeting
of two extraordinary yet singular and independent musical minds. Yet Bach
clearly wished to excel, and he intended his work to exhibit what he considered
to be the latest and most sophisticated stage in the art of keyboard music.

Even though the complete part I of the *Clavier-Übung* did not appear in
print until 1731, the collection as such appears to have been essentially finished by the time the first installment containing Partita 1 appeared in 1726.
No autograph manuscript of all six partitas survives, but autograph scores of
Partitas 3 and 6 open the second *Clavier-Büchlein* for Anna Magdalena Bach,
dating from 1725 (Fig. 5-2). This of course means that the last partita was
already finished when Partita 1 went to the engraver in 1726. As the autograph
sequence of Partitas 3 and 6 indicates, the six suites were not composed in
their eventual numerical order. Yet the entire collection presents a group of
similarly conceived and closely related suites that all originated around 1725,

FIGURE 5-2

Sarabande of Partita in E minor, BWV 830/4, autograph score in the
Clavier-Büchlein for A. M. Bach of 1725.

when Bach began the second keyboard album for his wife—after her first
album (begun in 1722) was completely filled. Since the content of the second
album following the two entries of Partitas 3 and 6 was determined by Bach's
wife, the most likely location for the entries of the other four partitas would
have been the first album. Unfortunately, the first album of 1722 for Anna
Magdalena survives in a fragmentary state, with only about one-third of its
original contents remaining—including five of the six *French Suites* at the
beginning of the book and entirely in the composer's hand. Hence it makes
good sense to assume that the six compact suites *sans prélude* were followed
in the same album by a set of six larger suites *avec prélude*, both dedicated to
Anna Magdalena, but that Bach ran out of space and had to start a second
album. Two external criteria support this conjecture: a block of eighty-plus
pages is missing from the album begun in 1722 (about the appropriate amount
of space for four partitas), and an autograph sketch of a sequential pattern in
A minor at the end of the first album relates to Partita 3, thereby supplying a
bridge to the beginning of the second album of 1725.[8]

As the two autograph versions of Partitas 3 and 6 in the *Little Clavier Book* of 1725 illustrate (see Table 5-2), Bach made no substantive changes to the existing movements for their publication, though he did carry out some careful editing and polishing, and also added an extra movement to both. Moreover, his revision of Partita 3 included a change in the heading of "Menuet" to "Burlesca"—which represented a more than merely cosmetic alteration. This change highlights the unusual makeup of the minuet movement: its imitative features, free-style polyphony, and unexpected syncopations. By renaming it Burlesca, the composer underscored its special character—in effect, it presents a parody or caricature of a conventional minuet. As if wishing to top this exquisitely original movement, he placed just after it another imaginative and witty character piece as movement 6, the Scherzo. Alteration to Partita 6 is confined to a moderation of the sharp contrast between the Corrente (with its pointed rhythmic bite) and the heavily decorated Sarabande, via the insertion of a new movement in the form of an evenly flowing and melodious Air that culminates in a chain of virtuoso leaps.[9]

Finally, the finale movement of the Partita 3 serves as an example of the fact that Bach never ceased to work on improvements. Well over six years after composing the piece for Anna Magdalena's *Clavier-Büchlein* and even some time after the undated first reprint of Opus 1 of 1731, he realized that in the contrapuntally conceived Gigue the theme was suitable for strict inversion in the second half of the movement.[10] He thus made an alteration at measure 25 and similar spots, so that the theme would no longer be mirrored merely in a mildly modified way, but would conform to a strict *thema inversum*. He made this belated correction on several copies of the publication, by erasing and overwriting the second and fourth group of beamed eighth notes.

EXAMPLE 5-1

BWV 827, Gigue: subject in first section and two stages of its inversion in second section.

The first installment of the collection, introducing Partita 1 with its seven movements, was manifestly designed to impress and to illustrate a genuinely innovative approach, one that went well beyond the achievements of the *English* and *French Suites*. The earlier manuscript collections and their individual contributions to the genre of keyboard suite were completely unknown outside the closest Bach circle. Therefore part I of the *Clavier-Übung*, a publication clearly meant to announce to the larger public a not yet widely known composer, quietly built on the considerable yet hidden experience of the *English* and *French Suites* and beyond—a systematically layered background apparently lacking for Handel's *Eight Great Suites*. Each of the first partita's seven movements displays a remarkable combination of fashionable melodic qualities, rhythmic vitality, and unobtrusive polyphonic design. This is as true of the elegant Praeludium, whose imitative design only gradually unfolds (reminiscent of certain preludes from the *Well-Tempered Clavier*), as it is of the Allemande and Courante, both of which benefit from the transparent style of the Inventions. Likewise the dance step pattern of the sarabande, with its emphasis on the second beat, is realized here by an emphatic combination of varied vertical harmonies and contrapuntally connected ornamental phrases. Even the two unadorned Menuets, with their simple and tuneful lines, constitute distinctly stylish examples, the first a charming treble-bass dance, the second a dance in perfect four-part counterpoint. An Italian giga, a variant of the French gigue that abstains from dotted rhythms and imitative elements and emphasizes triadic harmonies, concludes the cycle of movements with virtuosic fireworks, passages that require the player to demonstrate complete command of the most advanced contemporary keyboard technique.[11] Here, and for the first time, Bach adopted the *pièce croisée* manner in which two parts, one for each hand, cross and recross one another in the same range (Fig. 5-3). The technique is first traceable to volume 3 of François Couperin's *Pièces de clavecin* (Paris, 1722). But while Couperin applied the technique to performance on a double-manual harpsichord, Bach enhanced the keyboard acrobatics by presenting this passage to be played on a single-manual instrument.

The Giga of Partita 1 sets the stage for the finales of all other partitas. Even though Partita 2 concludes with a decidedly virtuosic Capriccio instead of a gigue, it was in fact a capricious character that defined the Italian giga. That same genre character also gave rise to the virtuosic nature of the French-style gigues of Partitas 3–6, all conceived as strict fugato movements based

FIGURE 5-3

Giga of Partita in B♭ major, BWV 825/7, *Clavier-Übung*, part I (1726 and 1731).

on capricious subjects, at times with melodic inversion. These intricate and sophisticated contrapuntal finales are reminiscent of the elaborate fugal sections that notably occur within the introductory movements of Partitas 2, 4, and 6. Their polyphonic logic contrasts with the effective but less consistent designs of Handel's fugues in the *Great Suites*. As Carl Philipp Emanuel Bach put it in 1788, in comparing the two masters of fugue:

> Handel's fugues are good, but he often abandons a voice. Bach's clavier fugues
> can be set out for as many instruments as they have voices; no voice fails to
> receive its proper share, and every one is carried through properly.[12]

By coyly stating that "Handel's fugues are good," the Bach son did not go so far as to denigrate them, but at the same time he certainly drew attention to the fundamentally dissimilar (and presumably superior) approach that his father had adopted—one that allowed of no shortcuts or convenient elisions.

The renaming of movement headings in part I of the *Clavier-Übung* notably centers on the opening movements. As the two titles in Anna Magdalena's album indicate (Table 5-2), they seem initially to have been designated Prelude. For the publication, however, the titles were changed to Praeludium, Sinfonia, Fantasia, Ouverture, Praeambulum, and Toccata, choices that emphasize the individuality of each multi-movement structure as signified in its first-movement heading. And although "praeludium," "fantasia," and "praeambulum" do not imply any particular musical specifics, the terms "sinfonia," "ouverture," and "toccata" ordinarily suggest the kinds of multi-divisional structures that these movements indeed embody. Beyond the terminological variety in naming the preludes, this seemingly external feature has its immediate internal implications, signifying the composer's departure from prevailing models and his thoroughly original approach to each individual partita, as well as his determination to publish a work that would have no equivalent.

Further, there is compelling evidence regarding the planning process for Opus 1, that from the outset Bach intended not to present merely another standard set of six suites but to offer a momentuous collection of substantial keyboard works in which nothing was left to chance, including the choice of keys. The initial plan included seven rather than six partitas, as the publication announcement for the installment containing Partita 5 reveals (May 1, 1730):

> Because the fifth suite of the Bachian Clavier-Übung is now finished and because, with the final two resting ones, the whole little work will be completed at the upcoming Michaelmas Fair, let such be known to the amateurs of the clavier.[13]

As mentioned above, Kuhnau's two volumes of Clavier-Übungen served as a template for Bach's general title, for his choice of the term "partita," and for the number and organization of this set of suites. Kuhnau's volumes contain seven partitas each, Book I of 1689 in seven major keys (C, D, E, F, G, A, and B♭) and Book II of 1692 in seven minor keys (c, d, e, f, g, a, and b). With this organization of fourteen major and minor keys, Kuhnau offered works in all the common keys used in the seventeenth century, prior to the gradual evolution toward equal temperament. Furthermore, since according to traditional music philosophy the modes or keys were related to the seven planets, seven weekdays, seven emotional qualities, and seven virtues, the grouping of works in sets of seven presumably communicated the God-given interrelationship of the universe and human creations. A representative mid-seventeenth-century diagram explains those connections as they were then understood (Fig. 5-4 and Diagram 5-1) and as composers applied them, naturally with individual modifications.[14] Dietrich Buxtehude, for example, is said to have written seven keyboard suites in which he "artfully depicted the nature or quality of the planets."[15] Although the cycle has not survived, it must have had the same general goal as did Kuhnau's suites in their modernized major-minor organization.

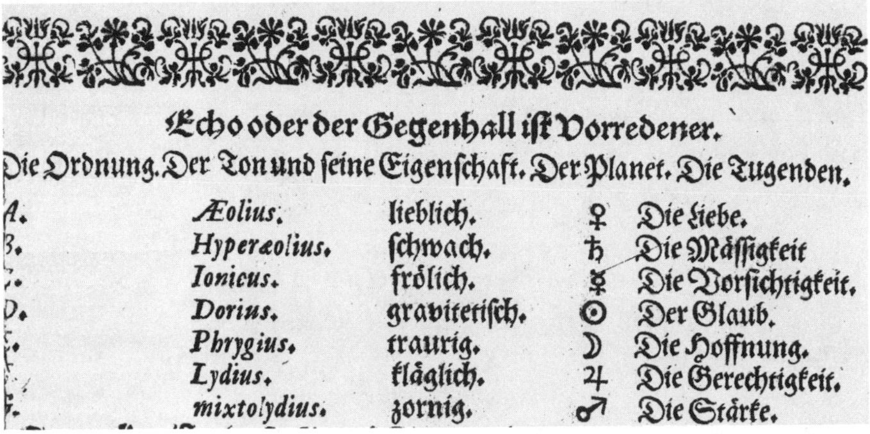
Echo oder der Gegenhall ist Vorredener.

Die Ordnung.	Der Ton und seine Eigenschaft.		Der Planet.	Die Tugenden.
A.	*Æolius.*	lieblich.	♀	Die Liebe.
B.	*Hyperæolius.*	schwach.	♄	Die Mässigkeit
C.	*Ionicus.*	frölich.	☿	Die Vorsichtigkeit.
D.	*Dorius.*	gravitetisch.	☉	Der Glaub.
E.	*Phrygius.*	traurig.	☽	Die Hoffnung.
F.	*Lydius.*	kläglich.	♃	Die Gerechtigkeit.
G.	*mixtolydius.*	zornig.	♂	Die Stärke.

FIGURE 5-4

J. S. Staden, *Der VII Tugenden, Planeten, Töne oder Stimmen Aufzug* (Nuremberg, 1645).

DIAGRAM 5-1

The Seven Modes (after Staden, Fig. 5-4)

ORDER AND MODE [KEY*]	CHARACTER	WEEKDAY†	VIRTUE
A Aeolian [A minor]	Loving	Friday (Venus)	Love
B♭ Hyperaeolian [B♭ major]	Weak	Saturday (Saturn)	Moderation
C Ionian [C major]	Cheerful	Wednesday (Mercury)	Caution
D Dorian [D minor]	Serious	Sunday (Sun)	Faith
E Phrygian [E minor]	Sad	Monday (Moon)	Hope
F Lydian [F major]	Miserable	Thursday (Jupiter)	Justice
G Mixolydian [G major]	Angry	Tuesday (Mars)	Strength

* Approximate tonal equivalent. † Indicated by planet symbol.

For reasons unknown, Bach did not realize his original plan of seven partitas for his Opus 1 but reverted to a set of six instead. The installment projected in May 1730 for the autumn Michaelmas Fair contained only Partita 6,[16] and about half a year later in the spring of 1731, the collected edition of six partitas appeared in print. The intended seventh partita had most likely been eclipsed by other projects. Nonetheless, the carefully designed tonal plan for an original set of seven suites hints clearly at F major as the envisioned key for the missing last piece. Unlike Kuhnau, however, Bach mingled major and minor modes in his key scheme. He also did not use a straightforward ascending succession of keys as he had done previously in both the *Well-Tempered Clavier* and the Inventions and Sinfonias, but instead chose a sequence of keys based on intervals expanding stepwise in alternating upward and downward directions (see Table 5-3).

TABLE 5-3. Key order in *Clavier-Übung* I

Partita:	1	2	3	4	5	6	[7]
Key:	B♭	c	a	D	G	e	[F]
Interval:	2nd↑	3rd↓	4th↑	5th↓	6th↑	7th↓	

The key scheme of the Bach partitas has neither precedent nor parallel (Diagram 5-1). Though based on the seven-note scale from c to b♭, it uses only six of the keys (a, B♭, c, D, e, and G), such that the key order no longer fully serves the intended purpose. The purposeful application of all seven steps of the diatonic scale, symbolically aligning them with music for each day of the week and also associating them with seven distinctive characters of expression, was a generally valid and vastly expandable idea—regardless of the various differing views on assigning affective properties to specific keys.[17] But Bach the ruminator gave way to Bach the pragmatist. He settled on a standard opus of six, and what resulted is a key order that is rational in its own way—three partitas each in the major and minor modes, but in two reversed sequences: B♭–c–a | D–G–e, that is, one major, two minor, followed by two major, one minor.

The new title page produced for the collected reprint of the six partitas bore the same wording as the earlier installments, describing its contents as "consisting in preludes, allemandes, courantes, sarabandes, gigues, minuets, and other gallantries" (Fig. 5-1). It also provided, in addition to the composer's title as Music Director in Leipzig, his new court title as Ducal Capellmeister of Saxe-Weißenfels—this in view of the fact that his Anhalt-Cöthen capellmeistership (as specified on the previous installments) had expired in 1728 with Prince Leopold's death. Moreover, the 1731 title page designated the collected edition quite deliberately as "Opus 1"—a number clearly suggestive of more to come. With its 73 densely filled pages of keyboard score, the finished print contained more music than the spaciously laid-out 1720 edition of Handel's *Eight Great Suites*, and in fact more than any other single-volume keyboard print of the era. Achieving publication in this manner fulfilled two of Bach's long-cherished ambitions: to encourage a broader following, and to secure his place as a performer-composer to be reckoned with.

At the same time, the composer's uncompromising demands on both performer and listener likely limited the popularity of these works. When the Leipzig literary scholar and philosopher Johann Christoph Gottsched, who considered Bach "the greatest of all musicians in Saxony,"[18] sent a copy of the freshly published *Clavier-Übung* to his keyboard-playing bride Luise Adelgunde Kulmus, she responded with the following: "The pieces you sent by Bach for the keyboard . . . are as difficult as they are beautiful. When I have played them ten times I still feel like a beginner."[19]

CLAVIER-ÜBUNG, PART II: ITALIAN CONCERTO AND FRENCH OVERTURE

While in many respects Bach's Opus 1 stood out from similar collections of suites, it generally followed the market, which preferred keyboard dances and suites by a wide margin. No such attempt to cater to the public was in play, however, in the *Clavier-Übung's* part II. Its fundamental idea of presenting, in juxtaposition, two substantial and challenging works in the two preeminent national styles of European music was without any precedent for any keyboard publication (Table 5-4). The title page describes the contents of the volume in quite specific terms: "Second Part of the Clavier-Übung Comprising a Concert in the Italian Taste and an Ouverture in the French Manner for a Harpsichord with Two Manuals" (Fig. 5-5). The print

FIGURE 5-5

Clavier-Übung, part II: title page
(Nuremberg, 1735).

bears no reference to an Opus 2, because this time it was not self-published but was instead issued by the engraver and publisher Christoph Weigel Jr. of Nuremberg; the change of publishing venue probably spoke against the continuation of opus numbers. That Bach was able to line up a publisher, who had probably established contact with him by way of the Leipzig trade fairs, means that Weigel had reasonable confidence in the success of the project. And indeed, after a year or so a second printing was called for.

The new publication appeared during the Easter Fair of 1735, making the interval between the first two parts of the *Clavier-Übung* about four years. It seems, however, that the concept for the second volume originated from around or even before the publication date of Opus 1 in 1731, although no composing scores are extant. In the case of the *French Ouverture*, BWV 831, a manuscript exists that was apparently copied from the autograph score by Anna Magdalena Bach prior to 1733/34, and perhaps as early as around 1730. The title "Ouverture pour le clavecin par J. S. Bach," the headings of the individual movements, and a number of corrections are in the composer's own hand. The manuscript represents an earlier version of the piece in the key of C minor, and with a simplified notation of the slow (dotted) sections of the opening overture movement. An undatable earlier version of the *Italian Concerto*, BWV 971, survives in a pre-1762 copy by the second-generation Bach student Johann Christoph Oley, under the title "Concerto in F dur del Sigr: Johann Sebastian Bach."[20] The insignificant variants in this manuscript stem from an older version of the concerto now lost.

TABLE 5-4. *Clavier-Übung* II (C. Weigel, Nuremberg, 1735)

Concerto in the Italian Taste **in F major, BWV 971**	1. [Allegro] $\frac{2}{4}$
	2. Andante (D minor) $\frac{3}{4}$
	3. Presto ¢
Ouverture in the French Manner **in B minor, BWV 831**	1. Ouverture **C** | $\frac{6}{8}$ | **C**
	2. Courante $\frac{3}{2}$
	3. Gavotte 1ʳᵉ **2** 4. Gavotte 2ᵈᵉ (D major) **2** 3. *da capo*
	5. Passepied 1ʳᵉ $\frac{3}{8}$ 6. Passepied 2ᵈᵉ $\frac{3}{8}$ 5. *da capo*
	7. Sarabande $\frac{3}{4}$
	8. Bourée 1ʳᵉ **2** 9. Bourée 2ᵈᵉ **2** 8. *da capo*
	10. Gigue $\frac{6}{8}$
	11. Echo $\frac{2}{4}$

The two works in *Clavier-Übung* II (Figs. 5-6 and 5-7) represent keyboard adaptations of two different orchestral genres, concerto and overture. Their characteristic differentiations of orchestral dynamics, as reflected in the *forte* and *piano* indications of the scores, call for the gradated sonic resources of a double-manual harpsichord, as is directed by the specific wording of the title—in contrast to the requirements of the first volume. According to Johann Mattheson's discussion of style categories, the two principal genres within the *stylus symphoniacus* are concerto and ouverture,[21] the one of Italian and the other of French origin. Yet contemporaneous discussions of which factors actually define the Italian style and which the French tend to be on the vague side. For example, according to Johann Gottfried Walther's influential music dictionary of 1732, for which Bach served as the Leipzig distributor, "The Italian style is sharp, colorful, and expressive whereas the French style is natural, fluent, tender, etc."[22] Given his strong preference for practical explanations, Bach decided to address this matter in purely musical terms within *Clavier-Übung* II. There he vividly exemplified the contrasting realms of Italian and French styles, setting them against each other as two fundamentally discrete approaches to composition involving two distinct musical languages.

Here Bach once again made purposeful use of key, so as to highlight even further the extent and depth of the stylistic contrasts in question. The juxtaposition of two pieces in F major and C minor would not have made enough of a point in terms of the incompatibility of the two styles. Thus for the publication, the composer transposed the *Overture* from its original C

FIGURE 5-6

Italian Concerto, BWV 971, *Clavier-Übung*, part II (1735).

minor down to B minor. In this way, he accentuated the contrast between major and minor modes by using keys represented by the notes *F* and *B*, which form the interval of an augmented fourth or tritone (three whole steps)—the very definition of dissonance, in medieval times termed the *diabolus in musica* (the devil in music).

FIGURE 5-7

French Overture, BWV 831, *Clavier-Übung*, part II (1735).

As its title suggests, part II of the *Clavier-Übung* clearly delineates the distinctions between concerto and overture, and defines the contrasting stylistic principles with great clarity on both large- and small-scale levels. Bach counterposes Italianate three-movement form (fast–slow–fast, with the middle movement in a different key) with French-style multiple-movement structure (prelude and sequence of short dances, all in the same key, with major/minor variants possible). Other contrasts abound, including melodic-melismatic versus rhythmic-metric emphasis, ritornello (tutti-solo) and aria forms versus homogeneous dance types and character pieces, strict versus irregular part-writing, and free-style polyphonic continuity versus quickly passing harmonic effects—to mention only the prevailing traits that are brought into play (see Figs. 5-6 and 5-7).

In its first movement, indeed within the very opening measures of its arresting thematic beginning, the *Italian Concerto* exemplifies the essence of Italianate concerto style. It also sets out an exemplary model of a methodically conceived tonal plan, with resourceful harmonic variation involving and balancing all significant scale degrees—tonic, dominant, subdominant, submediant, and mediant:

> **Ritornello** (R) 1 (F) – **Solo** (S) 1 (F → C) – **R2** (C → d) – **S2** (a → B♭) – **R3** (B♭ → C) – **S3** (d → F) – **R4** (F → C) – **S4** (C → F) – **R5** (F)

In comparable fashion, in its own first measures the opening movement of the *French Overture* forcefully projects a typically French musical atmosphere. This overall character is immediately communicated via the overture's majestic "signature" opening section, with its slow, sharply pointed, and pervasive dotted rhythms and intermittent short runs. Other features typical of French practice include deliberate renunciation of melodic focus at times, the introduction of unexpected dissonances, and the employment of sudden and unpredictable harmonic shifts.

The *Concerto* BWV 971 represents an original composition, but it is one that must be understood within the context of the many transcriptions of Italian orchestral concertos that Bach had prepared for organ and harpsichord in Weimar. Such transcriptions, mainly of violin concertos by such composers as Giuseppe Torelli, Alessandro and Benedetto Marcello, and most notably Antonio Vivaldi, continued to play a role in Bach's Leipzig teaching studio, as corroborated by the collection of concerto transcriptions BWV 972–982 in the possession of his nephew, the St. Thomas School student Johann Ernst Bach.[23] Since Johann Sebastian Bach himself, according to his own words, learned from the modern Italian concerto style "how to think musically,"[24] he apparently continued to make use of this repertoire for the benefit of his students. He likewise enjoyed performing such concerto transcriptions at the

Collegium Musicum concerts in the 1730s. There are also two original Bach keyboard concertos composed in the spirit of orchestral transcription: the Concerto in C major, BWV 1061, for two harpsichords, from around 1732/33, and the *Italian Concerto*, from about the same time.

The *Overture* BWV 831 is completely unrelated to transcription technique and belongs in a different compositional realm, one that includes part I of the *Clavier-Übung*. Yet even though the Partitas are in general linked to the French genre of suite, they are in no way representative of French style. On the contrary, Bach demonstrated in the Partitas his personal adaptation of the genre. His overall approach to the reimagining and recasting of keyboard dances is particularly evident in their subtle polyphonization, involving virtually omnipresent strains of elegant counterpoint quite uncommon in the French style.

The *Overture* in B minor presents a distinctly contrasting conception, as is immediately evident from its movement structure. The work abstains from the German core settings of allemande–courante–sarabande–gigue, and also lacks the latent polyphonic textures that distinguish the *English Suites*, the *French Suites*, and the Partitas. On the other hand, Bach does not follow any specific French models, such as François Couperin's *Second* and *Troisième Livre de Pièces de Clavecin* (1717 and 1722), which he knew[25] but whose movement organizations are conceived in very different ways. It seems, therefore, that Bach came up with his own idea of what he deemed a typically French-style suite, in much the same way as he put together his orchestral suites. Of these, the *Overture* in C major, BWV 1066, from the mid-1720s, comes closest to the organization of BWV 831, this time with eleven movements (Ouverture–Courante–Gavottes I and II–Forlane–Menuets I and II–Bourrées I and II–Passepieds I and II).

CLAVIER-ÜBUNG, PART III: A GERMAN *LIVRE D'ORGUE*

The information available regarding Bach's library of organ literature is as accidental and fragmentary as that regarding his music library as a whole. Nevertheless, the historical dimension, breadth, and depth of the substantial organ portion can well be judged by: (1) starting with the oldest item that bears his ownership mark, the printed tablature book *Orgel oder Instrument Tabulatur* by Elias Nicolaus Ammerbach (Leipzig, 1571); (2) continuing with works by his early idols Pachelbel, Reincken, Böhm, and Buxtehude; and (3) taking into account the contemporary organ repertoires of the 1720s and 1730s that Bach would presumably have known. This method affords results, even though many specifics are perforce lacking. Bach definitely owned a manuscript copy of Girolamo Frescobaldi's *Fiori Musicali* (Rome, 1635), on which he had inscribed "J. S. Bach 1714," and also a manuscript copy he made around 1710 of Nicolas de Grigny's *Premier Livre d'Orgue* (Paris, 1699).[26] These were two of the most influential and widely circulated publications of seventeenth-century organ music. Indeed, the Weimar court organist likely nourished the hope of one day publishing an organ book of his own. And when he did finally produce a *Clavier-Übung* volume dedicated to organ music, he modeled it closely after the Frescobaldi and de Grigny prototypes. While the organ pieces of de Grigny are devoted entirely to the liturgy of the Roman Catholic Mass, the Frescobaldi volume presents settings for three different categories of the Roman Mass but also includes some secular pieces. Bach combined these concepts, translated them into the familiar realm of the Lutheran worship service with Kyrie, Gloria, and catechism chorale settings, and also added an appropriate nonliturgical portion, with a prelude and fugue for large organ[27] and four duets, extended two-part pieces for any type of keyboard (Table 5-5).

Part III of the *Clavier-Übung* appeared in time for the Michaelmas Fair of 1739, according to a September 28 letter of the same year from the composer's nephew Johann Elias Bach. Acting at the time as Bach's private secretary, he informed a colleague "that the copper-engraved work of my cousin is now finished and a copy may be had from him for three reichstalers."[28] Evidently the work had originally been intended to make an earlier appearance, since a previous message of January 10 to the same recipient states: "that my honored cousin will bring out some keyboard pieces that are principally intended for organists and are exceedingly well composed. They will probably be ready for the coming Easter Fair and make up some 80 pages."[29] The delay in Bach's publication of this extensive work was most likely due to the fact that he had been forced to change engravers after more than half of the plates had been completed.[30] If the engraving process involving shops in Leipzig (Krügner) and Nuremberg (Schmid) was fairly advanced by the beginning of 1739, the work must have been delivered to the engravers during the fall of the previous year. This means, in turn, that the compositional genesis of such an extensive and complex collection of organ music would most likely have taken up much of

TABLE 5-5. *Clavier-Übung* III (Leipzig, 1739)

SETTINGS AND SECTIONS	PEDALITER PIECES	MANUALITER PIECES
Praeludium in E♭ major	1. BWV 552/1	
Hymns for the Kyrie and Gloria of the Mass		
Kyrie, Gott Vater in Ewigkeit	2. BWV 669	5. BWV 672
Christe, aller Welt Trost	3. BWV 670	6. BWV 673
Kyrie, Gott heiliger Geist	4. BWV 671	7. BWV 674
Allein Gott in der Höh sei Ehr	8.–9. BWV 675–676	10. BWV 677
Hymns on the six articles of the Catechism		
Dies sind die heiligen zehn Gebot	11. BWV 678	12. BWV 679
Wir glauben all an einen Gott	13. BWV 680	14. BWV 681
Vater unser im Himmelreich	15. BWV 682	16. BWV 683
Christ unser Herr zum Jordan kam	17. BWV 684	18. BWV 685
Aus tiefer Not schrei ich zu dir	19. BWV 686	20. BWV 687
Jesus Christus, unser Heiland	21. BWV 688	22. BWV 689
Duets		
Duetto I in E minor		23. BWV 802
Duetto II in F major		24. BWV 803
Duetto III in G major		25. BWV 804
Duetto IV in A minor		26. BWV 805
Fuga in E♭ major	27. BWV 552/2	

the year 1738, if not more. Yet in the absence of a composing score, no further details arc known.

Curiously, the title page of the publication (Fig. 5-8) describes its contents rather tersely, expressly mentioning only "various preludes on the Catechism and other hymns." At the same time, considering the heterogeneous nature of a collection that no concise phrase could adequately have described, the title's emphasis on the catechism chorales seems to have been a deliberate decision. Just as the term "catechism" implies a summary or exposition of doctrine, this volume of the *Clavier-Übung* was intended to serve as a summary of the art of the organ; indeed, it might well have been called Bach's *Livre d'orgue*, or Organ Book, instead being assigned the serial title. Yet just as important to the composer as the program of integrating the full range of keyboard instruments was the overall didactic impetus of the *Clavier-Übung*. Evidence for the latter

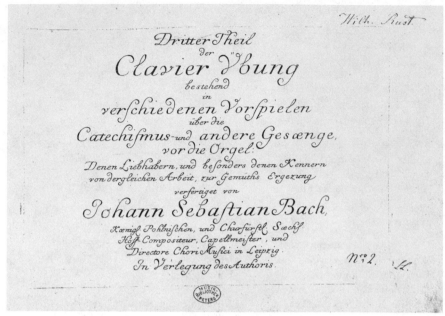

FIGURE 5-8

Clavier-Übung, part III: title page (Leipzig, 1739).

is also present on the title page in the emphatic and unique phrase "especially for connoisseurs of such work" in addition to the standard dedication line "for music lovers."

The choice of chorale repertory differs notably from the content of Bach's other two collections of organ chorales: the Weimar *Orgel-Büchlein*, with its short chorale settings, and the Leipzig compilation of earlier large-scale chorale fantasias and preludes known as the Great Eighteen Chorales (BWV 651–668), which were being edited while he was still at work on *Clavier-Übung* III. Both collections, as well as the 1746 publication of the Six "Schübler" Chorales (BWV 645–650), focus on hymns for the ecclesiastical year and other religious themes. In the *Clavier-Übung*, by contrast, Bach set seasonally independent hymns for the Sunday Mass Ordinary (Kyrie and Gloria) as well as for the six weekday catechism services held throughout the year on the chief parts of Luther's Catechism (The Ten Commandments, The Apostles' Creed, The Lord's Prayer, Baptism, The Office of the Keys and Confession, and The Lord's Supper). In other words, the chorale repertoire for both Sunday and weekday services in the published collection was chosen by Bach for unrestricted use *in ogni tempo*—that is, for any time within the church year, a concept that somehow recalls the abandoned initial idea of seven suites in *Clavier-Übung* I associated with the seven weekdays.

The principle of unrestricted use also pertains to the free choice of keyboard instruments, since each chorale is set in both *pedaliter* and *manualiter* versions—such that each could be played on a large church organ with at least two manuals and pedal, and also on instruments without pedals (organ, harpsichord, and clavichord). By implication, this dual option extends as well to venues—meaning both larger and smaller churches, and even private homes. Comparably broad options were also available for the non-chorale-based pieces in *Clavier-Übung* III, the Prelude and Fugue for a large organ and the four duets for keyboards without pedal. This deliberate flexibility in instrumental realization seems to have been inspired by two related motivations: to avoid excluding music lovers with access only to smaller keyboard instruments, and also to broaden the market appeal of a particularly sophisticated and demanding publication.

Despite their unquestionably liturgical background and character, the organ chorales of *Clavier-Übung* III were in fact not designed to be played at services. This applies in particular to the larger settings, whose durations range well beyond what was customary for the regular preluding that preceded congregational singing; even the small-scale chorales are generally not suitable for the purpose of preluding. Moreover, the settings of all three strophes of Luther's Kyrie hymn (BWV 669–674) provide clear evidence that they were not meant to serve as separate intonations for every strophe to be sung. They were instead intended as stand-alone works, suitable either for organ recitals or for supplying music during Communion, which was the sole interval in the Lutheran liturgy suited to the presentation of extended organ pieces. The overall organization of the published collection reflects the structure of a typical Bachian organ recital, which usually extended "over two hours or more," beginning with a prelude and ending with a fugue, "both with the full organ" (*organo pleno*). In between "he showed his art of using the stops for a trio, a quartet, etc." and elaborations of chorale melodies "in the most diversified manner."[31] This sort of program resembled in principle the framing device of the *Goldberg Variations*. Yet the 27 movements of the *Clavier-Übung* III certainly do not represent a cyclical performing sequence to be played in consecutive order, but instead put forward the general idea of a thematically or topically conceived recital. Part II of the *Clavier-Übung* juxtaposes the two major national styles; part III sets forth in its core material another quite unique and meaningful conception: the spirit of a musical presentation that highlights, in general terms, the regularly repeated hymns of the Sunday and weekday liturgies.

All the chorales that were selected for part III feature pre-Reformation and early-sixteenth-century melodies. Thus Bach continued to demonstrate his preference for the classic Lutheran hymns and their modal tunes, just as he had taken them up in the chorale cantata cycle. He now paid far more attention, however, to the harmonic idiosyncrasies of the various church modes, specifically Dorian ("Wir glauben all an einen Gott"; "Vater unser im Himmelreich"; "Christ unser Herr zum Jordan kam"; "Jesus Christus, unser Heiland"), Phrygian ("Kyrie, Gott Vater in Ewigkeit"; "Aus tiefer Not schrei ich zu dir"), and Mixolydian ("Dies sind die heilgen zehn Gebot"). In these realizations, the composer was at pains to underscore the singularities of the modes, clearly distinguishing his treatments from the ways in which the modern major-major modes were typically handled. He accordingly emphasized particular melodic traits (such as the unusual half step that begins the Phrygian mode), made use of specific cadential formulas, and gave attention to the application of real and tonal answers in fugal counterpoint. Such ideas and practices also seem to be in line with his teaching interests in the later 1730s and '40s, as reported by Johann Philipp Kirnberger with explicit reference to the *Clavier-Übung*.[32] Likewise, the collection's prominent occurrences of canonic counterpoint and its predilection for contrasts in the patterns of style reflect Bach's prevailing compositional and theoretical interests.

The raison d'être for bringing to the public this particular opus of organ music certainly involved Bach's manifest sense of pride, and also his eager wish to demonstrate that his fame and reputation rested on accomplishments representing the very highest level in organ composition and performance. With its seventy-seven pages of music,[33] the volume stood as the weightiest portion of the *Clavier-Übung*, and as an organ publication it did not have any counterpart whatever in the eighteenth century. Within the collection, it is the *pedaliter* works (the pieces with *obbligato* pedal parts) that truly document the distinctive achievements of Bach the organist. It should also be noted that the entire *pedaliter* contingent is governed by a methodical structural plan. This is most evident in the positioning of the Prelude and Fugue in E-flat major as distinctive and prominent bookends for the entire collection (Table 5-6), a frame that signifies the newly elevated standard for organ music with obbligato pedal—which is in fact promulgated throughout all the larger chorale settings.

TABLE 5-6. Large (*pedaliter*) settings in *Clavier-Übung* III: Configuration of design elements

	SCORE	CANTUS FIRMUS	GROUPING
Praeludium	5–6	—	*organo pleno*
Kyrie, Gott Vater in Ewigkeit	4 parts	soprano	
Christe, aller Welt Trost	4 parts	tenor	
Kyrie, Gott heiliger Geist	5 parts	bass	*organo pleno*
Allein Gott in der Höh sei Ehr	3 parts	alto	
Allein Gott in der Höh sei Ehr	3 parts	cited in all 3 parts	
Dies sind die heilgen zehn Gebot	5 parts	canon: alto/tenor	
Wir glauben all an einen Gott	4 parts	compressed; ostinato	*organo pleno*
Vater unser im Himmelreich	5 parts	canon: soprano/tenor	
Christ unser Herr zum Jordan kam	4 parts	alto (ped)	
Aus tiefer Not schrei ich zu dir	6 parts	bass I (double ped)	*organo pleno*
Jesus Christus, unser Heiland	3 parts	bass (ped)	
Fuga	5 parts	—	*organo pleno*

The function of the framing Prelude in E-flat and Fugue in E-flat is replicated in the corresponding musical symmetry of their respective tripartite formal organizations. The substantial prelude consists of three sections (A = French overture style, B = echo phrases, C = contrapuntal texture) that keep alternating, finally concluding with the A material. The fugue is conceived as a triple fugue with three distinct subjects (I, II, and III), the first of which is eventually combined with each of the other two according to the scheme I–II + I–III + I, in three extended sections.

The large chorale settings enclosed by this frame showcase a wide spectrum of compositional designs, bound together within a carefully prepared order. Not only are Mass and catechism hymns delimited from one another as distinct groups, they also present themselves in variously tiered relationships. Hence the Kyrie-Gloria settings have their central axis in the five-part Kyrie chorale, a piece for *organo pleno* (full organ). Similarly, the catechism chorales form a unit that divides into two triplet subgroups, with two parallel axes marked by the *organo pleno* settings of "Wir glauben all" and "Aus tiefer Not"—pieces that additionally feature ostinato bass and double pedal, respectively. The three individually set strophes of the Trinitarian Kyrie hymn form a bundle of four- and five-part settings unified by their retrospective polyphonic style and serious character, with plain melodies carried from soprano through the tenor to the bass. The two following settings of the Gloria hymn are set as trios, with the three-part texture echoing the Trinitarian character of the Gloria. The first piece places the plain chorale melody in the alto register, while the second distributes it freely amongst all three parts of the score.

The densely imitative setting of "Wir glauben all an einen Gott" has no equivalent anywhere in Bach's organ music. Its only counterpart can be found in the two ricercars *con obligo del basso* (with required bass) in Frescobaldi's *Fiori musicali* of 1635, which Bach took as models for his chorale setting. Bach obscures the plain cantus firmus, turns the first line of the chorale melody into a fugal subject for the three upper parts, and transforms the sweeping range of the Dorian cantus firmus into a six-measure-long pedal bass pattern that occurs five times on different pitches. This imposing setting is surrounded by two five-part chorales with highly sophisticated treatments of their plain melodies, in two-part canons, for alto and tenor and soprano and tenor. "Vater unser im Himmelreich" stands out on account of its differentiated and eccentrically mixed declamation of snapping Lombard rhythms, and also its staccato triplets—radically progressive stylistic features without counterpart anywhere else in Bach's output (Fig. 5-9).

The second group of three chorales is centered around the penitential psalm song "Aus tiefer Not," in the retrospective style of a vocal chorale motet. This is Bach's only organ work in strict six-part polyphony, and the only setting that requires double pedal-playing for two independent contrapuntal lines: bass I (cantus firmus, right foot) and bass II (left foot). The two settings that surround it place the unadorned cantus firmi in the pedal part, yet in two different registers (alto and bass). Their compositional makeups, however, could not be more dissimilar. The score of "Christ, unser Herr" constitutes a concertato quartet of treble duo (right hand), alto chorale melody (pedal), and basso continuo (left hand). By contrast, the trio score of "Jesus Christus, unser Heiland" presents the plain cantus firmus in the pedal bass, over which two virtuosic counterpoints for the right and left hands move in rapid motion, with technically challenging leaps and tricky syncopated rhythms.

There is no question that the core pieces of *Clavier-Übung* III, those for grand organ with pedal, were designed to represent an organistic tour de force, a model of what could be accomplished by application of consummate skill. They stand most impressively as a cyclically planned, rationally diversified, and carefully constructed group of demanding and evocative organ pieces.

FIGURE 5-9

"Vater unser im Himmelreich," BWV 682, *Clavier-Übung*, part III (1739).

The interspersed *manualiter* pieces, generally less exacting but in their own fashion no less elaborate, are by no means randomly inserted. These works display elements of cyclical planning also, as is evident in the ascending key order and modal symmetry of the duets: E minor–F major–G major–A minor. Other settings evince comparably thoughtful coordination, as in the case of the three "Allein Gott in der Höh" chorales in F, G, and A major, and respectively in $\frac{3}{4}$, $\frac{6}{8}$, and **C** time. In view of the largely dogmatic nature of the hymn texts, Bach emphasized a serious and contemplative character in the musical language of the compositions. He did not, however, pass up opportunities for text-related expressive gestures. An outstanding example occurs at the very end of the third Kyrie chorale, BWV 671, whose text refers to the hour of death and whose last line reads, "when we depart from this misery, Kyrie eleison."[34] For this special passage, the music abruptly transitions from diatonic to chromatic counterpoint and employs extremely dissonant harmonies, thereby emphatically enhancing Luther's moving poetic phrase (see Ex. 8-1 in Chapter 8).

As a varied collection of chorale-based and free compositions, part III of the *Clavier-Übung* is united by an extraordinary and multifaceted program that encompasses multiple aspects of the liturgical, theological, and hymnological background and context. Bach employed a comprehensive range of compositional methods, including ingeniously varied contrapuntal tech-

niques, and provided a panoramic overview of historical and contemporary
style elements and patterns. The published set furthermore associates the
compositions with specific keyboard instruments and addresses all keyboard
playing methods: included are compositions calling for either one or two manuals, works requiring *obbligato* pedal (simple and double), and pieces playable
without pedals. In his brief review of 1740, Lorenz Mizler summarized the
merits of this organ volume, referencing Johann Adolph Scheibe's notorious
critique[35] of Bach's "turgid and confused style":

> The author has here presented a new example of his experience and success in
> this kind of composition. No one will surpass him in it, and few will be able to
> imitate him. This work is a powerful refutation of those who have made bold
> to criticize the composition of the Hon. Court Composer.[36]

However, before attacking Bach's manner of composition for its lack of "amenity" (*Annehmlichkeit*), Scheibe, the son of Bach's organ builder in Leipzig,
had expressed his honest admiration for Bach, albeit within the context of his
extraordinary skills as an organist:

> One is amazed at his ability, and one can hardly conceive how it is possible for
> him to achieve such agility, with his fingers and with his feet, in the crossings,
> extensions, and extreme jumps that he manages, without mixing in a single
> wrong tone, or displacing his body by any violent movement.[37]

Mizler, for his part, did not address the real issue at hand, namely Bach's
penchant for the extremes in performance difficulty and contrapuntal
complexity—both habitual with Bach, and likely making it impossible for the
composer to find a publisher for his *Clavier-Übung* III. Thus the composer
was left to finance this particularly demanding organ volume out of his own
pocket. About a decade later, his colleague and friend Georg Andreas Sorge
pursued a different approach when preparing his own publication of chorale preludes. Sorge acknowledged in his preface that the chorale preludes of
Clavier-Übung III "deserve the great renown they enjoy," but he then made
the pitch for his own approach: "because works such as these are so difficult as
to be all but unusable by young beginners and others, who may lack the considerable proficiency they require . . . I herewith present . . . simple preludes,
to be played only on the manuals."[38]

In *Clavier-Übung* III, Bach's obvious aversion to lowering standards, and his conspicuous disregard for trendy musical inclinations, went hand in hand with an increased emphasis on a deliberate and systematic integration of historical, theoretical, and didactic musical considerations. Such purposeful overall planning anticipated certain procedures that were to become ever more prominent in the composer's compositional activities, perhaps most notably in the *Art of Fugue* and the *B-minor Mass*.

CLAVIER-ÜBUNG, PART IV: GOLDBERG VARIATIONS

In the concluding part of the *Clavier-Übung*, Bach directed his attention to yet another category of keyboard composition: the structured, multi-movement harpsichord opus of extraordinary length. The entirety of the fourth *Clavier-Übung* volume is taken up by the *Aria with 30 Variations*, BWV 988 (Table 5-7). Just as with part II, this composition required a larger double-manual harpsichord (specified on the title page, Fig. 5-10). Moreover, given that the engraved score was only a few pages longer than part II, Bach was able to attract Balthasar Schmid as publisher, and thus did not have to bear the sole financial risk for the project; Bach's connections with this publisher had long since been established through Schmid's partial involvement with ear-

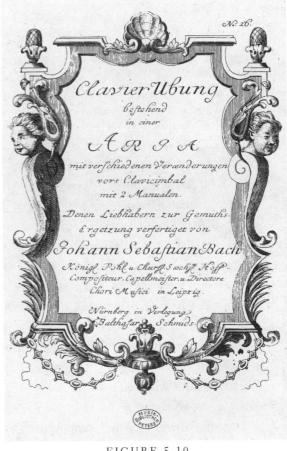

FIGURE 5-10

Clavier-Übung, part IV: title page (Nuremberg, n.d. [1741]).

lier parts of the *Clavier-Übung*. Part IV appeared in 1741, probably at the Michaelmas Fair in September, but its title page carries no mention that the print represented the fourth or final volume of a series. The plain heading *Clavier-Übung*, without reference to a volume number within the series, was presumably employed because the publisher preferred to begin as if making a fresh start; Schmid later published Bach's Canonic Variations on "Vom Himmel hoch" (BWV 769) as well (Chapter 8, page 303).

TABLE 5-7. *Clavier-Übung* IV (B. Schmid, Nuremberg, 1741)

Aria ($\frac{3}{4}$)		
Var. 1 ($\frac{3}{4}$)	Var. 2 ($\frac{2}{4}$)	Var. 3: *Canone all' Unisono* ($\frac{12}{8}$)
Var. 4 ($\frac{3}{8}$)	Var. 5 ($\frac{3}{4}$)	Var. 6: *Canone alla Seconda* ($\frac{3}{8}$)
Var. 7 ($\frac{6}{8}$): al tempo di Giga	Var. 8 ($\frac{3}{4}$)	Var. 9: *Canone alla Terza* (**C**)
Var. 10 (**¢**: Fugetta)	Var. 11 ($\frac{12}{16}$)	Var. 12: *Canone alla Quarta* ($\frac{3}{4}$)
Var. 13 ($\frac{3}{4}$)	Var. 14 ($\frac{3}{4}$)	Var. 15: *Canone alla Quinta* ($\frac{2}{4}$: andante, G minor)
Var. 16 (**¢** | $\frac{3}{8}$: Ouverture)	Var. 17 ($\frac{3}{4}$)	Var. 18: *Canone alla Sexta* (**¢**)
Var. 19 ($\frac{3}{8}$)	Var. 20 ($\frac{3}{4}$)	Var. 21: *Canone alla Settima* (**C**: G minor)
Var. 22 (**¢**: alla breve)	Var. 23 ($\frac{3}{4}$)	Var. 24: *Canone alla Ottava* ($\frac{9}{8}$)
Var. 25 ($\frac{3}{4}$: adagio, G minor)	Var. 26 ($\frac{18}{16}$)	Var. 27: *Canone alla Nona* ($\frac{6}{8}$)
Var. 28 ($\frac{3}{4}$)	Var. 29 ($\frac{3}{4}$)	Var. 30: *Quodlibet* (**C**)
Aria *da capo e Fine*		

It was the biographer Forkel who related the famous anecdote to the effect that this variation work came into being at the request of one of Bach's major patrons. According to Forkel, Count Hermann Carl von Keyserlinck of Dresden "once said to Bach that he should like to have some keyboard pieces for his house harpsichordist and former Bach pupil Johann Gottlieb Goldberg, which should be of such a soft and somewhat lively character that he might be a little cheered up by them in his sleepless nights."[39] The evidence, however—including not only the volume's lack of any formal dedication as required by eighteenth-century protocol, but also Goldberg's tender age of fourteen—indicates that the so-called "Goldberg Variations" did not in fact originate as a commissioned work, but were instead envisioned from the outset as a part of the overall framework of the *Clavier-Übung* series, for which they provide the thoroughly splendid finale.

In the absence of the composer's autograph score, the work's genesis remains largely unknown, but there is ample evidence that the idea for an opus of variations was once again triggered by a Handel publication: this time his second volume of the *Suites de Piéces de Clavecin*, HWV 434–442

TABLE 5-8. Handel, *Suites de Pièces pour le Clavecin*, vol. II (London, 1733)

Suite I in B♭ major, HWV 434	1. Prélude 2. Sonata 3. Aria con [5] Variazioni 4. Menuet
Suite II in G major, HWV 435	1. Chaconne and Variatio 1–21
Suite III in D minor, HWV 436	1. Allemande 2. Allegro 3. Air 4. Gigue 5. Menuetto and Variatio 1–3
Suite IV in D minor, HWV 437	1. Prélude 2. Allemande 3. Courante 4. Sarabande and Variatio 1–2 5. Gigue
Suite V in E minor, HWV 438	1. Allemande 2. Sarabande 3. Gigue
Suite VI in G minor, HWV 439	1. Allemande 2. Courante 3. Sarabande 4. Gigue
Suite VII in B♭ major, HWV 440	1. Allemande 2. Courante 3. Sarabande 4. Gigue
Suite VIII in G major, HWV 441	1. Allemande 2. Allegro 3. Courante 4. Aria 5. Menuetto
	6. Gavotte and Variatio 1–5 7. Gigue
Suite IX in G major, HWV 442	1. Prélude 2. Chaconne and Variatio 1–62

(London, 1733), which includes several sets of variations (Table 5-8). The suites presented in the first volume of 1720 all originated from before 1717, but the second volume offered works that were even earlier, including some from Handel's Hamburg years (1703–6)—among them the two German-style suites HWV 439–440 and the extended variation sets HWV 435 and 441–442. Whether Bach became familiar with the second volume during the 1730s cannot be definitively established. And he likely would not have known that these recently published works were two or even three decades old. Yet it does seem that he took a particular interest in the last piece of the set. This work, *Prelude and Chaconne with 62 Variations*, HWV 442, also existed in an earlier pirated print, *Prélude et Chaconne avec LXII Variations*, published by Gérard Witvogel (Amsterdam, c. 1732). In both editions, the final movement of the chaconne (Variation 62) is printed in incomplete form as a two-part canon at the octave, though the riddle is easy to solve by adding the missing ostinato bass under the notated upper parts (here as cue notes):

EXAMPLE 5-2

HWV 442, *Variation 62: canon at the octave above ostinato bass.*

It is safe to assume that Bach would have been unimpressed by this unsophisticated canonic setting. Yet it apparently made him curious to discover what sorts of different contrapuntal solutions, and how many, he himself could devise over the same ground bass. Given the missing composing manuscript, the when, how, and full extent of Bach's manifold mental exercises remain unknown. But he did later enter into his personal copy of *Clavier-Übung* IV the end result of his experimental musings, in the form of a systematically structured and carefully edited selection of fourteen canons (see Fig. 8-6, page 299). This calligraphic autograph version of the canon cycle BWV 1087, from which Bach eventually took the six-part canon BWV 1076 for his portrait painting (see Prologue), postdated the *Clavier-Übung*. Yet its Handelian link and the origin of BWV 1087 points to the compositional genesis of the thirty variations in general, and to the presence and plan of its canonic movements in particular.

Bach had not directed his attention to ostinato bass variations since composing the *Aria variata alla maniera italiana*, BWV 989, around 1704. The principal difference between an aria *alla maniera italiana* such as the famous *romanesca* aria (a melodic-harmonic formulation popular in Italy in the early Baroque) on the one hand, and the passacaglia or the French chaconne on the other, lies in the construction of their differing bass lines. The latter normally entails an ostinato bass pattern of four or sometimes eight measures—as may be seen in Bach's Ciaccona for unaccompanied violin, BWV 1004/5, his Passacaglia in C minor for organ, BWV 582, and the opening chorus of the cantata "Jesu, der du meine Seele," BWV 78.[40] By contrast, the aria *alla maniera italiana* consists of a longer ostinato bass divided into two sections, each of which is repeated, as in the arias BWV 989 and BWV 988. With this structural difference in mind, and with an eye to enhancing the overall musical potential, Bach extended and transformed Handel's eight-measure chaconne bass into an ostinato bass with the unusual length of 32 measures, made up of two sixteen-measure halves:

EXAMPLE 5-3

BWV 988: Bach's extended version of the ostinato bass.

In the first half of Bach's binary aria, the bass cadences in G major (m. 8) and then in the dominant key of D major (m. 16); the second half moves to E minor (m. 24) and finally returns to the tonic (m. 32). While it is typical for a chaconne and passacaglia to present an uninterrupted sequence of ostinato bass variations in a single movement, an Italianate "aria variata" habitually proceeds in separate ("strophic") movements, each based on the ostinato pattern—the model for Bach's *Aria with Variations*.

Bach's construction of an unprecedentedly lengthy ostinato bass led him to design an aria featuring an extended and delicately embellished treble melody in the style of a sarabande, such that the opening movement of the set represented a full-length suite-type unit. This in turn made it possible to treat the entire "suite" of thirty variations as a dynamic cycle of highly individualized movements that follow absolutely no conventional organizational pattern. However, the composer must have realized from the beginning that such a large-scale instrumental performing cycle was sustainable only if it offered a wealth of variety while at the same time being structured according to a rational and carefully deliberated plan. Crucial above all was to avoid monotony. To this end, Bach broke new ground by bringing into play a wide range of meters ($\frac{3}{4}$, $\frac{3}{8}$, $\frac{6}{8}$, $\frac{9}{8}$, $\frac{12}{8}$, ¢, $\frac{2}{4}$, $\frac{12}{16}$, and $\frac{18}{16}$ against $\frac{3}{4}$), tempos (al tempo di Giga, andante, alla breve, and adagio, to list only the indicated modifiers), texture (canon, fugetta, and ouverture, again to mention only the indicated terms), and finally, musical expression (not readily categorizable, but including two stirring movements in the minor mode, the andante canon variation 15 and the adagio variation 25, and a variety of other movements representing diverse characters and genre models).

Despite the freely chosen organization of the non-canonic variations, for which no standard order exists, and the constant element of surprise, Bach nevertheless established a highly cogent formal framework. First, he decided to employ the aria in a double function, as both a point of departure and a point of return. He also located at the very center of the cycle a clear inflection point by introducing to the first minor-mode variation (15)—which, with its pervasive sigh motifs, offers what might be understood as an acknowledgment of exhaustion. He then gave the second half of the work a fresh and energetic start, beginning it with a minature French overture (16), thus creating an intriguing link back to part II of the *Clavier-Übung*. Within the overall cycle, a notable evolution toward ever-increasing technical demands steadily unfolds, requiring utmost virtuosity on the part of the player.

FIGURE 5-11

Variations 28 and 29, *Goldberg Variations*, BWV 988,
Clavier-Übung, IV (1741).

Beyond all this, the sequence of thirty variations is punctuated by canons that mark the groupings of three movements. The canons themselves are arranged in ascending intervals from unison to ninth, with the final variation (30) then supplying a striking climax in the form of a quodlibet. The strictly graded sequence of canon movements, representing a third of the entire work, provides a structural scaffolding of unrelenting contrapuntal logic, while the pieces between them—two-thirds of the whole—offer great freedom for a rich panoply of variations, which present an exceptionally broad array of metric schemes and contrasts of musical character.

The concluding quodlibet (Fig. 5-12) is not a canon, but instead another kind of artful composition, one that simultaneously combines two well-known melodies over the ground bass of the aria. Bach's choice for this special finale movement once again reveals a characteristically astute assessment of his compositional options within the overall design of a multi-movement work, particularly in view of the virtuoso fireworks of the preceding variations 28 and 29 (Fig. 5-11). While it could not have been easy to conclude a variation cycle of such unprecedented dimensions and challenges, he certainly succeeded in devising a last movement that was both appropriately complex, and tuneful and memorable. Musical quodlibets usually combine popular and lighthearted melodies, often with humorous texts, and both the tunes used here fit admirably within this tradition.

The first melody that Bach chose for the quodlibet is a German dance tune from the early seventeenth century, known alternatively as the "Grossvatertanz" (Grandfather dance) and the "Kehraus" (literally, sweep-out = last dance). This round dance and its associated melody were ordinarily performed as the grand finale at a dance festival, wedding, or similar event, and remained popular into the earlier nineteenth century.[41] The second melody is the "Bergamasca" tune, related to a rustic dance from northern Italy that came to be widely employed as a variation theme in seventeenth-century keyboard music. Frescobaldi's *Bergamasca* variations in G major, at

FIGURE 5-12

Variation 30: Quodlibet, *Goldberg Variations*, BWV 988: *Clavier-Übung*, IV (1741).

the end of his *Fiori musicali* of 1635, are among the best-known variations on the tune. Some fifty years later, Buxtehude wrote a set of 32 Bergamasca variations in the same key, referring to the tune as "La capricciosa." By integrating the Bergamasca into the conclusion of his massive variation cycle, Bach—familiar with the music of these illustrious keyboard masters of the previous century—evidently sought to acknowledge them and to associate his grand composition with the heritage they had established. Few if any of his contemporaries would even have known Frescobaldi's name, let alone his music, and only the keyboard cognoscenti would have recognized the reference to Buxtehude's unpublished variation set. Yet the allusions to both composers at the very end of the *Clavier-Übung* stand as Bach's clear affirmation of the debt he owed to those who had opened the way for him.

The "Grandfather" dance tune cited at the very beginning of the quodlibet (mm. 1–2) forms a two-part canon at the octave. It is followed (mm. 2–3) by the "Bergamasca" tune, as a two-part canon at the fifth. Subsequently, different segments of both tunes appear in resourceful contrapuntal manipulations above the aria ground. Both melodies are associated with various popular texts, which differed from region to region. According to a note attributed to Bach pupil Johann Christian Kittel in a copy of the original print,[42] the "last dance" tune Bach quoted was a love song of farewell character:

Ich bin so lang nicht bei dir g'west,	I have been away from you for so long,
Rück her, rück her, rück her.	Come closer, closer, closer.

And the folk song to the Bergamasca tune carried these lyrics:

Kraut und Rüben haben mich vertrieben,	Cabbage and turnips have driven me away;
Hätt' mein' Mutter Fleisch gekocht, wär' ich länger blieben.	If my mother had cooked meat I would have stayed longer.

Regardless of which specific texts, if any, the composer may have had in mind, he succeeded in turning the thirtieth and last variation into a relaxed, humorous, evocative, and highly satisfactory culmination. Moreover, he miraculously managed to make his sophisticated contrapuntal combinations sound anything but complicated: the movement is cheerful in affect, and most certainly entertaining.

Part IV of the *Clavier-Übung* drew benefit in many ways from Bach's experiences with the three preceding parts. Though cast very much on its own terms, it effectively engages with the prevailing *Clavier-Übung* themes: formal, textural, and stylistic variety, advanced technical demands, contrapuntal sophistication, and ingenious logic of musical architecture. In one fundamental way, however, part IV distinguishes itself. In the first three volumes of the *Clavier-Übung*, there is no expectation whatever that the works included call for a consecutive performance from cover to cover. Yet the concluding volume clearly invites and indeed requires such treatment. It thus represents a truly large-scale instrumental work meant to be performed in such a manner. Undergirding the dazzling and extraordinary surface variety of the *Goldbergs*, the monothematic focus and firm structural grounding lend remarkable cohesion to the grand variation cycle, one of the most impressive ever created. In summary, the several new challenges posed by the *Aria with 30 Variations* reinforced Bach's resolve to have the four-volume compendium of his *Clavier-Übung* define the state of the art and make history in the realms of both composition and performance.

CHAPTER 6

A Grand Liturgical Messiah Cycle

Three Passions and a Trilogy of Oratorios

Bach's six oratorio-style works and his *Clavier-Übung* series fit intriguingly into the same time frame of the 1720s and 1730s. This overlap perhaps suggests an association of sorts between the two series, though they are admittedly quite distinct as groupings of opus-like works. In both cases Bach moved in novel directions, conceptualizing and realizing instrumental and vocal works of unparalleled scale. Moreover, in neither case did the composer anticipate how that particular series of compositions might eventually evolve. When conceiving the *St. John Passion* he surely intended to add, over the course of time, one or more similar works based on other gospels, shaping them in different ways. Indeed, the *St. John Passion* of 1724 was followed by two more Passion oratorios—according to St. Matthew in 1727 and St. Mark in 1731—works originating under dissimilar conditions and incorporating divergent compositional procedures. After Bach had dealt three times with the dramatic story and theologically central message of the suffering and death of Jesus Christ, a parallel oratorio project evolved between 1734 and 1738, when Bach added works corresponding to the three other principal events in the life of the biblical Jesus, as traditionally celebrated at the jubilant holidays of Christmas, Easter, and Ascension Day. While each of the six oratorio-style works was designed to function as an independent opus, any one of the Passions plus the supplementary oratorio trilogy completed the traditional liturgical cycle of the four major Christological feasts of the ecclesiastic year—a logical sequence of individual works covering the same thematic range that Charles Jennens and George Frideric Handel would draw upon a few years later for their *Messiah* oratorio of 1741.

Even though Bach, in his first year as Thomascantor, had to do considerable scrambling in order to manage the weekly church music program, he did not shy away from additional and rather ambitious projects right from the start. He made his presence notably felt just months after his arrival, opening the 1723 Christmas season with an opulent and richly instrumented Latin Magnificat that was premiered at the Vespers service on Christmas Day. Twice as long as a regular cantata and scored for five rather than the standard four voices, it represented Bach's lengthiest piece performed in Leipzig to that point. In its musical design, he paid particular attention to the handling of the extended form as it related to the content of this ancient and renowned canticle of Mary. As a framing device, he repeated the opening movement "Magnificat anima mea" (My soul doth magnify the Lord) as the final movement, using its closing verse "Sicut erat in principio" (As it was in the beginning), thus making the sense of this phrase vividly apparent. This sort of referencing and framing would become one of his hallmark devices for handling extended musical structures, notably in the oratorio-style works.

After Christmas 1723, the next occasion for a major performance was Good Friday, the highest Lutheran holiday, and Bach responded admirably to this opportunity in 1724. Easter was traditionally preceded by a *tempus clausum*, the seven-week period of Lent during which no concerted music was presented during worship services (save for the feast of the Annunciation). This break afforded Bach the working time to surpass his own splendid Magnificat, and to demonstrate yet again his undiminished ambitions as he neared the end of his first year in office. Now in charge of what was the oldest and arguably most distinguished church music establishment in Lutheran Germany, the composer considerably expanded his musical horizons by turning to the most extended—and at the time the most modern—genre of sacred music. Only three years earlier in 1721, a concerted oratorio-style Passion had been presented for the first time at the two Leipzig main churches of St. Thomas's and St. Nicholas's, by Bach's predecessor Johann Kuhnau. This had taken place as a response of sorts to the performance in 1718 of a Passion oratorio by Georg

Philipp Telemann at Leipzig's New Church (one of Leipzig's lesser churches), conducted by its music director Johann Gottfried Vogler. The highly favorable reception of the Telemann work by Leipzig audiences prompted the establishment in 1721 of a special endowment to support a Passion oratorio for the Good Friday Vespers at Leipzig's main churches. This new Vespers service, alternating annually between St. Thomas's and St. Nicholas's, was intended to replace the long-standing tradition of a musical afternoon service involving a simple liturgy of prayers, lessons, and congregational singing of hymns from the rich repertory of Passion songs, the most extensive section of the Lutheran hymnal.

At the request of the Leipzig clergy, the format of Kuhnau's *St. Mark Passion* was to comprise the unaltered text of the biblical Passion story, chorale strophes from the Lutheran hymnal, and lyric contemplations. This format purposely contrasted with the Hamburg prototype of the "modern" Passion oratorio as created by Barthold Heinrich Brockes, in which poetic paraphrases replaced the verbatim gospel text. The Brockes libretto, entitled *Der für die Sünden der Welt gemarterte und sterbende Jesus* ([The story of] Jesus, tortured and dying for the sins of the world) and published in 1712, was first set by Reinhard Keiser in the year of its origin. Its popularity began to grow quickly, especially through Georg Philipp Telemann's composition of 1716, also performed two years later at the New Church in Leipzig, where Telemann had been music director in the early 1700s.

The newly established Vespers service was held for the first time at the Leipzig main churches on Good Friday of 1721, when Kuhnau presented his *St. Mark Passion* at St. Thomas's; he once again performed it the following year at St. Nicholas's. The music of this work is mostly lost,[1] and the few surviving portions reveal a piece of modest proportions. It was built on the tradition of the seventeenth-century Passion *historia*, in the form of music set exclusively to the biblical text following the classic opening formula of the liturgical *invitatorium*: "Höret an das Leiden unsers Herren Jesu Christi nach dem heiligen Marco" (Listen to the suffering of our Lord Jesus Christ after St. Marcus). Kuhnau added chorale strophes and a few short arias with lyric reflections, but avoided all the fashionable elements that had contributed to the ever-growing popularity of the Brockes-style oratorio.

No Passion was performed in 1723, during the interim after Kuhnau's death, so it fell to his successor to pick up where he had left off. Bach turned directly to the task, electing to continue the newly established practice of the "musicalische Passion." But in doing so he followed his own agenda, transforming the Good Friday Vespers into the musical pinnacle of the year by offering a modern work of unprecedented scope and ambition. It was quite exceptional that a work of music would dominate the liturgy and take up more time than the sermon, the traditional centerpiece of the Lutheran service. The shorter first part of the musical Passion was timed in such a way that the sermon could start near the beginning of the second hour of the service. Yet there were no time restrictions for the second part of the musical work, the longer one by far in all of Bach's Passions.

ST. JOHN PASSION

The *St. John Passion*, BWV 245, was premiered at St. Nicholas's on Good Friday of 1724. Bach's first truly large-scale composition, with a performance time of almost two hours, it set the stage for what would become the high point in the annual sacred music program for the Leipzig main churches (Fig. 6-1). Since Bach, as the composer, was entirely free to choose his cantata texts, it is safe to assume that he himself selected the texts from the Gospel of John. He also followed the same general format that Kuhnau had employed, one that featured three textual-musical components: biblical narrative, chorale strophes, and lyric meditations in madrigalian poetry. Yet Bach elevated all three to a new level of musical sophistication and

FIGURE 6-1

"Herr, unser Herrscher," BWV 245/1: autograph fair copy (c. 1738).

elaboration, as he was so fond of doing in virtually every genre that he took up. Unconstrained by doctrinal considerations, he brought to the settings of contemplative poetry in particular a modern cast and an expansive structure. He also realized that the literal use of John Chapters 18 and 19, the traditional liturgical lesson for Good Friday, offered more varied and more powerful dramaturgical possibilities than did the condensed poetic paraphrases of the Brockes libretto. A brief contemplation of Brockes's poetic rendering of the scene of Jesus before Pilate will readily reveal just why Bach found it to be unpromising:

[Evangelist:] Wie nun Pilatus
    Jesum frag't,
ob er der Juden König wär?
sprach er: [Jesus:] Du hast's gesag't.
[Chor:] Bestrafe diesen Übeltäter,
den Feind des Kaisers, den Verräter.
[Pilatus:] Hast du denn kein Gehör?
Vernimmst du nicht, wie hart sie dich
    verklagen?
Und willst du nichts zu deiner Rettung
    sagen?
[Evangelist:] Er aber sag'te
    nichtes mehr.

  Aria (duet)
[Tochter Zion:] Sprichst du denn
    auf dies verklagen
kein einzigs Wort?
[Jesus:] Nein, ich will euch itzo zeigen,
was ihr durch's Geschwätz verlor't.

[Evangelist:] And when Pilate
    asked Jesus
whether he was the King of the Jews,
he spoke: [Jesus:] You said it.
[Chorus:] Punish this culprit,
the enemy of the emperor, the traitor.
[Pilate:] Can you not hear?
Do you not take in how harshly they
    accuse you?
And will you not say anything to save
    yourself?
[Evangelist:] But he said
    no more.

  Aria (duet)
[Daughters of Zion:] Are you speaking
    about these accusations
not a single word?
[Jesus:] No, I want to show you now
what you lost by the gossip.

By contrast, Luther's straightforward "classic" prose translation of this same extended scene, with its rapid dialogues, had the clear advantage not only of offering the accustomed and more immediately dramatic rendition of the story, but also of providing the crucial theological emphasis on John's particular portrayal of Christ the King. Moreover, Bach and his contemporaries would certainly not have deemed the literary style of Luther's version dated or overly stilted. Therefore Bach let the unabridged gospel serve as the principal conduit of action throughout the oratorio. Despite its being the first work of its kind, the *St. John Passion* illustrates in an exemplary way just how the composer began the process of designing a large-scale work of vocal music: as a keenly attentive reader of its basic text. It also demonstrates the remarkably varied musical solutions that he devised based on his perusal of the gospel, both in his settings of dramatic prose and also in the creation of contemplative inserts. It is entirely evident that for the composer, it was the scriptural text that primarily defined the form, content, scope, and overall character of the entire multi-movement work.

Though we can take for granted Bach's intimate familiarity with the Bible and hymnal, and also his eager study of pertinent theological litera-ture, we can only speculate as to what exactly he read, what he took away from it, and how specific passages may have served as sources of inspiration and possible bases for concrete musical decisions. The composing of can-tatas had provided Bach with considerable experience in setting librettos of biblical verse, reflective poetry, and chorale strophes. For the very different task of composing two entire gospel chapters, however, his challenge was to come up with a distinctive and aesthetically successful solution, notably in the absence of a suitable libretto. He therefore chose to supplement the extended biblical text with an appropriate array of strophes from the hymnal and also suitable contemplative lyrics from a variety of authors, including the seventeenth-century poets Christian Weise and Christian Heinrich Postel (Table 6-1). The heterogeneous choices of the non-biblical inserts and their placement suggest that Bach made these decisions himself. He also consid-ered it important to reference the famous and influential Brockes libretto of 1712, and he therefore adopted no fewer than five Brockes poems, albeit with significant alterations.

Bach was well aware of the differences between John's account and the synoptic gospels of Matthew, Mark, and Luke; for example, John's Passion story does not contain the Last Supper. In response, the composer proceeded to amend John's text by adding two short passages from Matthew, both of which enhanced the dramatic impact of specific scenes in preparation for a contemplative musical moment. He first inserted Peter's lament from Matthew 26:75 at the end of the betrayal scene, leading directly to the aria "Ach, mein

TABLE 6-1. *St. John Passion* "Herr, unser Herrscher," 1724 version;
1725 changes

BIBLICAL NARRATIVE	CHORALE STROPHES	CONTEMPLATIVE POETRY (AUTHOR)
Part I. Before the Sermon		
		1. Herr, unser Herrscher (after Psalm 8:1)
2. John 18:1–8	3. O große Lieb, o Lieb ohn alle Maße	
4. 18: 9–11	5. Dein Will gescheh, Herr Gott, zugleich	
6. 18:12–14		7. Von den Stricken meiner Sünden (after B. H. Brockes)
8. 18:15a		9. Ich folge dir gleichfalls mit freudigen Schritten (unknown)
10. 18: 15b–23	11. Wer hat dich so geschlagen (2 strophes)	
12. 18:24–27; Matthew 26:75		13. Ach, mein Sinn (Christian Weise)
	14. Petrus, der nicht denkt zurück	
Part II. After the Sermon		
	15. Christus, der uns selig macht	
16. 18:28–36	17. Ach, großer König (2 strophes)	
18. 19:18:37–19:1		
		19–20. Betrachte, meine Seel / Erwäge (after Brockes)
21. 19: 2–12a	22. Durch dein Gefängnis Gottes Sohn	
23. 19: 12b–17		24. Eilt, ihr angefochtnen Seelen (Brockes)
25. 19:18–22	26. In meines Herzens Grunde	
27. 19:23–27a	28. Er nahm alles wohl in acht	
29. 19:27b–30a		30. Es ist vollbracht (C. H. Postel)
31. 19:30b		32. Mein teurer Heiland, laß dich fragen (Brockes)
	(32.) Jesu, der du warest tot	
33. Matthew 27:51–52		34–35. Mein Herz (Brockes) / Zerfließe, mein Herze (unkown)
36. 19:31–37	37. O hilf, Christe, Gottes Sohn	
38. 19:38–42		39. Ruht wohl, ihr heiligen Gebeine (unknown)
	40. Ach Herr, laß dein lieb Engelein	

St. John Passion "O Mensch bewein" (1725 version) *substitutions and additions*

1.	III. O Mensch, bewein dein Sünde groß (figural chorale)
after 11.	11+. Himmel reiße, Welt erbebe
13.	13II. Zerschmettert mich, ihr Felsen und ihr Hügel (aria/chorale)
19–20.	19II. Ach windet euch nicht so, geplagte Seelen
40.	40II. Christe, du Lamm Gottes (figural chorale)

Sinn, wo willt du endlich hin" (Ah, my conscience, where will you flee at last), which is a reflection on Peter's desperate state of mind. The later added passage, from Matthew 27:51–52, involves the earthquake following the death of Jesus, a striking occurrence not reported by John but quite important for Bach's dramaturgy as a preparation for the subsequent arioso, which offers a reflection on the earth-shattering event: "Mein Herz, in dem die ganze Welt bei Jesus Leiden gleichfalls leidet" (My heart, while the whole world also suffers as Jesus does).

In his reading of John's narrative, Bach noted literary features not present in the other gospels, namely verbatim repeats of text and substantial textual correspondences in the quick dialogue exchanges, especially within the scenes of the trials before the High Priests and Pilate. He took these into account by giving to the crowd (*turba*) identical choruses and closely related musical treatments for the corresponding portions of text (Table 6-2). These immediately noticeable textual and musical parallelisms have long been observed,[2] but are more often than not explained as superimposed musical structures rather than text-derived design features.

TABLE 6-2. Repeated and corresponding text passages,
John 18 and 19

18:5	a*	**Jesum von Nazareth.** (Jesus of Nazareth.)
18:7	a	**Jesum von Nazareth.**
19:3	b	Sei gegrüßet, lieber **Jüdenkönig!** (Hail, King of the Jews!)
19:6	c	**Kreuzige ihn!** (Crucify him!)
19:7	d	Wir haben ein Gesetz, und nach dem Gesetz soll er sterben; denn er hat sich selbst **zu Gottes Sohn gemacht** (We have a law, and by our law he ought to die, because he made himself the Son of God)
19:12	d	Lässest du diesen los, so bist du des Kaisers Freund nicht; denn wer sich **zum Könige machet**, der ist wider den Kaiser. (If thou let this man go, thou art not Caesar's friend: whosoever maketh himself a king, speaketh against Caesar.)
19:15	c	Weg mit dem, **kreuzige ihn!** (Away with him, crucify him!)
19:21	b	Schreibe nicht: **der Jüden König**, sondern dass er gesaget habe: Ich bin **der Jüden König**. (Write not, The King of the Jews; but that he said, I am King of the Jews.)

* Letters a–d designate musical correspondences.

Another text-related musical decision involved the accumulation of *turba* choruses in the scene of Jesus before Pilate. The central and lengthy passage John 18:2–17, in which the mob functions as the driving force continually impelling Pilate, actually contains roughly half of the *turba* choruses in the entire Passion. Bach—well aware of the advantages the biblical text had over the bland treatment of Brockes—chose not to interrupt this particularly dynamic biblical section with an aria, instead inserting only the single meditative chorale strophe "Durch dein Gefängnis Gottes Sohn" (Through your captivity, Son of God).

Bach's composing score of the *St. John Passion* has not survived, but he most likely conceived the narrative *en bloc*, such that the gospel text could function as the primary structural frame of the musical score. Since the Passion had no uniform libretto and included poetic reflections by various authors from different sources, Bach was able to fold in at will the non-biblical poetic reflections as well as the chorale strophes. Removing them from this setting of the biblical narrative reveals a completely continuous composition. The coherent setting of the biblical text thus provided for the possibility of replacing certain arias and chorales with others—a potential the composer realized in the work's later versions (see page 209 below). Central to the composer's account of the Passion, however, are three particularly evocative movements that portray the biblical Jesus according to St. John in the form of three distinct yet intertwined musical vignettes as they are illuminated in the following sections.

Christ the King: "Herr, unser Herrscher"

In the Gospel of John, the scene of Jesus before Pilate comes to its climax when the Roman governor places at the top of the cross the inscription "Jesus of Nazareth, King of the Jews" in Hebrew, Greek, and Latin (John 19:19). He emphatically underscores his action by stating, "What I have written, I have written" (John 19:22). This inscription represents the grounds for Jesus's conviction, and at the same time conveys the gospel's principal theological theme, one that is more prominently incorporated in John's account than in the three synoptic gospels. Bach in turn made the theme of Christ the King the focal point of this Passion, emphasizing it through particularly assertive musical declamation in the extensive exchange between Pilate and Jesus at the beginning of part II (John 18:28–37). He set off the elaborate dialogue with two strophes of the chorale "Ach, großer König" (O great King; no. 17). Revealing Christ as the King, whose "kingdom is not of this world" (18:36), is the theological theme that originates in this central scene of John's gospel. This provided Bach with a justification for assigning to Jesus the Christological title of Lord, which thoroughly penetrates the concept of the piece as a whole—as is evident not only in the opening and concluding choral movements, but also in the internal solo movements.

The text and music of the opening chorus of the *St. John Passion* overtly and unmistakably address the Lord and Ruler. The choice of the opening phrase "Herr, unser Herrscher" (Lord, our Ruler) is an unusual, indeed a unique Passion opening, especially in the initial threefold acclamation of "Herr." The uncommon treatment continues when the movement later transitions to become a hymn of praise, with the word "verherrlichen" (glorify, magnify).

The idea of glorifying the Lord is based on the opening verse of Psalm 8, "O Lord, our Lord, how excellent is thy name in all the earth! Who hast set thy glory above the heavens." In Martin Luther's "Psalm summaries," found as psalm headings in many Lutheran Bibles and hymnals, Psalm 8 is referred to as "Weissagung von Christo, seinem Reich, Leiden und Herrlichkeit" (Prophecy of Christ, his empire, suffering, and glory). The unknown author of the poetically rather awkward text of the opening chorus took the word "Ruhm" (glory) from the psalm verse, but otherwise made verbatim use of the invocation of a daily prayer from the principal Saxon hymnal by the seventeenth-century Dresden court preacher Matthias Hoe von Hoenegg.[3] Selecting what was needed to lend a proper character to John's narrative, Bach set the text of the movement in two parts: the prayer invocation "Herr, unser Herrscher . . . ," followed by a modified and extended version of the traditional *invitatorium* (Kuhnau: "Listen to the suffering . . ."; Bach: "Show us through your Passion . . ."), with five metrically unequal lines in an overall rhyme scheme of ABBCCA:

Herr, unser **Herr**scher,	Lord, our ruler,
dessen Ruhm in allen Landen **herr**lich ist!	whose praise is glorious in all the lands!

Zeig uns durch deine Passion,	Show us through your Passion
daß du, der wahre Gottessohn,	that you, the true Son of God,
zu aller Zeit,	at all times,
auch in der größten Niedrigkeit,	even in the greatest humiliation,
ver**herr**licht worden bist.	have been glorified.

In a particularly effective musical translation of the words, Bach did not strictly observe the form of the given text: he has the da capo of the first section begin prematurely, overlapping with the last line of the second section. This clever manipulation underscores the pointed alliteration in the words "Herr, Herrscher, herrlich, verherrlichen." At one point the composer also establishes a strong contrast to the glorifying character and *forte* dynamics that dominate the music, with a sudden retreat to *piano* dynamics at the penultimate line in the second section, which speaks of "the greatest humiliation." The oratorio's sorrowful central subject is in fact musically accentuated by "crown of thorns" imagery throughout the opening movement, which acts to moderate and restrain the glorifying tone. The moving instrumental introduction translates directly into the score the imagery of the suffering Lord and King bearing the crown of thorns (eventually the focus of the arioso no. 19; see the next section). The two violins and later the basso continuo play the rolling-note pattern of the traditional musico-rhetorical figure of *circulatio*, which here suggests the Lord's crown (Fig. 6-2). This repetitive pattern constitutes the primary instrumental motif, which from measure 21 also shapes the vocal lines of "Herrscher" and "verherrlichen" throughout the entire movement. Also, again from the very beginning of the movement on, a second basic motif is introduced by the oboes and transverse flutes via consecutive dissonant intervals of minor seconds and tritones—$d/e^{\flat}$″ in measure 1, c″$/f^{\sharp}$′ in measure 2, g″$/a^{\flat}$″ in measure 3—establishing a recurrent pattern that eventually circulates through all twelve chromatic scale degrees. The sharp and piercing dissonances represent stinging thorn-pricks, and define the Lord's coronet as a crown of pain. The cumulative effect of these haunting initial instrumental sounds very much projects the dark *lamento* character appropriate for the opening of a musical Passion.

The hymn-of-praise nature of the opening movement adds a significant new facet to the pattern of lamentation that prevails in Passions by both earlier and later composers, and it differs even from the treatments in Bach's own *St. Matthew* and *St. Mark Passions*. The unusual musical character that the composer settled upon for the opening of the *St. John Passion* also gave him the idea for the corresponding final movement. Rather than having the work end with the funerary chorus "Ruht wohl, ihr heiligen Gebeine" (Rest well, you blessed limbs), he added the concluding chorale strophe "Ach Herr, lass dein lieb Engelein" (Ah, Lord, let your dear little angels). This chorale in effect echoes the beginning of the Passion, opening conspicuously with the acclaim-

FIGURE 6-2

"Herr, unser Herrscher," BWV 245/1: autograph fair copy, detail (c. 1738).

ing phrase "Ach, **Herr**" (O Lord), and ending in symmetric correspondence
to the opening chorus with a line that elevates the final chorale to a hymn of
eternal praise, "**Herr** Jesu Christ . . . / ich will dich **preisen** ewiglich" (Lord
Jesus Christ . . . / I will praise you eternally).

Man of Sorrows: "Betrachte, meine Seel"

A dramatic high point in the scene of Jesus before Pilate occurs at the moment
when the governor asks the crowd to choose between Jesus and another con-
victed man. The mob cries out that the murderer Barabbas should be the one
who is spared. Immediately thereafter, Pilate proceeds to have Jesus scourged.
The gospel (John 19:2–3) describes the action in graphic detail: "And the
soldiers plaited a crown of thorns, and put it on his head, and they put on
him a purple robe, and said, Hail, King of the Jews! and they smote him with
their hands." In the St. Matthew Passion, Bach's music conveys the imagery
of the brutal flagellation through the fierce and insistent dotted rhythm in the
accompanied recitative no. 51, "Erbarm es Gott!" (Have mercy, God!). In the
St. John Passion, however, and exactly at the midpoint of this gruesome event,
Bach places an arioso and aria (nos. 19–20) that seem completely detached
from the violent scene. The composer enhanced the contrast by setting the
immediately preceding words of the Evangelist ("und geißelte ihn"—and
scourged him, end of no. 18) in a particularly agitated manner, using the same
rhythmic pattern as he would later use in no. 51 of the St. Matthew Passion.
The subsequent arioso in E-flat major then introduces an abrupt retreat into
adagio mode in an unexpected shift of mood, presenting an entirely new and

delicate instrumental color heard neither before nor thereafter: in soft dynamics, two violas d'amore, an obbligato lute, and the *pianissimo* notes of the bass (in the 1749 performance additionally colored by a contrabassoon) set forth a highly distinctive texture and timbre (Fig. 6-3).

Evangelist (no. 18): . . . Da nahm Pilatus
    Jesum und geißelte ihn.

    Arioso (no. 19)
Betrachte, meine Seel,
    mit ängstlichem Vergnügen,
Mit bittrer Lust
    und halb beklemmtem Herzen
Dein höchstes Gut in Jesu Schmerzen,
Wie dir auf Dornen, so ihn stechen,
Die Himmelsschlüsselblumen blühn!
Du kannst viel süße Frucht
    von seiner Wermut brechen,
Drum sieh ohn Unterlaß auf ihn!

    Aria (no. 20)
Erwäge, wie sein blutgefärbter Rücken
In allen Stücken dem Himmel gleiche geht,
Daran, nachdem die Wasserwogen
Von unsrer Sündflut sich verzogen,
Der allerschönste Regenbogen
Als Gottes Gnadenzeichen steht!

Evangelist (no. 18): Then Pilate
    took Jesus and scourged him.

    Arioso (no. 19)
Behold, my soul,
    with anxious delight,
with bitter joy,
    and torn, anguished heart,
your highest good in Jesus' sorrow,
how from the thorns that pierce him
heavenly primroses bloom!
You can pick much sweet fruit
    from his bitter wormwood,
so gaze upon him without ceasing!

    Aria (no. 20)
Consider how his bloodstained back
in every aspect is like Heaven,
in which, after the watery deluge
was released upon our flood of sins,
the most beautiful rainbow
was placed as God's sign of grace!

The texts of the arioso and aria represent reworkings by an unknown author of two poems from the Passion libretto by Brockes, where they appear in two adjacent arias in the reverse order, which are connected by a short Evangelist passage.[4] The revamped arioso-aria poems invoke specific religious imagery by asking the faithful soul first to behold ("betrachte") and then to consider ("erwäge"). While the aria relates the blood-stained back of Jesus to the metaphorical rainbow, God's sign of peace, over Noah's ark, the preceding arioso serves to set up the unexpectedly quiet and reflective mood. It is inspired by the traditional image of the "Schmerzensmann" (Man of Sorrows), a trope originating in late medieval mysticism and kept alive through the later centuries. For example, it serves as the subject of the seventeenth-century Lutheran Passiontide hymn "Du großer Schmerzens-Mann" (You great Man of Sorrows),[5] taken up by Bach in the form of the four-part chorale BWV 300.[6] The Man of Sorrows represents the iconic devotional image of the suffering Jesus, portrayed wearing a crown of thorns and surrounded by flowers. In the arioso no. 19 the flowers are termed "Himmelsschlüsselblumen," keys to the heavenly gate. The well-known image of the Man of Sorrows, as seen here in the fifteenth-century painting by the Dominican friar Master Francke (Fig. 6-4), was widely disseminated through the centuries and found a place in many churches, chapels, and homes, and also in illustrated Bibles and hymnals.

FIGURE 6-3

"Betrachte, meine Seel," BWV 245/19: copy J. N. Bammler (1749).

The reversal of the two poems in Bach's Passion from their order in the Brockes libretto creates a more logical and more effective sequence: the contemplation of the Man of Sorrows now comes first, before the meditation on the rainbow sign of peace and grace. Bach's arioso no. 19 places the King with the crown of thorns at the center of the extended Pilate scene, in which the subdued music serves to obscure the noise of the cruel flagellation. Even before the bass voice of the allegorical faithful soul utters the words "Behold, my soul," the first measure of Bach's instrumental score brings to a

FIGURE 6-4

Frater Francke, "Man of Sorrows" (1435).

complete standstill the dramatic action from the preceding recitative ("and scourged him"). The ensuing movement projects an atmosphere of peaceful reflection on the image of Christ the King wearing the crown of thorns. The melody and the quiet instrumental accompaniment of the arioso perfectly complement—and indeed enhance—the expressive qualities of the poetic lines. The devotional image of the Man of Sorrows, which inspired both the tranquil sacred poem and Bach's quiet, lyrical, and surpassingly delicate musical setting, depicts the crowned King at the moment of "his greatest humiliation," as anticipated in the words of the opening chorus. The Lord and Ruler glorified in that opening movement is in fact the very same Lord now made to bear the painful crown.

Christus Victor: "Es ist vollbracht"

The special pair of solo movements within the scene of Jesus appearing before Pilate (nos. 19–20) have their weighty counterpart in the death scene, the only other solo piece in the *St. John Passion* that abruptly introduces a unique and previously unheard instrumental sonority, one well outside the realm of the contemporary orchestral vocabulary. In the aria "Es ist vollbracht" (no. 30), a viola da gamba is employed as an instrumental obbligato, accompanied only by the continuo. The aria text is derived from a poetic model by Christian

Heinrich Postel.[7] It consists of seven lines in two parts (4 + 3), possesses a clear rhyme scheme (abab | aca), and accommodates the standard ABA da capo form. Yet Bach did not adhere to the customary structuring, overriding it in unconventional fashion and creating a modified design with a significantly shortened da capo (ABA'):

A

Es ist vollbracht!	It is finished!
O Trost für die gekränkten Seelen,	O comfort for the afflicted souls,
Die Trauernacht	The night of mourning
Läßt mich die letzte Stunde zählen.	Now lets me reckon the final hour.

B

Der Held aus Juda siegt mit Macht	The hero from Judah triumphs with power
Und schließt den Kampf.	And brings the battle to a close.

A'

Es ist vollbracht!	It is finished!

Furthermore, Bach created a special sense of closure by returning in line 7 to the music of line 1. In the vocal part, however, instead of literally repeating the A section, the composer twice set only the final words of Jesus, "Es ist vollbracht" (measures 40 and 44). This phrase is taken verbatim from the text

FIGURE 6-5a

"Es ist vollbracht," BWV 245/30, copy J. N. Bammler (1749): A section.

FIGURE 6-5b

"Es ist vollbracht," BWV 245/30, copy J. N. Bammler: B section, with autograph
dynamic markings.

and music at the very end of the preceding recitative (no. 29)—in other words,
verbatim from the gospel. The initial A section had presented the same line
from no. 29 (mm. 13–14), picking up and embellishing the final words in the
manner of a French musical *tombeau* (Fig. 6-5a).

The reshaped B section allowed the composer, at this unlikely moment of
the death scene, to reintroduce the image of Christ the King as the triumphant
Hero of Judah. Amid the placid and somber sound of the trio for alto, viola da
gamba, and continuo, the composer called for the full string orchestra to erupt,
with a sudden change of tempo from ¢ *molt' adagio* to ¾ *vivace* (Fig. 6-5b).
By way of this explosive gesture, the dead Jesus is brought back to life in the
guise of the allegorical figure of the Lion of Judah (Revelation 5:5), and claims
victory over death. Bach underscores the stark juxtapositions of life and death,
triumph and defeat, by inverting the traditional ABA structure—in which the
A section ordinarily presents a full sound, and the B, reduced dynamics. In this
crucial aria, the B section is designed to overpower the framing A sections in
order to underscore the image of *Christus victor*—Christ the King defeating
the powers of death and all evil.[8]

This foreshadowing of—and indeed unmistakable reference to—the biblical event of Easter is emphasized by Bach immediately after the subsequent two-measure recitative (no. 31), with the text "and he bowed his head, and gave up the ghost." There is no other known work by Bach in which two extended arias are separated by such a very brief recitative. In the *St. John Passion*, however, he presents a victorious Christ the King, in considerable contrast to the figure of Jesus "tortured and dying for the sins of the world," as it was in the title of the Brockes libretto (see above, page 194). This dichotomy is further highlighted by the triumphant D-major bass aria "Mein teurer Heiland, lass dich fragen" (My dear Savior, let me ask you; no. 32), with its chorale interpolation "Jesu, der du warest tot, lebest nun ohn Ende" (Jesus, you who were dead live now unendingly). And in the ensuing imaginary dialogue between the faithful soul and Jesus, the answer to the pivotal double question ("Am I made free from death? Can I . . . inherit the kingdom of Heaven?") is an emphatic "Yes":

Bin ich vom Sterben frei gemacht?	Am I made free from death?
Kann ich durch deine Pein und Sterben	Can I, through your pain and death,
Das Himmelreich ererben?	Inherit the kingdom of Heaven?
. . . . . .	
Doch neigest du das Haupt	Yet you bow your Head
Und sprichst stillschweigend: Ja.	And say silently: Yes.

The two key solo numbers of the *St. John Passion*, as well as its opening chorus and concluding chorale, make abundantly clear Bach's aim and purpose in characterizing the Passion story as the story of Christ the King, lending to his first oratorio-style composition a unique unifying focus. In its setting of two full chapters of John, the work and its overall musical design drew inspiration directly from the composer's close reading of John's text and his understanding of John's theology.

The different versions of the *St. John Passion*—a Note

Bach performed four different versions of the *St. John Passion*, continuing to return to the work over a period of twenty-five years.

In addition to these presentations, he embarked around 1738 on a revision of the original score of 1724, a project that was left unfinished (BWV 245.4).[9] Only one year after the very first performance of the work, the composer decided to make significant changes. Following the example of Kuhnau, who had presented his *St. Mark Passion* in two consecutive years (first at the St. Thomas Church and then at St. Nicholas's), Bach also performed the *St. John Passion* twice in succession: in 1724 at St. Nicholas's and a year later at St. Thomas's.

The second performance of the work was not, however, a mere repeat like Kuhnau's, as Bach made considerable adjustments to the character of the Passion so as to fit the work into the continuing chorale cantata cycle of 1724/25. In this second version (BWV 245.2) he replaced the opening and concluding movements with large-scale chorale choruses: "O Mensch, bewein dein Sünde groß" (O mankind, bemoan your great sin; no. 1^{II}) and "Christe, du Lamm Gottes" (Christ, you Lamb of God; no. 40^{II}) (see Table 6-1). This change alone resulted in a distinct departure from the emphasis on John's narrative of Christ the King that Bach had so effectively pursued in the 1724 version (BWV 245.1). Moreover, he inserted in the first part of the work the additional aria "Himmel reiße, Welt erbebe" (Crack open, Heaven, tremble, World; no. 11+), a chorale elaboration, and replaced the aria "Ach, mein Sinn" (Ah, my soul; no. 13) with the aria "Zerschmettert mich, ihr Felsen und ihr Hügel" (Crush me, you rocks and hills; no. 13^{II}). Moreover, in the second part he quite understandably deleted the paired arioso-aria "Betrachte"–"Erwäge" (nos. 19–20), since the pair now lacked the opening chorus as a reference point; he replaced the two movements with the single aria "Ach windet euch nicht so, geplagte Seelen" (Ah, do not writhe so, tormented souls; no. 19^{II}).

When Bach performed the work for the third time in the early 1730s (BWV 245.3), he essentially restored the original version of 1724 with its opening chorus "Herr, unser Herrscher" but eliminated the two passages from the Gospel of St. Matthew (with some related adjustments, in order to avoid any overlap with the now extant *St. Matthew Passion*). Altogether, these changes represented a cut-and-paste process that would have been inconceivable within the uniform poetic libretto of the later *St. Matthew Passion*.

Further adjustments made to the Passion—first in the unfinished revision of the original score in a fair copy of twenty pages from the late 1730s (BWV 245.4), and then for a final performance in 1749 (BWV 245.5)—essentially restored the character and movement structure of the 1724 version. These modifications were either purely musical revisions designed to improve the score (as in the unfinished revision BWV 245.4) or involved alterations of a few text passages and the enlargement of the orchestra (as in BWV 245.5), amendments which clearly indicate that the composer never brought the ongoing process of revising his *St. John Passion* to a definitive end. Nevertheless, none of the changes made after the second version of 1725 affected the essential design of the first version, which so brilliantly embodied Bach's original musical response to John's gospel.

ST. MATTHEW PASSION

The creative premises for the St. Matthew Passion, BWV 244, were fundamentally different from the conditions under which the first Passion had originated. Besides benefitting from the earlier example, Bach also now enjoyed time for advance planning, having brought to a conclusion the consummately demanding 1724/25 chorale cantata cycle. That year had been the busiest of his life, and now in his third academic season he purposefully tapered off his production of cantatas. Moreover, in the spring of 1725 he began collaborating with an ambitious twenty-five-year-old amateur poet, Christian Friedrich Henrici. When and how the two met remains unknown, but Bach must have taken notice of him in late 1724 when Henrici, under the pen name Picander, began publishing in installments a series of devotional poems for the Sundays and feast days of the ecclesiastical year, under the title Sammlung erbaulicher Gedanken (Collection of edifying thoughts). The composer proceeded to hire Henrici for the text of the secular Tafel-Music "Entfliehet, verschwindet, entweichet, ihr Sorgen" BWV 249.1, which had been commissioned for the birthday celebrations of Duke Christian of Saxe-Weißenfels on February 23, 1725. It was Henrici, then, who most likely also created the sacred substitute text (termed a parody) that was later combined with the same music to create the parody composition "Kommt, fliehet und eilet, ihr flüchtigen Füße" for the Easter Cantata BWV 249.3. Around that same time, Henrici's installment series published a libretto for a Passion oratorio[10] that was closely modeled after the Brockes example. Even though Bach was not interested in this kind of libretto, given its paraphrased biblical narrative, he apparently came to an agreement with Henrici about a new Passion libretto that would meet his requirements.

Just when Bach actually asked Henrici/Picander for a St. Matthew Passion libretto remains unknown, as does the date of its delivery. The most likely time for this commission would have been spring 1725, in the immediate aftermath of two events: the second performance of the St. John Passion, which undoubtedly raised the question of what would be offered on Good

Friday 1726, and the successful debut collaborations with Picander on the secular and sacred versions of BWV 249. The deliberate and indeed dramatic slowdown in Bach's cantata schedule for the academic year 1725/26 (see above, page 146) further suggests that he intended to carve out time for special projects, and that he initially aimed at presenting a new Passion in 1726. Yet because he eventually selected for 1726 the *St. Mark Passion* by Gottfried Keiser[11] (a work he had performed more than a decade earlier in Weimar), we can assume that the new composition was not yet ready. But there was another and likely more important reason for the pragmatic decision to perform the Keiser Passion, which related to the double-choir requirement for the *St. Matthew Passion*. As soon as the composer settled on the double-choir structure of his new Passion, he realized that the performance of the projected work would have to wait until 1727. The St. Nicholas Church, where the Good Friday Vespers would be held according to the rotational schedule, offered insufficient space for a work so ambitiously scored. A work for double choir and orchestra could be performed only at St. Thomas's, where in fact all *St. Matthew* performances would take place during Bach's lifetime. The decision that the premiere of the new work would have to be delayed until 1727 must have been made early in the planning process—a not unwelcome circumstance that afforded additional time for both librettist and composer.

TABLE 6-3. *St. Matthew Passion* (1727)

POETRY BY PICANDER	BIBLICAL NARRATIVE	CHORALE STROPHES FROM HYMNAL
Part I. Before the Sermon		
*The Daughters of Zion (I) and the Faithful (II):**		(1.) O Lamm Gottes, unschuldig
1. Kommt, Ihr Töchter (I/II)	2. Matthew 26:1–2	3. Herzliebster Jesu
	4. 26:3–13	
When the woman anointed Jesus:		
5–6. Du lieber Heiland / Buß und Reu (I)	7. 26:14–16	
When Judas took the 30 silver pieces:		
8. Blute nur, du liebes Herz (II)	9. 26:17–22	10. Ich bins, ich sollte büßen
	11. 26:23–29	
When Jesus kept the Passover:		
12–13. Wiewohl mein Herz / Ich will dir mein Herze (I)	14. 26:30–32	15. Erkenne mich, mein Hüter†
	16. 26:33–35	17. Ich will hier bei dir stehen†
	18. 26:36–38	

When Jesus quailed at the Mount of Olives:

19–20. O Schmerz / Ich will bei meinem Jesu wachen (I/II)	**21.** 26:39	**(19.)** Was ist die Ursach

After the words "O my Father, . . . let this cup pass from me":

22–23. Der Heiland fällt / Gerne will ich mich bequemen (II)	**24.** 26:40–42 **26.** 26:43–50	**25.** Was mein Gott will

When Jesus was captured:

27. So ist mein Jesus nun gefangen (I, II)	**28.** 26:51–56	**29.** Jesum lass ich nicht von mir‡

Part II. After the Sermon

The Faithful and Zion:

30. Ach, nun ist mein Jesus hin (I, II)	**31.** 26:57–59 **33.** 26:60–63a	**32.** Mir hat die Welt

After the words "But Jesus kept silent":

34–35. Mein Jesus schweigt / Geduld (II)	**36.** 26:63b–68	**37.** Wer hat dich so geschlagen

When Peter wept:

39. Erbarme dich (I)	**38.** 26:69–75	
		40. Bin ich gleich von dir gewichen
	41. 27:1–6	

After the words "It is not lawful . . . because it is the price of blood":

42. Gebt mir meinen Jesum wieder (II)	**43.** 27:7–14 **45.** 27:15–22 **47.** 27:23a	**44.** Befiel du deine Wege† **46.** Wie wunderbarlich

After the words "What evil has He done?":

48–49. Er hat uns allen wohlgetan / Aus Liebe (I)	**50.** 27:23b–26	

When Jesus was scourged:

51–52. Erbarm es Gott / Können Tränen meiner Wangen (II)	**53.** 27:27–30 **55.** 27:31–32	**54.** O Haupt voll Blut und Wunden†

When Simon of Cyrene was compelled to bear His cross:

56–57. Ja freilich will in uns / Komm, süßes Kreuz (I)	**58.** 27:33–44	

When Jesus was crucified:

59–60. Ach Golgatha / Sehet, Jesus hat die Hand (I; I, II)	**61.** 27:45–50 **63.** 27:51–58	**62.** Wenn ich einmal soll scheiden†

When Jesus was taken down from the cross:

64–65. Am Abend / Mache dich, mein Herze, rein (I)	**66.** 27:59–66	

After the words "And they sealed the stone":

67–68. Nun ist der Herr / Wir setzen uns mit Tränen nieder (I, II)		

* Section headings from Picander's libretto (1729), in translation. Roman numerals indicate choir I or II.
† Melody "Herzlich tut mich verlangen."
‡ No. 29: In 1736 replaced by "O Mensch, bewein dein Sünde groß," no. 1ᴵᴵ from the 1725 version of the *St. John Passion*.

Composer and librettist: A productive partnership

The close collaboration between Bach and Picander, as it emerged while they were working on this composition of quite unprecedented scale, is a unique aspect of the *St. Matthew Passion*. It is unmistakably and impressively documented by none other than the composer himself in the calligraphic fair copy of the work he made in 1736, nearly ten years after its first performance. There he penned in Latin on the title page, "Poesia per Dominum Henrici alias Picander dictus," and below in Italian, "Musica di G[iovanni]. S[ebastiano]. Bach" (Fig. 6-6). No other Bach score carries the name of the librettist, let alone identifies one so conspicuously. For Bach to have acknowledged his librettist so expressly in the score seems a clear indication that in the composer's view, the creative partnership had been exceptionally successful.

During the work's genesis over a period of nearly two years, Bach set three more secular librettos by Picander to music: the *dramma per musica* "Der zufriedengestellte Aeolus," BWV 205 (August 1725), the *dramma per musica* "Die Feier des Genius," BWV 249.2 (August 1726), and the birthday cantata "Steigt freudig in die Luft," BWV 36.2 (November 1725 or 1726). This activity speaks to an evolving and especially close partnership, one that would endure for more than two decades. While the composer and librettist consulted extensively during the joint Passion project, Bach the initiator and senior partner apparently exercised strong influence. Only he could have made the most fundamental decisions of immediate musical relevance, including first and foremost the establishment of a full-scale dialogue between the allegorical figures "Die Tochter Zion" (the Daughters of Zion) and "Die Gläubigen" (the Faithful), to be realized by a unique double-choir configuration. These allegorical figures had already appeared in Picander's *Erbauliche Gedanken* (1725), and as such were borrowed from the famous Brockes libretto of 1712— though neither Brockes nor Picander had placed them in juxtaposition within an overall dialogue structure. In addition, none of the numerous settings of the Brockes libretto—by Keiser and Telemann (see above), Handel (1716), Johann Mattheson (1718), Johann Friedrich Fasch (1723), and Gottfried Heinrich Stölzel (1725)—call for double choir, let alone double orchestra, which was after all the foundation for the monumental dimensions of Bach's new Passion. Absent the composer's direct input, Picander would hardly have devised the entirely unique design component of two choirs placed in poetic and musical juxtaposition.

Other libretto elements of the *St. Matthew Passion* that are driven by musical ideas include the notion of working into the poem of the opening chorus the German Agnus Dei (Lamb of God) hymn and melody, with direct implications for the movement's triple-choir scoring; and also the plan of having most arias preceded by an arioso, a decision that dictated the expansive overall format of the work. Moreover, it can be taken for granted that Bach, so intimately familiar with the Lutheran hymnal, surely took the lead in the choice of chorales. This pertains most obviously to the quintessential Passion tune "Herzlich tut mich verlangen" (I heartily request for a blessed end), related to Paul Gerhardt's "O Haupt voll Blut und Wunden" (O Head, full of blood and wounds). The chorale is strategically positioned throughout the work, with varying

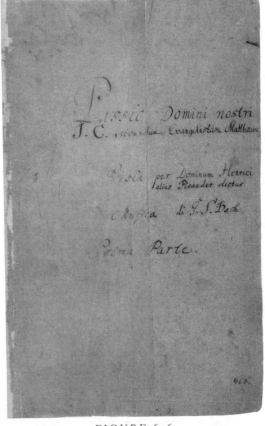

FIGURE 6-6

St. Matthew Passion, BWV 244: autograph title page (1736).

keys carefully attuned to its changing musical context, as in no. 15: *g♯'*; 17: *g'*; 44: *f♯'*; 54: *a'*; and 62: *e'*. The composer's active role in shaping the libretto is also suggested by Henrici's taking into consideration the Passion homilies by Heinrich Müller, a seventeenth-century North German theologian and devotional author whose writings the composer kept in his library.[12]

Henrici, who made a living as executive administrator of the postal service and later as chief tax collector for the city of Leipzig, published five sizable volumes of occasional poetry under his pen name Picander. Despite the impressive quantity of his output, he is frequently written off as a "Gratulantendichter" (congratulory poet), and he is definitely not counted among the more illustrious German literati. Nevertheless, given Bach's particular requirements, Picander seems to have been an ideal choice. And in the libretto of the *St. Matthew Passion*, he generally surpassed himself. Among Passion lyrics of the German Baroque, few examples can be found to equal the poetic quality and cogent theology offered up in the following verses:

No. 13

Ich will dir mein Herze schenken,	I want to give my heart to thee,
senke dich, mein Heil, hinein.	sink thyself in it, my salvation.
Ich will mich in dir versenken,	I want to immerse myself in thee,
ist dir gleich die Welt zu klein,	and if the world is too small for thee,
ei, so sollst du mir allein	ah, thus for me shalt thou alone be
mehr als Welt und Himmel sein.	more than world and heaven.

No. 27a

Mond und Licht	Moon and light
ist vor Schmerzen untergangen,	are quenched for sorrow,
weil mein Jesus ist gefangen.	because my Jesus is taken prisoner.

No. 64

Am Abend, da es kühle war,	In the evening, when it was cool,
ward Adams Fallen offenbar;	Adam's fall became manifest;
Am Abend drücket ihn der Heiland nieder.	in the evening the Redeemer laid himself down.
Am Abend kam die Taube wieder	In the evening the dove returned
und trug ein Ölblatt in dem Munde.	carrying an olive leaf in its mouth.
O schöne Zeit! O Abendstunde!	O beautiful time! O evening hour!
Der Friedensschluss ist nun mit Gott	Peace is now made with God,
gemacht,	
denn Jesus hat sein Kreuz vollbracht.	for Jesus has fulfilled his cross.

Without such strong poetry to work with, Bach would hardly have been able to create his refined and deeply moving masterwork. Indeed, he was the first to acknowledge the librettist's contribution when he prominently displayed Picander's name above his own in the autograph fair copy of the Passion.

The choir loft as virtual stage

The *St. John Passion* had no self-contained libretto, but instead consisted of interchangeable poems of diverse provenance, scattered throughout the biblical account of the events it describes. The *St. Matthew Passion*, by contrast, is built upon a poetic foundation that is complete in itself, one that provides a robust framework for the composition. The synthesis of poetry and music is underscored by Bach's collocation on the title page of the terms "Poesia" and "Musica" (Fig. 6-6), for the musical outline of the entire work was primarily determined by its madrigalian poetry and the individual meditations on scenes of the Passion story. As such, the libretto constituted a decisive precondition for the scale and musical originality of the work. And indeed, for this very reason, the biblical narrative as a whole could be excluded from the libretto in its published form,[13] which in fact offered only brief cues to pertinent gospel passages, such as "When the woman anointed Jesus" (before nos. 5–6), "When Judas took the thirty silver pieces" (before no. 8), or "When Jesus celebrated the Last Supper" (before nos. 12–13). These references sufficiently identified the moments of action around which the respective contemplative and devotional texts were focused.

True to the concept of oratorio as sacred opera, the biblical references in the libretto clearly established the organization of the biblical text into fifteen main scenes. The poetic meditations relate to these, in line with the theological tradition of the Passion story's division into separate actions. Thus the choir loft of the church became a virtual stage on which the dramatic story unfolded—without literal theatrical effects, but with an abundance of inward-directed imagery.

TABLE 6-4. *St. Matthew Passion:* Scenic organization

— Introduction to Part I (no. 1)	— Introduction to Part II (no. 30)
I. The anointing in Bethany (nos. 5–6)	VII. The interrogation by the High Priests (nos. 34–35)
II. The betrayal of Judas (no. 8)	VIII. Peter's denial (no. 39)
III. The Last Supper (nos. 12–13)	IX. Judas in the Temple (no. 42)
IV. Jesus's despair on the Mount of Olives (nos. 19–20)	X. Jesus before Pilate (nos. 48–49)
V. The prayer on the Mount of Olives (nos. 22–23)	XI. The scourging of Jesus (nos. 51–52)
VI. The seizure of Jesus (nos. 27a–b)	XII. Simon of Cyrene (nos. 56–57)
	XIII. The crucifixion (nos. 59–60)
	XIV. The descent from the cross (nos. 64–65)
	XV. The burial (nos. 67–68)

The virtual actors consist of two allegorical groups: (1) the Daughters of Zion (Choir I), representing the biblical Jerusalem, which includes the Evangelist and the historical witnesses, in dialogue with (2) the Faithful (Choir II), representing the souls of the believers or the contemporary Christian community. This diachronic scheme must be understood as a poetic idea connecting the past and the present, invoked in order to draw listeners more directly into a timeless story. Yet unlike in a staged opera, the characters—the biblical figures of Jesus, Peter, Pilate, the High Priests—were not to be personified by individual singers. Instead, Bach's original performing parts consisted of three part-books for the bass of Choir I: one for Jesus and all the bass arias of Choir I, another for Judas and Pontifex 1, and a third for Petrus, Pontifex (Caiaphas), Pontifex 2, and Pilatus. The other choir parts were designated similarly, making it clear that singers did not assume specific individual roles but instead shared them. For example, the bass concertist of Choir I was assigned the part of Jesus and all the bass arias. The virtual stage of sacred opera made possible what would not work at all on an actual stage.

The double-choir feature of the Passion is introduced in quasi-programmatic style at the very beginning of the work, in the massive opening chorus that calls for a third choir to present a chorale from the distant swallow's-nest organ gallery on the eastern (altar) end of St. Thomas's, opposite the main music gallery on the western end. The elaborate and expressive movement in E minor sets the tone for the whole, and provides a summation of what the oratorio aims to achieve in its religious, poetic, and musical messages. With its intense initial exhortation "Kommt, ihr Töchter, helft mir klagen" (Come, Daughters, help me lament), the first choir, representing the Daughters of Zion (meaning earthly Jerusalem, the biblical site of Christ's suffering), engages the second choir of the Faithful in a dialogue about the story of the innocent Lamb of God, Ruler in Zion (the celestial Jerusalem according to the New Testament Apocalypse). The first of several crowning effects occurs when the sound of the double choir in "terrestrial" E-minor mode, emanating from the rear gallery of the church, is penetrated by the liturgical Agnus Dei song, the radiant unison melody "O Lamm Gottes unschuldig" in the "celestial" G-major mode, echoing from the front balcony of the church and proclaiming Christ's innocence.

In this introductory movement, Picander's poetry achieves seamless integration, with freely conceived verse in da capo form (ABA) and a chorale strophe in bar form (AAB) blending elegantly into each other. The first line of the chorale, "O **Lamm** Gottes unschuldig" (O guiltless *lamb* of God), provides an affirmative answer to the dialogue "Seht ihn!—Wie?—als wie ein **Lamm**" (See him!—How?—Like a *lamb*). The third chorale line, "allzeit erfunden geduldig" (found *patient* at all times), answers to "Sehet!—Was?—seht die Geduld" (See!—What?—See the *patience*); and the fourth line, "all **Sünd** hast du getragen" (you have borne all *sin*), responds to "Seht!—Wohin?—auf unsre **Schuld**" (Look!—Where?—upon our *guilt*).

Although the idea of integrating the Agnus Dei song in the opening chorus may have originated with Bach,[14] Picander's meticulous poetic construction opened the way for him to compose a setting that merges the various interlocking components. At the same time, the modal E-minor/G-major dichotomy of the opening chorus creates a profound harmonic tension, one that is never resolved. Quite to the contrary, over the course of the Passion, tonal and modal contrasts grow increasingly acute across a labyrinth of keys, with a constant oscillation between sharp and flat keys leading up to the C minor of the final chorus, a tonality extremely remote from the E minor of the opening. Yet, the dominant of C minor is G major, the key of both the Agnus Dei tune and also the very first recitative that begins the biblical narrative, "Da Jesus diese Rede vollendet hatte" (When Jesus then had finished with all these sayings). G major thus functions as a key that bridges the whole, from the opening E minor/G major to the closing C minor (no. 68), including the darkest moment of the story, at Jesus's last words, "Eli, Eli, lama asabthani" (no. 61a), set in the remote keys of B♭ minor and E♭ minor.

In Picander's libretto, the opening and concluding poems in both parts of the oratorio function as prominent framing devices. Bach accordingly translated these frames into substantial aspects of musical architecture involving double-choir technique and nuanced musical effects for the virtual stage. Thus he composed the twin poem at the end of part I, "So ist mein Jesus nun gefangen" (Thus my Jesus is now captured, no. 27a), as an aria for Choir I with *bassetto* accompaniment (dispensing with low-register basso continuo) and with starkly contrasting interjections by the full Choir II: "Laßt ihn, haltet, bindet nicht!" (Leave him, stop, don't bind him!). This section leads most effectively into the fully scored chorus no. 27b, "Sind Blitze, sind Donner in Wolken verschwunden?" (Have lightning and thunder disappeared in the clouds?), projecting the high drama of a thunderstorm invoked by the seizure of Jesus. Bach's setting of the twin poem at the end of part II, devoted to the burial of Jesus (nos. 67–68), begins with a *recitativo a quattro* for Choir I, "Nun ist der Herr zur Ruh gebracht" (Now the Lord is brought to rest), with the full Choir II responding to each line of the solo voices: "Mein Jesu, gute Nacht" (My Jesus, good night). The recitative is followed by a calming and comforting minuet (no. 68) in which Choirs I and II unite in the closing text of "Wir setzen uns mit Tränen nieder" (We sit down in tears). The final C-minor chord of the Passion incorporates the piercing dissonance of a quarter-note appoggiatura (b''♮), whose delayed resolution signifies the falling of the imaginary curtain.

Bach's subtle sense of dramaturgy, effectively realized in the double-choir treatment of key numbers in Picander's libretto, is applied in equal measure to the setting of the biblical narrative, the actual core of the Passion story as told by the Evangelist. The core is in turn flanked by the various soliloquists for Jesus, Judas, Peter, Pilate, and other characters as well as the *turba* choruses for the High Priests, disciples, and other groups. In taking up this procedure, the composer benefitted significantly from the experience he had gained in writing the *St. John Passion*. In the new work, the presence of a larger perform-ing apparatus opened an array of new possibilities for composing the crowd choruses, which could now draw on double-choir scoring. Additionally, the extended overall format of the *St. Matthew Passion* (despite the work's decid-edly devotional character) allowed for a rather deliberate move in the direction of sacred opera. For example, the composer decided to emphasize the words of Jesus through *accompagnato* recitatives, with fully scored instrumental accompaniment rather than basso continuo only. This was a practice borrowed directly from opera seria, where such recitatives served in the representation of divine and royal figures.

In employing the *accompagnato* style as flexibly as he did, Bach in fact went well beyond the operatic practices of his time, which tended to make use of plainly harmonized *secco* recitatives and arioso declamation. In his ceremonial recitation of the liturgical text for communion (no. 11), Jesus's words are further accentuated through the employment of textual parallelisms. The treatment of these words exemplifies Bach's subtle mode of functional thinking: once he had settled upon an idea—here, the emphasis-laden string accompaniment— he sought to exhaust its possibilities through all possible means. For example, "Mein Vater, ist's möglich" (My father, if it is possible) in the twice-uttered prayer in Gethsemane (nos. 21 and 24) appears first in B-flat major, then in B minor, in order to intensify its impact. Bach also incorporated the inverse of this gesture, as in the setting of Jesus's last words, "Eli, Eli, lama asabthani?" (My God, my God, why have you forsaken me?," no. 61a). Here he withholds the strings at the moment of death, thereby symbolically revealing the dual nature of Christ as both God and man. Only at this juncture does Jesus's voice descend to the same level as that of all the other soliloquists. In its treatment of various kinds of text passages, the setting of the biblical narrative throughout shows a degree of sophisticated stylistic differentiation that well exceeds the more uniform text handling in the *St. John Passion*. Compare, for instance, the different treatment of the two short sentences "Wahrlich, dieser ist Gottes Sohn gewesen" (*St. Matthew*, no. 63b) and "Sei gegrüßet, lieber Jüdenkönig!" (*St. John*, no. 21b). The compact two-measure *turba* setting "Wahrlich, dieser ist Gottes Sohn gewesen" (Truly, this was the son of God) is a highly effective and moving melodic phrase in A-flat major. In the twelve-measure-long setting of a text with one less syllable, "Sei gegrüßet, lieber Jüdenkönig!" (Hail, King of the Jews!) in the *St. John Passion*, a more spontaneous and immediate sense of staged drama is apparent. Yet in the second Passion, the musical dramaturgy not only is more comprehensive but also assumes more of a liturgical character, as is made clear from the very beginning by the multidimensional opening chorus.

Human characters and emotions

Thanks to a congenial libretto and the large number of arias in the *St. Matthew Passion*, Bach could focus on the varied sorts of poetic meditations through which the human psyche—in Baroque terminology, the faithful soul—responds to the various segments of the Passion story. The music sets out a broad range of emotional and affective reactions, which were directly and unambiguously articulated by Picander in the first line of every poem (see Table 6-5). The librettist constructed the text incipit of each aria such that either the initial keywords or the opening phrase would serve to articulate the aria's basic character. Representative examples include "Repentance and remorse rips the sinful heart in two" (no. 6); "Bleed out, you loving heart!" (no. 8); "I will give you my heart" (no. 13); and "I will watch with my Jesus" (no. 20). Picander thereby provided a crucial semantic focus that served a triple function: it inspired the composer to invent a proper musical idea and suitable musical expression for the declamatory vocal part and its embracing instrumental score, it suggested a suitable *Affekt* to the singers and instrumentalists, and it guided listeners toward perceiving and internalizing the intertwined meanings of words and music.

TABLE 6-5. *St. Matthew Passion*: Scenes, arias, and individual contemplation

No.	Voice (choir)	Scene	Aria text incipit
	A(I)	I: Bethany	Buß und Reu knischt das Sündenherz entzwei (Repentance and remorse rips the sinful heart in two)
8	S(II)	II. Judas's betrayal	Blute nur, du liebes Herz! (Bleed out, you loving heart!)
13	S(I)	III. Last Supper	Ich will dir mein Herze schenken (I will give you my heart)
20	T(I)	IV. Jesus's despair	Ich will bei meinem Jesu wachen (I will watch with my Jesus) + Choir II: So schlafen unsre Sünden ein (So our sins fall asleep)
23	B(II)	V. Prayer on Mt. of Olives	Gerne will ich mich bequemen, Kreuz und Becher anzunehmen (I gladly bring myself to take on the cross and the chalice)
35	T(II)	VII. Before High Priests	Geduld! wenn mich falsche Zungen stechen (Patience! when false tongs pierce)
39	A(I)	VIII. Peter's denial	Erbarme dich, mein Gott (Have mercy, my God)
42	B(II)	IX. Judas in the Temple	Gebt mir meinen Jesum wieder! (Give me back my Jesus!)
49	S(I)	X. Jesus before Pilate	Aus Liebe will mein Heiland sterben (Out of love my Savior wants to die)
52	A(II)	XI. Scourging of Jesus	Können Tränen meiner Wangen nichts erlangen (If the tears on my cheeks can do nothing)
57	B(I)	XII. Simon of Cyrene	Komm, süßes Kreuz (Come, sweet cross)
60	A(I)	XIII. Crucifixion	Sehet, Jesus hat die Hand uns zu fassen ausgespannt, kommt! (Look, Jesus has stretched out his hands to embrace us, come!) + Choir II: Wohin? wo? (Where? where?)
65	B(I)	XIV. Descent from cross	Mache dich, mein Herze, rein (Make yourself pure, my heart)

For the majority of the madrigalian texts, the librettist halted the narration or action and then introduced the moment of contemplation, supplying a few short descriptive verses before continuing on to the main devotional reflection. The introductory features and the devotional core ideas were each time realized by the composer with a quasi-preluding arioso followed by the aria. For example, the relevant moment in the Bethany scene is realized in arioso no. 5, which focuses on the central imagery of the scene: the woman of Bethany pouring precious water upon Jesus's head. This is set by Bach in the form of an arioso recitative, with a word-painting instrumental motif of trickling water, preparing for the extended contemplative meditation (no. 6) on the woman's gracious gesture, and the unworthy reaction of Jesus's disciples in the spirit of "repentance and remorse" that "rips the sinful heart in two." As this happens to be the very first aria of the Passion, it also encourages the audience to adopt a penitent attitude as they listen devoutly to the unfolding Passion story.

The various ariosos that precede almost all the arias of the *St. Matthew Passion* play a particularly critical role. They offer a broad spectrum of intensive solo writing, realized with a great variety of instrumental scoring and with distinctive motifs, illustrative musical imagery, and notably expressive harmonic textures. A special case in point is "Ach Golgatha, unselges Golgatha!" (Alas, Golgotha, unfortunate Golgotha, no. 59), a piece in A-flat major that has no parallel in terms of extreme harmonic progressions, over a continuo bass that ranges as far as G♭, c♭, and F♭. The arioso ends strikingly, with the final g′ in the vocal line over an incomplete A-flat-major cadence that is resolved only by the two oboi da caccia.

The varieties of highly individualized human expression called for in the libretto of the *St. Matthew Passion* are by no means typical of ordinary church cantata texts, in that they tend to address complex issues of faith, symbolism, and theological doctrine. This is not to say, however, that Picander's libretto places the entire emphasis on abstruse doctrinal content. On the contrary, he also at times employed easy-to-understand keywords and phrases that relate to individual emotional expression, such as "Ich will dir mein Herze schenken" (I will give you my heart), or "Mache dich, mein Herze, rein" (Make yourself pure, my heart). Such straightforward and unpretentious language stood in contrast to the more convoluted literary style of the Brockes libretto, and helped Bach to generate vivid musical ideas that would underscore, illuminate, and enhance the meanings of the poetic incipits. In this regard, and even within Bach's own works, the *St. Matthew Passion* stands alone as a conceptually unified and thoroughly original opus.

ST. MARK PASSION

Although the 1731 *St. Mark Passion*, BWV 247, is commonly referred to as Bach's "lost" Passion setting, a good deal can nevertheless be said regarding its genesis, structure, and content. The compositional procedures for this opus were somewhat different from those followed in the two earlier Passions, in that this "new" work made substantial use of preexisting musical material, thereby also establishing a model for the later oratorio trilogy. While the *St. John* and *St. Matthew Passions* were founded conceptually on biblical narrative and madrigalian poetry, respectively, the point of departure for the *St. Mark* lay in the composer's desire to find a home within his permanent sacred repertoire for a secular work originally created for a single performance on a particular occasion. The composition in question was the Funeral Ode, BWV 198, a remarkably exquisite work that Bach had composed in November 1727, on a joint commission also involving the Leipzig university professor and poet Johann Christoph Gottsched. The Ode was destined for performance at an academic memorial service in honor of the Saxon Electress and Polish Queen Christiane Eberhardine.

In terms of functionality and character, there could hardly be a more suitable match for a musical Passion than this royal *Tombeau*. It is not known when and how Bach's plans for a Passion based on the music of the Funeral Ode emerged, but they are likely related to two events in the spring of 1729. On April 15, the second performance of the *St. Matthew Passion* took place. And about three weeks earlier in Cöthen, on March 23 and 24, Bach had presented funeral music for his former employer Prince Leopold, who had died in November of 1728. That funeral work (for which only the texts survive) was a large-scale offering that incorporated movements from both the 1727 Funeral Ode and the *St. Matthew Passion*, a combination that seems to have inspired the third Passion project. The versatile Henrici, librettist for the Cöthen funeral piece and by now Bach's house poet, agreed to parody the Gottsched text of the Funeral Ode for the projected *St. Mark Passion*, the premiere of which was set for Good Friday of 1731, a date that allowed for sufficient preparatory time.

Bach had previously reused works composed for special, nonrecurring secular occasions by adapting them for liturgical functions. But the *St. Mark Passion* represents the first instance of a large-scale secular adaptation that required the integration of preexisting music into a larger structure, one comprising both multiple chorale strophes and extended biblical narrative with newly composed settings. In other words, this third Leipzig Passion presented the composer with a completely new set of self-imposed musical challenges. Alas, since the score of the *St. Mark Passion* is lost without a trace, one of the most regrettable casualties of the division of Bach's estate in 1750, the only concrete evidence that exists (besides the two published librettos of 1731 and 1744) consists of the parody models from the Funeral Ode, BWV 198, and various chorale settings transmitted in manuscripts and early prints (Table 6-6).

TABLE 6-6. *St. Mark Passion* (1731)

PARODY SOURCE	POETRY BY PICANDER*	BIBLICAL NARRATIVE	CHORALE STROPHES	BWV
Part I. Before the Sermon				
98/1	1. Geh, Jesu, geh zu deiner Pein	2. Mark 14:1–5a	3. Sie stellen uns wie Ketzern nach	257†
		4. 14:5b–11	5. Mir hat die Welt trüglich gericht'	248/46†
		6. 14:12–19	7. Ich, ich und meine Sünden	393†
		8. 14:20–25		
98/5	9. Mein Heiland, dich vergeß ich nicht	10. 14:26–28	11. Wach auf, o Mensch, vom Sündenschlaf	397†
		12. 14:29–31a		
		12. 14:31b–34	13. Betrübtes Herz, sei wohlgemut	
	12+.* Ich lasse dich, mein Jesu, nicht	14. 14:35–36	15. Machs mit mir, Gott, nach deiner Güt	
		16. 14:37–42		
98/3	17. Er kommt, er kommt, er ist vorhanden	18. 14:43–45		
	19. Falsche Welt, dein schmeichelnd Küssen	20. 14:46–49	21. Choral: Jesu ohne Missetat	355
		22. 14:50–52	23. Choral: Ich will hier bei dir stehen	271†
Part II. After the Sermon				
98/8	24. Mein Tröster ist nicht mehr bei mir	25. 14:53–59	26. Was Menschenkraft und -witz anfäht	257†
		27. 14:60–61a	28. Befiehl du deine Wege	270†
		29. 14:61b–65	30. Du edles Angesichte	
		31. 14:66–72	32. Herr, ich habe mißgehandelt	331†
	33+.* Will ich doch gar gerne schweigen	33. 15:1–14		
	34. Angenehmes Mordgeschrei	35. 15:15–19	36. Man hat dich sehr hart verhöhnet	353†
		37. 15:20–24	38. Das Wort sie sollen lassen stahn	302†
		39. 15:25–34	40. Keinen hat Gott verlassen	369
		41. 15:35–37		
	42. Welt und Himmel, nehmt zu Ohren	43. 15:38–45	44. O Jesu, du	404
		45. 15:46–47		
98/10	46. Bei deinem Grab und Leichenstein			

* Includes additions made prior to 1744: Aria texts nos. 12+ and 33+, most likely by Picander.
† A group of four-part chorales from the manuscript collection of Bach's pupil Johann Ludwig Dietel, 1734–35.[15]

The overall plan for the *St. Mark Passion* reveals a shift in the proportions allotted to the three principal components: madrigalian poetry, biblical narrative, and chorale strophes. While the biblical text was a given, the madrigalian pieces initially numbered only eight, compared to ten in the *St. John* and seventeen in the *St. Matthew Passion*—not including ariosos, which the *St. Mark* lacks completely. Five of the contemplative poems (nos. 1, 9, 17, 24, and 46) originated as parodies of the Funeral Ode, and thus provide insight into the original musical character of these settings, if we adopt the reasonable assumption that the composer made no major changes. Movements 19, 34, and 42 may also stem from extant works, but could just as well have been newly composed. The same applies to the two movements of unknown origin that were added in the revised version (nos. 12+ and 33+), which increased the number of madrigalian pieces to a total of ten. Yet meditative lyrics are associated with only three biblical scenes in each of the two parts of the oratorio (four in the 1744 libretto). On the other hand, there are sixteen four-part chorales in the *St. Mark Passion*, thirty percent more than are present in either of the other two Passions. Nine of them happen to be transmitted together in a manuscript compilation made in 1734–35 by Bach's student Johann Ludwig Dietel, in which certain patterns typical of copying suggest that this group of chorales in fact belonged to the *St. Mark Passion*. Moreover, their manner of four-part chorale harmonization shows a consistently greater degree of contrapuntal intricacy and rhythmic animation than Bach had typically brought to bear in the past, particularly in the inner voices[16]—a trend that would continue in the *Christmas Oratorio*. Finally, there is no question that the striking preponderance of chorale settings, at the expense of extended arias, resulted in a notable reduction in overall musical density and complexity.

Bach's goal of according the *St. Mark Passion* its own profile as a less complex and dramatic musical structure is also reflected in its subdued orchestral sound, with a unique timbre derived from the unusual scoring of the Funeral Ode. The instrumental ensemble consists of two transverse flutes, two oboi d'amore, two viole da gamba, and two lutes, plus the standard strings and basso continuo. The rare additions of the viols and lutes to the orchestral tutti not only created an especially distinctive sound, but also afforded to Bach an array of possibilities for dividing the instrumental ensemble into smaller units of varied sonorities for the accompaniment of arias, without having to add special instruments to the standard string ensemble as he had done in both the *St. John* and *St. Matthew Passions*.

Since the score of the *St. Mark Passion* has not survived, however, only movements 3, 5, and 8 of BWV 198 can suggest something of the enhanced range of sonorities that Bach was able to cultivate thanks to the uncommon makeup of the ensemble. The *St. Mark Passion* also likely shared with the Trauer Ode a comparably focused tonal architecture, with a return to the home key in the final movement (Table 6-7).

TABLE 6-7. *St. Mark Passion:* Parody movements from the Funeral Ode

PASSION SCENE	MADRIGALIAN POETRY	PARODY MODELS AND SCORING
Introduction to Part I	1. Geh, Jesu, geh zu deiner Pein (Go, Jesus, go to your suffering)	← 1. Laß, Fürstin, lass noch einen Strahl (Give one backward glance, o Princess)—tutti; **C**; B minor
The Last Supper	9. Mein Heiland, dich vergeß ich nicht (My Savior, I do not forget you)	← 5. Wie starb die Heldin so vergnügt (How died our heroine so content)—alto, va da gamba I, II, lute I, II, bc; $\frac{12}{8}$; D major
Peter's denial*	12+. Ich lasse dich, mein Jesu, nicht (I will not leave you, my Jesus)	
Prayer on Mt. of Olives	17. Er kommt, er kommt, er ist vorhanden (He comes, he comes, he is here)	← 3. Verstummt, verstummt, ihr holden Saiten (Be mute, be mute, you lovely strings)—soprano, vn I, II, va, bc; **C**; B minor
Betrayal of Judas	19. Falsche Welt, dein schmeichelnd Küssen (False world, your flattering kisses)	
Introduction to Part II	24. Mein Tröster ist nicht mehr bei mir (My consoler is no longer with me)	← 8. Der Ewigkeit saphirnes Haus (Eternity's sapphired halls)—tenor, fl trav I, ob d'am I, strings, bc; $\frac{3}{4}$; E minor
Jesus before Pilate*	33+. Will ich doch gar gerne schweigen (Even though I want to remain silent)	
Scourging of Jesus	34. Angenehmes Mordgeschrei (Pleasant bloodthirsty clamor)	
Death of Jesus	42. Welt und Himmel, nehmt zu Ohren (Earth and Heaven, listen)	
Burial	46. Bei deinem Grab und Leichenstein (At your grave and tombstone)	← 10. Doch Königin! du stirbest nicht (No, Queen, you shall not die)—tutti; $\frac{12}{8}$; B minor

* Added before 1744.

The treatment of the biblical narrative from the Gospel of St. Mark, a particularly critical area, eludes any judgment because the musical setting could only have been originally composed throughout (as with the subsequent *Christmas Oratorio*), and not a trace of it is extant. While the two framing choruses and three arias from the Funeral Ode, together with a substantial body of chorale strophes, offer significant information regarding the general musical character of the Passion, no comparable substantiation regarding the dramaturgical design is available, since the aesthetic identity of the *St. Mark Passion* was rooted first and foremost in the musical treatment of the unfolding biblical story. The settings for the various soliloquists (Evangelist,

Jesus, Peter, Judas, Witnesses, High Priest, Pilate, Female Servant, Soldier, Centurion) and for the turba choruses remain completely unknown, as do the dynamic dialogues and the general pacing of the action. Therefore it is impossible, for example, to compare the settings of the words of Jesus in *St. Mark* to those in the other two Passions. While many sections in the Gospel of St. Mark have close parallels in St. Matthew, including the nearly identical "Wahrlich, dieser Mensch ist Gottes Sohn gewesen" (Truly, this man was the son of God), one would suppose that Bach composed such passages differently from the corresponding passages in the *St. Matthew Passion*, though certainly no less effectively. But in what ways would this have been? Although it is safe to assume that the musical design of the biblical narrative benefitted from Bach's experience in composing the two earlier Passions, the degree of advancement in the treatment of the drama cannot be determined—and on account of their far shorter biblical narratives, the later oratorios offer no general guidance, let alone specific information. Again, the complete disappearance of the score of the third Passion represents one of the most painful of the losses from Bach's overall output. This major oratorio-style work would, like no other, stand as a key document revealing the composer's mature command of musical dramaturgy.

This misfortune is only compounded in light of certain evidence regarding a later revision of the score, which is provided in a single surviving copy of the original libretto from 1744. A *St. Mark Passion* performance took place at the St. Thomas Church on March 27 of that year, but the amended *St. Mark* libretto with two additional arias stems from before 1744. The process of revising the Passions, which included compositional changes and additional or replaced movements, apparently began around 1736. In that year, Bach made considerable changes to the *St. Matthew Passion* and wrote out an entirely new fair copy. His revision of the *St. John Passion*, dating from the second half of the 1730s, also involved substantial musical modifications, and resulted in the beginning of a new fair copy of the score, which then broke off after twenty pages and remained incomplete. Changes he made to the *St. Mark Passion* included the addition of two arias (nos. 12+ and 33+), adjustments to the recitatives, and most likely a polishing of the entire score, which (by analogy to the other two Passions) probably necessitated the preparation of a new score copy as well. These revisions were carried out around 1740 and surely in conjunction with a performance of the work, which was followed by still another presentation in 1744. That Bach re-performed, reviewed, and made improvements to his third Passion certainly indicates that he continued to keep it in line with its sister works. The *St. Mark Passion* in its final version was smaller in scale than the other two, and definitely lacked the monumentality of the double-choir *St. Matthew Passion* (dubbed within the Bach family "die große Passion"). Yet it was chronologically the last of the three, and as such perhaps the most modern in terms of concept and style.

THE ORATORIO TRILOGY

The three sacred works specifically designated as "oratorio" form a coherent, topically interrelated group of works for the three jubilant ecclesiastical feasts of Christmas, Easter, and Ascension (Figs. 6-7a–c). They also continue the parody pattern of the mid-1730s that shaped the *St. Mark Passion*. The Latin titles that all three of them received (*Oratorium Tempore Nativit: Xsti*;[17] *Oratorium Festo Paschatos*; *Oratorium Festo Ascensionis Xsti*) emphasize their close connections and their conceptual coherence as a complementary liturgical addendum to the Good Friday Passions. For the scores of those Passion oratorios, Bach had chosen Latin titles as well (*Passio secundum Joannem*; *Passio secundum Matthaeum*); a 1728 reprint of the 1725 libretto of the *St. John Passion* refers to the work as *Actus Oratorium*.[18] Thus a grand overall design emerges in this group of six oratorio-style compositions, which were created to commemorate the major stations of the biblical Jesus's life as articulated by the Christian creed: his birth, his suffering and death, his resurrection, and his ascension to heaven.

There is no musical precedent for a coherent scheme like the one Bach conceived in the mid-1730s, one that would encompass all four of the principal Christological feast days of the ecclesiastical year. Although a notable revival of Passion oratorios had by then taken root in Lutheran Germany, following primarily from the popular 1711 Passion libretto by Brockes, there was no comparable trend involving musical settings of the biblical Christmas, Easter, and Ascension stories. Bach's cyclical embedding, as it were, of the three Passions within a complementary trilogy of oratorios therefore represented a decidedly original conception.

The jubilant character of the *Christmas, Easter*, and *Ascension Oratorios*, highlighted by the brilliant sonorities of orchestral brass, separated them as a group from the Passions, which focused on a much broader and darker spectrum of expression related to the suffering and death of Jesus. Liturgical dis-

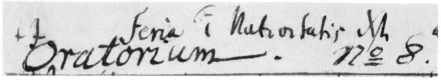

FIGURE 6-7a

Christmas, Easter, and *Ascension Oratorios:* autograph head titles (1734/35 and 1738).

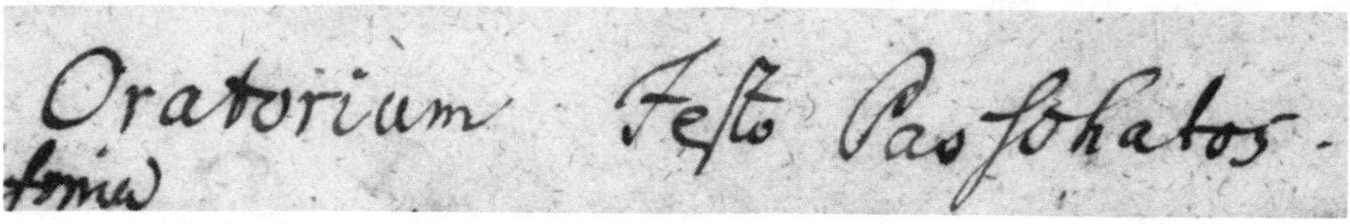

FIGURE 6-7b

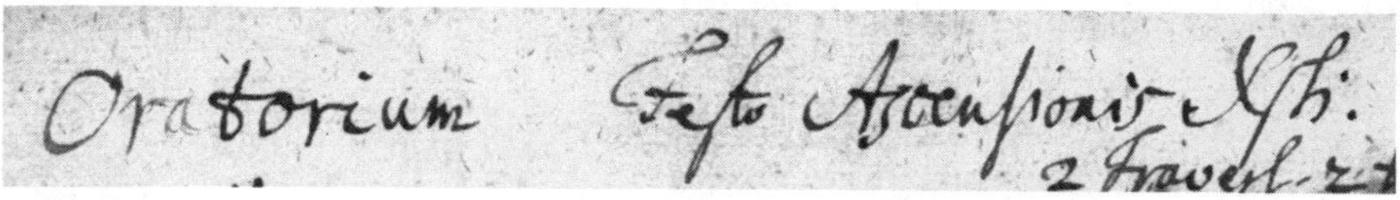

FIGURE 6-7c

tinctions also arose because the three oratorios were destined, like cantatas, to be performed as festive *Haupt-Music* (principal music) on the particular feast days, and in their proper place: before the sermon at the principal morning service and at the Vespers service (in the customary alternation between the St. Nicholas and St. Thomas churches). Therefore their duration was restricted to about half an hour (in the case of the *Christmas Oratorio,* applying to each part individually). The Passion oratorios, on the other hand, had their unique place in the afternoon Vespers on Good Friday, a true musical service with no similar restrictions regarding the length of the composition.

By focusing on the biblical narration of the life of Jesus, the three oratorios offered an alternative to the regular cantatas for Christmas, Easter, and Ascension Day that were based on non-narrating texts, and ordinarily began with biblical verses related to the prescribed liturgical lessons and ended with seasonal chorales. The *Christmas Oratorio* offers a contrasting case in point. In its omission of the liturgical readings, it underscores the deliberate conceptual distinction between an oratorio and a regular church cantata—the former serving as a musical vehicle for coherent biblical narrative and related lyric contemplation, the latter working as an exegetical and interpretive musical sermon on a biblical text. Though they may take the place of a cantata within the order of the worship service, the oratorio-style works constitute a separate type, one that accords with the contemporary definition of oratorio as "sacred opera."

Bach's oratorios are linked with his Passions in that they both feature biblical narrative as the structural backbone, although the traditional *historia* format is far more pronounced in the Passions owing to their lengthy scriptural texts. Nonetheless, Bach's renewed interest in the *historia* concept, which began with the *Christmas Oratorio* of 1734/35, may well have prompted the subsequent major revisions of his Passions, all undertaken with the goal of completing and unifying his large-scale musical cycle relating the story of the biblical Jesus.

The *historia* tradition in sacred music provided a strong common denominator, such that Passion and oratorio represented essentially the same genre for Bach, with respect to their verbatim inclusions of biblical narrative along with madrigalian poetry and chorales. The term "Passion," or "musicalische Passion," however, had for some while been firmly established in Lutheran Germany, whereas the term "Oratorium" (derived from the Italian *oratorio*) was only rarely applied and long remained loosely defined. Even Johann Christoph Gottsched, an influential critic of the time, remained rather vague in his *Versuch einer Critischen Dichtkunst* (Leipzig, 1751):

> Church pieces, generally called oratorios—that is, prayer pieces—resemble cantatas in that they, too, contain arias and recitatives. They also generally introduce various speaking personae so that there might be variety among the singing voices. Here now the poet must introduce biblical persons, from the gospels or other texts—even Jesus and God himself—or allegorical figures representing religious functions such as Faith, Love, Hope, the Christian Church, Sacred Bride, Shulamite, the Daughters of Zion, or Faithful Soul, and the like, in a speaking manner so that the outcome corresponds to purpose and place.[19]

As this passage makes clear, oratorio was generally understood as a work of narrative or dramatic content based on a text that introduced dialogue between biblical or allegorical persons. Therefore opera invariably served as a point of reference. Johann Gottfried Walther accordingly defined oratorio in the following way, in his influential *Musicalisches Lexicon* (Leipzig, 1732):

> Oratorium . . . a sacred opera, or musical performance of a sacred *historia* in the chapels or chambers of certain great lords, consisting of dialogues, duos, trios, ritornellos, large choruses, etc. The musical composition must be rich in everything that art can muster in terms of ingenious and refined ideas.[20]

The definition of oratorio as sacred opera posed a dilemma to Bach, given his contractual obligations as Thomascantor. Prior to his election, Town Councilor Steger had the town scribe record in the minutes of the meeting that he had voted for Bach, but that the latter "should make compositions that were not theatrical."[21] Not surprisingly, Bach's final pledge to the town council of May 5, 1723, included a paragraph that specified that the music "shall not last too long, and shall be of such a nature as not to make an operatic impression, but rather incite the listeners to devotion."[22]

Bach addressed the controversies regarding length and operatic character within devotional music by simply ignoring them. His church pieces were, from the beginning, considerably longer than those of his predecessors, and yet no complaints were ever recorded. As to theatrical compositions, since medieval times there had been a tradition of presenting the biblical Passion story in dramatized chanted style, with the Evangelist as musical narrator. The roles of Jesus, Peter, and Pilate were assigned to soliloquists, while the crowds of the High Priests, the people, and soldiers were represented by *turba* choruses. In his Passion oratorios Bach adhered to this tradition, making use of the biblical narrative as a structural backbone and adding contemplative sacred poetry and congregational hymns, all with the goal of "inciting the listeners to devotion." In this regard the overall shape and character of the Passion was clearly distinct from the prevailing conventions of opera. It may well be for this reason that Walther modified his definition of oratorio by expressly adding, following the term "sacred opera," the reference to "sacred *historia*" and its required biblical narrative. Bach's oratorios for Christmas and Ascension Day go in exactly the same direction, by adhering conceptually to the biblical *historia* tradition. However, as the genesis of the *Easter Oratorio* and in particular the absence of any verbatim biblical narrative therein demonstrates (see below, page 241), Bach by no means drew a strict line between *historia*, oratorio, and opera.

Another essential connection between the genres of opera and oratorio manifests itself in sacred arias borrowed from secular models. These typically dealt with human virtues, qualities, and emotions, and in their new positions in Bach's sacred oratorios, their protagonist characters still embodied correspondences to the original dramatis personae. For example, in the *dramma per musica* BWV 214, *Fama* (the mythological personification of popular rumor) enunciates the praise of the Electoress in the aria "Kron und Preiß gekrönter Damen" (Crown and prize of crowned ladies, no. 7); in the *Christmas Ora-*

torio, essentially the same character, though now a bass vocalist, pronounces the Christ child "Großer Herr und starker König" (Great lord and strong king, no. 8). In the wedding serenata BWV 1163, *Die Schamhaftigkeit* (Chastity) in dialogue with *Natur* (Nature), *Tugend* (Virtue), and *Verhängnis* (Destiny) likewise alludes to the image of "das Lilien Kleid unberührter Reinigkeit" (the lily-white gown of untouched purity) in "Unschuld, Kleinod reiner Seelen" (Innocence, jewel of pure souls, no. 5); the sacred parody in the *Ascension Oratorio*, "Jesu, deine Gnadenblicke . . . deine Liebe bleibt zurücke" (Jesus, your mercy's glances . . . your love remains, no. 5), preserves this imagery of pure love, in conjunction with the appearance of two men in white garments. Similarly, in the Serenata BWV 249.1, "Entfliehet, verschwindet, entweichet, ihr Sorgen," the nymph Doris (her Greek name meaning "pure" or "unmixed"), offers up "Hunderttausend Schmeicheleien" (A hundred thousand flatteries, no. 5); the same soprano voice and character representing the pure soul also figures in the *Easter Oratorio* parody "Seele, deine Spezereien" (Soul, your spices, no. 5). Even though such associations would have remained obscure to the oratorio listener unfamiliar with the secular models, they played a decisive role in the literary and musical process of parodying. In each such case, both poet and composer meant to preserve, if not intensify, the original character along with the related functions of theatrical expression.

Christmas Oratorio

The *St. Mark Passion* of 1731 provided the immediate point of departure for all three oratorios, as it was similarly grounded in the principle of borrowing major parts from preexisting works. This practice also related directly to Bach's activities as director of the Collegium Musicum, a position that he assumed in 1729. This association lasted for more than a decade with only brief interruptions, and represented a substantial commitment for Bach beyond his principal post of Thomascantor. The autumn of 1733 saw the beginnings of a series of performances by the Leipzig Collegium in honor of the royal family in Dresden. Following the death of Augustus "the Strong" in early 1733, Bach decided it would be advantageous to offer a suitable tribute to his musically interested son and successor, the Saxon Elector Friedrich August II (King Augustus III of Poland), whose spouse Maria Josepha (a former Hapsburg princess) was especially devoted to music.

The series of festive congratulatory compositions for the Dresden court, performed at the Collegium's "extra-ordinairen Concerten" (extraordinary concerts), began on September 5, 1733. First came the *dramma per musica Hercules am Scheidewege*, BWV 213, on the occasion of the birthday of the electoral prince Friedrich Christian. It was followed a few months later by "Tönet, ihr Pauken! Erschallet Trompeten!" BWV 214, which was presented on December 8, the birthday of the Electress Maria Josepha. Since the texts for such occasional works rendered impossible any repeat performances without major changes, the composer would have been thinking from the outset about possible opportunities for repurposing the music. For Bach, transplanting such compositions into the church repertory was a logical and highly workable solution.

When it came to sacred parody of lavish and elaborate congratulatory works originally written in honor of a royal family, only the most prominent and celebratory events of the church year were truly appropriate. The feast days from Christmas to Epiphany in the following year, 1734/35, presented to Bach an early and ideal opportunity for adapting quite a number of these newly composed occasional pieces. The *Christmas Oratorio*, BWV 248, owes its origin to plans most likely formed in 1733, during the time when Bach and Picander were jointly devising the first congratulatory cantata, BWV 213. Since festive occasions like a royal birthday and the birthday of the King of Heaven were practically interchangeable from a musical point of view, certain natural affinities were already present. Apt textual and musical allusions, such as those in the cradle song "Schlafe, mein Liebster" (BWV 213/3), could be transferred easily from the young electoral prince to the Christ Child (and BWV 248/19). This was in fact true for the Hercules Cantata, BWV 213, as a whole: six out of seven arias and choruses were incorporated into the *Christmas Oratorio*. The mythological tale of young Hercules, destined to be the strongest human on earth, could not have been more fitting both for the original occasion (anticipating the future of the young prince as ruler of Saxony and Poland) and for its sacred parody (celebrating the Christ child as the future ruler of heaven and earth). The relatively quick conversion of these compositions for the sacred context suggests a premeditated strategy for reusing both poetic and musical ideas, with the ultimate goal of creating a permanent repertoire piece.

Among Bach's large-scale vocal works, the *Christmas Oratorio* presents a quite special case. He conceived the work, both text and music, as a self-contained whole, yet its performance was spread over the six feast days of the twelve-day Christmas period, and was furthermore divided between the two main churches in Leipzig. Its creation linked the idea of a subdivided oratorio to the practice of performing cantatas for the Sundays and feast days of the church year, as indicated in the original score and in the original libretto of the 1734/35 premiere (which provides information on the alternating performance venues and times).[23] In order to make the scheme work and to create a coherent biblical narrative for the oratorio as a whole, Bach bypassed the sequence of prescribed gospel lessons for the six holidays that the regular cantatas ordinarily followed.[24] Instead he selected the story of Jesus's birth from Luke 2:1–21 for parts I–IV, followed by the stories of the flight into Egypt and the Adoration of the Magi from Matthew 2:1–12 for parts V–VI. This arrangement established a framework for the madrigalian texts that Bach commissioned from an exceptionally skilled author, in this case unnamed. Picander, the poet of the Hercules Cantata, is by far the most plausible candidate, though his printed collections do not in fact contain the text of the oratorio. Whoever accomplished the parody work was extremely skillful in recasting the original texts. Not only did meter, rhyme, and form have to be preserved in order to make the underlay of the new poems technically successful, their expressive character also had to be in accord with the *Affekt* and character of the existing music.

The text of the opening chorus of the cantata BWV 214 provides musically suggestive imagery that is lost in the *Christmas Oratorio*. For example, the successive entries of timpani, trumpets, and violins correspond only to the original text:

Cantata, BWV 214/1: "Tönet, ihr Pauken! Erschallet Trompeten! Klingende Saiten, . . ." (Resound, you drums! Ring out, you trumpets! Sonorous strings . . .)
Christmas Oratorio, BWV 248/1: "Jauchzet! Frohlocket! Auf preiset die Tage, Rühmet . . . (Exult, rejoice, arise, praise these days, extol . . .)

Nonetheless, the two texts are in complete agreement in presenting a general call to exult and rejoice. There are only a very few instances where the original and parodied texts do not match, as in the case of these two arias:

Cantata, BWV 213/9: "Ich will dich nicht hören, ich will dich nicht wissen" (I will not listen to you, I will not learn from you)
Christmas Oratorio, BWV 248/4: "Bereite dich, Zion, mit zärtlichen Trieben" (Prepare yourself, Zion, with tender efforts)

Yet Bach managed to transform the character of the later sacred movement by making two crucial changes: rescoring from unison violins in BWV 213/9 to

oboe d'amore solo with violin I in BWV 248/4, and softening the harsh articulation of the jagged staccato notes in BWV 213 (which underscore the harsh
character of the original poetic lines) via eighth-note slurs, which support a
tender declamation of the new words.

Such modifications demonstrate that beyond his perpetual concern for
overall structure, the composer was ever attuned to fine expressive details. This
emphasis extended to the subdivision of the biblical passages, the choice of
suitable chorale stanzas and the responses to text in their harmonizations, and
the placement of reflective lyrics involving parodied material. The amount of
work involved in this tailoring of music and content cannot be overestimated.
Furthermore, there is more new material in the *Christmas Oratorio* than
borrowed. New composition was supplied for the entire biblical narrative,
including such extended choruses as "Ehre sei Gott in der Höhe" (Glory be
to God in the highest), and also for all the chorale strophes. New as well were
a number of major madrigalian pieces including the opening chorus of part
V, the trio no. 51, and the aria for alto and solo violin no. 31, a particularly
intimate and introspective B-minor movement in unusual $\frac{2}{4}$ time, with refined
and exquisite vocal-instrumental articulation. Combining existing and newly
composed music toward a new end was far from a matter of mere convenience,
let alone expediency (Table 6-8): it actually presented a considerable challenge, one that in the *Christmas Oratorio* actually went well beyond what the
composer had faced in preparing the *St. Mark Passion*.

TABLE 6-8. *Christmas Oratorio* (1734/35)

PARODY MODELS	MADRIGALIAN POETRY*	BIBLICAL NARRATIVE	CHORALE STROPHES
BWV	*Part I: First Day of Christmas*		
214/1	1. Jauchzet, frohlocket, auf, preiset die Tage	2. Luke 2:1, 3–6	
*	3. Nun wird mein liebster Bräutigam		
213/9	4. Bereite dich, Zion, mit zärtlichen Trieben		5. Wie soll ich dich empfangen
		6. Luke 2:7	
*	7. Wer will die Liebe recht erhöhn		(+ Er ist auf Erden kommen arm)
214/7	8. Großer Herr, o starker König		9. Ach, mein herzliebes Jesulein
	Part II: Second Day of Christmas		
	[10. Sinfonia]	11. Luke 2:8–9	12. Brich an, o schönes Morgenlicht
		13. Luke 2:10–11	

	14. Was Gott dem Abraham verheißen		
14/5	15. Frohe Hirten, eilt, ach eilet	16. Luke 2:12	17. Schaut hin, dort liegt im finstern Stall
	18. So geht denn hin, ihr Hirten geht		
13/3	19. Schlafe, mein Liebster, genieße der Ruh	20–21. Luke 2:14	
	22. So recht, ihr Engel, jauchzt und singet		23. Wir singen dir in deinem Heer

Part III: Third Day of Christmas

14/9	24. Herrscher des Himmels, erhöre das Lallen	25–27. Luke 2:15	28. Das hat er alles uns getan
13/11	29. Herr, dein Mitleid, dein Erbarmen	30. Luke 2:16–19	
	31. Schließe, mein Herze, dies selige Wunder		
	32. Ja, ja mein Herz soll es bewahren		33. Ich will dich mit Fleiß bewahren
		34. Luke 2:20	35. Seid froh dieweil
	24. Herrscher des Himmels (repeated)		

Part IV: New Year's Day

13/1	36. Fallt mit Danken, fallt mit Loben	37. Luke 2:21	
	38. Immanuel, o süßes Wort		(+ Jesu, du mein liebstes Leben)
13/5	39. Flößt, mein Heiland, flößt dein Namen		
	40. Wohlan, dein Name soll allein		(+ Jesu meine Freud und Wonne)
13/7	41. Ich will nur dir zu Ehren leben		42. Jesus richte mein Beginnen

Part V: Sunday after New Year's Day

	43. Ehre sei dir, Gott, gesungen	44. Matthew 2:1	
	45. Wohl euch, die ihr dies Licht gesehen		46. Dein Glanz all Finsternis verzehrt
15/7	47. Erleucht auch meine finstre Sinnen	48. Matthew 2:2	
	49. Warum wollt ihr erschrecken?	50. Matthew 2:4–6	
	51. Ach, wenn wird die Zeit erscheinen		
	52. Mein Liebster herrscht schon		53. Zwar ist solche Herzensstube

Part VI: Epiphany

48.1/1	54. Herr, wenn die stolzen Feinde schnauben	55. Matthew 2:7–8	
48.1/2	56. Du Falscher, suche nur		
48.1/3	57. Nur ein Wink von seinen Händen	58. Matthew 2:9–11	59. Ich steh an deiner Krippen hier
		60. Matthew 2:12	
48.1/4	61. So geht! Genug, mein Schatz		
48.1/5	62. Nun mögt ihr stolzen Feinde schrecken		
48.1/6	63. Was will der Höllen Schrecken nun		
48.1/7			64. Nun seid ihr wohl gerochen (figural chorale)

Newly composed madrigalian texts.
BWV 213: "Laßt uns sorgen, laßt uns wachen" Dramma per musica *Hercules at the Crossroads* (Sept. 9, 1733)
BWV 214: "Tönet, ihr Pauken! Erschallet Trompeten"   Dramma per musica (Dec. 8, 1733)
BWV 215: "Preise dein Glücke, gesegnetes Sachsen"   Dramma per musica (Oct. 5, 1734)
BWV 248.1: Church cantata (text, date, and occasion unknown)

A comparison of the *Christmas Oratorio* with the three Passions reveals significant differences in conceptual approach and formal design, notwithstanding numerous comparable features. The later work clearly drew benefit from Bach's background in the Passion oratorio, and it embodies both enhanced compositional sophistication and forward-looking stylistic orientation. The sophistication is particularly noticeable in the treatment of the four-part chorales, where the subtle polyphonization of the four-voiced texture goes well beyond the chorale harmonizations of the 1720s. The chorale treatments expand even beyond the threshold set in the *St. Mark Passion*, emphasizing a stronger contrapuntal treatment of the inner parts (alto and tenor) as more active and independent vocal lines. Now each part is itself a splendid individual melody, resulting in a sublime balance of vertical and horizontal elements. The chorale settings also display notably animated rhythmic profiles, and examples of direct response to text are now a more frequent feature of the realizations. Musical elements of the choruses and arias also strongly reflect stylistic adjustments that Bach made in the 1730s. These traits were surely influenced by the diversified modern repertoire of vocal and instrumental music that had been included in the programs of the Collegium Musicum, works by Telemann, Johann Adolph Hasse, Nicola Porpora, and others. Thus the madrigalian pieces in the *Christmas Oratorio* feature a meticulous stylistic tailoring unknown in Bach's vocal music before 1730. To some extent this evolution had its roots in the secular origin of many of these numbers. Yet the stylistic advancement also reflects Bach's willingness to employ conventions currently in fashion. This trend is exemplified in the two choruses "Ehre sei dir, Gott, gesungen" (Let honor be sung to you, God, no. 43) and "Herr, wenn die stolzen Feinde schnauben" (Lord, when our proud enemies snarl, no. 54). Both of these are in a quick $\frac{3}{8}$ time *a la passepied*, displaying the memorable melodic phrases and rhythmic patterns of dance—despite the fact that they are newly composed and not of secular origin. In fact, there are other movements clearly in the dance mold, including nos. 1, 24, and 36 (similarly in fast $\frac{3}{8}$) and the minuet chorale no. 42. In these pieces, semi-concealed contrapuntal polyphony is combined with colorfully variegated instrumental scoring.

Owing primarily to its multipart structure and the distribution of its performance over several days, formal planning was necessarily a central consideration in the large-scale design of the *Christmas Oratorio*. Bach aimed at musically discernible distinctions between the six separate parts, while at the same time maintaining overall coherence. Toward this end, he established a complex organizational structure that was governed predominantly by keys, instrumental colors, and musical correspondences. According to a symmetric scheme unequaled in Bach's first two Passions, the tonal organization and the instrumental scorings were logically planned and closely interconnected (Table 6-9). All six parts of the work stand as distinct and self-contained units in both tonality and sonority. Each part is based on an individual yet closed cycle of tonally stable choruses, arias, and chorales, and is further differentiated by its use of brass and woodwinds. The home key of D major and identical instrumental scorings bookend the first three Christmas feast days, and also enclose the entire cycle. New Year's Day and the beginning of the second half of the work are announced in the sharply contrasting flat key of F major and by the distinctive sound color of paired horns.

TABLE 6-9. *Christmas Oratorio:* Keys and scorings

Part	Key structures	Strings, continuo, +
I	D—a—e—G—D	trumpets I–III, timpani, flute I–II, oboe/oboe d'amore I–II
II	G—e—C—G	flute I–II, oboe I–II, oboe da caccia I–II
III	D—A—b C—f♯—D	as in part I
IV	F—C—d—F	corno da caccia I–II, oboe I–II
V	A—f♯—b—A	oboe d'amore I–II
VI	D—A—G—b—D	as in part I

The varied orchestral scoring serves not only a formal function, but also a symbolic one. The regal sound of the trumpet choir and the brilliant trumpet solo in no. 8 set the tone for the entire work, while the singular appearance of horns in part IV underscores the threefold significance of New Year's Day, which coincides with the Feast of the Circumcision of Christ and the Feast of the Holy Name of Jesus. In part II, strings along with transverse flutes define the angelic choir, while a unique grouping of four oboes provides the pastoral backdrop for the shepherds. The combination of flutes and oboes in the Sinfonia that opens part II celebrates the arrival of the Christ child with the symbolism of music made both in heaven and on earth. The reduced scoring of the orchestra in part V communicates the lesser importance of this day within the hierarchy of the feast days. At the same time, its A-major tonality means that the arrival of part VI in D provides a sense of closure to the whole.

Beyond all this, motivic correspondences of different kinds support and emphasize the musical architecture of the oratorio. Part III is rounded off by a simple da capo design that brings a repeat of the opening chorus. The closing chorale of part I reintroduces the trumpet battery for short interludes, thus providing a reminiscence of the oratorio's beginning. The same effect occurs in part II, with the return of a motivic idea from the introductory Sinfonia. Part IV frames each line of its closing chorale with a ritornello and once again makes use of the scoring of its opening chorus. The final chorale in part VI is an extended figural setting of 68 measures that fulfills a double function, as the conclusion of the entire work and a framing reminiscence of the opening. The importance attached to the large-scale musical form—and concurrently, to the liturgical integration of the entire work—prompted Bach to devise a strong relationship between the oratorio's outer parts. He did so by employing the melody "Herzlich tut mich verlangen" for both no. 5 and no. 64, the first and last chorales. The restrained harmonized melody of the first chorale reappears in the magnificent setting of the closing chorale, where it is triumphantly elevated by the obbligato use of the orchestra. Yet the jubilant ending of this oratorio celebrating the nativity of Jesus Christ at the same time foreshadows his suffering and death: the well-known chorale melody had a tradition of dual use in Leipzig, for both the Advent hymn "Wie soll ich dich empfangen" (How should I receive You) and the Passion hymn "O Haupt voll Blut und Wunden" (O Sacred Head, full of blood and wounds). This usage links Advent and Passiontide, and it surely figured into Bach's thinking as he planned and composed the oratorio.

Easter Oratorio

External evidence suggests that Bach developed the idea of a follow-up to the *Christmas Oratorio* at the same time that this composition was taking shape. In the first place, all the works that would serve as models for *Ascension* and *Easter Oratorio* parodies predate the models for the *Christmas Oratorio*. Hence from early on the composer was fully in a position to envision an oratorio trilogy. Furthermore, Bach wrote out the score of the *Christmas Oratorio* and began the *Ascension Oratorio*, BWV 11, on the same stock of paper, which he acquired in the late fall of 1734.[25] For reasons unknown, he broke off work on the *Ascension Oratorio* after the first movement and postponed its completion to 1738, when both the *Easter* and *Ascension Oratorios* were eventually premiered.[26] Yet the overall context strongly implies that the planning for at least the first and last pieces of the trilogy dates back to the same time period. Given his suspension of work on the *Ascension Oratorio*, Bach's initial plan to prepare all three oratorios in fair copies for performances in the church year 1734/35 could not be realized. Nevertheless, the three matching titles (Fig. 6-7) document the composer's intention of serial planning. While the causes for postponing the project's completion over several years remain uncertain, we do know that in the summer of 1736 he entered into an extended conflict with the new rector of the St. Thomas School, Johann August Ernesti, who had been appointed in November 1734. This prolonged wrangle could not alone account for the delay, but possibly contributed to it.

The *Easter Oratorio* as such required relatively little preparation because it substantially duplicated the Easter Cantata, BWV 249.3, which had been based in turn on the Weißenfels Serenade, BWV 249.1. Both of these were products of the initial collaboration of Bach and Picander in 1725 (see above, pages 211 and 214), and that joint project stands as further possible evidence for Picander's later involvement in the ambitious oratorio trilogy. The Weißenfels *dramma per musica* is a theatrical Arcadian scene involving four mythological characters (Doris, Sylvia, Menalcas, and Damoetas), who playfully serenade Duke Christian. It begins with the line "Entfliehet, verschwindet, entweichet, ihr Sorgen" (Flee, vanish, yield, you sorrows), and its finale movement begins with the words "Glück und Heil, bleibe dein beständig Teil" (Fortune and health will be with you enduringly). The work's celebratory function and nature thus made it readily suitable for conversion into festal music in praise of the risen Lord. For the Easter Cantata, the roles of the four pastoral characters were exchanged for the biblical figures of four of Jesus's disciples: Mary (wife of James), Mary Magdalene, Peter, and John. As indicated by the opening line, "Kommt, fliehet und eilet, ihr flüchtigen Füße" (Come, flee and hurry, you speedy feet), Peter and John encourage the two women to join them as they run to the empty grave. The secular libretto was thus easily adapted to the biblical Easter morning scene.

The music of the arias and choruses remained the same, as the metrical structure of the new text followed the patterns of its secular model exactly. Only the recitatives had to be newly composed for the new biblical narrative. Yet the traditional gospel reading for Easter Sunday, the short lesson Mark 16:1–8, was not kept verbatim. Instead, the biblical story according to all four gospels was transformed into a poetic dialogue of exactly the sort that

Barthold Heinrich Brockes had introduced in his 1711 Passion libretto, one that differs substantially from the scriptural recitatives in Bach's Passions. Moreover, the newly created Easter Cantata included not a single chorale, thereby making it truly exceptional within Bach's output of church music. But when the composer realized that an accommodation might be desirable, he settled on performing a second cantata after the sermon on the same Easter Sunday. The piece selected for this purpose, "Christ lag in Todesbanden" (BWV 4), consisted exclusively of chorale-based movements. Another unusual feature of the Easter Cantata of 1725 was its extended instrumental introduction, a two-movement sinfonia that requires about seven minutes to perform. This may well have been the longest instrumental piece to have been performed as part of a Leipzig cantata to that point. (In 1726/27, Bach would go even further, exceeding this duration with various ambitious sinfonias for obbligato organ and orchestra, a daring innovation in cantata style that apparently faced no objections following the accepted precedent from Easter 1725.)

TABLE 6-10. *Easter Oratorio* (1738/1743)

PARODY MODEL*	EASTER CANTATA (1725)	EASTER ORATORIO (1738/1743)	BIBLICAL REFERENCES
BWV 249.1*	Picander	[Picander]	John, Matthew, Mark, and Luke
1–2. Sinfonia: *Allegro–Adagio*	=	=	
3. Aria (Duet T, B–S, A)	3. Kommt, fliehet und eilet	3. Chorus: Kommt, eilet und laufet	John 20:4
4. Recitative (Quartet)	4. O kalter Männer Sinn	=	Matthew 27:61; Mark 16:10
5. Aria (S)	5. Seele, deine Spezereien	=	Mark 16:1; Luke 24:1
6. Recitative (Quartet)	6. Hier ist die Gruft	=	John 20:1–3
7. Aria (T)	7. Sanfte soll mein Todeskummer	=	John 20:7
8. Recitative (B, A)	8. Indessen seufzen wir	=	Luke 24:32
9. Aria (A)	9. Saget, saget mir geschwinde	=	Luke 24:10
10. Recitative (B)	10. Wir sind erfreut	=	Matthew 28:8; Mark 16:10; Luke 24:23
11. Aria à 4 (S, A, T, B)	11. Preis und Dank	11. Chorus: Preis und Dank	

* **BWV 249.1:** *Tafel-Music* "Entfliehet, verschwindet, entweichet, ihr Sorgen"—Serenata for the birthday of Duke Christian of Saxe-Weißenfels (February 23, 1725).

In light of the availability of no more than three cantatas of his own composition for Easter Sunday, it seems likely that Bach performed BWV 249.3,
his first and only Leipzig work for this major holiday,[27] several times during the
decade after 1725. When he finally adopted the work for the oratorio trilogy,
he made relatively few changes for the performance of 1738—though these
were quite remarkable. First, in the revised version BWV 249.4 and the newly
written-out fair copy he renamed the work "Oratorium Festo Paschatos" to
match the other two oratorios (Fig. 6-7b). Then he not only polished the text
and refined the musical score,[28] he also quite strikingly eliminated the roles of
Peter, John, and the two Marys, rendering their parts simply as choral voices
of soprano, alto, tenor, and bass. More notable changes affected the opening
vocal movement: in the "aria duetto," originally sung by Peter and John (first
and third sections) and the two Marys (middle section), the revised text incipit
now read "Kommt, eilet und laufet" (Come, hasten and race). In a further
revision of 1743, BWV 249.5, the duet no. 3 was completely rewritten and
rescored so that it became a full-fledged four-part opening chorus; similarly,
the concluding no. 11 became a choral movement as well. Despite the reuse
of most of the existing words, the four-part choruses no. 3 and 11 neutralized
the function of the original operatic duet by simultaneously addressing and
representing the congregational audience. The exhortation "Come, hasten
and race" (to see the miracle of the empty grave) was meant to involve all.
Despite the continued absence of chorales, Bach managed to alter markedly
the oratorio by skillfully transforming its character from theatrical into devotional music.

Even in its new guise, the *Easter Oratorio* differs in certain basic aspects
from its two sister compositions, notably in the absence of scriptural text and
hymns. At the same time, the genesis of the work serves as a reminder of the
close connection between opera and oratorio, and of Bach's emerging concept
of a devotional oratorio based on a biblical story without dramatic dialogue.
He seems to have become quite fond of his *Easter Oratorio*, presenting it more
than once after 1738 and for a last time on Easter Sunday 1749, some fifteen
months before his death.

Ascension Oratorio

The conceptual aspects of the conversion of the 1725 Easter Cantata to the
Easter Oratorio in the 1730s correspond well with Bach's general concep-

tion for the oratorio trilogy. In stark contrast to the Passion story, the biblical accounts of the Christmas, Easter, and Ascension stories in all four gospels are short and contain little if any dialogue. Thus the only soliloquists in the *Christmas Oratorio*, for example, are *Angelus* (the Angel, in no. 13) and *Herodes* (King Herod, in no. 55), and both appear only in brief passages. The Angel in part II (Luke 2:10–12, "Fear not: for, behold, I bring you good tidings . . .") is assigned to the soprano voice, but the continuation of his words (verse 12, "And this shall be a sign unto you . . .") is taken up by the Evangelist—indicating that here too, Bach intended to de-emphasize the theatrical impact of music within the liturgy of the main service. The biblical text of the *Ascension Oratorio*, BWV 11, is taken from the "gospel harmony" by Luther's colleague Johannes Bugenhagen, a compilation of the biblical accounts of the four gospels and, in the case of the Ascension story, taken from Luke, Acts, and Mark.[29] The resulting short narrative consists of eight verses altogether, and was distributed over four recitatives that include but a single dialogue, in no. 7: "Two men in white garments stood beside them, who also said: You men of Galilee, why do you stand and gaze up to heaven?"

TABLE 6-11. *Ascension Oratorio* (1738)

PARODY MODELS*	MADRIGALIAN PIECES	BIBLICAL NARRATIVE	CHORALE STROPHES
	Picander (?)	Luke 24 and Acts 1	
BWV 1162/1	1. Chorus: Lobet Gott in seinen Reichen	2. Luke 24:50–51	
—	3. Accompagnato: Ach, Jesu, ist dein Abschied		
BWV 1163/3	4. Aria (A): Ach bleibe doch, mein liebstes Leben	5. Acts 1:9	6. Nun liegt alles unter dir
		7. Acts 1:10–11	
—	8. Accompagnato: Ach ja, so komme bald zurück	9. Luke 24: 52; Acts 1:12	
BWV 1163/5	10. Aria (S): Jesu, deine Gnadenblicke		11. Wenn soll es doch geschehen (figural chorale)

* BWV 1162: "Froher Tag, verlangte Stunden," cantata on a text by Johann Heinrich Winckler for the rededication of the renovated St. Thomas School (June 5, 1732); re-performed with a text by Picander under the headline "Frohes Volk, vergnügte Sachsen" BWV 1158, for the name day of Elector Friedrich August II of Saxony (August 3, 1733).
  BWV 1163: "Auf! süß entzückende Gewalt," cantata for the wedding of Peter Homann and Sibylla Mencke (November 27, 1725).

The structure of the *Ascension Oratorio,* whose unnamed librettist was most plausibly Picander, closely resembles the design of the individual parts of the *Christmas Oratorio.* Three of its five madrigalian pieces were borrowed from two lost secular cantatas of different origins and times, while everything else was newly composed (Table 6-11). The festive cantata "Froher Tag, verlangte Stunden" (Happy day, long-awaited hours, BWV 1162), performed at the rededication of the renovated and enlarged St. Thomas School on June 5, 1732,[30] provided the model for the spectacularly upbeat introductory chorus in fashionable $\frac{3}{4}$ time. The two subsequent arias were both taken from the 1725 wedding cantata "Auf! süß entzückende Gewalt" (Up, sweet enchanting force, BWV 1163). The exquisite original text by Johann Christoph Gottsched had inspired the composer to set them in a particularly delicate and expressive manner, and they preserved their gentle character in the oratorio version.

Since the original scores of all three of these parody movements have not survived, the extent of the composer's editorial adjustments and improvements to the music cannot be determined. Yet to touch upon only one example of possible alteration, the detailed articulation marks in the unison violin part of the alto aria no. 4 (which eventually would form the basis for the Agnus Dei movement of the *B-minor Mass*) introduced a new kind of stylish slurring involving slurs that cross bar lines, a detail not found in Bach's scores prior to the mid-1730s (Fig. 6-8). Corrections in the autograph score of the oratorio further indicate that the composer revised the instrumental scoring of the soprano aria no. 10. In the original, a chamber-like ensemble of two transverse flutes presents the two upper parts, while two oboi da caccia set forth the bassetto (high bass). In the oratorio, the sonority is more voluminous, with two unison flutes and one oboe for the two upper parts, and unison violins plus violas for the bassetto.

The share of new composition in the *Ascension Oratorio* is proportionally just as substantial as in the *Christmas Oratorio,* and involves the *accompagnato* recitative or arioso movements nos. 3 and 8 and also the chorale strophes. The two *accompagnato* movements, of only 11 and 7 measures respectively, very much resemble their equivalents in the *Christmas Oratorio* (nos. 7, 14, 18, 32, 40, 52, and 61), those being movements that similarly serve as quasi-preludes to the arias or, less frequently, as postludes. In this regard, the *Ascension Oratorio,* with its two particularly refined and harmonically sophisticated ariosos of the pre- and postlude types, capped the development of what seems to have been a Bachian specialty: the combination of arioso (*recitativo accompagnato*)

FIGURE 6-8

Ascension Oratorio, BWV 11/4: autograph fair copy (1738), detail.

and aria as extended points of repose for reflective meditation. Such a double feature occurred for the first time and on a more modest scale in the *St. John Passion* (nos. 19–20 and 34–35), then in a systematic fashion throughout the *St. Matthew Passion* (see Table 6-3). Strangely, this approach is totally absent from the *St. Mark Passion*, perhaps as a consequence of its greater austerity and restraint.

The two chorale movements of the *Ascension Oratorio* are distinct in character: no. 6 is a simple four-voice setting, while the concluding figural chorale "Wenn soll es doch geschehen" (sung to the melody of "Von Gott will ich nicht lassen," Erfurt 1572) is of great length, presenting the chorale tune in the soprano with a dense polyphonic underpinning that involves the entire orchestra in extended *concertato* ritornellos. In its compositional design and outsized format of 71 measures, this movement has only a single counterpart in Bach's entire vocal oeuvre: the concluding figural chorale of part VI of the *Christmas Oratorio* (68 measures). The analogous treatment extends to bimodal construction: though the chorales are based on melodies in Phrygian and minor modes, respectively, but harmonized in the key of B minor, they are in fact embedded in a radiant D-major orchestral context. This phenomenon recalls the reverse tonal and modal dualism (E minor/G major) of the opening chorus in the St. Matthew Passion, and demonstrates the range of artistic means at Bach's disposal in the 1730s. The parallel finale movements of the *Christmas* and *Ascension Oratorios* imply a carefully planned correspondence, and reveal an intention to provide an overarching device for connecting the first and last movements of a biblical story told in music. Bach in fact achieved a grand musical narration of the entire salvation story, the centerpiece of which is the Passion, framed and elevated by a trilogy of jubilant oratorios.

Around 1738, at the time when Bach was making fair copies of the scores of the *Easter* and *Ascension Oratorios,* he was also preparing a thorough revision of the *St. John Passion,* though he never completed it (see above, page 210). The fragmentary state of the *St. John Passion's* revision and the interruptions affecting the *Ascension Oratorio* between 1735 and 1738 may in fact be entirely unrelated. Nevertheless, they support the notion of persistent frustrations with the school administration that were the lot of the Thomascantor in the later 1730s. This unfortunate situation ultimately led Bach to focus increasingly on musical projects of personal interest, though at the expense of his creative investment in the Leipzig church music. The deliberate cultivation of large-scale sacred compositions and the close interconnections between the oratorio-style works of this period can hardly be coincidental, and certainly bespeak the composer's interest in expanding his musical perspectives. For example, the concluding line of the *Easter Oratorio,* "Der Löwe von Juda kommt siegend gezogen" (The lion of Judah comes marching victoriously), forms a striking link with the phrase "Der Held aus Juda siegt mit Macht" (the hero of Judah triumphs with might), from the center section of aria no. 30 in the *St. John Passion,* and this correspondence invites one to seek out further associations. The image of Christ the King in the opening chorus of the *St. John Passion,* "Herr, unser Herrscher" (Lord, our ruler), closely relates to the opening of the *Ascension Oratorio,* "Lobet Gott in seinen Reichen" (Praise God in his kingdoms), as well as to the concluding vision of Christ's "Herrlichkeit" (Lordship). The latter phrase in turn parallels the concluding line of the opening chorus in the *Christmas Oratorio,* "lasst uns den Namen des Herrschers verehren" (let us glorify the name of the Lord) and the initial line of its part III, "Herrscher des Himmels" (Lord of heaven).

In sum, Bach created a remarkable network of textual and musical correspondences across these works. The cited cross-references suggest a special and likely intentional affinity of the *St. John Passion* with the three oratorios. In fact, it appears that he had long wished to realize a cyclical performance of all four works within a single church year. He finally succeeded in 1748/49, the penultimate year that was granted to him, when he indeed arranged for performances of the complete cycle on the proper liturgical dates: the *Christmas Oratorio* from Christmas Day to Epiphany at the turn of the year 1749,[31] followed by the *St. John Passion* on Good Friday, the *Easter Oratorio* on Easter Sunday, and the *Ascension Oratorio* on Ascension Day.

Bach's sacred compositions were ultimately all intended to fulfill one and the same purpose—that of arousing, enhancing, and guiding the devotion of believers, this following from his solemn pledge upon taking the office of Thomascantor.[32] Perhaps significantly, he repeated that pledge in a personal annotation he recorded in the margins of his 1681 Bible with commentary by Abraham Calov, which he acquired in 1733. Sometime thereafter, perhaps even within the period of the genesis of the oratorio trilogy and the revisions of the Passions, he pondered the circumstances of invoking the presence of God's grace by musical means and wrote, "With a devotional music God is always in his presence of Grace."[33] This can certainly stand as a fitting motto for all of Bach's sacred music, but in particular for his imposing group of large-scale works for the major Christological feasts of the church year, the composer's grand liturgical Messiah cycle.

CHAPTER 7

In Critical Survey and Review Mode

Revisions, Transcriptions, Reworkings

F ollowing his move to Leipzig, Bach's compositional output in the 1720s increased dramatically, with a consistent production of church cantatas and an impressive output related to his other musical activities. Hence the music shelves of the "Componir Stube" (composing room), as the cantor's office at the St. Thomas School was called, must have been overflowing by 1729, when he took on the further and considerable responsibility of directing the Leipzig Collegium Musicum. Two years later, in June of 1731, the Bach family had to leave their apartment for a major expansion and renovation of the school building where they had lived for the previous eight years.[1] During the eleven-month construction phase, the entire family relocated with their belongings to temporary quarters in Hainstrasse, not far from St. Thomas Square. At the end of April 1732, they were able to return to their enlarged and renovated apartment in the school building. It remains uncertain whether the contents of Bach's office, including his instruments and substantial library, could have been accommodated without compromise at the interim quarters. He may well have been forced to place some things in temporary storage, and he surely expected better conditions upon returning to an improved and more spacious dwelling. The highly disruptive moves must have necessitated some sort of stock-taking, likely prompting the composer to examine his musical possessions closely and to separate out the more important materials from the less significant. This process might very possibly have encouraged him to purge at least a portion of his sizable collection of scores and parts, and to dispose of items no longer needed or wanted—including manuscripts of his own works.

DISPOSAL VS. PRESERVATION

The temporary relocation Bach confronted in 1731–32 was the last but by no means only forced occasion for discarding dispensable materials. The moves from Cöthen to Leipzig and from Weimar to Cöthen would certainly have prompted such actions as well, but it remains particularly curious that of all the music Bach composed in his youth, not a single piece survives in autograph manuscript. A key to this mystery might lie in the later behavior of his second son Carl Philipp Emanuel, who, while preparing an inventory of his own keyboard works in 1772, used the occasion to dispose of all early compositions. His explanatory note at the beginning of the chronological list of works stated, "I have discarded all works from before the year 1733" (the year he turned nineteen) "because they were too youthful."[2] Whether or not Carl Philipp Emanuel knew of some similar destruction by his father, the fact is that of all Johann Sebastian's music composed by age eighteen, nothing has been transmitted in autograph manuscripts. Additionally, since only a very few of his works written after 1703 and up to around 1714 exist in original scores,[3] a substantial part of Bach's early output most probably fell victim to one or more house-cleaning operations. That would also explain why the transmission of works from the period before 1715 is based largely on copies, made primarily by his students, family members, and close colleagues. Though he certainly wished in his role as teacher to supply valuable paradigms, it is understandable that later on he might have withdrawn from circulation works he no longer cared for or approved. In the absence of direct evidence, the actual volume of discarded works remains uncertain, but it seems unlikely that he waited beyond the Weimar and Cöthen years to dispose of early works he wished to disown. Yet even so, the special situation of 1731–32 offered an opportunity for him to sort things out even more thoroughly, and with a mature critical eye. It also afforded him a chance to organize for more practical access the mass of accumulated scores and parts that he did retain—a necessary precondition for much of the surveying, selecting, and borrowing from earlier works that would preoccupy him throughout the 1730s. Finally, it would have permitted him to make conscious decisions about what he wanted to preserve, not only for his own future use but beyond.

There is no question that in the early 1730s Bach developed an evolving consciousness regarding his family's and his own musical legacy. No one had done it before, so it was he who in 1735 compiled a multi-page document under the heading *Ursprung der musicalisch-Bachischen Familie* (Origin of the Bach family of musicians), an annotated family tree and genealogy with more than fifty names of musicians from six generations extending back to the sixteenth century.[4] The *Ursprung* was complemented by an analogous collection entitled *Alt-Bachisches Archiv* (Old Bach Archive) that comprised musical compositions by several seventeenth-century ancestors. Thus Bach not only saw himself as embedded in a long family tradition, he also grasped what his own (fifth) generation would pass on to the next. Two members of the sixth generation, Wilhelm Friedemann and Carl Philipp Emanuel, had by 1735 entered their own professional careers in Dresden and Frankfurt, and the proud father could content himself with strong hopes for their futures. By the same token, he had surely made his offspring well aware of their origins and their individual responsibilities for carrying on the family's estimable traditions. At the same time, he occupied himself with defining his own place in history, not merely within the family but in a broader sense, paying increased attention to considerations of posthumous reputation. Comments made in the genealogy regarding Johann Christoph Bach (1642–1703), without a doubt the most distinguished of the ancestors, set forth a discerning assessment. Johann Sebastian termed him "the profound composer," the only family member receiving such an accolade, and Carl (who eventually inherited the document and recalled his father's verdict) later added "the great and expressive composer."[5] "Profound" and "expressive" articulate the decisive qualities required of a great composer, and represent the threshold Bach set not only for his sons and pupils, but primarily for himself. They likewise would have served him as criteria for discriminating between music to preserve and pieces better disposed of.

Bach's relentless self-criticism, leading to rejection of inadequate work, was closely related to the concern for his legacy. This is made evident in a persistent quest for improvement, a constant pursuit of revision, and the ultimate aim of true "musical perfection"—a Bachian term and goal at the center of

Johann Abraham Birnbaum's essay of 1738.[6] This approach to compositional refinement was always present, deeply grounded in the composer's character and readily traceable throughout his creative life. It was further enhanced in the 1730s, however, not so much by newly written music but notably by the factor of recurring performances of a very large number of his own extant compositions. Such presentations pervaded nearly all areas of his activities: the sacred music repertoire, the Collegium Musicum programs, and the teaching of private keyboard and composition students.

The year 1731 marked something of a turning point in Bach's overall approach to the planning of future compositional projects. This was the year that brought the proud publication of Opus 1 (the collected edition of *Clavier-Übung* I) and also the initial performance of the *St. Mark Passion*, the first large-scale vocal composition based on preexisting material. Both events functioned as capstones, as it were, for they essentially concluded his involvement with the genres of suite and Passion oratorio. They also set the composer free to take up new challenges in both instrumental and vocal realms. Moreover his Opus 1, representing a significant step in terms of public exposure, had placed Bach definitively and irreversibly in the company of major composers to be reckoned with—and its three equally groundbreaking sequels only reinforced his own sense of having reached a position second to none. At the same time, and also contributing to the securing of his legacy, the third Passion paved the way for further reworkings of larger secular settings, in a manner that would greatly expand his sacred repertoire.

The emerging pattern of Bach's composing activities confirms this conclusion. He avoided returning to old routines, and to the kinds of works he now wished to leave behind: cantatas, sonatas, suites, and concertos. Naturally there were sporadic circumstances that caused him to break the pattern, and he continued to produce the occasional instrumental or vocal work, which he customarily accomplished with particularly original results. Representative examples include church cantatas, almost exclusively additions to the chorale cantata cycle, including "Wachet auf, ruft uns die Stimme," BWV 140 (1731), "Ich ruf zu dir, Herr Jesu Christ," BWV 177 (1732), "Es ist das Heil uns kommen her," BWV 9 (1734), "Wär Gott nicht mit uns diese Zeit," BWV 14 (1735), and the opening chorus of "Ein feste Burg ist unser Gott," BWV 80 (1739). There was also further instrumental ensemble music, notably the Concerto in C major for two harpsichords, BWV 1061 (1732–33), the sonatas for obbligato harpsichord and transverse flute in B minor, BWV 1030, and A major, BWV

1032 (both c. 1736), and the orchestral overture with obbligato transverse flute in B minor, BWV 1067 (c. 1738).

NO RANDOM YIELD

Apart from the examples just mentioned, and a few similar instances of individual works in the traditional genres, virtually all of Bach's major compositional projects from the 1730s onward either concentrated on groundbreaking new ideas—such as parts II–IV of the *Clavier-Übung* (Chapter 5), the *Musical Offering*, Canonic Variations on "Vom Himmel hoch," and the *Art of Fugue* (Chapter 8)—or else primarily involved the review, assembly, revision, and reuse of extant compositions. The latter encompass a rather complex set of activities that can essentially be divided into three categories: assembling extant works in revised versions, transcribing or arranging existing pieces, and integrating both extant material and new composition into larger units.

The Great Eighteen Chorales for Organ

Bach's involvement in his most ambitious project of organ music, part III of the *Clavier-Übung* (published in 1739), prompted him to look back on, appraise, and in some cases build upon what he had earlier achieved in this area. The most obvious link between the 1739 publication and earlier organ music is found in part III's large trio on the Lutheran Gloria chorale "Allein Gott in der Höh sei Ehr" (Alone to God on high be glory), BWV 676 (see Table 5-6), whose theme derived from two organ chorales that Bach had composed more than twenty years earlier:

EXAMPLE 7-1

Three ways of developing the tune "Allein Gott in der Höh sei Ehr."

In addition to the short chorale settings of the *Orgel-Büchlein*, the Weimar years had yielded many extended organ chorales built on the tradition of the large-scale settings by Dietrich Buxtehude and other North German masters— compositions that were directly associated with the long heritage of free fantasias and preludes for organ. These expansive Bach settings were not gathered in a volume, however, but were instead apparently kept in a portfolio of single manuscript fascicles, as suggested by the sole extant autograph manuscript of the Weimar version of "Nun komm, der Heiden Heiland," BWV 660.[7] The substantial chorale settings exist primarily as copies by Bach's Weimar student Johann Tobias Krebs and his Weimar cousin Johann Gottfried Walther. Since no other autograph manuscripts from the original portfolio survive, its contents and range remain essentially unknown. Yet a Leipzig manuscript, primarily in Bach's hand and comprising seventeen fair copies of revised Weimar organ chorales, offers at least a glimpse of that portfolio, in the form of a representative selection of older pieces that the composer deemed worthy of retaining.

This manuscript,[8] which Bach began around 1739, presents a highly informative picture (Table 7-1). The eighteen chorales included represent some of the most popular Lutheran hymns, and they seem to have been assembled for the purpose of preserving what the composer considered to be his finest pieces from an earlier period. The rather haphazard choice of chorales and the duplication of a number of them would not have been suitable for a collection to be published. The first fifteen chorales (BWV 651–665) were entered in Bach's own hand around 1739–1742, and reflect various degrees of revision in comparison with the earlier versions (Fig. 7-1). The alterations range from editorial polishing of individual settings, fine-tuning of voice-leading, and additions of ornaments, to more substantial revisions of the polyphonic settings, including expansions, some minor and others more significant. Nevertheless, more than half of the selected pieces were left essentially unchanged and received only minor editorial touch-ups. The prevailing calligraphic impression of most copies suggests that Bach first made the changes in the older manuscripts, before entering fair copies into the new manuscript and then disposing of the now-superfluous earlier copies. Work on the project seems to have been interrupted after about 1742, but it was resumed around 1746–47. Thereafter, apparently troubled by vision problems, Bach asked his student (and, as of 1749, son-in-law) Johann Christoph Altnickol to make fair copies of the two chorales BWV 666 and 667, while BWV 668 was still in the works.

TABLE 7-1. The Leipzig revision manuscript of the Great Eighteen Chorales, BWV 651–668

BWV	WORK	CHORALE TREATMENT	SCRIBE	VARIANCE FROM PRE-LEIPZIG VERSION
651	*Fantasia* Komm, heiliger Geist, Herre Gott	plain c.f./B (ped.); organo pleno	JSB (1739–42)	substantially expanded by 80 measures
652	Komm, heiliger Geist, Herre Gott	embellished c.f./S; 2 clav./ped.		meticulously edited, 6 measures added
653	An Wasserflüssen Babylon	embellished c.f./T; 2 clav./ped.		thoroughly revised, 6 measures added
654	Schmücke dich, o liebe Seele	embellished c.f./S; 2 clav./ped.		slightly edited
655	*Trio* Herr Jesu Christ, dich zu uns wend	plain c.f./B (ped.); 2 clav./ped.		slightly edited
656	O Lamm Gottes unschuldig (3 var.)	plain c.f./S, alto, bass (ped.)		slightly edited
657	Nun danket alle Gott	plain c.f./S; 2 clav./ped.		slightly edited
658	Von Gott will ich nicht lassen	plain c.f./T (ped.)		meticulously edited
659	Nun komm, der Heiden Heiland	embellished c.f./S; 2 clav./ped.		slightly edited
660	*Trio super* Nun komm, der Heiden Heiland	embellished c.f./S; "a due bassi"		meticulously edited
661	Nun komm, der Heiden Heiland	c.f./B (ped.); organo pleno		slightly edited, notational change
662	Allein Gott in der Höh sei Ehr	embellished c.f./S; 2 clav./ped.		slightly edited
663	*Trio super* Allein Gott in der Höh sei Ehr	embellished c.f./T; 2 clav./ped.		slightly edited, 1 measure added
664	Allein Gott in der Höh sei Ehr	plain c.f./B (ped.); 2 clav./ped.	JSB (1716–17)	thoroughly revised, notational change
665	Jesus Christus, unser Heiland	plain c.f./B (ped.)		slightly edited
666	Jesus Christus, unser Heiland	plain c.f./S	Altnickol (1747–48)	slightly edited
667	Komm, Gott Schöpfer, heiliger Geist (2 var.)	plain c.f./S, B (ped.); org. pleno		slightly edited
668	Wenn wir in höchsten Nöten sein	plain c.f./S; 2 clav./ped.	Anon. 12 (1750)	substantially expanded by 36 measures

c.f. = cantus firmus (chorale melody); S = soprano, A = alto, T = tenor, B = bass.
organo pleno = full organ; 2 clav./ped. = left and right hand on two different manuals, feet on pedal.

FIGURE 7-1

Fantasia "Komm, heiliger Geist, Herre Gott" BWV 651: autograph fair copy (c. 1739/40).

The last chorale, BWV 668, represents a special case, as it apparently occupied the composer during the last months, and perhaps even weeks, of his life. The composition represents an extended elaboration of a short setting from the *Orgel-Büchlein*. (Similarly, the immediately preceding chorale, BWV 667, "Komm, Gott Schöpfer, heiliger Geist," is a 26-measure expansion of the eight-measure-short chorale BWV 631 that originated in Weimar.) In the 1740s if not before, Bach worked on a similar enlargement of the short chorale "Wenn wir in höchsten Nöten sein" (When we are in the greatest distress, BWV 641), expanding it from nine measures to 45. Yet in the late 1740s, this longer version was apparently still not ready to be copied by Altnickol. The work in this form actually surfaced in the posthumous first edition of the *Art of Fugue* (1751), still under its original heading "Wenn wir in höchsten Nöten sein." A note in the print provides further information by explaining the inclusion of "the chorale added at the end, which the deceased man in his blindness dictated on the spur of the moment to the pen of a friend."[9] It is actually unlikely that Bach dictated the expanded chorale on that occasion, since it already existed. Relevant details are not mentioned, but the unknown friend may well have played the expanded version on Bach's pedal harpsichord for the ailing composer, who had lost his vision but was still in a working mood. Upon hearing it, Bach realized that the work could still benefit here and there from editorial improvements, and he may have proceeded to dictate some contrapuntal, melodic, and rhythmic adjustments.

Finally, in the expectation of near death, he seems to have asked the friend to change the heading to "Vor deinen Thron tret ich hiermit" (Before your throne I now appear). That final version of BWV 668 was eventually entered at the very end of the Great Eighteen manuscript, in a fair copy by a scribe provisionally called Anonymous 12.[10]

The compositional designs adopted for the extensive chorale elaborations are every bit as varied and resourceful as those found in the *Orgel-Büchlein*, while eschewing the latter's compression to small scale. Ten of the eighteen settings have a duration of more than five minutes, and the largest score, BWV 652, comprises no fewer than 199 measures. As in the *Orgel-Büchlein*, cantus firmus treatments are diverse in register placement (soprano to bass) as well as presentations in plain, moderately ornamented, and highly embellished forms. Stylistically, the pieces range from the concertato fantasia on "Komm, heiliger Geist, Herre Gott" (Come, Holy Spirit, Lord God) to the virtuoso chorale trios BWV 655 and 664, to more contemplative and expressive settings like those of BWV 654 and 659.

A comparison between the Great Eighteen and earlier versions of these works proves quite instructive. The setting of "An Wasserflüssen Babylon" (By the rivers of Babylon), BWV 653, of which two older versions exist, seems to typify the process of selecting and revising. The earliest version, probably pre-Weimar, is in a five-part score of exceptional harmonic density that makes use of double pedal—both feet simultaneously on the pedal keyboard—to facilitate presentation of the decorated chorale melody in the tenor position, played by the left hand. In Weimar Bach converted this somewhat clumsy and overly dense version into a more transparent four-part setting. The thoroughly revised Leipzig version then turned that intermediate version into a still more transparent and differentiated polyphonic score, employing elements from both earlier versions but in a realization that is now clearly distanced from the venerable North German models.

That Bach assembled an anthology of his most successful and felicitous organ chorales in a designated manuscript raises the question of whether he also prepared a corresponding collection of exemplary organ works not based on chorales, possibly including toccatas, fantasias, fugues, and other large-scale free works that were core pieces from his virtuoso recital repertoire. No Leipzig manuscript anthology containing such pieces in fact exists, but as suggested by the reference in the posthumous list of works (see Table 1-1), Bach evidently did keep together a parallel collection of individual autograph or scribal fair copies of such organ compositions. Out of what must have been a substantial number of works, however, only one autograph copy has survived, of the Prelude and Fugue in B minor, BWV 544.[11] The title page of the manuscript bears the name "Christel" in Anna Magdalena Bach's hand, indicating that it was assigned to the inheritance of her youngest son, Johann Christian, who also received his father's pedal harpsichord. When Johann Sebastian's estate was divided, the autograph of BWV 544 most probably was part of a batch of similar organ pieces destined for Johann Christian,[12] who then must have taken them all to Berlin, where he lived until 1755 with his half-brother and tutor Carl Philipp Emanuel. Although the fate of all the other organ manuscripts inherited by Johann Christian remains unknown, their temporary residence in Berlin would explain the existence and derivation of various copies made there after 1750. Several representative collections of free organ works may offer a glimpse of the youngest Bach son's inheritance, including, notably, a copy by Johann Gottfried Siebe of the Six Great Preludes and Fugues, BWV 543–548[13]—a homogeneous set of pieces quite possibly intended by the composer to be an opus-like collection.

Bach certainly devoted much care to the "legacy project" of the Great Eighteen. He eventually added to the manuscript, in his own hand, the performing version of the Canonic Variations on "Vom Himmel hoch" (Chapter 8). But during the mid-1740s his mind increasingly turned to major reexaminations, improvements, and revisions of his extant opus collections. These included the recently completed part II of the Well-Tempered Clavier (see below), and also the twenty-year-old set of six sonatas for obbligato harpsichord and violin, which received a thorough overhaul. Both working manuscripts, with autograph revisions, were replaced by fair copies made from Bach's originals by Altnickol, his trusted pupil.[14]

The Six "Schübler" Chorales for Organ

During the 1740s, Bach compiled pieces of comparable nature in two further opus-like collections, now in rearranged and revised versions: the Sechs Choräle von verschiedener Art (Six Chorales of Various Sorts), and a set of harpsichord concertos. Only the former collection was fully realized and published, around 1747/48 (Fig. 7-2). The so-called "Schübler" Chorales are transcriptions of chorale-based movements, most of them excerpted from the 1724/25 chorale cantata cycle (Table 7-2). In the 1740s, Bach re-performed most if not all of his chorale cantatas, and also made numerous revisions to these earlier works. This process apparently prompted the composer to consider transcribing a number of the movements for organ. Since the cantata movements actually originated as settings in the manner of organ chorales, the later transcriptions more or less returned the original cantata movements to their conceptual home.

TABLE 7-2. Cantata sources for *Sechs Choräle von verschiedener Art* ("Schübler" Chorales), BWV 645–650

BWV	"SCHÜBLER" CHORALE	BASED ON CANTATA MOVEMENT	DATE OF CANTATA
645	Wachet auf, ruft uns die Stimme	BWV 140/4: Zion hört die Wächter singen Scoring: tenor (c.f.), unison strings, bc	Nov. 25, 1731
646	Wo soll ich fliehen hin, or, Auf meinen lieben Gott	Lost cantata Scoring: alto, treble instrumental obbligato, bc	—
647	Wer nur den lieben Gott lässt walten	BWV 93/4: Er kennt die rechten Freudenstunden Scoring: soprano, alto, unison strings (c.f.), bc	July 9, 1724
648	Meine Seele erhebt den Herren	BWV 10/5: Er denket der Barmherzigkeit Scoring: alto, tenor, trumpet or 2 oboes (c.f.), bc	July 2, 1724
649	Ach bleib bei uns, Herr Jesu Christ	BWV 6/3: Ach bleib bei uns, Herr Jesu Christ Scoring: soprano (c.f.), violoncello piccolo, bc	Apr. 2, 1725
650	Kommst du nun, Jesu, vom Himmel herunter	BWV 137/2: Lobe den Herren, der alles so herrlich regieret / Scoring: alto, solo violin, bc	Aug. 19, 1725

FIGURE 7-2

Six Chorales, BWV 645–650: title page [Zella, 1747/48].

In 1747, Bach entrusted both the *Musical Offering* (BWV 1079) and his edition of the chorale transcriptions to the novice engraver Johann Georg Schübler of Zella, Thuringia. Just why he did so is difficult to explain. Perhaps the experienced and reputable Nuremberg publisher Balthasar Schmid, who in 1741 had printed the *Goldberg Variations* and in 1747 took on the Canonic Variations on "Vom Himmel hoch," was simply too busy to take on such time-sensitive work as BWV 1079. Or perhaps Schmid was too expensive, whereas Schübler may have been disposed to perform a favor for his former teacher Bach. However this may be, the technical quality of Schübler's engravings of both the *Musical Offering* and the chorales did not match that of Schmid. Furthermore, the print contained numerous flaws in the texts of the chorale transcriptions, which Bach subsequently corrected with ink in various printed copies that went through his hands.[15] The nature of these mistakes strongly suggests that the engraver had to work from a sloppily written and faulty manuscript, perhaps prepared by one of Bach's copyists. Since the composer did not—and at that time very possibly could not—participate in proofreading the plates, it also seems that he was not fully engaged in the project.[16] This situation may well reflect his concurrent preoccupation with elaborate compositional projects to which he assigned higher priority—namely the *Musical Offering*, the Canonic Variations, the *Art of Fugue*, and the *B-minor Mass*.

In Bach's eyes, the Six Chorales would likely have counted as a practical, homogeneous, and marketable spin-off product, one that would further elevate his status and reputation as an unrivaled composer of organ works. The collection consists of two pairs of trios (BWV 645–646, BWV 649–650) framing two four-voice settings at the center (BWV 647–648)—a symmetric organizational scheme very typical for Bach. Each setting serves as an elaboration of the given chorale melody, as indicated by the headings, which refer to the titles of the chorale melodies.[17] The organ realizations show no tendency toward establishing particular word-tone relationships (in response to the text of the specific hymn strophe of the pertinent cantata movements), but instead follow Bach's preferential approach to composing organ chorales, namely to evoke the general character of the given hymn. In this regard, the "Schübler" Chorales offer a very serviceable collection of popular Lutheran hymn tunes. Yet because this is a genuine Bachian opus, the collection also requires considerable technical facility on the part of the player.

Harpsichord Concertos

The posthumous work catalog (see Table 1-1) summarily lists "various concertos for one, two, three, and four harpsichords." The surviving repertoire of such compositions comprises thirteen works in total. A smaller group of concertos for solo harpsichord and orchestra formed a special collection in a voluminous autograph score of 53 folios, dating from the second half of the 1730s.[18] This manuscript, from around 1738 and without a title page, represents the last known major orchestral score prepared by Bach. It contains seven concertos and the very beginning of an eighth, none of them newly composed and all of them unnumbered (Table 7-3). For one reason or another, Bach did not complete what he had set out to do: he broke off the score for the last concerto after entering only the opening orchestral ritornello (leaving the last measure incomplete), and he also left empty the last system of the score (Fig. 7-3).[19]

The opening of the manuscript is quite typical of Bach's working scores. He begins with the standard formula "J. J." (*Jesu juva*, Jesus help), written just before the title entry of the first concerto (Fig.

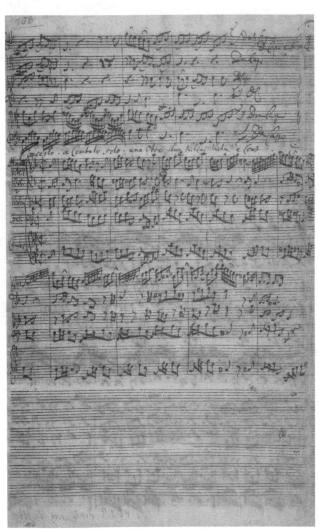

FIGURE 7-3

Harpsichord Concerto in D minor, BWV 1059/1: autograph (c. 1738).

FIGURE 7-4

Harpsichord Concerto in D minor, BWV 1052/1:
autograph (c. 1738).

7-4). Significantly, a corresponding concluding mark, "Fine. "S[oli] D[eo] G[loria]," appears after the sixth concerto, followed by eight empty staves, marking the clear end of a grouping of works (Fig.7-5). This suggests that Bach initially planned a conventional opus of six concertos. This opus would have concluded with a somewhat unusual concerto combining two recorders with the solo harpsichord, an imaginative and clever transcription of *Brandenburg Concerto 4*. Yet after completing the score containing the six concertos BWV 1052–1057, Bach apparently decided to add still more harpsichord concertos—but he somehow did not get much beyond the first of these, leaving BWV 1059 as a short fragment. There was no obvious reason for aborting the project at that particular moment.

This overall picture leaves the impression that the composer initially projected an opus of six concertos for solo harpsichord, perhaps for publication, and then considered enlarging the collection. Since the fresh start with BWV 1058 was again marked with the "J. J." initiation formula,[20] Bach had most likely envisioned an enlarged opus of two-times-six concertos—a possibility that would have allowed him to incorporate his extant concertos for two

FIGURE 7-5

Harpsichord Concerto in F major, BWV 1056/3: autograph (1738).

and three harpsichords, showcasing his innovations in this genre. He could easily have completed another collection of six concertos by appending two pairs each of works for two (BWV 1060, 1062) and three harpsichords (BWV 1063–1064).[21] Yet in the end, he did not do so. What shape and purpose Bach had in mind for a potential opus of two volumes must remain uncertain. It is possible that this ambitious endeavor may simply have grown too unwieldy and demanding in light of his many other concurrent projects. On the other hand, it is conceivable that he considered the publication of a concerto opus, perhaps in response to Handel's Opus 4, published in 1738. Balthasar Schmid, publisher of the *Goldberg Variations*, would have been a logical choice, especially since son Carl Philipp Emanuel published several keyboard concertos with him in the 1740s. Bach perhaps never fully abandoned such a plan, since during the 1740s he intermittently returned to his concerto collection in progress, continuing to enter additions and revisions in the unfinished manuscript.[22]

TABLE 7-3. Concertos for one, two, and three harpsichords and orchestra

BWV	WORK	SOLO OF ORIGINAL CONCERTO (ORIGINAL KEY)	ORGAN SOLO IN CANTATA	DATE OF CANTATA
[volume 1]				
1052	[1] Concerto in D minor	keyboard (organ or harpsichord)	BWV 146/1 and 2; BWV 188/1	1726; 1728
1053	[2] Concerto in E major	keyboard (organ or harpsichord)	BWV 169/1 and 5; BWV 49/1	1726
1054	[3] Concerto in D major	violin (BWV 1042: Concerto in E)	—	
1055	[4] Concerto in A major	? keyboard	—	
1056	[5] Concerto in F minor	mvt. 2: oboe (BWV 156/1: Sinfonia in F)		1729?
1057	[6] Concerto in F major	violin (BWV 1049: Brandenburg Concerto no. 4 in G)	—	
[volume 2]				
1058	[7] Concerto in G minor	violin (BWV 1041: Concerto in a)	—	
1059	[8] Concerto in D minor (frag.)	keyboard (organ or harpsichord)	BWV 35/1 and 5	1726
1060	[9] Concerto in C minor	oboe and violin (?)	—	
1062	[10] Concerto in C minor	2 violins (BWV 1043: Concerto in d)	—	
1063	[11] Concerto in D minor	3 harpsichords	—	
1064	[12] Concerto in C major	3 harpsichords	—	

In the manuscript as it stands, all concertos were entered by the composer as fair copies; none of the works were newly composed. The concertos no. 3 and 7 represent transcriptions of the violin concertos in E major and A minor respectively, while no. 6 is based on the *Brandenburg Concerto* 4 in G major for solo violin, two recorders, and strings. In all three instances the original solo violin is replaced by a solo harpsichord, with the orchestral parts largely unchanged. The editor Wilhelm Rust accordingly postulated in 1869 that all eight harpsichord concertos must have been transcribed from violin concertos.[23] Accordingly, no. 1, the most popular of the harpsichord concertos, has been reconstructed as a violin concerto in D minor.[24] Moreover, based on the fact that the model for the middle movement of no. 5 is a cantata sinfonia with solo oboe, various proposals of alternate melody instruments—transverse flute, oboe d'amore, viola, and others—have been suggested as solo instruments for concertos no. 2, 4, 5, and 8.[25] Recent scholarship, however, has called into question the premises for such hypotheses. The cantata sinfonia versions of nos. 1, 2, and 8 suggest that they most likely were based on earlier keyboard concertos,[26] probably to be performed on either organ or harpsichord; no. 4 may have originated as a keyboard concerto as well.

Finally, however, the prehistory, chronology, and original destinations of the various concertos is of secondary importance, since Bach's autograph score unequivocally presents them as harpsichord concertos. When he began to compile the collection, he clearly intended to add yet another category of exemplary compositions that would enhance his reputation as a keyboard composer and virtuoso. In undertaking this project in the late 1730s, he would certainly have realized that the genre of keyboard concerto was no longer novel. Indeed, Handel had published his organ concertos op. 4 and op. 7 in 1738 and 1739, although they had actually been composed somewhat earlier. Nevertheless, awareness of Handel's works in this category may well have motivated Bach to respond—and presumably excel—in presenting similar works of his own. As always, he certainly had no interest in ceding this territory to anyone else.

Ever since his Weimar years, Bach had been uniquely engaged with the idea of involving the organ and harpsichord in the Italian concerto genre, and thereby developing an autonomous keyboard alternative to the violin concerto. In the background for this process were his numerous transcriptions for organ and harpsichord of violin concertos by Vivaldi and others. The harpsichord cadenza for the *Brandenburg Concerto* no. 5 from 1721 presented a stunning and unparalleled prototype revealing the potential of the harpsichord as a solo instrument. Bach was also "greatly admired" in 1725 at the Dresden court for presenting organ concertos "with intervening soft instrumental music."[27] In subsequent years he made further use of the organ as solo instrument in a number of Leipzig cantata sinfonias, which were effectively precursors to three of the harpsichord concertos eventually entered in the autograph score (Table 7.3). Finally, his leadership role at the Collegium Musicum opened the way to the development of concertos for one, two, three, and four harpsichords. These innovative works were admittedly designed to provide attractive performing opportunities for the master himself, his sons, and his best pupils. At the same time, they opened the way to the cultivation of an entirely new genre.

The autograph working score of the harpsichord concertos illuminates in detail the nearly exclusive focus of Bach's revisions: he concentrated almost entirely on elaborating the solo part, while the orchestral scores of the extant works were only sparingly modified. Throughout the manuscript, corrections and embellishing additions in all seven concertos concentrate on the treble (upper or right-hand) part, which functions almost exclusively as the main carrier of the principal melodic lines as well as all figurative material and technical passagework. An offshoot of the Italian violin concerto, the early keyboard concerto assigned the true solo function exclusively to a single solo voice in the treble register, while the left-hand part generally hewed closely to the basso continuo line. The careful shaping of the treble part was directed toward finding optimal idiomatic solutions for keyboard figuration and passagework that would be analogous to the well-established Italian patterns of virtuosic violin vocabulary. Bach also paid close attention, however, to the role of the left hand, and he in fact opened essentially new territory in this regard. As the revisions indicate, freeing the left hand from the continuo line was a primary concern for Bach. Probably based on improvisational experiments that were not notated, the composer painstakingly rewrote major portions of the left-hand parts in order to make them more independent. These notable and significant changes in fact document one of the most decisive steps in the evolution of the keyboard concerto.

Most of the typical virtuoso concerto effects that eventually emerged, involving both hands of the player, did not previously exist in keyboard music and had to be borrowed from violin solo conventions. Bach had already begun this process in Weimar. A violinist himself, he sought the best and most effective ways to adapt to the keyboard various violin techniques, like the one known as *bariolage* (an effect produced by bowing two strings, one open, the other fingered, in rapid alternation; in the following example, there are two fingered strings, one open):

EXAMPLE 7-2

BWV 1004, Ciaccona: bariolage passage, mm. 236–37.

His goal was to transform such string idioms into idiomatic and elegant keyboard figuration. The adoption of such techniques can be clearly traced in the different stages of revision preserved in the sources of the D-minor Concerto, BWV 1052:[28]

EXAMPLE 7-3

BWV 1052/1: string ensemble score (S), with three versions of keyboard solo passages (bariolage adaptations), mm. 146–48.

Many such patterns are evident throughout the harpsichord concerto man-uscript, figurations designed for both hands and combined by Bach with the sort of virtuosic passagework cultivated in exemplary pieces like the *Fantasia chromatica* (BWV 903) and the C-minor Fantasia (BWV 906). The composer thus created an ingenious and visionary blueprint for raising the keyboard-concerto genre to an unprecedented level, which then became the point of departure for his sons and pupils.[29]

Throughout the 1730s, the keyboard concerto and keyboard music in general appear to have been areas of primary importance to Bach in the instrumental realm, clearly at the expense of chamber and orchestral music. Although there were abundant opportunities for performing instru-mental ensemble music between 1729 and 1741 in conjunction with the Collegium Musicum, Bach's creative investment in that area (as attested by the extant sources of pertinent works) was at best modest, notably in comparison with the remarkable productivity during the same period of Georg Philipp Telemann. If we take as representative only the three-volume *Musique de Table* (Hamburg, 1733), with its numerous overtures, concertos, quartets, trios, and sonatas, we see that Telemann energetically engaged in various approaches to a wide range of instrumental genres and scorings, frequently experimenting with the given formal norms. Bach, on the other hand, largely refrained from altering the formal models, as he only rarely departed from the three-movement concerto and sonata in concerto manner (fast–slow–fast), and the four-movement chamber sonata (slow–fast–slow–fast). Instead, he directed his attention chiefly to aspects of thematic and motivic elaboration within the individual movements. In this regard, his last original ensemble concerto, the "Concerto a sei" in D minor, BWV 1043, better known as the Double Violin Concerto and dating from around 1730, can stand as a case in point. Largely absorbed during the 1730s in his four-volume *Clavier-Übung* series and in the cre-ation of concertos for one and more harpsichords, Bach essentially appears to have left the larger field of instrumental composition to his Hamburg colleague and friend, whose works he certainly admired and on occasion performed.[30]

Even in the absence of a published opus, Bach's keyboard concertos exerted an immediate influence in Leipzig and Berlin circles and had long-term impact, with the keyboard concerto being firmly adopted into the genre categories of the era. Indeed, the overwhelming number of keyboard concertos composed in the mid-eighteenth century were written by members of Bach's circle, notably by the son Carl Philipp Emanuel. The latter began composing such works fairly regularly from 1733 on, while still under the guidance of his father, and he had one of his early concertos (Wq 11 in D major) printed in 1745 by Balthasar Schmid, his father's publisher. Carl alone composed some 55 concertos, and when we add the output of his brothers and cousins, the total production of keyboard concertos by the younger Bach family amounted to well over one hundred works.

Finally, at the place where the youngest Bach son left off, the young Mozart began. It can hardly be coincidental that when Leopold Mozart decided to familiarize his son with the genre so inseparably tied to the Bach name, he did so by assigning Wolfgang to recast Johann Christian Bach's sonatas op. 5, as concertos for keyboard and strings (K. 107). Just as Bach had learned from Vivaldi, thus did Mozart learn from a son of Bach.

Kyrie-Gloria Masses

The technical starting point for the Christmas, Easter, and Ascension Day oratorios was the reuse of ceremonial secular works, with the goal of converting suitable occasional music for recurring sacred functions. Bach's liturgical repertory of Latin Masses, embodying reworkings of sacred cantata movements and originating in the mid-1730s alongside the oratorios, offers a fascinating parallel. The composer's objective was once again to augment the repertorial choices available for the major church holidays. But the procedures he employed in creating music for the Latin Mass exhibit significant differences, not so much because of dissimilarities between the content of the German cantata texts and their Latin textual parodies, but rather because of the discrepancies between German and Latin prosody, that is, the fundamental differences in word lengths, stress patterns, and intonation when, for example, the phrase "Liebster Gott, erbarme dich" (/ ⌣ /, ⌣/ ⌣/) turns into "Qui tollis peccata mundi" (⌣/ ⌣ ⌣/ ⌣/ ⌣). It was perhaps precisely this challenge that tempted Bach to seek results that were not merely acceptable, but were in fact superior to the starting point in each case. The works in question (Table 7-4) demonstrate that he achieved this result in consummate fashion.

TABLE 7-4. The Kyrie-Gloria Masses and their parody models

Kyrie cum Gloria	B Minor BWV 232[I]	F Major BWV 233	A Major BWV 234	G Minor BWV 235	G Major BWV 236
Vocal and wind scoring	SSATB; 3 tr+timp, cor, 2 fl, 2 ob	SATB; 2 cor, 2 ob	SATB; 2 fl	SATB; 2 ob	SATB; 2 ob
Kyrie–Christe–Kyrie Gloria–Et in terra Laudamus te	1.* 2.† 3.* 4.† 5.* 6.†	1. BWV 233.1 2.†	1.† 2. BWV 67/6	1. BWV 102/1 2. BWV 72/1	1. BWV 179/1 2. BWV 79/1
Gratias agimus tibi	7. BWV 29/1			3. BWV 187/4	3. BWV 138/4
Domine Deus	8.†	3.†	3.†		4. BWV 79/5
Domine Fili				4. BWV 187/3	
Qui tollis	9. BWV 46/1	4. BWV 102/3	4. BWV 179/5	5. BWV 187/5	
Qui sedes	10.†				
Quoniam	11.†	5. BWV 102/5	5. BWV 79/2		5. BWV 179/3
Cum Sancto Spiritu	12.*	6. BWV 40/1	6. BWV 136/1	6. BWV 187/1	6. BWV 17/1

* Probably original composition.   † No parody model ascertainable.

The liturgical requirements at the Leipzig churches for the principal morning service on major feast days (Christmas Day, Easter Sunday, Whitsunday, etc.) included the performance of a polyphonic Mass typically consisting of Kyrie and Gloria only, according to Lutheran tradition. But the use of so-called Kyrie-Gloria Masses also prevailed in the Roman Catholic rite at the Saxon court and elsewhere. During the first decade of his cantorate, Bach had no interest in composing such "Kyrie cum Gloria" Masses. He instead chose to perform Masses by other composers, and focused on establishing a serviceable repertory of cantatas. In the spring of 1733, however, a special situation arose. After the death of Elector Augustus "the Strong" on February 1, the latter's son and successor, Friedrich August II, planned a visit to Leipzig for a reception by the city council on April 20–21. As part of the official *Erbhuldigung* (fealty celebration), a festive service was scheduled for Sunday, April 21, at St. Nicholas's Church,[31] with a sermon by Superintendent Deyling and music by Cantor Bach. The performance represented a permitted exception within the music-free mourning period that had been decreed by the Saxon court for the duration of six months, effective February 2, 1733. For this special occasion and in recognition of the Electoral family's Roman Catholic faith, the choice of a Latin Mass would have been most appropriate, since the Mass represented the only major liturgical genre common to both Lutherans and Catholics. Yet while the biblical text for the sermon was publicized in typical fashion, no details about the music were announced. Therefore, were it not for the following clues, no information on what was actually performed would be available to us.

A few months after the fealty celebration, in late July 1733, Bach traveled to Dresden and presented the new sovereign with a complete set of parts for a Kyrie-Gloria Mass in B minor, BWV 232[I]. In the dedication phrase on the title wrapper of the performing parts, the author of the work expressly referred to a past performance—"bezeigte . . . mit inliegender Missa . . . seine unterthänigste Devotion" (demonstrated with the enclosed Mass . . . his most humble devotion). Although no specifics are given, the performance might in fact have taken place at the Leipzig worship service on April 21, an occasion that was supposed to be attended by the Elector. At the last moment, however, the Elector decided not to attend the Lutheran service at Leipzig's oldest parish church. Yet the sovereign's entourage was present at the service, meaning that the performance of a Kyrie-Gloria Mass would still have been appropriate. However, if the liturgical Mass performance at St. Nicholas's had to be canceled (for whatever reason), an alternative option would have been a concert performance at St. Sophia's, the Protestant court church in Dresden where Wilhelm Friedemann Bach had just been installed as organist. This might have occurred immediately prior to the official presentation of the parts for the Mass to the Elector on July 27.[32]

Whatever happened, the origin of Bach's first Mass composition is closely tied up with the change of government in 1733 and Bach's plan to better his standing in Leipzig by gaining direct support from the Saxon Elector and King of Poland. The strategy ultimately worked, because in 1736 he received the appointment of "Electoral Saxon and Royal Polish Court Compositeur," whose title and privileges brought him considerable benefits for the remainder of his life.[33]

After Bach brought to an end the composition of church cantatas for the regular Sundays of the ecclesiastical year (excepting a few supplements to the chorale cantata cycle, as mentioned earlier), he turned his attention in the 1730s to the major church holidays. Toward this end, he spent considerable time with the extant large-scale works like the Passions and the *Magnificat*, revising them and putting them into final form. The oratorio trilogy then resulted in new works for Christmas, Easter, and Ascension Day. In 1738/39 the composer also added two extended cantatas, BWV 30 for St. John's Day, and BWV 80 for the Reformation Festival. The former was a parody of the secular piece "Angenehmes Wiederau," BWV 30.1, and the latter an expanded version of an already extant Reformation cantata. The solemn Kyrie-Gloria Mass BWV 232[1] of 1733 thus stood as a rather exceptional composition. Given its hour-long duration and majestic format (lavish scoring for five-part choir, trumpets, horns, and timpani, and woodwinds), it was not truly suitable for a major holiday service that would also have included performance of a cantata. Therefore Bach eventually chose this quite distinctive work for expansion into what would become a full Mass in B minor. In its earlier state, however, the work stimulated the composer's general interest in the genre of Mass, inspired him to study Masses by various (mostly Italian) composers, and finally resulted in the composition of several more serviceable and compact half-hour Kyrie-Gloria Masses. All of these were scored modestly, and each encompassed no more than six movements. Moreover, in contrast to the solemn Mass of 1733, the other four Kyrie-Gloria Masses made more extensive use of borrowings from church cantatas of the 1720s (Table 7-5). The Mass in F major, BWV 233, draws from an even earlier model, its Kyrie being based on an original single Kyrie from the early Weimar period.[34]

Dating of the four shorter Masses to around 1738 is based on the autograph scores of BWV 234 and BWV 236 (Fig. 7-6). Although the original sources for the other two, BWV 235 and BWV 233, have not survived, they can be linked to the first two, since all four appear as a group in a later fair copy (in the sequence BWV 234–236–235–233). Bach had his pupil Johann Christoph Altnickol prepare this copy around 1748, at around the same time that he himself was putting the finishing touches on his expansion of the Kyrie and Gloria of 1733 into the full Mass in B minor. The four Kyrie-Gloria Masses had emerged as part of a cluster of major projects that kept Bach particularly busy in the late 1730s, along with larger vocal settings like BWV 30 and BWV 80 (see above) and part III of the *Clavier-Übung*, as well as the beginnings of

TABLE 7-5. The Kyrie-Gloria Masses and their sacred parody sources

BWV	MASS MOVEMENT	BWV	CANTATA MOVEMENT
233/1	Kyrie–Christe–Kyrie eleison	233.1:	Kyrie "Christe, du Lamm Gottes" \<Weimar version\>
233/2	Gloria in excelsis Deo–	–	(?)
233/3	Domine Deus(?)	–	–
233/4	Qui tollis peccata mundi	102/3:	Weh der Seele, die den Schaden . . . (Woe to the soul which no longer knows any harm)
233/5	Quoniam tu solus sanctus	102/5:	Erschrecke doch, du allzu sichre Seele (Be terrified, you all-too confident souls)
233/6	Cum Sancto Spiritu	40/1:	Darzu ist erschienen der Sohn Gottes (For this the Son of God appeared)
234/1	Kyrie–Christe–Kyrie eleison	–	
234/2	Gloria in excelsis Deo	67/6:	Friede sei mit euch (Peace be with you)
234/3	Domine Deus	–	–
234/4	Qui tollis peccata mundi	179/5:	Liebster Gott, erbarme dich (Beloved God, have mercy)
234/5	Quoniam tu solus sanctus	79/2:	Gott ist unsre Sonn und Schild (God is our sun and shield)
234/6	Cum Sancto Spiritu	136/1:	Erforsche mich Gott (Search me, God)
235/1	Kyrie–Christe–Kyrie eleison	102/1:	Herr, deine Augen . . . (Lord, your eyes look for faith)
235/2	Gloria in excelsis Deo	72/1:	Alles nur nach Gottes Willen (Everything according to God's will)
235/3	Gratias agimus tibi	187/4:	Darum sollt ihr nicht sorgen (Therefore do not be anxious)
235/4	Domine Fili unigenite	187/3:	Du Herr, du krönst allein . . . (You Lord, you alone crown the year with your good)
235/5	Qui tollis peccata mundi	187/5:	Gott versorget alles Leben (God takes care of every life)
235/6	Cum Sancto Spiritu	187/1:	Es wartet alles auf dich (Everything waits for you)
236/1	Kyrie–Christe–eleison	179/1:	Siehe zu, daß deine Gottesfurcht (See to it, that your fear of God)
236/2	Gloria in excelsis Deo	79/1:	Gott der Herr ist Sonn und Schild (God the lord is sun and shield)
236/3	Gratias agimus tibi	138/4:	Auf Gott steht meine Zuversicht (My confidence is in God)
236/4	Domine Deus	79/5:	Gott, ach Gott, verlass die deinen nimmermehr (God, ah God, never abandon your own ones)
236/5	Quoniam tu solus sanctus	179/3:	Falscher Heuchler Ebenbild (Images of false hypocrite)
236/6	Cum Sancto Spiritu	17/1:	Wer Dank opfert, der preiset mich (He who offers thanks praises me)

work on the Great Eighteen Chorales, part II of the *Well-Tempered Clavier*, and the *Art of Fugue*. Original performance parts are available only for the Mass in A major, BWV 234, reflecting at least three presentations: around 1738, between 1743 and 1746, and 1748/49. Assuming this is representative, all four Masses would have been performed several times in the late 1730s and throughout the 1740s.

FIGURE 7-6

Mass in G major, BWV 236/1: autograph (c. 1738).

The general concept of a unified opus of Masses is manifest in a number of shared features. The works uniformly employ a six-movement structure, with the Gloria sections comprising symmetric arrangements of two choruses framing three solos. Each work also makes use of a methodically organized series of keys, modes, and wind scorings. Furthermore, while the solemn Mass of 1733 begins in B minor and ends in D major, the four shorter Masses exhibit tonal closure in coherent schemes that resemble the compact key organization of the six parts of the *Christmas Oratorio* (Table 6-9):

BWV 233: F–F–C–g–d–F
BWV 234: A–A–f#–D–b–A
BWV 235: g–g–d–B♭–E♭–g
BWV 236: G–G–D–a–e–G

Of particular importance for the cohesiveness of the group was Bach's exclusive use of sacred parody models from church cantatas of the 1723/24 and 1725/26 cycles, from which he selected movements of particular quality and refinement. Unifying the group as well was the composer's overlapping use of parody sources: together, the Masses in A major and G major have six movements from cantatas BWV 79 and BWV 179, while the Masses in G minor and F major between them have seven movements from cantatas BWV 102 and BWV 187 (Table 7-4).

Bach must have found it both intriguing and challenging to apply a novel and completely original procedure for converting into Latin movements models that were not only sacred but also in the German language, and of turning metric and rhymed poetry into liturgical prose. A central premise for the success of parody, whether from secular music to sacred or from one sacred work to another, involves the affinity of character and expression. Perhaps because Bach knew his output intimately and also had performed most cantatas several times, his choices of parody models succeeded with remarkable precision, both in principle and in detail. For the choruses, Bach consistently used suitable cantata movements with compatible biblical texts, mostly from the Psalms, the only exception being the Gloria chorus, BWV 235/2. For BWV 233/2 and BWV 234/1 the parody models are unknown (Table 7-6; cf. Table 7-5). In the case of the Gloria movement BWV 235/2, the original poetic text by Salomon Franck for its parody model BWV 72/1, with its focus on the resolve "Everything according to God's will alone, in joy as in sorrow, in good times as in bad times . . . this shall be my motto [*Losung*]," fits perfectly well the Gloria hymn of praise, with its emphatic "laudamus, adoramus, benedicimus, glorificamus te." The effect is only enhanced by the jubilant character of the music.

TABLE 7-6. Kyrie-Gloria choruses based on cantata choruses
with biblical text

BWV 233/6 (Cum Sancto Spiritu)	BWV 40/1 (1 John 3:8)
BWV 234/2 (Gloria in excelsis)	BWV 76/6 (John 20:19)
BWV 234/6 (Cum Sancto Spiritu)	BWV 136/1 (Psalm 139:36)
BWV 235/1 (Kyrie eleison)	BWV 102/1 (Jeremiah 5:3)
BWV 235/6 (Cum Sancto Spiritu)	BWV 187/1 (Psalm 104:27–28)
BWV 236/1 (Kyrie eleison)	BWV 179/1 (Sirach 1:34)
BWV 236/2 (Gloria in excelsis)	BWV 79/1 (Psalm 84:12)
BWV 236/6 (Cum Sancto Spiritu)	BWV 17/1 (Psalm 50:23)

The German texts of the chosen parody models were generally a very good fit for the new Latin text underlay, though Bach more often than not had to make carefully coordinated adjustments in the prosody and the musical scorings. Even though he could have dealt with the entire challenge simply by producing entirely new compositions, his decision to elaborate extant settings in order to achieve his desired result cannot be questioned. Bach must have derived particular satisfaction from the opportunity to undertake a second pass at a perfectly fine older piece, which he did in numerous other instances of revision and arrangement in the 1730s. In the autograph score of the G-major Mass (BWV 236), the various adjustments that Bach made, notably in the continuo part, indicate his obvious eagerness to improve the original five-part contrapuntal setting.

The approach to the opening chorus of the Gloria of the A-major Mass represents another case in point. The parody choice of the chorus no. 6 from cantata BWV 67 was clearly triggered by the phrase "Friede sei mit euch" as it relates to the "et in terra pax" of the liturgical hymn. Yet the composition of the cantata movement BWV 67/6 for three-part chorus and solo bass (representing the *vox Christi*) strictly followed the format of the poetry, with the biblical statement interjected four times:

A1 strings:	introduction (ritornello)—		
B1 bass:	Friede sei mit euch!		Peace be with you!
A2 chorus:	Wohl uns! Jesus hilft uns kämpfen	How blessed we are! Jesus helps us fight	
	Und die Wut der Feinde dämpfen,	and dampens the rage of the enemy,	
	Hölle, Satan, weich!	Hell, Satan, back!	
B2 bass:	Friede sei mit euch!		Peace be with you!
A3 chorus:	Jesus holet uns zum Frieden	Jesus brings us to peace	
	Und erquicket in uns Müden	and refreshes in us weary ones	
	Geist und Leib zugleich.	spirit and body together.	
B3 bass:	Friede sei mit euch!		Peace be with you!
A4 chorus:	O Herr, hilf und laß gelingen,	O Lord, help and let it be accomplished,	
	Durch den Tod hindurchzudringen	through death to be brought	
	In dein Ehrenreich!	to Your glorious kingdom!	
B4 bass:	Friede sei mit euch!		Peace be with you!

Bach composed this post-Easter cantata movement with two strongly contrasting and alternating musical ideas, which juxtapose two very distinct expressive *Affekts*: the calm, salutary words of the risen Jesus (B) and the animated, combative mood of the disciples waging war against Satan for the glorious kingdom of Christ (A). The choral A sections (**c**: *Vivace e forte*) are supported by an animated accompaniment of virtuoso strings (which also present the ritornello-style instrumental introduction), whereas the instrumental ensemble of the lyrical solo sections B ($\frac{3}{4}$: *Adagio e piano*) employs only flute and two oboi d'amore.

The shorter liturgical prose text of the A-major Gloria required not only major adjustments to the text underlay, but also a complete reorganization of the form and a reassignment of the *vox Christi* to three different soloists.

Gloria in excelsis Deo.
Et in terra pax hominibus bonae voluntatis.
Laudamus te, benedicimus te, adoramus te, glorificamus te.
Gratias agimus tibi propter magnam gloriam tuam.

Moreover, the opening text of the Gloria had to be integrated within the instrumental introduction, and the concluding verse needed to be recomposed in a four-part choral texture. Here is the scheme that Bach devised for the allocation of the text:

A1 chorus: Gloria in excelsis Deo.
B1 alto: Et in terra pax hominibus bonae voluntatis.
A2 chorus: Laudamus te, benedicimus te,
B2 bass: Adoramus te,
A3 chorus: Glorificamus te, laudamus te, benedicimus te,
B3 tenor: Adoramus te,
A4 chorus: Glorificamus te, laudamus, benedicimus, adoramus te,
B4 chorus: Gratias agimus tibi propter magnam gloriam tuam.

Notwithstanding all these complications, the resulting Mass movement (equal in length to the cantata movement) presents itself as anything but a makeshift or stopgap solution, but rather as a highly effective further evolution of the earlier vocal setting. This applies likewise to the solo movement "Qui tollis peccata mundi" of the same A-major Mass, which is derived from the cantata aria "Liebster Gott, erbarme dich," BWV 179/5—in which "miserere nobis" and "erbarme dich" (have mercy) are the matching words that define the focus of the musical expression. The cantata movement in A minor is scored for soprano, two oboi da caccia, and basso continuo (cello, double bass, and organ). The Mass setting, however, is transposed up to B minor and features the soprano accompanied by two flutes and a bassetto (high bass) fundament, executed by violins and violas in unison and without organ. This rescoring lends to the Latin piece a strikingly new sonic identity, and communicates the text within an unusually poignant atmosphere.

The examples cited above are representative of the considerable modifications that Bach undertook in the process of parodying extant cantata movements. Yet these impressive accomplishments in conversion were supplemented by substantial passages of new composition, which were often required to accommodate the Latin prosody as well as the meanings of specific phrases and words. Such cases include the completely fresh beginning that was added to the final movement of the Mass BWV 234, in order to afford the proper ceremonial weight to the phrase "Cum Sancto Spiritu." There was also a thorough revision and extension of the "Quoniam" in the Mass BWV 236, in a rescored version for solo oboe, tenor, and continuo (a movement based on the cantata aria BWV 179/3 for two oboes, two violins, tenor, and continuo). A still further example lies in the significant lengthenings of up to two dozen added measures in all three solo movements in the Mass BWV 235—these apart from the likely additions of newly composed movements for the Mass BWV 233 (Table 7-4).

The four Kyrie-Gloria Masses, which emerged as particularly refined parodies of selected sacred cantata movements, further validate the superb quality of their musical origins and stand as evidence of the unconventional, truly creative, and highly advanced nature of Bach's borrowing practice. His work with the Masses is comparable to his settings of the sacred oratorios from the same period, which also derived in large part from extant secular models. There is little question that the Mass opus was meant to stand on its own as a coherent grouping, taking its place among the very finest of Bach's vocal compositions. Given the growing distaste in the later eighteenth century for the empurpled baroque lyrics of the cantatas, Passions, and oratorios, it was the Kyrie-Gloria Masses and the *B-minor Mass* that cemented Bach's reputation as a vocal composer, and in decisive fashion. In fact, two entire movements—one each from the G-major and A-major Masses, respectively—were printed as examples in early composition treatises: Friedrich Wilhelm Marpurg's *Abhandlung von der Fuge* (Berlin, 1754) and Johann Philipp Kirnberger's *Die Kunst des reinen*

Satzes in der Musik (Königsberg, 1779). Furthermore, the Mass in A major, published in 1818, was among the first of Bach's works to appear in print in its complete version, this being one of the initial manifestations of the nineteenth-century Bach revival.

The Well-Tempered Clavier, Part II

A follow-up opus based on the very same idea as an earlier one represents an absolute anomaly in the composer's oeuvre. The preparation of a second volume of the *Well-Tempered Clavier* (WTC), BWV 870–893, seems to have been prompted by the extensive pedagogical application of the original, which had been put into final form in 1722. Through the subsequent years, that collection served successfully as a foundational text in Bach's teaching studio, while the composer sustained his enduring fascination with the first volume's three constituent essentials: improvisatory fantasy, learned imitative counterpoint, and tonal diversity. After almost two decades, these factors gave rise to a new companion volume of preludes and fugues in all keys. Yet Bach initially hesitated to designate it specifically as a second part. It was not until 1744 that he had his trusted copyist Johann Christoph Altnickol prepare a fair copy, under the heading "Des Wohltemperirten Claviers Zweyter Theil."[35] Understandably, Bach wished the second part to be clearly distinct from the first. In one of the earlier manuscripts from around 1739,[36] he in fact toyed with French headings like "Prélude" and "Fugue," presumably in order to suggest the modernity of the new pieces relative to the more traditional styles of the first set, which had used the Latin titles "Praeludium" and "Fuga." Eventually, however, he refrained from any sort of titular window dressing and kept the academic Latin, as Altnickol's authoritative fair copy indicates.

Structurally, part II of the WTC resembles its forerunner in virtually every respect. Yet although in part I the preludes and fugues in identical keys are numbered separately ("Praeludium 1," "Fuga 1," etc.), part II clearly presents them as pairs—as is shown in the London autograph score of 1739 and later, with the headings "Prælude et Fugue 1," etcetera (Fig. 7-7). Moreover, while in part I the Eb-minor prelude and D#-minor fugue, BWV 853, still projected a certain enharmonic ambivalence, the parallel pair in part II uniformly present the key of D# minor. In terms of overall stylistic orientation, part II clearly reflects not only an accommodation to the preferences and needs of a

FIGURE 7-7

Prelude in C major, BWV 870/1: autograph working score (1739–42); "par J." added
later by W. F. Bach.

younger generation of students, but also the shifting priorities of the composer
himself. This is most evident in some of the preludes. Those in c, D, d♯, E,
e, f, G, g♯, and B♭ feature full-fledged binary structures, with repeat signs for
both sections, and an explicit nod toward the sonata format favored by his
composing sons and students. In the preludes in F♯, A♭, and b, on the other
hand, ritornello-style format prevails. In the D, f, g♯, B♭, and B settings, *galant*
melodic gestures reign, while in the C, E♭, E, F, and g preludes, subtle strains
of counterpoint and small-scale motivic elements abound.

In line with the general stylistic trend toward leaner polyphony, the majority of fugues in part II (fifteen in all) are scored for three parts, with the
remaining nine scored for the more traditional four parts. By comparison,
part I contains two five-part, ten four-part, and eleven three-part fugues,

along with a single two-part setting. Although both volumes of the collection present comparable arrays of relatively straightforward fugues (with the occasional application of special techniques, such as thematic inversion and augmentation, or the introduction of one or two fixed countersubjects), part II also introduces several double fugues as well as examples with fixed countersubjects of thematic weight, in the keys of c♯, g, g♯, B♭, B, and b. These works are unmistakably related to the more systematic exploration of multiple-theme fugues in the *Art of Fugue*, a compositional project that overlapped in time with part II.

The most notable distinction between the two parts of the WTC lies in the greater length of both preludes and fugues in part II: the pieces in the second collection are on average a quarter to a third longer than those in part I. In the fugues, the increased length is achieved not through the incorporation of extended interludes, but rather through the adoption of longer themes and more substantive elaboration overall of the given musical material.

The compositional history of part II is for the most part obscure, since the composing scores that Bach used to prepare the incomplete autograph fair copy of an intermediate version (1739–42) have not survived. Yet the chronology of the volume's origins apparently extends over several years, and in fact it may not have begun as a second volume but rather as a haphazard assemblage of individual preludes and fugues. The evolution of part II also seems to have overlapped with revisions Bach entered into his copy of part I, first in 1732, then around 1736, and again after 1740, leading to the conclusion that part II was not intended to replace but rather to continue and supplement part I. The principal stages in the genesis of part II are summarized in Table 7-7. For the early versions of the pieces no original sources exist, and therefore their chronology remains unknown. Secondary sources, however, in the form of copies taken from lost autographs, document early versions for a number of the works.[37] Original sources for the first revision are available in an incomplete manuscript that combines two originally separate copies: A1 in the composer's hand (preludes headed "Praeludium") with later yet minor entries made by his son Wilhelm Friedemann, and A2 in the hands of Bach and his wife Anna Magdalena (preludes headed "Prélude"). The second revised version is not known from any copy in the composer's hand, and is represented only by the aforementioned fair copy in the hand of Bach's pupil and later son-in-law, Johann Christoph Altnickol.

TABLE 7-7. Compositional history of the *Well-Tempered Clavier*, Part II

STAGE	DATE	SOURCE	SCRIBE†	PRELUDES AND FUGUES
Early versions*	before 1739	composing scores (lost)	JSB	All
1st revised version A1	1739–42	fair copy ("Praeludium")	JSB, WFB	C, C♯, d♯, F♯, A♭, g♯, B♭, b♭, B
A2		fair copy ("Prélude")	JSB, AMB	c, d, E♭, E, e, F, f♯, G, g, A, a, b
2nd revised version B	1742–44	revised score (lost)	JSB	All
	1744	fair copy	Altnickol	All

* Transmitted not in autograph copies but only in secondary sources for the Preludes in C, C♯, d, G and the Fugues (some named Fughettas) in c, C♯, E♭, G, A♭.[38]
† JSB = Johann Sebastian Bach; AMB = Anna Magdalena Bach; WFB = Wilhelm Friedemann Bach.

An important group of works in the prehistory of part II appears to have come from a probably incomplete in-progress collection of five preludes and fughettas in C, d, e, F, and G, BWV 870.1 and BWV 899–902, which date from before 1730. The Prelude in C, BWV 870.1, and the Fughettas in F, BWV 901, and G, BWV 902, were included in part II, all in substantially revamped form (and in one case also transposed) as Prelude in C, BWV 870/1, Fugue in G♯, BWV 886/2, and Fugue in G, BWV 884/2. These concrete relationships indicate that part II began to some degree—the full extent remains unknown—as a compilation of more forward-looking preludes and fugues that would form a suitable point of departure for the creation of a companion to part I. In this sense, part II fits well into Bach's numerous wide-ranging projects of the 1730s, all conceived under the rubric of a review and critical assessment of his earlier compositions, as he sought appropriate homes for those he did not wish to fall between the cracks. Though part II of the WTC represents a unique instance of a Bach opus closely tied to an earlier work, it nonetheless demonstrates that the composer's intention was hardly to repeat himself, but instead to remain ever in search of novel and original solutions.

The overall picture of Bach's compositional endeavors after 1730 reveals a clear focus on what he considered to be his principal domains: demanding keyboard music and intricate vocal composition. His musical projects were centered in his areas of particular expertise, and they resulted in many of the achievements of which he was most proud. In sum, the issue of musical legacy mattered very much to him. After the 1720s, the pace of Bach's creative productivity began to ease. Yet all of his projects, including those undertaken in review mode, still demonstrate an undiminished eagerness to widen and deepen the scope of his musical objectives, and to explore new territory without repeating what had already been accomplished. He could thereby augment and bolster his standing—for himself, for the people around him, for posterity, and above all "soli Deo Gloria."

CHAPTER 8

Instrumental and Vocal Polyphony at Its Peak

Art of Fugue *and* B-minor Mass

I f there is one category of musical composition most closely identified with the name of Bach, it is surely fugue—not a specific genre or form *per se*, but rather a process of imitative polyphony in which, as the Latin term *fuga* suggests, "one voice chases the other."[1] The nearly infinite possibilities for developing an artful piece out of a single succinct musical idea fascinated Bach the composer and performer for a lifetime. And the two works that preoccupied him during the later and final years of his life, the *Art of Fugue* and the *B-minor Mass*, bear eloquent testimony to this truly passionate devotion—the *Art of Fugue* being a work entirely dedicated to an intensive exploration of fugal composition, and the *B-minor Mass* standing out among Bach's vocal works for its large number of choral fugues. Together they mark the end point of Bach's musical oeuvre, though neither work was initiated with any such prospective outcome in mind.

The beginnings of the *Art of Fugue* in the late 1730s overlapped with the genesis of the last two parts of the *Clavier-Übung* and the second book of the *Well-Tempered Clavier*. A complete first version was set down in an autograph fair copy around 1742, at a time when the solemn Kyrie-Gloria Mass of 1733 had long been written but the *B-minor Mass* as such was barely on the horizon.

Though these two late works emerge as dual capstones to Bach's career, they might well have been supplanted by further achievements had the composer's health permitted. But as the 1740s drew to a close, he was handicapped by ever-worsening vision problems. In the spring of 1750, driven by an irrepressible will to live and an unwavering zeal to continue his creative work, he made the courageous decision to undergo a decidedly risky eye operation. Alas, the procedure did not bring the desired outcome, and following the surgery Bach suffered a steady decline that led to his death a few months later.

The wider context that determined the direction in which these two major works eventually unfolded during the 1740s seems clear. First of all, Bach took full advantage of the title bestowed upon him in December 1736, "Electoral Saxon and Royal Polish Court Compositeur." The appointment conferred a new elevated status that insulated him from the petty struggles and constant minor conflicts with the Leipzig municipal authorities. Whether or not he was motivated by the deep frustrations brought about by deteriorating working conditions—in part caused by a protracted dispute with the rector about the appointment of choir prefects—Bach in his later years adopted an increasingly relaxed attitude toward official obligations. He continued to conduct and administer the cantor's office with the student assistance available to him, but without the remarkable creative energy he had once applied to the musical program for the Leipzig churches. His changed priorities, above all with respect to official duties versus free artistic inclinations and pursuit of personal musical interests, were as conspicuous as they were significant.

Bach's tendency toward ever more sophisticated contrapuntal study and composition manifested itself first and most clearly in part III of the *Clavier-Übung* (see Chapter 5), particularly in its retrospective Palestrina-style settings and canonic chorale elaborations. His favored intellectual pursuit appears also to have been directly related to his private teaching activities, which at that time involved a number of academically inclined students, including Lorenz Christoph Mizler, Johann Friedrich Agricola, and Johann Philipp Kirnberger—all three of whom would emerge as leading music theorists. In fact, Mizler lectured on counterpoint at the University of Leipzig, and in 1742—practically under Bach's eyes—he published an annotated German translation of the Latin counterpoint treatise *Gradus ad Parnassum* by Johann Joseph Fux (Vienna, 1724). Although he owned a copy of the Latin original, he did not approve of Fux's pedagogical method. He instead expanded on the traditional practice of teaching counterpoint, which had customarily been accomplished within the framework of two-, three-, and four-part polyphony. But Bach also elected to go further and to address problems occurring in settings for five and more voices, matters not previously considered by theorists. His pupils Agricola and Kirnberger both transmitted their teacher's newly advanced set of rules for dealing with five-part counterpoint. Agricola did so in German, and entered the rules by hand in his personal copy of Mizler's Fux translation; Kirnberger eventually published them in the original Latin under the heading "Regula Ioh. Seb. Bachii" (Fig. 8-1) in his treatise *Die Kunst des reinen Satzes in der Musik* (Königsberg, 1774–79). Always with an eye to balancing horizontal lines and complex vertical harmony, Bach's rules focus on the tones within a chord of five or more voices, specifically on augmented and diminished intervals, whose doublings he prohibited.[2] These rules were exemplified collectively for the first time in the final section of his five-part organ chorale "Kyrie, Gott heiliger Geist," BWV 671, composed for the *Clavier-Übung* III of 1739 (see page 181). Any doubling of the circled individual notes in the following example, all representing augmented and diminished intervals, would have violated Bach's rules:

* Intervals, the doubling of which Bach's rule prohibited, are marked by circles.

EXAMPLE 8-1

Organ chorale BWV 671: five-part chromatic ending.

Composing, teaching, and performing were inseparable acts for Bach throughout his career, yet beginning in the mid-1730s, elaborate and erudite counterpoint attracted his particular attention as never before. Even though he clearly enjoyed and kept abreast of popular musical trends, as demonstrated in his 1742 *Cantate burlesque* "Mer hahn en neue Oberkeet" (BWV 212), the greater number of his major works throughout the 1740s display evidence of ever more frequent and varied applications of special contrapuntal techniques. Teaching notes he prepared around 1739–42 corroborate his focus on techniques of double counterpoint and canonic writing. They also make extensive reference to historical materials treating canonic and fugal procedures, notably the writings of Gioseffo Zarlino and Seth Calvisius (Fig. 8-2).[3]

FIGURE 8-1

"Regula J. S. Bachii," BWV 1129: Johann Philipp Kirnberger, *Die Kunst des reinen Satzes in der Musik*, vol. II/3 (Berlin, 1779).

Knowledge of Bach's expertise in such matters must certainly have spread in Leipzig intellectual circles. For example, one Johann Friedrich Mentz, university professor of philosophy and physics, at one point asked him to assist in solving an enigmatic canon by Teodoro Riccio (c. 1540–c. 1600), which had turned up in an old friendship album in Mentz's possession.[4] Moreover, Bach apparently liked to engage his oldest son, Wilhelm Friedemann, in considerations of contrapuntal matters, as is made clear by a manuscript from the later 1730s that documents various contrapuntal studies shared by father and son (Fig. 8-3). Notably, such theoretical activities were complemented by a clustering of Bach's church performances of several Masses by Palestrina, the classic master of traditional vocal polyphony. He presented Palestrina's *Missa sine nomine* of 1590 for six voices and the *Missa Ecce sacerdos magnus* of 1554 for four voices, as well as Francesco Gasparini's *Missa canonica* of 1706 for four voices, in retrospective counterpoint (Fig. 8-4). The relevant performing materials originating from the period around 1740–42 were for the most part prepared by Bach himself, and offer vivid testimony to his preference for combining study and performance.

Finally, the principle of elaboration was one of the most characteristic

FIGURE 8-2

Canones aliquot per Josephum Zarlinum, BWV 1130: autograph teaching notes (1742/43), detail.

aspects of Bach's method of composition. From very early on, he was strongly inclined toward sophisticated elaborations of musical ideas—regardless of whether they were preexisting, like chorale tunes, or self-devised, like fugue subjects. In his systematic explorations of their musical potential, he invariably attempted to penetrate the material at hand as deeply as possible, in the process revealing "the most hidden secrets of harmony."[5] Uncovering such secrets as were implicit in musical material was a genuine and abiding passion

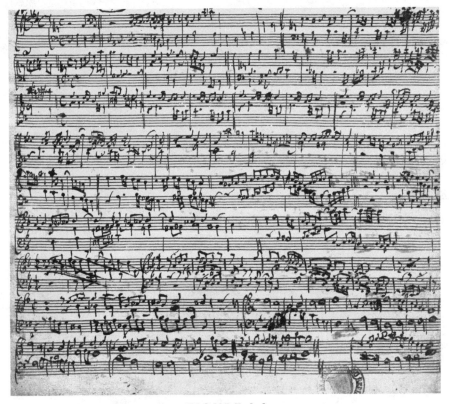

FIGURE 8-3

J. S. and W. F. Bach, joint counterpoint studies, BWV 1132: dual autograph (1736–39), detail.

for him, as was the process of bringing a setting to a point of near perfection. As a student of composition who was essentially self-taught, he is said to have "learned chiefly by the observation of the works of the most famous and proficient composers of his day and by the fruits of his own reflecting upon them."[6] Also, and again in the words of Carl Philipp Emanuel, "through his own study and reflection alone he became even in his youth a pure and strong fugue writer."[7] His own habit of deep reflection ("eigenes Nachsinnen") complemented his ongoing study of *exempla classica*, especially in relation to fugue. From the very outset, the composition of a fugal setting based on contrapuntal elaborations of a given or self-devised subject held his intense interest. The obituary celebrated his ability when hearing a theme to be "aware—it seemed, in the same instant—of almost every intricacy that artistry could produce in its treatment."[8] This exceptional talent was the fountainhead of his working procedure in elaborating on thematic ideas, and explains his astonishing gift

FIGURE 8-4

Francesco Gasparini, *Missa canonica*: oboe/violin part, copy J. S. Bach (1740–42).

for uncovering their latent contrapuntal potential.

The close association of elaboration and variation relates to Bach's compositional method, as manifested in his characteristic manner of pursuing in the context of imitative polyphony "the development of a single subject through the keys with the most agreeable variation."[9] This he consistently accomplished across the various genres, and the principles of elaboration and variation were ultimately on display even in transcriptions and parody procedures. The close relationship between the two shows itself perhaps most clearly in the *Clavier-Übung*, first in the paired chorale settings of part III (Table 5-5), and then on a more systematic level in part IV (Table 5-7).

THE ART OF FUGUE COMPLETED: THE MANUSCRIPT VERSION

The prevailing trend of polyphonic orientation and design in Bach's late instrumental compositions was recognized rather early on in the history of Bach scholarship, with Bach's final masterpieces often being compared to Beethoven's late works. By this line of reasoning, the *Art of Fugue* was reckoned as the remarkable finale of a unique series of monothematic works, one that commenced with the *Goldberg Variations* of 1741 and continued with the 1747 *Musical Offering* and the subsequent Canonic Variations on "Vom Himmel hoch." Only in the later 1970s did new research compel a change of view, after it turned out that the *Art of Fugue* actually stood at the beginning of this development—meaning that the pattern of influences had to be read in reverse.[10] The *Art of Fugue*'s extended genesis—from the later 1730s through the first completed version of about 1742 (BWV 1080.1) up to the expanded but incomplete final version of 1749/50 (BWV 1080.2)—affected the other pieces in very much the same way that the *Art of Fugue* itself benefitted from the composer's engagement with what had formerly been considered forerunners. In sum, Bach's monothematic instrumental projects of the 1740s ultimately stand as a complex of multifarious and interlocking projects, all related to the composer's ever-evolving preoccupation with artful contrapuntal writing.

A trace of the *Art of Fugue*'s origin, in the form of a germinal cell, is preserved in the aforementioned joint contrapuntal studies undertaken with Wilhelm Friedemann. At the very beginning of lines 1–2 of the score, as shown in Fig. 8-3, Bach notated the head motif of the work's principal theme in D Dorian and in quarter notes, together with its diminution in eighth notes, as a study in contrapuntal augmentation. The subsequent measures further contribute to the shape of the thematic idea as it eventually emerged—though it cannot be determined whether these references represent a retrospective allusion to something already in the works, or instead foreshadow a prospective venture. Although the actual beginnings cannot be dated exactly, the general plan for an instrumental cycle of monothematic imitative counterpoint and fugal polyphony took shape at some point after 1736—that is, in the immediate vicinity of part III of the *Clavier-Übung* and of part II of the *Well-Tempered Clavier*. At the same time, the referential occurrence within Bach's counterpoint studies with Wilhelm Friedemann strongly suggests that the initial focus of the project was centered around contrapuntal theory in general rather than the technique of fugue in the narrower sense. Bach in fact pursued in the collection the core idea of using the vehicles of fugal design and fugal technique in order to exemplify contrapuntal processes. This procedure is confirmed by his later designation of the individual movements as "Contrapunctus" rather than "Fuga." Only toward the end of the laborious endeavor, and for the published version, did he settle on the title *Die Kunst der Fuge* (*The Art of Fugue*); see below, page 310.

Bach based the cycle of fugues on a number of premises that contribute to its unique character. First of all, he decided to use a single theme to achieve his purpose of fully expounding the concept of fugal counterpoint and its various types, a plan that differed fundamentally from the role and broad variety of fugues in both books of the *Well-Tempered Clavier*. To this end, he devised a subject of notable simplicity, striking melodic efficacy, and unmistakable harmonic implications (given the prominent position of the leading tone *c#*):

EXAMPLE 8-2

The Art of Fugue, BWV 1080 *principal theme.*

The subject is equally strong both in its original and inverted forms, which combine in highly satisfactory counterpoint. Its key of D minor was a deliberate choice, given the traditional associations of D minor with the Dorian church mode (*modus primus*), and also its role as the *modus chromaticus*, as Bach had explored it in his *Fantasia chromatica*, BWV 903—and as he would survey it to a far greater extent in the *Art of Fugue*.

The second premise consists in the principle of variation, which the entire cycle represents, and indeed in a triple sense: (1) variations on the single principal theme in progressive melodic-rhythmic iterations tailored to its contours and flow, extending from its straightforward original statement (the first four notes forming a plain D-minor triad) to highly florid versions; (2) variations of scoring and style encompassing two- to four-part writing and achieved via the application of *stile antico, stile francese*, and a mix of older and newer manners of composition; and (3) variations of contrapuntal techniques. Among the latter are such devices as imitation of the principal theme at different intervals and pitches, inversion of the theme (extending even to the inversion of an entire movement), employment of the theme at double and half speeds, and combinations of the theme with new countersubjects. The idea that Bach was—at least partially—considering a cycle of consecutive variation movements is suggested by the ending of fugue no. III on the dominant key of A major in the autograph manuscript (see Table 8-1), such that fugue no. IV had to follow immediately in order to facilitate a return to the home key. While the later published version abandoned such obligatory linking of movements, the idea of coherent cyclic variation was present in the early stages of the work's evolution.

TABLE 8-1. *The Art of Fugue*: Early version in the autograph manuscript, c. 1742

NO.*	TYPE OF SETTING	STRUCTURAL ELEMENTS: METER, THEMES, COUNTERSUBJECTS, AND CONTRAPUNTAL DEVICES†	CATEGORY OF COUNTERPOINT
I	4-pt fugue	¢ Th ♩: ASBT, diatonic contrapuntal continuation	1. Contrapunctus simplex:
II	4-pt fugue	¢ Th ♩ *inv*: TASB, chromatic contrapuntal continuation	three simple fugues
III	4-pt fugue	¢ Th ♩: BTAS, dotted contrapuntal continuation (ends in A-major half cadence)	
IV	4-pt fugue	¢ Th ♩ *mod-inv*+Th *mod*: ABST, at the octave	2. Contrapunctus duplex:
V	4-pt fugue	C Cs-A: SBAT; → Cs-A+Th ♩, at the twelfth	Th with Cs-A and Cs-B,
VI	4-pt fugue	C Th ♩ *mod-inv*: STBA; → Th+Cs-B, at the tenth	at three different intervals
VII	4-pt fugue	C Th ♩ *mod* +Th ♩ *mod-inv-dim*: BSAT, at the octave	3. Contrapunctus duplex:
VIII	4-pt fugue	C Th ♩ *mod*+Th ♩ *mod-inv*+Th 𝅝 *mod-inv-aug* 𝅝: TSAB, at the octave	Th *mod*, at three different speeds
IX	2-pt canon	⁹⁄₁₆ Th ♪ *var-inv*+Th *var*: SB, perpetual "Canon in Hypodiapason" (at the octave)	4. Contrapunctus duplex: Th *var*, as canons and
X	3-pt fugue	²⁄₄ Cs-C: TBS; → Cs-C+Cs-D; Th +Cs-C+Cs-D	with Cs-C, Cs-D, and
XI	4-pt fugue	²⁄₄ Th ♪ *var*: ASBT; → Cs-C+Cs-D; Cs-C+Cs-E; Cs-C+Cs-D+Cs-E+Th *var-inv*	Cs-E
XII	2-pt canon	C Th ♩ *var*+Th ♩ *var-inv-aug*: SB, perpetual "Canon in Hypodiatesseron" (at the fifth)	
XIII	4-pt fugue	³⁄₄ Th ♩ *var*: SATB, Contrapunctus simplex	5. Contrapunctus inversus:
	4-pt fugue	³⁄₄ Th ♩ *var-inv*: BTAS (mirroring of previous fugue)	3- and 4-part scores
XIV	3-pt fugue	²⁄₄ Th ♪ *var*: SAB, Contrapuntus duplex	entirely inverted
	3-pt fugue	²⁄₄ Th ♪ *var-inv*: BAS (mirroring of previous fugue)	
XV	Addendum	revised version of augmentation canon no. XII (no longer perpetual canon)	Version expanded by 11 measures

* In the autograph score, pieces are numbered (Roman numerals, added after 1800) but were not given titles (neither "Fuga" nor "Contrapunctus").

† For the fugal openings; the themes, counterpoints, and countersubjects defining the movements; answering intervals (octave, fifth, etc.); special devices applied or involved.

Abbreviations and explanations:

Th Principal theme; *aug* = augmented; *dim* = diminished; *inv* = inverted; *mod* = slightly modified; *var* = varied; *var-inv* = varied and inverted; *mod-inv* = slightly modified and inverted

Cs-A–E Countersubjects (new themes, distinct from principal theme) A to E; Cs-E beginning with B♭-A-C-B♮ = BACH

SATB Soprano, alto, tenor, bass (indicate initial sequence of thematic entries)

→ Indicates combinations after first fugal exposition

+ Indicates simultaneous combination of themes and countersubjects

♩ . . . Speed (basic motion) of principal theme: quarter ♩, half ♩, and whole 𝅝 notes

The third premise taken up by Bach involves systematic organization in combination with increasing contrapuntal complexity, beginning with fugues based on simple counterpoint, continuing to fugues applying double counterpoint, and finally proceeding to fugues whose mirror images are not only correct but also as musically attractive as their original forms. The structure of the collection's early version reveals in its sequence of movements a scheme that seems intended to evoke the logical methodology of a counterpoint treatise, moving forward step by step with the goal of seeking variety and diversity through the application of abundant melodic, rhythmic, and harmonic resources. An important and related external aspect involves the composer's decision to notate the work in open score and in the traditional vocal clefs (C-clefs for soprano, alto, and tenor, along with the F-clef for bass), so as to be able to assign each instrumental voice to its proper space. Although the pieces were intentionally designed for keyboard performance (additional voices and chords, up to seven parts total in final cadential passages, represent typical keyboard effects), Bach underscored the study aspect by setting out a score image that would show with optimal clarity the contrapuntal texture in general and individual voice-leading in particular.

In the autograph score of the completed early version of the *Art of Fugue* (Fig. 8-5), the fourteen numbered but untitled movements of the main group form five unmarked yet distinct sections, each with its own makeup (see Table 8-1). The first section in simple counterpoint (*contrapunctus simplex*) comprises three fugues on the unaltered principal theme, all in the retrospective style of the seventeenth-century ricercar (the Italian term for a *recherché* or "well-researched" fugal or canonic instrumental movement). This section expounds the theme with extreme clarity and transparency, dispensing with all instrumental virtuosity. No. II, the centerpiece, introduces the inversion of the theme and, through its contrapuntal extension and accompaniment, the element of chromaticism.

Beginning with the second section in double counterpoint (*contrapunctus duplex*), all movements use modified (IV–VII) and then varied (IX–XIV) versions of the main theme, following the principle of theme with variations. The movements then gradually pass into more current stylistic territory and incorporate the technique of double counterpoint, in which each part or voice can be placed either above or below the other. Number IV introduces this possibility by placing the principal theme (mildly modified with dotted rhythms) and its inversion alternately above and below each other at the interval of an octave. Nos. V and VI employ two entirely new themes (countersubjects A and B) in combination with the principal theme at intervals of a twelfth and a tenth. The third section (nos. VII and VIII) presents the techniques of diminution and augmentation, combining the principal theme in straight and inverted forms with versions in halved and doubled note values, with these layers proceeding at three different speeds.

In the fourth and fifth sections, which are announced by the two-part canon no. IX, the principal theme takes on even more varied shapes and is presented in an array of metric configurations, as the changing time signatures indicate. Now more suitable for further combinatorial possibilities, the varied principal theme is combined with two and three new subjects,

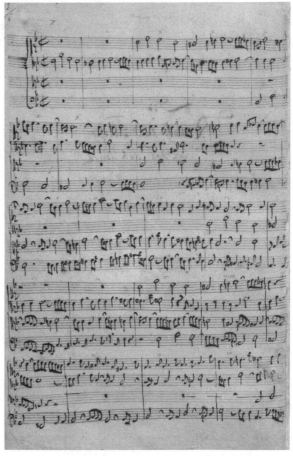

FIGURE 8-5

Opening fugue (untitled) of *The Art of Fugue*, BWV 1080.1/1: autograph fair copy (c. 1742).

C+D and C+E+D, all used in regular and inverted forms and resulting in a closely interrelated pair of movements comprising the triple and quadruple fugues, nos. X and XI (all four subjects are shown in Ex. 8-4). The quadruple fugue no. XI does not, however, introduce its countersubjects in separate expositions—as Bach would later plan to do in Contrapunctus 14 of the expanded version—but instead presents in fixed combinations the subjects C and D (from m. 27), then C and E (from m. 89). At the halfway point of the quadruple fugue, countersubject E (initially starting on the note *eb*) clearly spells out twice in the two upper voices and in the proper pitches the melodic sequence of Bach's name (Bb–A–C–B♮, which in German reads B-A-C-H), mm. 90–91 and 93–94.

EXAMPLE 8-3

BWV 1080/11: B-A-C-H theme (countersubject E), mm. 90–91.

At the very end of the piece, however, the varied principal theme in the top voice appears contrapuntally and harmonically supported by its three countersubjects (subject E starts again on *eb*)—an extraordinary tour de force in advanced chromaticism as well as a climactic and highly effective fugal conclusion:

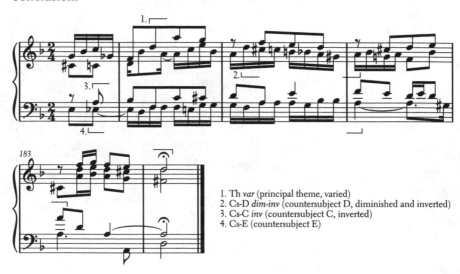

1. Th *var* (principal theme, varied)
2. Cs-D *dim-inv* (countersubject D, diminished and inverted)
3. Cs-C *inv* (countersubject C, inverted)
4. Cs-E (countersubject E)

EXAMPLE 8-4

BWV 1080/11: crowning simultaneous combination of four subjects.

Both fugues are set in modish $\frac{2}{4}$ meter, exploit daring dissonances, and move into advanced regions of harsh as well as expressive chromatic harmony, and in this particular respect they go much further than any previous composition by Bach. This modest finale effect was to be superseded eventually by the more pointed B-A-C-H subject used in the closing quadruple fugue of the published version. Yet no. XI delivers the evidence that the composer's idea of weaving his name like a signature into the score of the concluding fugue with multiple themes occurred early on, and can only be interpreted as a subtle but self-assured reminder of the personal hand he had taken in defining the art of the fugue.

The final section sets forth the apex of contrapuntal sophistication by offering two fugues and their mirror counterparts, no. XIII in simple counterpoint and no. XIV in double counterpoint, whose scores can also be read upside down and whose mirrored versions sound every bit as good as the originals. Bach had never written anything like this before, and he must have taken real satisfaction in drawing the set to a close with a little flourish that effectively illuminates the principle of mirrored sound:

EXAMPLE 8-5

BWV 1080/13: final flourish, mirrored, as an audible hint.

Concluding the work with two mirror fugues offered up the very ultimate in the catalog of intricate contrapuntal procedures. Yet the story here involves more than learned artifice, for even as Bach ingeniously resolved the formidable technical challenges that he had set for himself, he achieved at the same time extraordinarily elegant and gripping musical results.

The autograph manuscript containing the fourteen movements of the early version was begun and completed as a fair copy, one intended to replace preceding drafts that were most likely heavily corrected working scores of all fourteen movements. Since these preliminary materials were no longer needed, Bach likely disposed of them, as he had done in similar instances. He had never before undertaken a project of comparable complexity, and surely he would have gone through a process of experimental trials and errors. Yet there exist no details or clues whatsoever regarding the compositional prehistory of this first version. All the more important, therefore, is the partial evidence available regarding preparations for the printed final version. Although it cannot be determined just how soon Bach began to rethink the project after reviewing the early version, the last two pages of the autograph score offer the first signs of self-criticism and a quest for further improvement. Soon after copying out all fourteen movements, he entered as no. XV a substantially altered version of the augmentation canon no. XII. In the much longer replacement canon, Bach significantly increased the chromaticism of the harmonies, essentially recasting this movement in the form in which it was later published.

The bound autograph score of 1742 also included an appendix of three separate autograph fascicles and loose leaves containing (1) an alternative performing arrangement of the three-part mirror fugue no. XIV for two keyboards, dating from c. 1742–46; (2) the printer's copy of the augmentation canon no. XV, once again revised in alla breve (¢) notation with doubled note values, c. 1747/48; and (3) the final draft of the unfinished final quadruple fugue in two-stave keyboard notation from c. 1748–49 (breaking off at measure 239), probably a hint that all the fugues were originally drafted in keyboard notation rather than in open score. Although the three appendices cannot be precisely dated, they reveal that the preparations for publication of the expanded and reorganized version moved at a relatively slow pace. But despite his advanced age, the composer had his hands full with other projects, most of them not unrelated and comparably demanding.

CANONIC INTERMEZZI

Bach had always been fascinated by canonic technique. In this, the strictest category of imitative counterpoint, two or more vocal or instrumental parts present exactly the same melodic line, but begin at different times and at different intervals. The parts may move in different directions, at different speeds, or in any combination thereof. Relatively early but already mature examples of chorale canons show up in the *Orgel-Büchlein*, and various types of canons appear in instrumental concertos, suites, and cantatas as well as in the separate genre of short dedication canons for friendship albums. During the final decade of his life, however, Bach's interest in both the theory and practice of canonic counterpoint rose to new heights. The first prominent and extended examples occur in *Clavier-Übung* III and IV (Chapter 5) and in the newly added monumental opening chorale setting of the Reformation cantata "Ein feste Burg," BWV 80 (1739), with its prominent instrumental *cantus firmus* canon framing the vocal score.[11]

Fourteen Canons on the "Goldberg" Aria

In the later 1730s, most likely while preparing *Clavier-Übung* IV, the composer's attention turned to an extended and systematic exploration of canonic art. This is suggested by the genesis of the *Fourteen Canons* on the "Goldberg" aria bass, BWV 1087 (the source for the canon BWV 1076 depicted in the Haußmann portrait of 1746, as discussed in the Prologue).[12] Around 1748, long after the Goldberg Variations had been published, Bach entered these canons in calligraphic fashion on the last page of his personal copy of the *Clavier-Übung* (Fig. 8-6). It can be safely assumed, however, that their actual composition

FIGURE 8-6

Fourteen Canons, BWV 1087: autograph fair copy (c. 1748).

took place much earlier. The canons seem to have originated as a series of mental exercises with which Bach was amusing himself by exploring the potential of the Handel ostinato (Chapter 5, page 185), and they probably started out as some sort of canonic doodling that he wrote down while working on the *Goldberg Variations.* The notation "Etc." after canon no. 14 at the bottom of the autograph page suggests that he had more canonic solutions in mind and could easily have gone on. It appears that the edited and carefully organized collection was put together by the composer for his own use, with an eye to such purposes as entries for friendship albums (as with no. 11 =

BWV 1077, dedicated in 1747 to his student Johann Gottlieb Fulde). The title formulation, "Verschiedene Canones über die ersteren acht Fundamental-Noten vorheriger Aria" (Diverse canons on the first eight fundamental notes of the previous aria), makes clear that the series is intimately associated with the "Aria mit verschiedenen Veränderungen" (Aria with diverse variations) in the same book.

The collection of *Fourteen Canons* (Table 8-2) in the composer's autograph fair copy presents several intriguing aspects, including the linguistic mix of Latin, Italian, and German typical of Bach's method of instruction and also his characteristic gift for the logical and systematic organization of a serial project. But in particular, the manuscript reveals his success in creating musically appealing results even within the highly restrictive miniature format of four-measure canons. The autograph displays the entire series of canons in abbreviated enigmatic notation, such that the full series fits on a single page. For example, Canons 1 and 2 are written on the first staff, with key and time signatures in mirror image at both ends in order to indicate that the canonic parts are to be read forward and backward simultaneously. The combinations of notation and verbal instructions entered on the page—"all' roverscio" ([to be read] in inversion), "il soggetto in alto" (the subject [to be placed] in the alto part), or "in unisono post semifusam" ([succession of canonic part] in unison after a sixteenth note), and so forth—represent the full range of canonic vocabulary as it relates to the various techniques.

The subject of the canon series, the first eight fundamental notes that make up the initial section of the 32-measure Goldberg aria bass, was indeed borrowed from Handel (Chapter 5, page 186), and as an ostinato bass pattern it actually goes back to the seventeenth century.[13] Yet Bach seems to have been the first to discover, or at least to make known, the inherent canonic potential of this subject: Canons 1–4 demonstrate that the subject, if read forward and backward in both regular and inverted or mirrored forms, always yields correct counterpoints and harmonically satisfactory results. It therefore constituted the ideal vehicle for him to employ in illustrating the contrapuntal principles of inversion and retrograde motion. It also provided a point of departure for him to experiment with further technical manipulations, in which he combined the given subject with countersubjects to form independent and distinct contrapuntal lines.

In this exemplary series, Bach methodically demonstrated the workings of the various canonic categories and contrapuntal techniques, as they progress from simple canons to the more complex double and triple canons (i.e.,

TABLE 8-2. *Fourteen Canons* on the first eight fundamental notes of the
Aria from the *Goldberg Variations*

NO.	ORIGINAL HEADING	CANON CATEGORY*	COMBINATION OF THEME AND COUNTERSUBJECTS
1	Canon simplex	Simplex: Th, in unison	Th/Th *retro*
2	all' roverscio	Simplex: Th *retro*, in unison	Th *retro*/Th *retro+inv*
3	Beede vorigen Canones zugleich, motu recto e contrario	Simplex: Th, at the fifth	Th/Th *inv*
4	motu contrario e recto	Simplex: Th *inv*, at the fifth	Th *inv*/Th
5	Canon duplex à 4	Duplex: Th+A, at the fifth	(Th/Th *inv*)+(A/A *inv*)
6	Canon simplex über besagtes Fundament à 3	Simplex: Th+B, at the third	Th+(B/B *inv*)
7	Idem à 3	Simplex: Th+Th *ext-dim* ♪, stretto at the fifth	Th+(Th *ext* ♪/Th *ext* ♪-*inv*)
8	Canon simplex à 3, il soggetto in Alto	Simplex: Th+C, at the twelfth	Th+(C/C *inv*)
9	Canon unison post semifusam à 3	Simplex: Th+D, extreme stretto in unison	Th+(D/D)
10	Alio modo, per syncopationes e ligaturas à 2	Duplex: Th+E, with syncopations and suspensions	Th+(E/E)
	Evolutio	Duplex: mirrored resolution	Th+(E *inv*/E *inv*)
11	Canon duplex übers Fundament à 5	Duplex: Th+F+ G, both counterpoints at the octave	Th+(F/F *inv*) + (G/G *inv*)
12	Canon duplex über besagte Fundamental-Noten à 5	Duplex: Th *aug* ♩+Th *ext-dim* ♪+ Th *ext-dim* ♪, stretto at the fifth	Th ♩+(Th *ext* ♪/Th *ext* ♪-*inv*) +(Th *ext* ♪/Th *ext* ♪-*inv*)
13	Canon triplex à 6	Triplex: Th at the twelfth+H at the fifth +I at the fifth	(Th/Th *inv*)+(H/H *inv*) + (I/I *inv*)
14	Canon à 4 per Augmentationem et Diminutionem	Quadruplex: Th *ext*, at the twelfth, the octave, the fifth, and at 4 different speeds (proportional)	Th *ext* ♪-*inv*/Th *ext* ♪/ Th *ext* ♩-*inv*/Th ♩

* Abbreviations and explanations:

Th Principal canon theme (eight fundamental notes of the "Goldberg" aria); *aug* = augmented; *dim* = diminished; *ext* = extended; *inv* = inverted; *retro* = retrograde; *retro+inv* = retrograde and inverted

A–I Counterpoints A to I; *inv* = inverted

+ Indicates combination of themes and counterpoints

♩ . . . Speed of theme: sixteenth ♪, eighth ♪, quarter ♩, and half ♩ notes

(x/x) Two or more parts—theme or counterpoints—forming a canon

with two and three subjects), and imitation in close and very close succession
(stretto, in which the leader and follower overlap). In Canon 12, he introduced
proportional principles: two canons on the extended and varied theme at two
different speeds (both sixteenth-note and eighth-note motion) over and above
the regular theme in half notes. As a culmination point in Canon 14, Bach
presents a quadruple proportional canon, in which all four parts move at

different speeds (in half, quarter, eighth, and sixteenth notes)—an absolutely unique specimen among his canonic compositions. Even though the nature of the cycle was determined by theoretical principles and systematic organization, and despite the extreme limitations of the miniature format, Bach had no interest in creating purely laborious-sounding cerebral music. Indeed, he kept the notion of musically engaging and charming variety very much alive throughout the series, notably with the unexpected chromatic harmonies in Canons 6 and 11, the energetic rhythms in Canons 9 and 14, and the sophisticated and captivating five- and six-part textures of Canons 11 to 13.

Canonic Variations on the Christmas song "Vom Himmel hoch"

In the course of working on the *Fourteen Canons*, Bach would have noticed that the eight fundamental notes resembled the melody of the Lutheran Christmas song "Vom Himmel hoch, da komm ich her" (From heaven high I come). Each of the four phrases of the tune consists of eight notes (without passing tones), with their diatonic components generally related to the subject of the *Fourteen Canons* and its triadic harmonic underpinning:

EXAMPLE 8-6

(a) *BWV 1087: main subject of the canons.*

(b) *"Vom Himmel hoch, da komm ich her," last section of the melody resembling the fundamental notes of BWV 1087.*

While the *Fourteen Canons* were not designed as a performing series but rather as a lesson in canonic theory and practice, the Christmas tune offered the possibility of composing an elaborate set of chorale variations designated and suitable for organ performance. Bach embraced and realized this opportunity in a set of five variations under the title "Einige canonische Veränderungen über das Weyhnacht-Lied: Vom Himmel hoch, da komm ich her vor die Orgel mit 2. Clavieren und dem Pedal" (A few canonic variations on the Christmas hymn "From heaven high I come," for the organ with two manuals and pedal).

The set of Canonic Variations, BWV 769, as published by Balthasar Schmid, the Nuremberg publisher of the *Goldberg Variations*, appeared around 1747 (Figs. 8-7 and 8-8). The actual genesis of the work remains largely obscure, however, because the only extant original source other than the first edition is a later fair-copy manuscript, which Bach prepared for organ performance and entered into the manuscript of the Great Eighteen Chorales (Chapter 7). As he had done with the canon BWV 1076 (Prologue, pages 3–4), he included a copy of the print in one of the packages later circulated by the Leipzig-based Corresponding Society of Musical Science, which he had joined in June 1747.[14] Though not specifically composed for the organization, the set of chorale canons was eminently suitable for presentation to this learned society, as it

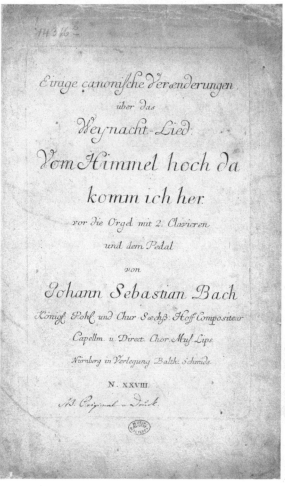

FIGURE 8-7

Canonic Variations, BWV 769: title page
(Nuremberg, n.d. [c. 1747]).

enabled the composer to share with fellow members his profound knowledge and ingenious practical application of complex canonic procedures.

The compositional history of the "Vom Himmel hoch" Variations (Table 8-3) can be conjectured only on the basis of their inner relationship with the fourteen Goldberg canons—that is, they most likely originated some time after the *Goldberg Variations* proper were published. Like the nine canonic movements of the *Goldbergs*, all five chorale variations are designed as stretto canons. The first three of the set closely resemble their technical models, even using three different imitation intervals for leader and follower. The close rela-

FIGURE 8-8

Variation 5, Canonic Variations, BWV 769
(Nuremberg, c. 1747).

tionship is especially evident in no. 3, a slow movement with *cantabile* designation, which carries a clear association with Variation 15 of the *Goldbergs* in *andante* motion. While the augmentation canon no. 4 has no equivalent in *Clavier-Übung* IV, it relates directly to the augmentation canon in the early version of the *Art of Fugue* and also to the revised form of this same canon at the very end of the autograph manuscript (see page 293). The two versions represent the earliest examples of an extended movement constructed as an augmentation canon, demonstrating that the interrelationship of the various canonic projects played an obvious role.

Whereas all canonic parts in variations 1–4 consist of free counterpoints, the chorale melody itself is finally subjected to canonic treatment in the last variation, and in a particularly sophisticated manner that has no equivalent elsewhere. In relatively short sequential order, Bach applied canonic imitations at the intervals of a sixth, third, second, and ninth, intervals that had not been used in the four preceding variations (Fig. 8-6). Beyond that, variation 5 concludes with a notable intensification of texture over and above the last chorale line in the organ pedal. Here Bach created a climax in two stages: first in a five-part texture, with four parts expounding the opening chorale phrase in diminution, and then in a six-part texture, which finally combines all four chorale lines in diminution and stretto—a dazzling and masterful conclusion.

TABLE 8-3. Canonic Variations on the Christmas hymn "Vom Himmel hoch," c. 1747

ORIGINAL HEADING (CANON CATEGORY)	SCORE (PARTS)	STRUCTURAL COMPONENTS: CANTUS FIRMUS AND COUNTERPOINTS*
Variatio 1. Canone all' ottava	3	(A, r.h./A, l.h.) = stretto canon at the octave + c.f., ped.
Variatio 2. Canone alla quinta	3	(B, r.h./B, l.h.) = stretto canon at the fifth + c.f., ped.
Variatio 3. Canone alla settima (cantabile)	4	C + c.f., r.h. + (D, l.h./D, ped.) = stretto canon at the seventh
Variatio 4. Canone all'ottava, per augmentationem	4	(E, r.h./E *aug*, l.h.) = canon at the octave + F, l.h. + c.f., ped.
Variatio 5. L'altra sorte del' canone all' roverscio,		
1) alla sesta [mm. 1–14]	3	(c.f., r.h./c.f. *inv*, l.h.) = stretto canon at the sixth + G, ped.
2) alla terza [mm. 14–27]	3	(c.f. *inv*, r.h./c.f., l.h.) = stretto canon at the third + H
3) alla seconda [mm. 27–39]	4	I, r.h. + K, l.h. + (c.f. *inv*, l.h./c.f., ped.) = stretto canon at the second
4) alla nona [mm. 39–52] è	4	(c.f. *inv*, ped./c.f., r.h.) = stretto canon at the ninth + L, r.h. + M, l.h.
diminutio [mm. 52–54]	5	(c.f. *dim*/c.f. dim, l.h.) + (c.f. *dim*/c.f. *inv-dim*, r.h.) + c.f.-4, ped.
alla stretta [mm. 54–56]	6	c.f.-1+c.f.-2+c.f.-3+c.f.-4

Abbreviations and explanations:

c.f.	Cantus firmus (chorale melody); c.f.-1 (2,3,4) 1st (2nd, 3rd, 4th) phrase of c.f.
A–M	Different counterpoints, A to M
(x/x)	Two or more parts forming a canon, e.g. (A/A), (c.f./c.f. *inv*), etc.
+	Indicates combination of c.f. and counterpoints
r.h., l.h., ped.	Placement of parts for organ performance: right hand, left hand, pedal

For publication, Bach decided to issue the first three canons in abbreviated scores of two staves, which notated the leader of each canonic part but marked only the entry point of the follower, without including the part as such. This abbreviated notation was meant to demonstrate visually the rigor and exactitude of the canonic structure. Anyone reading the complete score, let alone performing the work, would have been obliged to work out on paper the realizations of the three- and four-part movements. Even the composer himself had to copy out the missing parts! Indeed, he prepared for himself a performing edition of the complete set in the autograph fair copy mentioned above.

The canons of the *Musical Offering*

Bach used a similar combination of abbreviated and complete notation in the *Musical Offering*, BWV 1079, a cyclical work comprising three distinct components: two keyboard fugues, a trio sonata, and ten canons, all based on one and the same "royal theme." As with no other Bach work, the genesis of the opus (published in September 1747) can be dated precisely to May 7 of that same year, when the composer was visiting the Potsdam court of King Friedrich II of Prussia. On that day Bach attended the evening chamber music gathering, and in a passage of the published work's characteristically adulatory dedication, he recalled the event:

> With awesome pleasure I still remember the very special Royal Grace when, some time ago, during my visit in Potsdam, Your Majesty's Self deigned to play to me a theme for a fugue upon the clavier, and at the same time charged me most graciously to carry it out in Your Majesty's Most August Presence.[15]

Upon returning home, the composer proceeded to notate the piece he had improvised on one of the king's new Silbermann fortepianos, namely a three-part fugue on the theme given to him by the king, now in edited and polished shape. He added to it a remarkably intricate keyboard fugue for six voices,[16] and entitled both of these pieces "Ricercar." He then composed a sonata for flute (the king's instrument), violin, and basso continuo "sopra Soggetto Reale" (on the royal subject), and finally supplemented the whole with ten canonic elaborations "super Thema Regium" (on the royal theme). These canonic pieces were distributed as follows over the three fascicles in which the work was published: (1) three in the keyboard fascicle, one after the three-part ricercar and two in enigmatic notation, that is, without indicating canon solutions in the form of entry points for the follower parts; (2) one in the set of three performing parts for the trio; and (3) the remaining six in a separate fascicle under the Latin heading "Thematis Regii Elaborationes Canonicae" (Canonic elaborations on the royal theme), with a title page bearing an ingenious Latin acrostic for the word "ricercar": "**R**egis **I**ussu **C**antio **E**t **R**eliqua **C**anonica **A**rte **R**esoluta" (the theme given at the king's command and the remainder resolved according to canonic art). Bach seems to have offered this rubric as a reference to the inner musical coherence of the otherwise rather heterogeneous collection (Fig. 8-9 and Table 8-4).

TABLE 8-4. *Musical Offering*: Thematis Regii Elaborationes
Canonicae, 1747

ORIGINAL HEADING, CANON CATEGORY	SCORE (PARTS)	STRUCTURAL COMPONENTS
Canon fascicle		
Canones diversi super Thema Regium		
Canon 1. a 2 [cancrizans—in retrograde motion]	2	Th *ext*/Th *ext-retro*
Canon 2. a 2 violini in unison	3	(A/A) + Th, bass part
Canon 3. a 2 per Motum contrarium	3	(B/B *inv*) + Th *var*, top part
Canon 4. a 2 per Augmentationem, contrario Motu	3	(C/C *inv-aug*) + Th *var*, center part
Canon 5. a 2 [per tonos—modulatory, ascending by whole steps]	3	(D/D) + Th *var*, top part
[6.] Fuga canonica in Epidiapente [at the fifth]	3	(Th *ext*/Th *ext*) + E, basso continuo, with Th quotes
Trio fascicle		
[7.] Canon perpetuus [for flute, violin, and basso continuo]	3	(Th *ext*/Th *ext-inv*)+ F, basso continuo
Keyboard fascicle		
[8.] Canon perpetuus super Thema Regium [at the octave] Quaerendo invenietis [Seek and you will find]	3	(G/G) + Th, center part
[9.] Canon a 2 [at the octave, inverted—in enigmatic notation]	2	(Th *ext*/Th *ext-inv*)
[10.] Canon a 4 [in unison and at the octave—in enigmatic notation]	4	(Th *ext*/Th *ext*/Th *ext*/Th *ext*)

Abbreviations and explanations:

Th Royal theme (in various forms): *ext* = extended; *var* = varied; inv = inverted; *retro* = in retrograde motion; *aug* = in augmentation; *dim* = in diminution
A–G Counterpoints A to G
(x/x) Two or more parts forming a canon
+ The plus sign indicates combination theme and counterpoints

The *Musical Offering*'s conceptual design, which far exceeded Bach's typical approaches in such regular performing genres as keyboard fugue and trio sonata, was clearly inspired and shaped by the special situation of 1747. Following a series of extensive canonic experiments, that year saw the beginnings of his preoccupation with preparing the *Art of Fugue* for publication. Moreover, the canonic movements of the *Musical Offering* very much reflect the dual nature of canonic composition, embodying as they do abstract contrapuntal construction and appealing musical qualities. Some of the pieces are more weighted to the latter category, being of lesser technical complexity

FIGURE 8-9

Musical Offering, BWV 1079/4a–f: *Canones diversi*
(Leipzig, 1747).

and eminently suitable for performance. Intricacy prevails in the longer movements, notably in the Fuga canonica [6] and in the perpetual canon [10] appended to the trio sonata. All these movements, specifically the sequence of "Canones diversi," numbered 1–5, take their departure from, and clearly recall the systematic theoretical approach of, the *Fourteen Canons*, yet they also evince a somewhat different progressive evolution. A one-line retrograde "crab" canon is followed by three settings that introduce regular, inverted, and augmented canonic follower parts. The "Canones diversi" subseries then culminates in two canon types without parallel in Bach's oeuvre: a modulatory canon ascending in whole steps, and finally a three-part canonic fugue (a fugue in which the two upper parts form a canon).

As a variegated assemblage of two keyboard fugues, a chamber sonata, and ten canons, the *Musical Offering* has no equivalent among the composer's monothematic works of the 1740s.[17] Its contents were carefully put together as a formal offering, a gift most appropriate for its musically proficient royal recipient and also truly worthy of its resourceful and imaginative creator. The work is conceived as a kind of self-portrait of a musicians' musician, one equally competent as a keyboard virtuoso, a capellmeister, and a masterful composer in all styles, including the most elaborate and erudite counterpoint. The two ricercars embody complementary realizations of both extemporaneous and ruminative fugal art, as well as differing types of keyboard virtuosity. In fact, the six-part fugue stands as the only such piece for performance with two hands ever written by Bach—or by any other composer. The trio sonata was meant as a special contribution by the Saxon capellmeister to the chamber repertoire of the acclaimed Prussian court ensemble, which included his own son and several former students. Particularly in the sonata's slow movements, Bach paid homage to the king's preferred style of delicate sensitivity (*Empfindsamkeit*), and he certainly demonstrated the suitability of the royal theme for such mannerist treatment, even if in contrapuntal disguise.

Finally, the canons were intended to appeal to the intellectual side of the philosopher-king. Bach most likely overestimated the ruler's taste for complex musical constructions. Still, the king might well have enjoyed the allegorical references attached to the augmentation canon no. 4 ("Notulis crescentibus crescat Fortuna Regis"—As the note values increase, so may the fortune of the King) and to the modulatory canon no. 5 ("Ascendente Modulatione ascendat Gloria Regis"—As the modulation moves upward, so may the King's glory).[18] Twenty-seven years later, the monarch recalled his Leipzig visitor with great admiration and also with some exaggeration when, as reported by Gottfried van Swieten, then Austrian ambassador to Berlin, "he sang aloud a chromatic fugue subject that he had given the old Bach, who on the spot had made of it a fugue in four parts, then in five parts, and finally in eight parts."[19]

In light of an ever-decreasing interest all across of Europe in strict musical composition generally and in the art of counterpoint in particular, Bach seemed to be suggesting an alternative (notably in the sonata), demonstrating how a subject as baroque and knotty as the "royal theme" could in fact be treated in an emphatically galant and expressive manner. Regarding the prevailing musical aesthetics in Berlin, with which Carl Philipp Emanuel and the younger generation identified, his father allegedly once remarked "'s ist Berlinerblau! 's verschießt!" ('Tis Prussian Blue! It fades!).[20] Given that skeptical point of view, Bach's steadfast adherence to traditional and "made-to-last" counterpoint might be understood as a program of contrast. He must certainly have been aware that the *Musical Offering*, widely available as a published work and further burnished by the dedication to the King of Prussia, provided him with a unique platform to make his case.

THE ART OF FUGUE UNFINISHED: THE PUBLISHED VERSION

Either before or after completing the *Musical Offering* but sometime around 1747, Bach decided to bring to the public in a printed edition a monothematic cycle of twelve fugues and two canons, a group of works then in manuscript. Since the collection still lacked a title, at some point he had his pupil and copyist Johann Christoph Altnickol enter "Die | Kunst der Fuga | d. Sign. Joh. Seb. Bach." onto the blank first page of the autograph fair copy, a programmatic title without any precedent and a title that also reflected the expansion and revisions he had in mind. The ordering of untitled movements in the manuscript version primarily followed the principles of contrapuntal technique and, subordinate to this, the concept of thematic variation, while fugue types played no major organizational role. The published version, however, would eventually order the movements not by contrapuntal categories but instead unequivocally by types of fugue, although Bach refrained from using the heading "fugue" throughout and chose the umbrella term "contrapunctus," in order to stress the primacy of strict contrapuntal writing.

The changed movement sequence in the print gave rise to what might in fact be considered a treatise, or "practisches Fugenwerk" (practical work of fugue), as its posthumous editor Carl Philipp Emanuel Bach later referred to

FIGURE 8-10

The Art of Fugue, BWV 1080.2: title page (n.d., n.p. [Berlin, 1751]).

it.[21] The collection comprised chapters, organized in terms of logical units and according to progressive difficulty (Table 8-5; the second column provides a concordance with the early version), which contained:

(1) simple fugues, based solely on the principal theme embedded in individual contrapuntal fabrics of distinct character;

(2) *counterfugues*, these being a type of fugue based on the juxtaposition of the principal theme with its inverted form (*fuga contraria*) and also introducing the techniques of diminution and augmentation;

(3) fugues on multiple subjects, including the principal theme, at different intervals;

(4) mirror fugues in simple and double counterpoint;

(5) strict canons of different kinds;

(6) a culminating finale in the form of a quadruple fugue.[22]

In its thorough exploration of fugal types, the *Art of Fugue* is the very first systematic and comprehensive practical guide in the history of music. It paved the way for the first published treatise on fugue, the *Abhandlung von der Fuge* (Berlin, 1753) by Friedrich Wilhelm Marpurg, who had visited with Bach in 1746 and apparently discussed with him issues of fugal composition.[23] Based on this connection, Marpurg was later asked by Carl Philipp Emanuel to write the preface to the second printing of the *Art of Fugue* (1752).

Bach's reorganization of the work for the purpose of publication strengthened its musical logic through the addition of a number of crucial elements. The group of simple fugues was augmented by a fourth, highly chromatic fugue of unusual length (138 measures). This late addition of Contrapunctus 4 speaks to Bach's ambitious musical goal, namely his desire to probe the nearly endless possibilities for treating new motivic ideas deriving from and coalescing with the given material, thereby extending contrapuntal techniques to their very limits. Thus, the fourth simple fugue demonstrates impressively that the first three simple fugues had by no means exhausted the potential of dealing with the fundamentals. Contrapunctus 4 also added the traditional pattern of syncopations and suspensions to its rhythmic vocabulary (see Table 8-2, Canon no. 10: "per syncopationes e ligaturas"), which in turn generated ideas for sequential patterns in the interludes and lent notable coherence to the entire movement. Finally, it features (in its third section) a special variant of the inverted principal theme. In purposeful violation of traditional rules, Bach expanded the theme's melodic contours to the span of a seventh, a gambit that

TABLE 8-5. *The Art of Fugue*: Version of the original edition, 1751
(cf. Table 8-1)

ORIGINAL HEADING (TYPE OF SETTING)	CONCORDANCE WITH EARLY VERSION	THEMES, COUNTERSUBJECTS, AND PROCEDURES	MAJOR CHANGES MADE TO EARLY VERSION
Simple Fugues		**Contrapunctus simplex**	
Contrapunctus 1.	I	¢ Th ♩: ASBT, diatonic contrapuntal continuation	mm. 74–78 with plagal cadence added
Contrapunctus 2.	III	¢ Th ♩: BTAS, dotted contrapuntal continuation	mm. 78–84 with plagal cadence added
Contrapunctus 3.	II	¢ Th ♩ *inv*: TASB, chromatic contrapuntal continuation	
Contrapunctus 4.	–	¢ Th ♩ *inv*: SATB, contrapuntal continuation with syncopations and suspensions	New composition
Counterfugues		**Contrapunctus duplex ("all' ottava")**	
Contrapunctus 5.	IV	C Th ♩ *mod*+Th *mod-inv*: ABST Time signature changed	Time signature changed
Contrapunctus 6. a 4 in Style Francese	VII	C Th ♩ *mod* +Th ♩ *inv*: BSAT	
Contrapunctus 7. a 4 per Augment: et Diminut:	VIII	C Th *mod* ♩ + Th ♩ *mod-inv* +Th 𝅝 *mod-inv-augm*: TSAB	
Fugues on multiple subjects		**Contrapunctus duplex** ("all' ottava, duodecima e decima")	
Contrapunctus 8. a 3 [at the octave, triple fugue]	X	¢ Cs-C: TBS; → Cs-D+Th ♩ *var-inv*	Time signature changed; note values doubled
Contrapunctus 9. a 4 alla Duodecima [double fugue]	V	C Cs-A: ASBT; → Cs-A+Th 𝅝	Note values doubled
Contrapunctus 10. a 4 alla Decima [double fugue]	VI	C Cs-B *inv*: ATBS; → Cs-B+Th ♩ *mod-inv*	mm. 1–22 added; note values doubled
Contrapunctus 11. a 4 [at the octave, triple fugue]	XI	¢ Th ♩ *var*: ASBT; → Cs-C +Cs-D; Cs-C+Cs-E; Cs-C+Cs-D+Cs-E+Th *var-inv*	Time signature changed; note values doubled
Mirror Fugues		**Contrapunctus inversus**	
Contrapunctus inversus 12ᵃ. a 4	XIIIᵃ	𝄴 Th ♩ *inv*: SATB, in Contrapunctus simplex	Note values doubled
Contrapunctus inversus 12ᵇ. a 4	XIIIᵇ	𝄴 Th ♩: BTAS (complete mirroring of 12ᵃ)	Note values doubled
Contrapunctus inversus 13ᵃ. a 3	XIVᵃ	¢ Th ♩ *inv*: SAB, in Contrapunctus duplex	Note values doubled

Contrapunctus inversus 13[b]. a 3	XIV[b]	¢ Th♩: BAS (complete mirroring of 13[a])	Note values doubled
Canons		**Canon**	
Canon alla Ottava	IX	$\frac{9}{16}$ Th ♪ *var-inv*/Th *var*: SB	
Canon alla Decima in Contrapunto alla Terza	–	$\frac{12}{8}$ Th♩ *var-inv*/Th *var*: BS	New composition
Canon all Duodecima in Contrapunto alla Quinta	–	¢ Th♩ *var*/Th *var*: BS	New composition
Canon per Augmentationem in Contrario Motu	XII	¢ Th♩ *var*/Th♩ *var-inv*: SB	Note values doubled
Quadruple Fugue		**Contrapunctus duplex et inversus**	
[Contrapunctus 14] Fuga a 3 Soggetti (unfinished)	–	¢ Cs-E: BTAS; → Cs-F/Cs-E/Th; Cs-G/Cs-F/Cs-E . . .	New composition, with separate expositions for three new countersubjects and final exposition mirrored

Abbreviations and explanations (see also Table 8-1, page 293):

Th   Principal theme; *aug* = augmented; *dim* = diminished; *inv* = inverted; *mod* = slightly modified; *var* = varied; *var-inv* = varied and inverted; *mod-inv* = slightly modified and inverted

Cs-A–G   Countersubjects (new subjects, distinct from principal theme), A to G; Cs-E and Cs-H beginning with B♭-A-C-B♮ = BACH

+   Theme (or countersubject) combined with countersubject (or theme)

→   Combinations after first fugal section

permitted daring modulations into harmonic areas far remote from the home key of D minor (Fig. 8-11). Along with this substantial and innovative addition, Bach reordered the simple fugues 1–2 and 3–4 according to the use of regular and inverted themes, and also extended each of the original three fugues by four to twelve measures, such that all four simple fugues end in plagal (IV–I) cadences. By this means he emphasized their retrospective stylistic profile, and established the chapter on simple fugues as the point of departure for further examples of fugal types and styles.

Bach's regrouping of the simple fugues (Contrapuncti 1–4) into a closed chapter also allowed for the creation of a separate chapter on counterfugues (Contrapuncti 5–7). These pieces incorporated the principle of imitation on different mensural scales, a move that resulted in a more logical reconfiguration of the entire first half of the work. In the subsequent group of fugues on multiple subjects, Bach consolidated the rhythmic notation such that related subjects appeared in the same note values. He also added a new opening section to Contrapunctus 10, in order to avoid starting with the principal theme

FIGURE 8-11

The Art of Fugue, BWV 1080.2: Contrapunctus 4, mm. 57–86 (Berlin, 1751).

at this juncture.[24] While the group of mirror fugues remained unchanged (apart from minor notational alterations), the canon group was enlarged to four movements by two newly composed pieces. The treatise-like chapter organization of the published version now departed from the original movement order based on the concept of cyclical variation (and performance), as realized in the gradual evolution of the principal theme's rhythmic-melodic shape.[25] The most substantial addition in the print, which ultimately also resulted in the work's unfinished state, occurred at the newly conceived conclusion. Whereas the earlier version ended with two mirror fugues framed by two canons, thereby amalgamating the two strictest forms of contrapuntal imitation in one group, Bach apparently intended to create an even more formidable culmination with a newly composed final movement.

According to Carl Philipp Emanuel Bach's description in the obituary, his father's

> last illness prevented him from completing his project of bringing the next-to-last fugue to completion and working out the last one, which was to contain four themes and to have them afterward inverted note for note in all four voices.[26]

Since the extant unfinished last fugue is not only the longest fugue of the cycle but also the longest one Bach ever wrote, it seems inconceivable that he would have planned to follow this piece with yet another fugue of equal length, to be subsequently "inverted note for note." The surviving autograph keyboard score of the unfinished fugue contains the expositions of three new subjects, the last one based on the letters B-A-C-H. The fourth section, which was supposed to combine the three themes with the work's principal theme in quadruple counterpoint, breaks off after only seven measures, leaving the piece incomplete. The process of composing a quadruple fugue, however, must of necessity begin with the section that has all four themes combined. And since precisely this concluding part of the fugue is missing, it seems indeed likely that what is preserved does not embody all that Bach had composed and left at the time of his death, and this in turn suggests the following scenario.

Carl Philipp Emanuel Bach, the first editor of the *Art of Fugue*,[27] had to deal with two different fragmentary manuscript sources for the conclusion of the work, one containing three fugal expositions and ending in a broken-off transition, the other containing four themes combined and inverted but still to be worked out. The first surviving fragment, the keyboard score of the unfinished fugue, served to prepare the open score for the print. It was misleadingly headed "Fuga a tre soggetti" because it treated only three subjects, the first of which looked a bit like the principal theme. The second fragment, containing one or more drafts that combine all four themes and their inversions, has not survived, but it apparently provided the basis for Carl Philipp Emanuel's assumption, cited above, that two fugues were planned for the work's conclusion—as opposed to the idea that the two fragments actually complemented each other as parts of one and the same projected Contrapunctus 14. This very long final fugue was to surpass the quadruple fugue of Contrapunctus 11, a composition that lacked the contrapuntal climax of combining and inverting all four themes.

The use of the B-A-C-H motif as the third fugal subject, less subtly threaded in than in Contrapunctus 11 but plainly spelled out, also speaks to the function of Contrapunctus 14 as the finale of the whole. Moreover, the chromatic nature of the name subject and the newly composed and heavily chromatic Contrapunctus 4 emphatically underscore the dual nature of the key of D as both minor mode and *modus chromaticus*, as had already been evident throughout the earlier version. The strikingly innovative use of chromaticism, particularly in Contrapunctus 4, Contrapunctus 11, the augmentation canon, and Contrapunctus 14, points to Bach's clear interest in demonstrating that contrapuntal writing does not set limits on the imaginative use of harmony.

The thorough reorganization of the *Art of Fugue*, prompted by a desire for systematic ordering, in no way overrode the composer's general musical priority: creating a work in which every movement offered an exhaustive exploration of the chosen contrapuntal technique—in fascinating combinations, with changing stylistic orientations, and employing a wide range of distinct and captivating ideas. Every single fugal or canonic movement possesses individual and sharply profiled musical contours. Bach seemed eager to demonstrate that "strict" contrapuntal composition offered a nearly endless variety of possible approaches. This final scheme also included a dynamic historical dimension by beginning with a set of fugues of notably retrospective character (though all of them display modern touches as well). The subsequent movements, however, explore a wide spectrum of rather fashionable melodic-rhythmic patterns, which are evident not only in the French style of Contrapunctus 6 but in virtually all of the following movements.

The *Art of Fugue* was the main instrumental project of Bach's final decade, evolving gradually and slowly reshaping itself over the course of time. In this work, the composer united with greatest consistency a monothematic cyclic conception, methodical contrapuntal procedures, and utmost musical resourcefulness. Although it is the work in which the theoretical component of his thinking is most overtly expressed, the results never congeal into recondite theory. The early version of the *Art of Fugue*, which presented a kind of "art of counterpoint in variation," led in due course to the published version in the form of a thoroughly systematic study of fugue and canon. The collection thus emerged as the "complete practical fugal work" of Carl Philipp Emanuel Bach's description, "in the deep and thoughtful execution of unusual, ingenious ideas, far removed from the ordinary run, and yet spontaneous and natural."[28] Theory and practice fused, while older and newer style elements and techniques of composition were integrated, all of this communicating Bach's individualistic approach to musical composition in an unmistakable and exemplary way. With the signature "B-A-C-H" woven into Contrapunctus 11 and even more prominently spelled out in the unfinished final fugue, the *Art of Fugue* stands as the most substantial and also the most personal instrumental opus ever to issue from Bach's pen.

As with no other composition by Bach, the *Art of Fugue* demonstrates in a decidedly focused manner just how the art of counterpoint can determine processes of compositional elaboration founded on rigorous and imaginative derivations from chosen or given musical themes and motives. The composer, who in the mid-eighteenth century clearly saw himself at the crossroads of musical style, surely knew from the outset that such exacting work would challenge rather than please performers and listeners alike. Yet he undertook the complex project without consideration for outside reactions or wider acceptance, not only because he himself was fascinated by the process itself, which surely gave him a wonderful pastime, but also because he likely wished to bequeath a legacy. Never even remotely popular in any era, the *Art of Fugue* nonetheless secured in professional circles, once and for all, the historical status of a musical technique, form, and genre that had already become inseparable from its author even before the work was published.

THE *MASS IN B MINOR*

It was no mere coincidence that after Bach's death his son Carl Philipp Emanuel ended up being entrusted with the manuscript and printing plates of the unfinished *Art of Fugue* and the barely completed autograph score of the *B-minor Mass*. The family and above all Wilhelm Friedemann, the executor of the estate,[29] realized that his younger brother was the one best suited to carry out responsible stewardship of the two major musical projects that had preoccupied the composer up until his demise. Thus Carl not only wrote the obituary with the summary list of works, which included a description of the unfinished state of the *Art of Fugue*, he also managed the remarkable task of bringing the work to posthumous publication within a year. In addition, and as a marketing device, he wrote an introductory essay for the collection, which he placed in the major intellectual journal of Berlin.[30] At the same time, he held the autograph score of "the great catholic Mass"[31] in safe custody. And going well beyond a merely custodial role, he saw to it that this particularly precious posthumous opus would not remain neglected, and took steps to ensure that the Mass would at minimum become something of a gift to musical insiders. Early on, he arranged for a number of professional manuscript copies to be prepared for Bach students and other Bach enthusiasts in Berlin, as well as for a number of serious connoisseurs. These included Baron Gottfried van Swieten of Vienna, who would eventually make the Mass available to Haydn and Mozart. As it turned out, however, more than three decades would pass before the Bach son was actually able to hear the music of the Mass, and only some of it, at that: in 1786 he conducted the first public performance of part II, the Symbolum Nicenum, at a concert in Hamburg to benefit a hospital for the poor.[32]

The manifold interrelationships between the *Art of Fugue* and the Mass, both of them peerless and exemplary works, were certainly not lost on the Bach son. The *Art of Fugue* focused on instrumental counterpoint in its most intricate and advanced realizations; the Mass, on the other hand, represented the art of vocal polyphony in all its remarkable diversity, offering as it did particularly profound settings of the venerable Mass text. The Mass in its entirety presents, both to the eye and the ear, the *summa summarum* of Bach's vocal art, bearing out in full the words of the 1733 dedication letter to the electoral court in Dresden. There, in subservient modesty befitting his rank, the composer had described the Mass—then comprising the Kyrie and Gloria, the work's initial unit—as "a humble work of the kind of *Wißenschafft* (knowledge, science, scholarship) I have attained in music." Such a characterization of what this music was intended to represent was surely true at the time, and applied all the more to the entire Mass as later completed (Table 8-6).[33]

The genre of Mass was especially well chosen for such an undertaking, and this choice led Bach, the seasoned cantor, capellmeister, and composition teacher, into new realms of conceptual thought. The oldest large-scale vocal form, the Mass had been the central genre of sacred vocal music since the fourteenth century. It therefore comes as no surprise that Bach should have wished to make his own contribution to this still unfolding chapter in the history of composition. The prospect must have seemed all the more attractive in that he had been witness to successive changes in contemporary tastes within his principal domain of vocal composition, the cantata repertoire. He had seen the interest in various types of cantatas wax and wane, with one sort supplanting another over time. And he had surely concluded that the linguistic, theological, and musical transience of the church cantata could in no way compare with the timelessness of the Latin Mass tradition.

Given this background, it is understandable that when Bach incorporated cantata movements into the *B-minor Mass*, he chose not only those that were the best suited in thematic terms, but also those that embodied exceptional compositional quality—doubtless with an eye to preserving these movements from the inevitable process of obsolescence. The pieces he selected (Table 8-7)

TABLE 8-6. The autograph score of the *B-minor Mass*, 1748–49

I. Missa* [1733]
Scoring: SSATB; 3 trumpets + timpani, horn; 2 flutes, 2 oboes, oboi d'amore; strings and continuo (2 bassoons, cello, violone, organ)

1.	Kyrie eleison†	B minor	Tutti (without tpt/timp)
2.	Christe eleison	D major	Duet: S I, II; 2 vn, bc
3.	Kyrie eleison†	F♯ minor	Tutti (without tpt/timp)
4.	Gloria in excelsis‡	D major	Tutti
5.	Et in terra pax†	D major	Tutti
6.	Laudamus te	A major	Solo: S II; vn, bc
7.	Gratias agimus tibi†	D major	Tutti
8.	Domine Deus	G major	Duet: S I, T; fl, str, bc
9.	Qui tollis peccata mundi†	B minor	Tutti (without ob, tpt/timp)
10.	Qui sedes ad dextram Patris	B minor	Solo: A; ob d'amore, bc
11.	Quoniam tu solus sanctus	D major	Solo: B; corno da caccia, 2 bsn, bc
12.	Cum Sancto Spiritu†	D major	Tutti

II. Symbolum Nicenum [1748–49]
Scoring: SSATB; 3 trumpets + timpani; 2 flutes, 2 oboes/oboi d'amore; strings and continuo

13.	Credo in unum Deum†	A Mixolydian	Chorus (plus 2 vn)
14.	Patrem omnipotentem†	D major	Tutti
15.	Et in unum Dominum	G major	Duet: S I, A; 2 ob d'amore, str, bc
16.	Et incarnatus est‡	B minor	Chorus (plus 2 vn)
17.	Crucifixus	E minor	Tutti (without ob, tpt, timp)
18.	Et resurrexit†	D major	Tutti
19.	Et in Spiritum sanctum	A major	Solo: B; 2 ob d'amore, bc
20.	Confiteor†	F♯ minor	Chorus, bc
21.	Et expecto†	D major	a (adagio): Chorus, bc; b (vivace): Tutti

III. Sanctus [1724]
Scoring: SSAATB; 3 trumpets and timpani; 3 oboes; strings and continuo

22.	Sanctus . . . Pleni sunt coeli†	D major	Tutti

IV. Osanna, Benedictus, Agnus Dei et Dona nobis pacem [1748/49]
Scoring: SATB (choir I); SATB (choir II); 3 trumpets and timpani; 2 flutes, 2 oboes; strings and continuo

23.	Osanna‡	D major	Tutti
24.	Benedictus	B minor	Solo: T; fl, bc
25.	Osanna (repeat)	D major	Tutti
26.	Agnus Dei	G minor	Solo: A; 2 vn, bc
27.	Dona nobis pacem†	D major	Tutti

* Sections I–IV numbered by Bach (as 1–4); numbering of movements is not original.
† Choral fugue.
‡ Imitative polyphony.

were of especially distinctive musical power. While it would undoubtedly have been easier for him to write many of the movements completely afresh, he chose not to do so. The "Crucifixus," the "Agnus Dei," and the other settings likewise based on earlier cantata movements all demonstrate that he considered extant compositions entirely worthy of revision and further improvement. Thus the highly expressive chaconne chorus "Weinen, Klagen, Sorgen, Zagen" (Weeping, lamenting, worrying, despairing), from the 1714 Weimar cantata BWV 12, achieved a more sophisticated shape and an even deeper profundity in its "Crucifixus" version (no. 17). The evolution is amply evident not only in the enhanced and more polished instrumental scoring, but also in the subtly intensified rhetoric—most notably when the final words "et sepultus est" are set with an unexpected a cappella sonority and a surprising modulation from E minor to G major, in preparation for the subsequent and triumphant "Et resurrexit" (no. 18).

A wide spectrum of styles for a timeless genre

In contrast to the Art of Fugue, there are no traces of a planning process for the B-minor Mass, at least not in terms of concrete compositional activities. The only telltale piece of chronological evidence consists of an early version of the Credo movement (no. 13), which has not survived in an autograph manuscript but is preserved in a copy by Bach's student Johann Friedrich Agricola, suggesting that the setting originated at some point after 1740. This Credo (BWV 232.3) happens to be in the key of G major, or rather, in the church mode of G Mixolydian, not the eventual key of A Mixolydian as used in the Mass (no. 13). Yet aside from the tonality, the early version is very close to the final movement. It also reveals Bach's intensive study and appropriation of the stile antico, the sixteenth-century vocal polyphony of Palestrina and his followers. That stylistic context was a significant point of departure for Bach's own Mass, which was conceived (much like the Art of Fugue) as a definitive statement within a timeless genre—deeply grounded in both past and contemporary styles.

While the Kyrie-Gloria of 1733 had already made use of retrospective polyphony, in the second "Kyrie" and the "Gratias" movements (nos. 3 and 7), the Credo of the B-minor Mass elevated the old style to an even higher level. Bach's experience with Palestrina was based not only on abstract study, but also on his performances of various Masses at the Leipzig main churches around 1740 and thereafter. Pertinent original performing materials in Bach's hand survive for Palestrina's *Missa sine nomine* and his *Missa Ecce sacerdos magnus*, the latter using the "Ecce sacerdos" chant as its theme. In both instances, Bach prepared doubling instrumental parts (woodwinds, strings, and continuo) to support the voices. Both works were also directly relevant to the Credo (no. 13), insofar as the six-part *Missa sine nomine* provided the stylistic model for the seven-part vocal texture of the score, while the four-part cantus firmus mass *Ecce sacerdos magnus* served as a model for Bach's use of the liturgical Credo chant as the theme.

Well aware of Palestrina's reputation as "the prince of musicians . . . for whose sake music was not banished from the church,"[34] Bach gave attention as well to more recent, mainly Italian masters of the *stile antico* tradition whose Latin works he performed in the early 1740s as well. These compositions included Antonio Caldara's *Magnificat in C major*, Antonio Lotti's *Missa Sapientiae*, and Francesco Gasparini's *Missa canonica*. The Caldara *Magnificat* provided a model of sorts, too, for Bach's Credo setting: Bach had rearranged its "Suscepit Israel" movement by expanding the original four-part vocal score to a six-part polyphonic texture with two violins as vocal substitutes, exactly as he would later expand the vocal score of the "Credo" to eight-part polyphony with two violins. Gasparini provided a further model in a quite different way. The systematic canonic construction of his Mass was certainly acceptable to Bach, or else he would not have performed the work. Yet this composition actually seems to have inspired him to employ various canonic devices—though rather sparingly and judiciously, as they appear in only three movements of the *B-minor Mass*. The "Confiteor" (no. 20) includes two cantus firmus canons, the second of which is in the form of an augmentation canon. The "Agnus Dei" (no. 26) contains several canonic passages, while the "Et incarnatus est" (no. 16) features a canon at its conclusion. These examples illustrate the decisive significance of the *stile antico* tradition in the conceptual planning of the *B-minor Mass*, as a comprehensive panorama of past and current polyphonic techniques.

The early version of the "Credo" stands somewhat isolated in the prehistory of the Mass. Its initial destination seems unclear, especially since it relates to and closely resembles a parallel work, the five-part Credo in F major, BWV 1081 (Fig. 8-12). Much shorter and less elaborate, it is a polyphonic Credo intonation that Bach composed around 1747/48, or even somewhat earlier, as an insert to precede the "Patrem omnipotentem" of the F-major Mass by Giovanni Battista Bassani. The considerably larger format of the Credo in

FIGURE 8-12

Credo in F major, BWV 1081: autograph (1747/48).

G major, however, made it unsuitable for inserting in any of the Latin Masses from Bach's performing library. Thus, it appears to signify a first step on the way toward the *B-minor Mass* before the rest of the work took shape. A subdominant opening in G for the Credo section in D major would indeed have worked well, but Bach settled on the dominant A major, and more suggestive in his overall planning process is the movement's conspicuous *stile antico* character, along with its focus on the pertinent medieval chant, whose continuation would eventually be reintroduced in the "Confiteor" movement (no. 20) of the Mass.

With the Credo completed, the actual composition of the ambitious full Mass, as reflected in the autograph score, seems to have progressed within a relatively narrow time frame, a genesis quite different from the decade-long gestation and maturation process of the *Art of Fugue*. Clearly the scope and form of the instrumental *Art of Fugue* project were utterly without precedent, meaning that Bach held control over—and was thus compelled to determine and realize—nearly all aspects of form and content. For the Mass, however, he was able to rely on guideposts of various sorts, and also on his familiar routines for setting given texts to music. In addition, he was drawing to a significant degree on extant compositions. Hence, after he had conceptualized the general shape of the expanded Mass, he was able to notate the bulk of the score quite efficiently from part II onward, movement by movement, a process that began in the second half of 1748 and continued through the fall of 1749. The many corrections in the autograph manuscript document a working score, one that Bach apparently put aside only when turning to the other major project he was pursuing simultaneously, the *Art of Fugue*, or else when failing eyesight compelled him to lay down his pen.

The parts and the whole

One of the final tasks that Bach carried out in compiling the score of the completed Mass was to prepare and number the title wrappers for the four individual parts of the work, which he kept in separate fascicles: I. *Missa*; II. *Symbolum Nicenum*; III. *Sanctus*; IV. *Osanna, Benedictus, Agnus Dei et Dona nobis pacem.* Each was inscribed with complete information on its respective scorings, along with the name of the composer (Fig. 8-13). Although this organizing task was in part an act of simple orderliness, it also related to the internal coherence and musical content of the work as a whole: the first two parts are set for five- and four-part choirs, part III requires a six-part choir, and part IV features an eight-part double choir. The overall result is a systematic display of diversity, covering the full range of possible scorings in vocal polyphony. Throughout the Mass, Bach mingled newly composed settings with carefully chosen extant music (Table 8-7). Typical examples in this regard are various of the choral fugues, including the "Qui tollis" (no. 9) of the Gloria, based on cantata BWV 46, "Schauet doch, und sehet, ob irgendein Schmerz sei" (Behold and see if there be any grief), and "Patrem omnipotentem" (no. 14) of the Symbolum Nicenum, based on cantata BWV 171, "Gott, wie dein Name, so ist auch dein Ruhm" (God, as your name, so is also your glory). The original movements were carefully selected from the cantatas, and corresponded closely in content and character to the destination movements in the Mass. In completing the full Mass, Bach continued the pattern of the 1733 Kyrie-Gloria in that the majority of movements were borrowed from extant cantata movements (though the reworked versions generally incorporated additional compositional refinement and often evinced enhanced expressive rhetoric).

TABLE 8-7. Parody movements in the *B-minor Mass*

Part I

7. Gratias agimus tibi   BWV 29/1 (1731): Wir danken dir, Gott (We give thanks to you, God)
9. Qui tollis   BWV 46/1 (1723): Schauet doch, und sehet, ob irgendein Schmerz sei (Behold and see if there be any grief)

[Nos. 2, 4, 6, 8, and 11 are based on unknown models.]*

Part II

14. Patrem omnipotentem   BWV 171/1 (1729): Gott, wie dein Name so ist auch dein Ruhm (God, as your name so is also your glory)
17. Crucifixus   BWV 12/1 (1714): Weinen, Klagen, Sorgen, Zagen (Weeping, lamenting, worrying, despairing)
21. Et expecto   BWV 120.2/1 (1729): Herr Gott, Beherrscher aller Dinge (Lord God, ruler of all things)

[Nos. 15, 18, 19, and 21 are based on unknown models.]*

Part IV

23, 25. Osanna   BWV 1157/1 (1732): Es lebe der König, der Vater im Lande (Long live the king, the father in the land)
26. Agnus Dei   BWV 1163/3 (1725): Entfernet euch, ihr kalten Herzen (Go away, you cold hearts)
27. Dona nobis pacem   No. 7 above: Gratias agimus tibi

[No. 24 is based on an unknown model.]*

---

* Fair-copy-like entries without formative corrections in the autograph score suggest reworking of, or borrowing from, extant movements.

As a genre, the Mass had long been a choral repertory *par excellence*, with relatively few opportunities for vocal solo parts. In this sense, it differed fundamentally from oratorios, in which vocal solos predominated. In dispensing with recitative, the Mass placed primary emphasis on the chorus, and thus provided opportunities for cultivating the full spectrum of vocal polyphony. Bach responded by offering a remarkable survey of retrospective and current choral styles and also of the many ways of treating solo voices, all in conjunction with colorful, varied, and virtuosic instrumental participation. In this regard, the *B-minor Mass* can indeed be viewed as an exemplary model for the creation of vocal-instrumental sacred music. In the domain of counterpoint, its spectrum of compositional approaches ranges from the concerto style of the "Gloria" (no. 4) to the motet style of the "Gratias" (no. 7), from the modern concertante fugue of the "Et in terra pax" (no. 5) to the retrospective fugue of the second "Kyrie" (no. 3), and from the freely expressive fabric of the "Et incarnatus" (no. 16) to the cantus firmus settings of the "Credo" and "Confiteor" (nos. 13 and 20), with their rigorous contrapuntal and canonic structures—to cite only a few examples from the choral numbers. In terms of their exemplary function, much the same can be said of the great variety of the solo movements. While eschewing for textual reasons the fashionable da capo form, Bach found sufficient compensation by capitalizing on the full range of solo aria and duet types, and by focusing in particular on differentiated and colorful orchestral accompaniments and instrumental obbligatos that avoid any repetition.

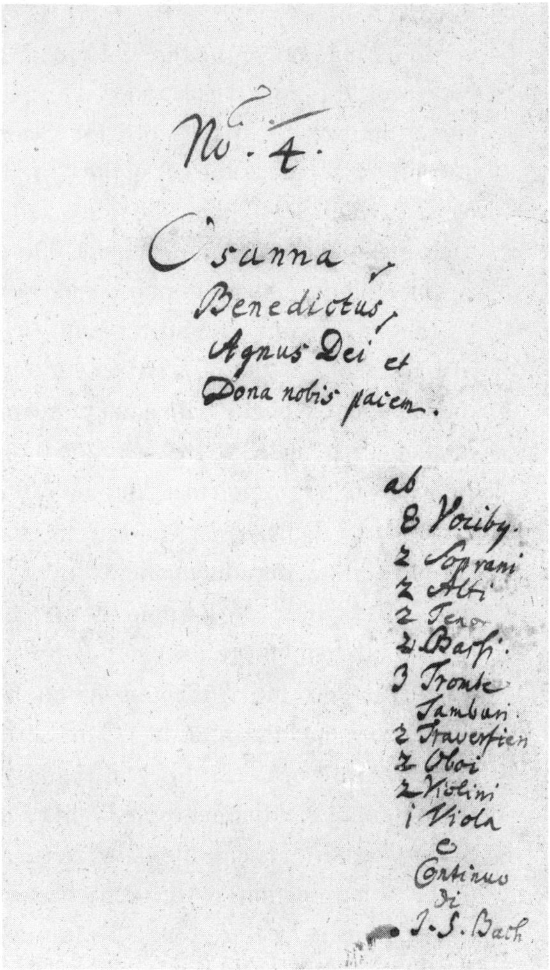

With his solemn Missa of 1733, Bach the capellmeister-cantor had taken the first step toward making his own contribution to the historic genre of Mass. That he did so with a particular

FIGURE 8-13

Mass in B minor, BWV 232: title wrapper (stub) for part IV, autograph (1749).

ambition to place himself in line for an honorary court title is immediately evident from the uncommon overall dimensions of that work: its five-part vocal sections, the large and diverse instrumental ensemble, the highly varied movement sequence, and the unusual degree of compositional elaboration. The 1733 *Missa* also reflects a well-designed and meaningful architecture. The two extended choral fugues of the Kyrie section—based on different chromatic subjects, one in modern style with an independent orchestra and the other in retrospective style with doubling instruments—frame a solo movement, the "Christe eleison" duet.[35] The key structure of this section (B minor–D major–F♯ minor) outlines the triad B–D–F♯, underscoring the Trinitarian character not only of the threefold Kyrie section but of the Mass as a whole. Moreover, the central position of D major, defined as such in the "Christe eleison" movement, underscores the Christological core of Bach's text setting and anticipates the home key of the Gloria section—and, indeed, of the entire Mass. After all, it is Christ who is invoked as the Lamb of God (Agnus Dei) in the concluding D-major movement "Dona nobis pacem."

The Gloria, a hymn of praise appropriately accompanied by an orchestra that includes trumpets and timpani, presents a wide-ranging spectrum of instrumental sounds and a virtuoso interplay of diversified vocal and instrumental forces. It begins with a magnificent concerto movement (no. 4), which employs triple meter for the first time in the work. The movement transitions sublimely into common time and simplified texture at "et in terra pax" (and on earth peace), then blossoms into an elaborate allegro fugue (no. 5). Three more choruses follow, introducing new varieties of choral polyphony. The "Gratias" (no. 7) is a retrospective fugue on the "Deo dicamus gratias" chant melody of the Lutheran liturgy, capped by a brilliant climax from the trumpet choir. The "Qui tollis" (no. 9) is a sensitive choral setting with a particularly expressive instrumentation, and the "Cum Sancto Spiritu" (no. 12) is an extended and dazzling vocal-instrumental fugue, calculated as the impressive finale movement of the original Kyrie-Gloria Mass of 1733. In between, four exemplary solo movements feature all five vocal soloists, as well as representatives of the various sections of the orchestra for the instrumental obbligatos: violin ("Laudamus te," no. 6), flute ("Domine Deus," no. 8), oboe d'amore ("Qui sedes," no. 10), and horn ("Quoniam," no. 11). In other words, all categories of instruments join in praise of the Holy Trinity.

Apart from minor editorial adjustments, Bach made no changes to what became part I of the full Mass. But he drew upon its overall design in creating a distinct yet comparably effective organizational structure for part II, the setting of the Nicene Creed. Solemn choral scoring, mainly for five voices, prevails throughout. Yet the movements now display a broader spectrum of styles, and bring into play various techniques and forms not employed in the Kyrie-Gloria sections. These include double fugue (no. 20), *stile antico* with liturgical cantus firmus (nos. 13 and 20), canonic treatment of a subject (no. 15), fugue of virtuoso character (nos. 14 and 21), cantus firmus canon (no. 20), ostinato variation (no. 17), chromatic madrigal manner (no. 21a), a cappella sonority with continuo (no. 17, at end; nos. 20 and 21a), and imitative setting in the tender and moving style of Giovanni Battista Pergolesi (no. 16).[36] Part II comprises only two solo movements, which are placed to mark the opening phrases of the second and third articles of the early Christian creed. They respectively address God the son and God the Holy Spirit, and set considerable amounts of abstract dogmatic text.

In their sheer technical demands, the choral fugues of the *B-minor Mass* generally have no counterpart in Bach's vocal music, nor in that of any other contemporary composer. However, as this difficulty of execution was not meant to be an end in itself, Bach in each case paid particularly close attention to underscoring the sense of the text. This is most obvious in his settings of "Et incarnatus," "Crucifixus," and "Et resurrexit" (nos. 16–18), where the texts lend themselves to intense musical expressivity. Yet even for words as abstract as "Credo in unum Deum" (I believe in one God), Bach was not at a loss in finding an arresting solution. The setting (no. 13) comprises three distinct musical building blocks: the medieval chant melody, an imitative texture of sixteenth-century polyphony, and an eighteenth-century basso continuo line (Fig. 8-14)—a deliberate diachronic combination of compositional devices from different eras. This approach animates and makes audible the timeless relevance of the words adopted in the year 325 by the Council of Nicaea: the Gregorian melody represents the faith of early Christianity, the sixteenth-century vocal polyphony reflects the renewal of this faith during the Reformation, and the modern basso continuo represents the faith of the congregation in Bach's own day. Only music can present simultaneously such a meaningful array of historical layers. Musical means can even summon a glimpse of the future, as encountered in the profound visionary musical rendering of the words "et expecto resurrectionem mortuorum, et vitam venturi seculi" (and I wait for the resurrection of the dead, and the life of the world to come). In this setting (no. 21), Bach addresses the dual aspects of death, both those pertinent to this world and those relating to a blissful afterlife. With the goal of depicting the misery and bitter end of human life, the dolorous expression of the *adagio* a capella section is generated by the most extreme and dissonant madrigalian chromaticism to be found anywhere in Bach's vocal output. By way of enharmonic modulation, this passage then gives way to a sharply contrasting and joyous tutti finale, marked *vivace e allegro*. This final segment projects a stunning vision of the anticipated eternal life in a different realm, reinforced by the triumphant sounds of trumpets and timpani.

After completing the score of the Symbolum Nicenum, Bach reviewed the structure of this section and decided that the words "et incarnatus est . . ."—included in the solo movement "Et in unum Dominum" (no. 15)—were not set with sufficient prominence. He consequently stretched and redistributed the text underlay of the solo (no. 15), opening the way for an additional chorus entirely dedicated to this theologically crucial pronouncement. Thus the Nicene Creed's Christological core—from incarnation and birth, suffering and death, to resurrection, ascension, and return—was now treated in a central group of three choral movements (nos. 16–18). Ever the self-critical reviser of his own work, Bach also apparently concluded that the stylistic range of the initial eight-movement version of part II still lacked a genuinely forward-looking setting. In response, he modeled the newly composed "Et incarnatus" chorus after a fashionable setting typified in the "Quis et homo" movement of Pergolesi's *Stabat Mater*, which Bach had arranged and performed around 1746/47 in a new German psalm cantata version, BWV 1083. Thus the "Et incarnatus" movement, Bach's very last vocal composition, turned out also to be his most modern. As a result of the inserted chorus no. 16, the overall musical architecture of part II also changed: the formerly balanced symmetry of choruses (nos. 13–14, 17–18, and 20–21) and solo movements (nos. 15 and 19) in the form of 2-1-2-1-2 now became a a more focused and arguably more meaningful axial-symmetric scheme of 2-1-3-1-2, with the "Crucifixus" no. 17 now as the centerpiece.

Part III of the score required only minimal compositional adjustments. Bach simply incorporated his single Sanctus from Christmas 1724, a work that he had performed several times in the subsequent decades. His principal alteration consisted in a rebalancing of the vocal scoring from what had been three sopranos, alto, tenor, and bass, to two sopranos, two altos, tenor, and bass. From the small group of extant single Sanctus pieces,[37] he selected what was by far the largest and most elaborate of his settings of the "thrice holy" from Isaiah 6:3 (Vulgate text).[38] In terms of external proportions, this setting was a perfect fit for the *B-minor Mass*. In representing the prophetic vision with its powerful imagery of the six seraphim angels in God's presence, the large seventeen-part score brings into play an intricate polychoral arrangement of six vocal-instrumental subsections consisting of high- (SSA) and low-register (ATB) choirs, brasses, reeds, strings, and the continuo groups. The Sanctus thus supplemented the mostly five-part choirs of parts I and II with a six-part vocal choir, which was in turn surpassed by the eight-part double-choir texture of the final part IV.

The four movements of the final section of the Mass were assembled exclusively from preexisting music (Table 8-7), beginning with the "Osanna" (no. 23), the revised double-choir version of a setting that had originated in the 1732 congratulatory cantata for King Augustus "The Strong." Since the parody model for the "Benedictus" (no. 24) remains unknown, the extent of the adjustments to the original cannot be determined. However, this setting for tenor, flute, and continuo is the only true trio setting in the entire Mass, and as such underscores the fact that Bach aimed at the strongest possible dynamic contrast between this delicate solo movement and the triumphant frame of the repeated "Osanna" chorus.

FIGURE 8-14

Mass in B minor, BWV 232/13: Credo, autograph (1748/49).

The parody model of the "Agnus Dei" (no. 26) is available, and allows for assessment of the changes Bach made when adapting the movement for the Mass, in which he actually uses only fifty percent of the model. In recasting this piece, he elected to modify the melodic contours of the instrumental ritornello with each reiteration; for the phrases containing the words "Agnus Dei," he interpolated newly composed passages that apply canonic counterpoint. The remarkable result is anything but a patchwork composition, and indeed it emerges as one of the most elegant, eloquent, and deeply moving segments of the entire Mass.

Bach's sense for overarching structural design is particularly evident at the conclusion of the work. First of all, his choice of the key of G minor for the

"Agnus Dei"—the lone occurrence of a flat key in the entire Mass—allows the entire Mass to end with a powerful plagal cadence, with G minor (the subdominant) resolving to D major. Bach also excised the formula "Dona nobis pacem" from the Agnus Dei (with which it traditionally ends), in order to generate a separate movement for a strong finale. For this purpose he turned again to the carefully considered prototype for the parodied "Gratias" from part I (no. 7). The model in question, the second movement of the cantata "Wir danken dir, Gott," BWV 29, is built on a fugal theme based on the identically chanted versicles of the Lutheran liturgy: [pastor:] "Benedicamus Domino" / [congregational response:] "Deo dicamus gratias" (Let us bless the Lord / Let us give thanks to God). It made complete sense to allude to the familiar Lutheran liturgical chant in both the cantata and the Gloria movements.[39] And since the chant melody represented the closing salutation at the end of every Sunday service in Leipzig, its reiteration at the very end of the Mass was particularly appropriate and provided a definitive conclusion for this monumental cyclical structure.

LEGACY

The 1786 benefit concert performance of the Symbolum Nicenum conducted by Bach's son, mentioned at the beginning of this section, also included works by Handel, Christoph Willibald Gluck, Antonio Salieri, and Carl Philipp Emanuel himself. A contemporary report singled out "in particular the five-part Credo of the immortal Sebastian Bach . . . which is one of the most superb pieces of music ever heard."[40] The composer himself never had the pleasure of performing this second part, let alone the B-minor Mass as a complete entity. Yet he must have had firm performing plans in mind, since he never composed anything without the intention of performance. The overall design of the Mass cycle strongly reflects the priorities and concerns of the performer-composer. But no concrete information regarding a projected performance is available, nor is it clear what possible function the work in its entirety could have served at the time. To be sure, any of the four parts of the Mass could have been presented individually within a festive Lutheran service, an undertaking that would certainly have been in line with the liturgical practices in Leipzig toward the mid-eighteenth century—when a new interest in Latin church music arose that also provided the context for Bach's

Kyrie-Gloria Masses.[41] As to a complete liturgical presentation, however, none of the various hypotheses of commissioned and potential performances at major cathedrals in Dresden or Vienna can be validated. Whether Bach the Lutheran could have reckoned on being invited for such occasions is no less problematic than the fundamental dilemma of slotting the oversized Mass into the liturgy of any sort of church service, regardless of religious orientation. Furthermore, the separation of the Osanna and Benedictus from the Sanctus and the splitting-up of the Agnus Dei into two unequal movements were in conflict with the norms of the Roman Catholic rite. This leaves open as the most likely possibility a performance outside the framework of a church service—in analogy to Carl Philipp Emanuel's concert presentation of the Symbolum Nicenum more than thirty-five years after his father's death.

In many European cities, presentations of oratorios and other sacred works in non-ecclesiastical venues occurred with increasing frequency toward the mid-eighteenth century. This was certainly the case in Leipzig, and notably at the performances presented by the *Grosses Concert* (Grand Concert) newly established in 1743. This organization largely continued the activities of Bach's Collegium Musicum and laid the groundwork for the later Gewandhaus concerts. Since its musical leadership team largely consisted of Bach's pupils and associates, he would have looked favorably upon this musical society and might well have considered it for a concert presentation of his Mass. In sum, while a performance of the Mass could perhaps have taken place during Bach's lifetime, we have no evidence that one actually occurred. In due course, the work came to be viewed—surely as its composer must have wished—as a superlative musical legacy, as did its instrumental counterpart, the *Art of Fugue*.

The two works did not arise in direct parallel because Bach worked on the various stages of the *Art of Fugue* on and off throughout the 1740s, which was for him a decade of nearly total withdrawal from creative involvement in new church music. During his first fifteen years in Leipzig, he had invested enormous effort in generously providing for the musical needs of the St. Nicholas and St. Thomas churches, but now the composition of cantatas, oratorios, Kyrie-Gloria Masses, and comparable pieces for regular practical use was for Bach a thing of the past. Certainly, when continuing to perform such works, he could not resist touching them up here and there. In this sense, and though he had already satisfied the practical needs of the Leipzig churches, his devotion to sacred music never ceased. But whatever improvements he chose to make were carried out in response to his own musical priorities and aesthetic values.

Increasingly over the final decade of his life, he took the liberty of setting his own agenda. And even as he intensified his ongoing work on the *Art of Fugue*, and also stood his ground in the face of advancing health problems, he finally took on the considerable challenge of adding his own contribution to the centuries-old tradition of the Mass.

The *Art of Fugue* uniquely exemplifies Bach's highest and most personal ideals of the art of instrumental counterpoint, presented in the form of a systematically organized and varied cycle of keyboard fugues. The finished score of the *B-minor Mass*, with its similarly exceptional cycle of twenty-seven movements (eleven of them choral fugues), surpasses all his other large-scale vocal compositions. It demonstrates his magisterial command of vocal poly-phonic art, consummating his achievements in that category, and indeed establishing a new threshold. This judgment applies not only to the wide-ranging compositional, stylistic, and timbral variety of the Mass, but also to the stirring, expressive, and theologically meaningful renderings of the venerable text, one that transcended confessional boundaries. In composing the *Art of Fugue*, Bach experienced and eventually exercised total freedom in determining form, content, and musical logic. By contrast, the Mass, as a musical genre like no other, brought a strict set of framework conditions that left no room for abstract systematic strategy, but nevertheless offered ample scope for Bach's imaginative architecture and his supreme command of mul-tifaceted vocal polyphony.

With a profusion of compositional techniques and stylistic approaches, the *Art of Fugue* and the *B-minor Mass* represent pinnacles of masterly crafts-manship, evincing extraordinary intellectual penetration of the material. Bach himself must have been fully aware of what he had achieved, in these two works, which so brilliantly enshrine his artistic credo.

"Praxis cum theoria"

Maxim of the Learned Musician

D uring the Age of Reason, no intellectually alert person in the city of Leipzig, then home of the largest university in the German lands, could have escaped the idea of combining scientific research with practical applications. This notion was in fact explicitly articulated by the philosopher Gottfried Wilhelm Leibniz in his famous dictum "theoria cum praxi." Public events—like the demonstrations of electrical experiments using a glass-globe machine that were staged by the young and flamboyant philosophy and physics professor Georg Matthias Bose of the University of Wittenberg—were a case in point, attracting many Leipzig spectators in the late 1730s. These presentations took place in the large music room of the stately house on St. Thomas Square belonging to the professor's father, the wealthy merchant Georg Heinrich Bose, a friend and patron of Bach's. The families lived right next door to each other, and Anna Magdalena Bach was the bosom friend ("Herzens-Freundin") of Bose's daughter Christiana Sybilla.[1] No records of just who attended these scientific demonstrations were kept, but it can be taken for granted that they included Johann Heinrich Winckler, the distinguished philosophy and physics professor of the University of Leipzig and faculty member of the St. Thomas School. Winckler was elected in 1747 to the Royal Society of London, and it was his research on electricity that formed the basis for Bose's experiments. He happened to be a close colleague of Bach's, and wrote the libretto for his (lost) cantata "Froher Tag, verlangte Stunden," BWV 1162, on the occasion of the rededication of the renovated St. Thomas School.

If Bach himself ever attended such a scientific demonstration, he would have realized immediately that the empirical method of the natural sciences, which emphasizes the search for evidence as discovered through practical experiments, had relatively little in common with the musical sciences (*musicalische Wissenschaften*) that he proudly represented—as he had specifically noted in his 1733 letter to the Saxon Elector (page 271). Though he was erudite in many facets of music theory, from the nuances of musical temperaments to the rules of counterpoint, and also intimately familiar with poetics and rhetoric, not to mention his expertise in the mechanics of musical instruments, Bach was concerned not with the abstract confirmation of theories, but instead with the skillful practical implementation thereof. Thus his governing maxim could more properly be expressed as "praxis cum theoria"—Leibniz reversed. The composer indeed subscribed to the close association of theory and practical application, yet with a differing order and weighting.

What the act of musical composition meant specifically to Bach is nowhere better summarized than in a concise explanation offered by Johann Abraham Birnbaum, his good friend and in many ways his official mouthpiece in print. In 1739, Birnbaum defined the process of composition as

> a musical exercise in which one should express partly one's own thoughts, partly given thoughts, correctly, clearly, orderly, coherently, and touchingly but not without scholarly contemplation.[2]

In other words, whether Bach was setting his own musical thoughts, or given thoughts in the sense of preexisting motifs and themes borrowed from other composers or from chorale melodies and the like, scholarly reflection upon them was a foundational aspect of his compositional method. The approach involved all the components of the climactic sequence of adverbial qualifiers listed above. These are notably prioritized from the "correct" and proper application of rules to "clear" articulation, from the "orderly" and "coherent" succession of thoughts to the ultimate goal of creating the effect of "touching" or moving the soul.

According to Birnbaum, Bach generally emphasized "experience and scholarship." He prized, in particular, the ability to quickly combine "the rules of the art of composition and learned reflection" when improvising and performing without preparation on the clavier or organ. The same applied to the formidable mental act of processing musical thoughts while rapidly setting down notes on paper, a procedure for which composers without comparable performing experience "perhaps need a whole day's worth of time," as Birnbaum put it. Furthermore, as Bach's pupil Johann Friedrich Agricola testified, he "needed only to have heard any theme to be aware—it seemed in the same instant—of almost every intricacy that artistry could produce in its treatment."[3]

This sort of instantaneous cognition and quick combinatorial aptitude typical of the mature Bach complemented the adopted process of musical thinking that played a formative role in the evolution of his personal style during the early Weimar years (page 103). Intensive study of the Italian concerto style exemplified in works by Vivaldi and contemporaries "taught him how to think musically." According to Johann Nicolaus Forkel, Bach had proceeded by examining "the chain of ideas, their relation to each other, the variation of the modulations, and many other particulars." Forkel obtained this information from the older Bach's sons, who themselves were taught how "order, coherence, and proportion" (Ordnung, Zusammenhang und Verhältnis) must be brought to bear on the treatment and setting of musical ideas.[4] For Bach, the concerto as a specific musical genre or form was of subsidiary significance here, for the larger principle applied across his activities in all categories, affecting his handling of counterpoint, thematic invention, and word-tone relationships in vocal works. What characterized Bach's musical thinking was, in fact, the swift mental processing of complex musical considerations and the conscious application of generative and formative procedures based on the musical material at hand—in other words, the meticulous rationalization of the creative act.

Applying the rubric "praxis cum theoria" to Bach is not to characterize him as merely a would-be theorist. As a teacher of composition, he naturally and regularly engaged his pupils in theoretical discourse and did not shy away from the occasional formulation of written rules, including thorough-bass guidelines and the "Regula Joh. Seb. Bachii" on five-part composition (page 287). Yet he clearly had neither the interest in nor the patience and the literary talent for emulating his treatise-writing composer colleagues like Johann David Heinichen and Jean-Philippe Rameau. The closest he ever came to a treatise-like work was the *Art of Fugue*, a tract with a bookish title but completely without a verbal component. Though less obviously, the *B-minor Mass* similarly functioned as a serious essay expounding the art of vocal polyphony. In both works, however, it is abundantly clear that what Bach expressed in terms of "praxis cum theoria" could only be adequately exemplified in his very own musical language. "His melodies were unusual, but always varied, rich in invention, and resembling those of no other composer" (page 8). Yet his musical idiom rested firmly and definitively on the ever-present theoretical background of polyphonic counterpoint.

Bach once characterized cantatas "of my own composition" in comparison with those by other composers as "incomparably harder and more intricate"[5] — a phrase whose two comparative adjectives complement one another, conveying that his works were "harder" to perform and "more intricate" in their construction. This characterization in fact extends well beyond the cantatas and applies to Bach's music in general, whether vocal or instrumental, ensemble or solo. He was fortunate to find appreciation and encouragement from his audiences for his virtuosic and learned approach. Those audiences were communities made up predominantly of connoisseurs, who in Weimar and Cöthen were led by an art-loving high nobility, and in Leipzig were spearheaded by an academic and mercantile elite. Moreover, all three venues offered him vocal and instrumental ensembles and collaborating musicians of a professional caliber second to none. Even if he complained in a 1730 memorandum to the Leipzig city council about general conditions and desirable improvements, he was apparently always able to assemble the kinds of performing forces needed for any given project. Like everyone else, he certainly encountered difficulties at times, yet he consistently avoided planning for anything he could not deliver. There is no documentation whatever that hints at unsatisfactory, let alone abortive, musical presentations for which he would have been held responsible.

As a member of the academic community and a noncitizen living in Leipzig under the jurisdiction of the University, Bach was well aware of his rather discriminating primary audience, and more often than not he tailored his music to the taste of a largely erudite and well-educated cohort. Before the professorial preachers at the St. Nicholas and St. Thomas churches took to their pulpits on Sundays to deliver their hour-long biblical exegeses and lofty spiritual advice, Bach regularly took his own turn and presented a comparably sophisticated yet never laborious musical sermon, a serious and enthralling twenty-minute display of exceptional artistry. His goal of achieving a proper balance also seems to have been noted since the only extant description of an actual Leipzig church performance confirms just that. On August 29, 1739, Bach conducted the cantata "Wir danken dir, Gott" (We give thanks to you, God), BWV 29, and the chronicler specially registered that the music was "as artful as it was pleasant."[6] One of the composer's regular listeners, the classicist Johann Matthias Gesner, summarized "the accomplishments of our Bach" by comparing them with "what not many Orpheuses, nor twenty Arions, could achieve."[7]

From the performers' perspective, things must have looked quite different, owing to the uncompromising demands that Bach placed upon singers and instrumentalists alike. Johann Philipp Kirnberger, a pupil of his and a participant in performances around 1740, remembered,

> The great J. Seb. Bach used to say, "Everything must be possible," and he would never hear of anything's being "not feasible." This has always spurred me onward to accomplish many difficult things in music, by dint of effort and patience, according to my own poor powers.[8]

The notion that "everything must be possible" recalls Bach's own reaction when the Prussian King Friedrich II asked him to improvise a six-part keyboard fugue on a theme the king had provided. Bach sidestepped the daunting request and instead performed a six-part fugue on a theme of his own choice, but afterward he apparently felt obligated to deliver a six-part ricercar on the royal theme, in published form. He never allowed anyone to surpass him on musical grounds. Yet his considerable demands probably demoralized some of his own students, even as they apparently encouraged others, including Kirnberger, to strive ever harder to achieve success.

After working for well over a decade with two professional court ensembles, Bach lost little time in challenging the prevailing general standards of performance when he took up his teaching post in Leipzig. This becomes abundantly evident when one compares his first cantata scores of 1723 with those of his predecessor Kuhnau, whose works he had immediately retired in order to launch a new regime. On the keyboard front as well, Bach quickly moved beyond the parameters of his earlier works. For example, in the very first installment (1726) of the *Clavier-Übung*, he required the player to come to terms with the latest in cross-hand technique, as set out in the Giga of Partita 1.

The reaction of a talented amateur musician, Luise Adelgunde Kulmus, to the collected edition of *Clavier-Übung* I (1731) may well have been typical. The fiancée of Johann Christoph Gottsched (professor of poetry at the University, a member of the St. Thomas congregation, and a librettist for Bach),[9] she had received from her future husband a copy of the print (see above, page 167), and remarked in acknowledging the gift: "Among the works . . . everything pleases me more than their caprices; these are inscrutably difficult."[10] She seems to have enjoyed the difficult-to-play dance movements, but she apparently felt intimidated by the more abstract contrapuntal preludes, in this context often referred to as "caprices." A young rationalist philosopher in her own right, she could see "no reason" for their complex contrapuntal design and related technical demands—most likely because she possessed no understanding of the theory of counterpoint, a necessary precondition for contrapuntal connoisseurship. At the same time, since she liked the dances, she must have appreciated their refined and often well-concealed strains of counterpoint, whether or not she noticed them as such.

This points up one of the most remarkable features of Bach's musical art: the natural, uncontrived, and truly effortless handling of polyphony in whatever musical context, from simple dance to strict canon, from two-part to multiple-voice counterpoint, from instrumental and vocal to mixed scores. What Johann Friedrich Agricola meant by singling out, in Bach's obituary, the phenomenon of "polyphony in its greatest strength" (page 8) corresponds closely to the ideal of "musical perfection" invoked by Birnbaum in his 1738 defense of Bach's style. Both of them point to the concept of composing music in which practice and theory coalesce, in which original thought, technical exactitude, and aesthetic beauty become congruent, all with the ultimate purpose—as the *Clavier-Übung* dedications put it—of the "renewal of the soul."

The opus-style benchmark works examined in this volume as separate entities provide, if considered together, a surprisingly coherent narrative of Bach's artistic evolution as he developed his musical universe, moving forward step by step without lingering, always setting new priorities and challenges for himself. The individual histories of these works run in parallel, to a certain extent, with the general narrative of Bach's professional life. Yet at the same time, the works in question exhibit remarkable individuality. They document the composer's unswerving pursuit of his wide-ranging personal musical interests, even when such pursuits caused him to defer the obligations of his office. Each single opus displays a distinct character, since each one was initiated, motivated, and shaped by an original and singular constellation of ideas, thereby setting the composer on a path not previously followed.

What began in the years after 1700, with the exuberant yet sophisticated virtuoso fugues embedded in the six toccatas, led to the refined advancement of multiple individualized fugue types and styles in the *Well-Tempered Clavier*, and eventually concluded with the profound and thoroughly systematized monothematic cycle contained in the *Art of Fugue*. This evolution speaks to Bach's ever-deepening scholarly quest for "the secret of fugue"—as Carl Philipp Emanuel put it, perhaps quoting his father. Revealing this secret as best he could, by thoroughly researching and testing the theories and techniques of counterpoint in all its many facets, remained a lifelong goal for Bach, one that influenced by quasi-magnetic force nearly everything else within his musical universe. The Weimar *Orgel-Büchlein*, along with the later *Clavier-Übung* III, complemented by the chorale cantata cycle, all combine contrapuntal logic with highly differentiated and expressive musical language, in small and large instrumental and vocal formats. This comprehensive approach was applied across an array of genres: suites, partitas, variations, sonatas, and concertos as well as choruses, chorales, recitatives, and arias of cantatas and oratorios. All were brought to new levels, thanks to Bach's abundant ingenuity and resourcefulness. Whenever and wherever reasonable, he enhanced and refined his works in each category with judicious infusions of contrapuntal art—an obsession which, in the view of his critics, compromised the actual functionality of his music. Yet in retrospect, such objections emerge as inconsequential. Viewed as a group, the opus-like works and collections exemplify in all possible ways Bach's "praxis cum theoria" approach, and they combine to offer, in distinct contours, a compelling intellectual portrait of this most learned of musicians.

Bach's ever-advancing cultivation of contrapuntal complexity accelerated during the 1740s. During this period he was more deeply immersed than ever before in the most involved techniques of strict-style composition. This activity apparently yielded both enjoyment and abundant satisfaction. It also required much abstract deliberation, and often resulted in formidably intricate musical creations. Yet Bach nevertheless remained committed to the primary goal of making the music speak engagingly and meaningfully, such that its sounds could succeed in moving the soul. This primary concern of his most definitely held sway in both the *Art of Fugue* and the *B-minor Mass*, if in differing ways.

During these same years, Bach was also casting a retrospective eye over much of his compositional output. For example, around 1744/45, he carefully reassessed his entire cycle of chorale cantatas, noting in several scores that they had been "completely reviewed" (page 23), and in many cases he made revisions in order to enhance the expressive eloquence of the music. In a further project of fine-tuning, he turned to another opus also dating back twenty years, the six harpsichord-violin sonatas BWV 1014–1019. And in the year 1744, Bach asked his student and son-in-law Johann Christoph Altnickol to prepare fair copies of several other major works that he had recently reviewed: the *Well-Tempered Clavier* (both books) and the four Kyrie-Gloria Masses BWV 233–236. Altnickol also assisted Bach with the fair copy of the Great Eighteen Chorales, BWV 651–668. This remarkable round of activity strongly suggests an increasing desire on the composer's part to prepare an appropriate and carefully curated musical legacy.

Although the *B-minor Mass* and the *Art of Fugue* were the last major works with which Bach was engaged, they are not to be understood as the absolutely final statements of a purposeful musical testament. They only coincidentally happened to be his last works, for he had firm plans extending beyond them and was eager and ready to move on, as clearly indicated by his decision to undergo eye surgery. Fate interfered with these plans, and thus the two great works indeed form the imposing endpoints of a logical sequence of milestones. Bach followed a long and varied—yet essentially straightforward—path of exploring all facets of the art of polyphony, from the virtual polyphony of a single melodic line as projected by an unaccompanied violin or cello, to the polyphony created by a multi-voiced choir and orchestra. His ultimate objective was to achieve a refined polyphonic sound in the sense of "fullness" (*Vollstimmigkeit*), completeness, and wholeness, thereby realizing the musical perfection[11] that became his ideal.

Curiously, this perhaps most characteristic aspect of Bach's musical language did not enter the discussion of his legacy that commenced immediately after his death, with Carl Philipp Emanuel Bach's *Versuch über die wahre Art das Clavier zu spielen* (Berlin, 1753) and Friedrich Wilhelm Marpurg's *Abhandlung von der Fuge* (Berlin, 1753). Bach's fundamentally polyphonic orientation was first truly expounded in Johann Philipp Kirnberger's two-volume treatise *Die Kunst des reinen Satzes in der Musik* (Berlin, 1771 and 1776–79). Although Kirnberger does not embrace Bach's particular pedagogical approach, his title formulation "The Art of Pure Composition" certainly reflects Bach's consistent focus on purity and clarity. He invokes the name of Bach, but takes his teachings only as a point of departure. Yet Bach's music is not in fact truly synonymous with any notion of "pure" composition. His widened concept of all-embracing polyphony is not covered in any author's chapters on harmony or counterpoint; nor are his distinctive melodic inventions and designs, his manifold and subtle departures from convention, or his purposeful violations of traditional rules.

In the end, it was Bach's highly personal and unorthodox approach to composition that resulted in music so exemplary, superlative, and transcendent. His voracious appetite for musical knowledge and his inquisitive and resourceful mind allowed the act of composition to become "praxis sine theoria"—practice not governed and directed by abstract rules, but instead inspired and guided by artistic imagination and inarguable musical genius. In Bach's musical universe philosophy, theory, composition, and performance were merged into a quite incomparable whole.

BIOGRAPHICAL DATES	BENCHMARK WORKS
Arnstadt—Mühlhausen—Weimar	
1685, March 21: born in Eisenach	
1703–7: Organist at the New Church in Arnstadt	
1707–8: Organist at St. Blasius Church in Mühlhausen	Six Toccatas (autogr. ms. lost), c. 1705–8
1708–17: Organist, chamber musician, and concertmaster (from 1714) at the court of Saxe-Weimar	Collection of Organ Chorales (autogr. ms., without title = *Orgel-Büchlein*), 1708–15; see 1723 Six "English" Suites (autogr. ms. lost), c. 1713–14 24 preludes and 24 fugues (autogr. ms. lost), c. 1717; see 1722
Cöthen	
1718–23: Capellmeister and Director of Chamber Music at the Princely Court of Anhalt-Cöthen	
1720: *Clavier-Büchlein* for Wilhelm Friedemann Bach	15 Praeambles and 15 Fantasias (= Inventions and Sinfonias); see 1723 Six Violin Solos (= Book I of unaccompanied solos, autogr. fair copy, 1720)
1721, March 24: Six Concertos dedicated to the Margrave of Brandenburg-Schwedt	Six *Brandenburg Concertos* (autogr. fair copy, 1721) Six Violincello Solos (= Book II of unaccompanied solos, autogr. ms. lost), c. 1721–23

BIOGRAPHICAL DATES	BENCHMARK WORKS
1722: First *Clavier-Büchlein* for Anna Magdalena Bach	Six "French" Suites (autogr. ms., fragmentary)
	Das Wohltemperirte Clavier (autogr. fair copy, 1722)
1723, February 7: Audition for post as Cantor and Music Director in Leipzig	*Orgel-Büchlein* (title added, 1723) *Aufrichtige Anleitung* = Inventions and Sinfonias (autogr. fair copy, 1723)
Leipzig	
1723–50: Cantor and Music Director in Leipzig	
1724: Good Friday vespers at St. Nicholas's Church	*St. John Passion* (autogr. ms. lost), see 1738
1724, June 11 through March 25, 1725	Chorale Cantata cycle (autogr. mss., 1724–25)
1725: Good Friday vespers at St. Thomas's Church	*St. John Passion*, 2nd version to fit chorale cantata cycle (autogr. ms. lost), see 1738
1725: Second *Clavier-Büchlein* for Anna Magdalena Bach	Six Partitas (autogr. ms. of two partitas, 1725; four partitas of the set most likely contained in fragmentary first *Clavier-Büchlein*, begun 1722)
1726: Michaelmas Fair	Partita 1 (first installment of *Clavier-Übung* I; further installments through 1729
1727: Good Friday vespers at St. Thomas's Church	*St. Matthew Passion* (autogr. ms. lost); see 1736
1729–41: Director of the Collegium Musicum	Six Sonatas for organ (autogr. ms., c. 1730)
1731: Good Friday vespers at St. Thomas's	*St. Mark Passion* (autogr. ms. lost); printed libretto survives
1731: Easter Fair	*Clavier-Übung*, part I (collected edition: op. 1), published
1733, July 27: Kyrie-Gloria Mass dedicated to Elector Friedrich August II of Saxony	Missa (Kyrie-Gloria) in B Minor (autogr. ms., 1733)
1734–35: Christmas Day through Epiphany	*Christmas Oratorio*, Parts 1–6 (autogr. ms., 1734)
1735: Easter Fair	*Clavier-Übung*, part II, published

BIOGRAPHICAL DATES	BENCHMARK WORKS
1736: Good Friday vespers at St. Thomas's	*St. Matthew Passion*, revised (autogr. fair copy, 1736)
1738: Easter Sunday Ascension Day	*Easter Oratorio* (autogr. fair copy, 1738) *Ascension Oratorio* (autogr. fair copy, 1738) *St. John Passion* (revised version, autogr. fair copy—fragmentary, c. 1738) Concertos for harpsichord (autogr. ms., c. 1738) Great Eighteen Chorales (autogr. ms., 1738–46
1739: Michaelmas Fair	*Clavier-Übung*, part III, published
Early 1740s	*Clavier-Übung*, part IV (*Goldberg Variations*), published 1741 *Well-Tempered Clavier*, Book II (autogr. ms., c. 1742) *The Art of Fugue*, complete early version, 14 movements (autogr. fair copy, without title), c. 1742 "Schübler" Chorales, published c. 1746–47
1747, May 10: evening concert at the court of King Friedrich II of Prussia in Potsdam	*Musical Offering* (dedicated to King Friedrich), published, Michaelmas Fair 1747
1747, June: joins Corresponding Society of Musical Science, Leipzig	Canonic Variations on "Vom Himmel hoch," published c. 1748; autogr. ms. for performance
Later 1740s	Chorale cantatas performed, reviewed, and partially revised *The Art of Fugue* expanded for publication, 18 movements (autogr. ms. additions, 1746–49); engraving initiated *Mass in B Minor* = Kyrie-Gloria of 1733, much expanded (autogr. ms., 1748–49)
1748–49: Christmas, Good Friday, Easter, and Ascension Day	Cyclical performance of oratorio trilogy with *St. John Passion*
1750, July 28: dies in Leipzig	
1751, spring	*The Art of Fugue*, published posthumously

NOTES

Prologue: On the Primacy and Pervasiveness of Polyphony

1. Mattheson requested such a note in *Das beschützte Orchestre* (Hamburg, 1717) and again in *Grosse General-Baß-Schule* (Hamburg, 1731); *BD* II, no. 83 and 303.
2. Birnbaum, a university lecturer, lawyer, and amateur musician, took up Bach's defense against the comments by Scheibe, who otherwise held Bach in high regard; for the Scheibe-Birnbaum controversy, see *NBR*, pp. 338–48.
3. Two versions of this only authentic portrait of the composer have survived, one painting dated 1746 and the other (better preserved) from 1748. Both originals are housed in Leipzig, the earlier painting at the Stadtgeschichtliches Museum, the later one at the Bach Museum (Bach-Archiv).
4. An oil portrait of one of Bach's predecessors, Johann Hermann Schein (1586–1630), shows the Thomascantor with a scroll; Maul 2012, fig. 12. Haußmann's 1727 portrait of Johann Gottfried Reiche (1667–1734) shows him holding a trumpet in his right hand and a music sheet with a virtuoso fanfare in his left; *BD* IX, fig. 353.
5. The penultimate canon no. 13 (BWV 1087/13) within the series.
6. *Musikalische Bibliothek*, vol. IV, p. 108; see NBA VIII/1, KB (C. Wolff, 1976), p. 34.
7. *BD* II, no. 559.
8. NBA VIII/1, KB, p. 22. The original reproduced in Fig. P-2 is the exemplar from the estate of Father Spieß (A-Wn: MS 64.460).
9. The extensive portrait collection assembled by Carl Philipp Emanuel Bach contains seven such portraits (of Samuel Friedrich Capricornus, Daniel Eberlin, Johann Andreas Herbst, Jacob Hintze, Hendrik Liberti, Michael Praetorius, and Samuel Scheidt), one or two of which may previously have been in the possession of his father; see CPEB-CW VIII/2, plates (A. Richards, 2012).
10. First published solution by Johann André, 1838 (NBA/KB VIII/1, p. 23); no eighteenth-century solution known.
11. *NBR*, p. 347.
12. *NBR*, p. 338.
13. *NBR*, p. 347.
14. Wolff 1968, p. 61; Dürr 1998, p. 312f. The subject in G (same rhythm as BWV 878/2) also occurs in a three-part fugue by Johann Joseph Fux, *Gradus ad Parnassum* (Vienna, 1724), Mizler trans. (Leipzig, 1742): Tab. 29, fig. 1.
15. *Musikalische Bibliothek*, III/1 (Leipzig, 1746), p. 354.
16. *NBR*, p. 297.
17. *NBR*, p. 305. For a related discussion, see "Epilogue: Bach and the Idea of 'Musical Perfection,'" in Wolff 2000.
18. *NBR*, p. 305.
19. The chapter "Von der Viel- und Vollstimmigkeit überhaupt," in Johann Mattheson's *Der vollkommene Capellmeister* (Hamburg, 1739), lumps "Vollstimmigkeit," "Harmonie im breiten Verstande" (harmony in the broad sense), and "Contrapunct"

together as equivalents, and defines the phenomenon as "an artful assemblage of different simultaneously sounding melodies, from which at once a multiple euphony originates" (p. 245).

20. NBR, p. 344.
21. "Kleine Schulrede, worin man die von GOTT bestimmte Harmonie in der Musik beurtheilt," in *Musikalische Bibliothek*, II/3 (Leipzig 1742), p. 63f.
22. NBR, p. 399.
23. NBR, p. 176.
24. NBR, p. 305.
25. BD II, p. 355.

Chapter 1: Revealing the Narrative of a Musical Universe

1. NBR, no. 306; regarding the division of the writing task, see BD VII (C. Wolff, 2008), p. 93.
2. Carl Philipp Emanuel was present for his father's funeral on July 31, 1750, immediately after which the musical estate seems to have been surveyed. He could not return to Leipzig in the fall when the details of the division of the estate were negotiated, and left a proxy with his brother Wilhelm Friedemann (Blanken 2018).
3. BD VII, pp. 104–110.
4. Omitted were the early Mühlhausen town council election cantata BWV 71 (published in 1708) as well as the separate individual prints of *Clavier-Übung*, part I.
5. Under the heading "Monument of three deceased members" (*Denkmal dreyer ver storbener Mitglieder*) of the Society of Musical Sciences in vol. IV of the *Musikalische Bibliothek* (Leipzig, 1754), Bümler's obituary is found on pp. 135–42, Stölzel's on pp. 143–57, and Bach's on pp. 158–76, along with the engraved attachment of the canon BWV 1076.
6. Ibid., p. 152.
7. See the introduction to the facsimile of *Clavierwerke-Verzeichnis* (1772), supplement of CPEB-CW (ed. C. Wolff, 2014).
8. Outside the estate proper, a few single scattered autograph keyboard manuscripts exist, some in the two anthologies compiled by Bach's brother Johann Christoph of Ohrdruf (D-B: Mus. ms. 40644; D-LEm: Becker III.8.7); see the listing in NBA IX/2 (Y. Kobayashi, 1989), pp. 206–10.
9. It remains uncertain whether all ten autographs were still held in Bach's library at the time of his death, or had instead been given to or acquired by students or patrons, like the partial autograph of the Sonata in G, BWV 1021, for violin and basso continuo.
10. To the instrumental collections in Table 1-1 must be added the six concertos dedicated to the Margrave of Brandenburg in 1721, and as such not included in Bach's estate.
11. "Ein gantzes mit Einschliessung aller darzu gehörigen Theile," definition of the term "universum" in Johann Heinrich Zedler, *Grosses vollständiges Universal Lexicon aller Wissenschafften und Künste* (Leipzig, 1731–54), vol. 49, col. 1819.

Chapter 2: Transformative Approaches to Composition and Performance

1. On Whitsunday 1721, Bach performed cantata BWV 172 at both St. Nicholas and St. Thomas churches, substituting for Johann Kuhnau. The printed cantata libretto has survived; see Schabalina 2008 and Simpfendörfer 2010.

2. For a preliminary list of Bach's students, see *NBR*, pp. 315–17; an updated and annotated catalog is in progress at the Bach-Archiv Leipzig.

3. This point is first discussed in Wolff 2002.

4. Maul 2012, Chapters 1 and 2.

5. He would return to the term "author" on the title pages of parts I and III of his *Clavier-Übung* when referring to self-publishing ("In Verlegung des Autoris"); see below, Figs. 5-1 and 5-8.

6. Bach's autograph score: D-B, Mus. ms. Bach P 283; several facsimile editions. The total of forty-eight chorales as counted by J. C. F. Bach (Fig. 2-1) includes the three separately set verses of BWV 627.

7. Heinz-Harald Löhlein, editor of the *Orgel-Büchlein* for NBA IV/1 (1983), following Dadelsen 1963, assumes four phases of the collection: Weimar 1713–14, 1714–15, 1715–16, and Leipzig additions. Stinson 1996 differentiates between five phases: Weimar 1708–12, 1712–13, 1715–16, 1716–17, and a few Leipzig additions. In the earliest entries, Bach's handwriting resembles closely the autograph copies of some instrumental works by Telemann and de Grigny from around 1709 (NBA IX/2, pp. 38–45). Stylistic arguments for a beginning of the *Little Organ Book* between 1708 and 1710 are presented in Wolff 2000 and Zehnder 2009.

8. For further details, see BWV³.

9. Facsimile: *Weimarer Orgeltabulatur: Die frühesten Notenhandschriften Johann Sebastian Bachs . . .*, ed. Michael Maul and Peter Wollny (Kassel, 2007).

10. The earliest known group of organ chorales by the young Bach as compiled around 1790 by Johann Gottfried Neumeister, first published 1985 as preprint of NBA V/9 (C. Wolff, 2003; updated edition, 2017). See also Wolff 1991[a], Chapter 9 ("The Neumeister Collection of Chorale Preludes from the Bach Circle"), pp. 107–27.

11. Schweitzer, J. S. *Bach le musicien-poète* (Leipzig, 1905); German ed., J. S. *Bach* (Leipzig, 1908); Eng. trans. Ernest Newman (Oxford, 1911), vol. II, p. 55. Schweitzer—theologian, physician, philosopher, humanitarian, and musician—was the first to discern this crucial aspect of Bach's musical language (Ger. ed., p. 424).

12. *Neu erfundene und Gründliche Anweisung . . . Zu vollkommener Erlernung des General-Basses* (Hamburg, 1711), early version of the expanded treatise *Der General-Bass in der Composition* (Dresden, 1728).

13. Bach's autograph score: D-B, Mus. ms. Bach P 415; several facsimile editions.

14. Bach's autograph manuscript: US-NHub Music Deposit 31; facsimile edition. NBA V/5 (Wolfgang Plath, 1962), pp. 19–37.

15. NBA V/6.1 (A. Dürr, 1989), pp. 132–42.

16. D-B, Mus. ms. Bach P 401. The scribe of this manuscript and of other important Bach sources for keyboard instruments was long designated "Anonymus 5," until Andrew Talle identified him (Talle 2003[a]).

17. *BD* III, p. 468.

18. *BD* II, p. 65.

19. *NBR*, p. 399

20. As arranged in the following (unexplained) sequence of minor and major keys: d–g–a–e–C–F–G–c–f–E♭–A♭–B♭–e♭–b♭–a♭–A–E–f♯–b–B–F♯–c♯–D♭.
21. NBR, p. 389.
22. NBR, p. 307.
23. BD III, p. 285.
24. The subdivision of the octave into twelve equal semitones, already described by Werckmeister, was first propagated in the publication *Beste und leichteste Temperatur des Monochordi* (Jena, 1706) by Johann Georg Neidhardt, a pupil of Johann Nicolaus Bach in Jena.
25. BD III, p. 304. Sharp thirds are tuned wider than pure thirds, and are a feature present in both Werckmeister's tunings and equal temperament.
26. Including BG and NBA.
27. NBR, no. 395.
28. NBR, p. 322.
29. This pertains likewise to the early versions of pieces from the *Well-Tempered Clavier* copied by Friedemann into his *Clavier-Büchlein* from his father's autographs.
30. For differences between the versions, see the editions in NBA V/3 (1970) and NBA V/5 (1962).
31. The same page layout also in Friedemann's *Clavier-Büchlein*.
32. Four inventions from Bonporti's collection were copied by Bach and his Cöthen-Leipzig student Bernhard Christian Kayser in a manuscript of 1723 (D-B, Mus. ms. Bach P 270); see Beißwenger 1992, p. 276f.
33. Letter to Forkel, 1775; NBR, p. 399.
34. Dreyfus 1996 imaginatively makes a case for the principle of invention well beyond the inventions and sinfonias.
35. See Bach's entry of an exercise with traditional fingering ("Applicatio") in Friedemann's *Clavier Book*; on the provenance of the Applicatio, see Wollny 2016.
36. Part I, Chapter 3.
37. Dürr 1978.

Chapter 3: In Search of the Autonomous Instrumental Design

1. The compilers of Bach's estate catalog in 1750 would hardly have been aware of the 1721 collection of selected works that later became known as the *Brandenburg Concertos*.
2. An exceptional case may be represented by the Prelude, Fugue, and Allegro in E-flat, BWV 998, from the late 1730s, with its unusual three-movement structure and the da capo form of its fugue.
3. New details on the prehistory of the Gewandhaus concerts are provided by Schulze 2018.
4. Listed in estate catalog; NBR, p. 252.
5. NBR, p. 397.
6. NBR, p. 318.
7. ". . . Weil Er, so bald er spielt, ja alles staunend macht." Poem by Micrander (pen name of Johann Gottlob Kittel), published as part of the review of Bach's recital in September 1731 at St. Sophia's Church "in the presence of all the court musicians

and virtuosos in a fashion that compelled the admiration of everyone." See *NBR*, p. 311.

8. *NBR*, p. 297.

9. *NBR*, p. 299.

10. D-B: Mus. ms. 40644 (Möller Manuscript). Besides works by the young J. S. Bach, the anthology comprises compositions by Tomaso Albinoni, Johann Adam Reincken, Georg Böhm, Nicholas Lebègue, Johann Pachelbel, and others; see inventory in Schulze 1984, pp. 41–43.

11. D-LEm: III. 8. 4 (Andreas Bach Book). In addition to works by the young J. S. Bach, the collection contains works by G. Böhm, Dietrich Buxtehude, Johann Kuhnau, J. Pachelbel, Louis Marchand, and others; see inventory in Schulze 1984, p. 43. A representative selection from both J. C. Bach anthologies was edited by Robert Hill: *Keyboard Music from the Andreas Bach Book and the Möller Manuscript* (Harvard Publications in Music, vol. 16), 1991.

12. BWV 913.1.

13. Based on source—and style—critical evidence, the following sequence may reflect the approximate chronological genesis of the pieces: Toccata in d, BWV 913–Toccata in D, BWV 912–Toccata in e, BWV 914–Toccata in g, BWV 915–Toccata in f#, BWV 910–Toccata in c, BWV 911–Toccata in G, BWV 916.

14. Mattheson 1739, p. 87f. For a discussion of Bach's stylistic relations to Buxtehude, see Wollny 2002 and Dirksen 2019.

15. The so-called Andreas Bach Book; see note 11.

16. As copies by his student Johann Martin Schubart (BuxWV 164) and his brother Christoph (BuxWV 165) indicate.

17. Buxtehude's much shorter and less complex Ciacconas are collected in the Andreas Bach Book (note 11).

18. See notes 10 and 11.

19. Three autograph copies (suites in F minor, B minor, and F major); see Beißwenger 1992.

20. D-B: Mus. ms. Bach P 803 (fasc. 13).

21. D-B: Mus. ms. Bach P 224; see detailed commentary in *Die Clavier-Büchlein für Anna Magdalena Bach 1722 & 1725* (ed. C. Wolff), Leipzig 2019.

22. Notable is the copy by Heinrich Nicolaus Gerber in D-B: Mus. ms. Bach P 1221.

23. D-B: Am.B. 50; see NBA V/7, KB (A. Dürr, 1981), p. 44.

24. D-B: N. Mus. ms. 365, in the hand of Bach's late principal copyist Johann Nathanael Bammler.

25. The music was copied by J. C. Bach while still at his parental home in Leipzig, but the remark is in another hand, possibly that of a Berlin student (communication kindly provided by Peter Wollny). Nevertheless, the information is likely to have been transmitted by J. C. Bach.

26. *NBR*, p. 468.

27. Beißwenger 1992.

28. See NBA V/7, KB (A. Dürr, 1981), p. 86f. The fact that Dieupart dedicated his suites to the Countess of Sandwich and from 1703 spent the rest of his life in England has been used to explain the name of the *English Suites*. On the other hand, Walther 1732 (p. 208) refers to Dieupart only as "ein Frantzösischer Componist," meaning

that Bach, if he had known about Dieupart's career in England, would have learned about it from other sources; see note 29.

29. D-B, SA 4274 ("VI. franz. Suiten from seel. Herrn Capellm. Bach"); *BD* VII, p. 71.

30. *BD* III, no. 715.

31. A revealing detail is offered in the early copy of the *French Suites* by Bach's student B. C. Kayser (Mus. ms. P 418), where the Gavotte of the Suite in B minor, BWV 814, is entitled "Anglois." The use of gavottes is standard in Dieupart's suites.

32. D-B: Mus. ms. P 418.

33. *Die Clavier-Büchlein für Anna Magdalena Bach 1722 & 1725* (ed. C. Wolff), Leipzig, 2019, pp. 128–42.

34. Gregorio Lambranzi's *Nuova e Curiosa Scuola de' Balli Theatrali* (Rome, 1716; German edition: *Neue und Curieuso Theatralische Tanz-Schul*, Nuremberg, 1716).

35. Arranged for melody instrument and bass, as indicated on the title page (". . . par un Violon & flûte avec une Basse de Viole & une Archilut").

36. See the Fugue in G major, BWV 577, and the related organ fugues by Buxtehude, BuxWV 142 and BuxWV 174.

37. Friedemann in the Menuet no. 11 of the 1722 Notebook and Carl in the Marches and Polonaises nos. 15–18 and 22 of the 1725 Notebook; see *Die Clavier-Büchlein . . .* (note 19, above), pp. 54, 110–13, and 116.

38. *Sechs Suiten für Violine solo* (facsimile of the 1696 original), ed. Wolfgang Reich (Leipzig, 1974).

39. D-B: Mus. ms. P 269.

40. Schwanenberger himself provided the combined title page: "Pars 1 | Violino Solo Senza Basso composée par S.ʳ Jean Seb. Bach. Pars 2 | Violoncello Solo Senza Basso composée par S.ʳ J. S. Bach, Maitre de la Chapelle et Directeur de la Musique a Leipsic. ecrite par Madame Bachen son Epouse."

41. *NV 1790*, p. 67: "Sechs geschriebene Suiten fürs Violoncell ohne Bass. Eingebunden."

42. D-B: Mus. Ms. P. 289. Schober (see Koska 2017) copied Suites 1–3, an anonymous copyist continued; NBAʳᵉᵛ 4 (A. Talle and J. E. Kim, 2016), introduction and report.

43. *NBR*, p. 397.

44. Suchalla 1994, p. 800f.

45. D-B: Mus. ms. Bach P 968 (Cöthen scribe), and D-LEm: Poel. mus. Ms. 31 (BWV 1001, Leipzig scribe); see NBAʳᵉᵛ 3 (P. Wollny, 2014), pp. 246 and 248.

46. Schletterer 1865, p. 140f.

47. *BD* III, p. 478.

48. AmZ, 21 (1819), col. 861.

49. In Bach's autograph "Partia."

50. A comparable counterpart, the Passacaglia in G minor for solo violin at the very end of Heinrich Ignaz Franz Biber's "Rosary Sonatas" of 1676, is based on the same ostinato bass, with 130 measures half as long, but similarly spiked with extremely virtuosic figurative material. While there is no evidence of any connections, the work by the Salzburg master might have been relayed to Bach by Westhoff, whose travels had led him through southern Germany, Italy, and France.

51. *Jenaische Allgemeine Literaturzeitung*, 282 (1805), p. 391.

52. "Viola de basso" is the instrument designation in J. P. Kellner's copy of the cello suites (D-B P 804) from around 1730.
53. As Gerber 1790 reports: "The stiff way in which the violoncellos were treated in his time compelled him, considering the lively basses in his works, to the invention of what he called viola pomposa, which at a little more length and height than a viola, but the depth and the four strings of the violoncello, had another fifth, e', and was placed on the arm; this convenient instrument put the player in the position to perform the existing high and fast passages more easily" (BD III, no. 948).
54. NBR, p. 252.
55. See note 38 (copyists different from the scribe of BWV 1001).
56. BD III, no. 808.
57. BD III, p. 219.
58. After the margrave's death it passed to his niece Princess Anna Amalia, and then to her capellmeister J. P. Kirnberger. The first edition was published by C. F. Peters, ed. Siegfried Wilhelm Dehn (Leipzig, 1850).
59. Some of the Weimar and Cöthen concertos entered the Leipzig performing repertoire. A few individual movements from the Brandenburg set even made it into church cantatas as instrumental sinfonias (BWV 1046/1, used in 1726 for cantata BWV 52, and BWV 1048/1, used in 1729 for cantata BWV 174).
60. "Flauto d'echo" refers to the echo effect in movement 2.
61. Preserved in the autograph set of parts, D-B: Mus. ms. Bach St 130.
62. For a more extensive discussion, see Wolff 2000, pp. 169–74: "'Musical Thinking': The Making of a Composer."
63. D-B: Mus. ms. Bach St 162 (harpsichord part only).
64. D-B: Mus. ms. Bach P 229.
65. Clark 1997, p. 67. At the time, the term "trio" or "clavier trio" was often used for duo sonatas with obbligato keyboard, counting as two independently active left- and right-hand keyboard parts.
66. Version II (D-B: Am. B. 61, from the collection of J. P. Kirnberger); version III (D-Bhm: 6138/21, in the hand of J. F. Agricola).
67. Mattheson 1739, p. 344.
68. J. F. Agricola's copy of 1739/40, see note 55.
69. One of the first examples, dated 1731, is the keyboard trio Wq 72 (early version).
70. Mattheson 1739, p. 344.
71. D-B: Mus. ms. Bach P 271.
72. D-B: Mus. ms. Bach P 272 (1732/35).
73. J. N. Forkel, 1802 (NBR, pp. 471–72).
74. US-NHub: LM 4718 [Ma21 Y11 B12], in the hand of J. G. Walther.
75. The G-minor Sonata, BWV 1029, is Bach's only three-movement chamber composition, probably arranged from an unknown four-movement model.
76. Scheibe 1740, p. 675.

Chapter 4: The Most Ambitious of All Projects

1. The cycle started at the beginning of the new academic year in June 1724, exactly one year after Bach took over the office of cantor and music director in Leipzig. Bach's cantata cycles follow the academic year—at the St. Thomas School, beginning on Monday after Trinity Sunday—and not the ecclesiastical year, which starts on the first Sunday in Advent and ends with the week following the last Sunday after Trinity.

2. The Lutheran Reformation referred to congregational hymns or church songs as "chorales" because the congregation took over the singing of the "cantus choralis" or plainsong from the clerical choir.

3. On Telemann's cantata cycles, see Jungius 2008 and Poetzsch 2017.

4. Krummacher 2018, pp. 42–43.

5. Dürr 1985, p. 50.

6. Bach held in his library the eight-volume anthology of more than 4,000 Lutheran hymns, compiled by P. Wagner, *Vollständiges Gesangbuch* (Leipzig, 1697); *BD* II, p. 496.

7. Birkmann belonged to the literary circle of Bach's friend Johann Abraham Birnbaum; see Blanken 2015.

8. On the 6th Sunday after Trinity 1724, for example, Bach and his wife stayed for guest performances in Cöthen; *BD* II, no. 134.

9. The ecclesiastical year runs from the first Sunday in Advent through the week after the last Sunday after Trinity, but the number of post-Trinity Sundays varies from twenty-two to twenty-seven. The liturgy for the 27th Sunday after Trinity automatically substitutes for the last Sunday after Trinity whenever it occurs. Therefore, the destination of BWV 140 is this last Sunday as well.

10. In Bach's choral library, these four chorale cantatas were apparently kept separate from the *de tempore* chorale cantatas, that is, those designated for a specific liturgical date, and therefore were not included in the inheritances of Anna Magdalena and Wilhelm Friedemann; see the final paragraph of this chapter.

11. The Dorian scale without key signature runs from *d* to *d'*, but with *b–c'* and not *b♭–c♯'* (as in the harmonic minor scale). It has a proper dominant on V (A-major triad) and in a Baroque context sounds much like D minor, but its most characteristic feature is the regular occurrence of *b* and the lack of the leading note *c♯*. BWV 121 is in transposed Dorian (*e* to *e'*, with a D-major key signature).

    The Phrygian scale *e to e'* (without key signature) begins with the characteristic half step *e–f*. Thus the continuo part in BWV 38 begins with the notes *e–f*, and the first line of the chorale melody ends *g'–f'–e'*. In BWV 2 it is transposed to D (with a D-minor key signature), with the half-step *d–e♭*. A salient harmonic feature of the Phrygian mode is the absence of V as dominant, such that E Phrygian in a Baroque context sounds more like A minor with an E-major triad as final chord.

12. In Leipzig, the music-free Lenten period (*tempus clausum*) began after Estomihi Sunday, the liturgical date for BWV 127; concerted music resumed with the Passion performance on Good Friday. As an exception, a cantata performance was always scheduled for the Marian Feast of the Annunciation (March 25). A second *tempus clausum* involved the 2nd, 3rd, and 4th Sundays in Advent.

13. Ziegler later published her cantata texts (*Versuch in Gebundener Schreib-Art*, Leipzig,

1728), with revisions and changes made by the author. There is no evidence for the frequently voiced view that Bach was responsible for the awkwardness of some passages in the texts as they were set in 1725.

14. On the basis of their opening chorale choruses, the original performing parts of BWV 68 and BWV 128 were initially kept together with the chorale cantatas (Wilhelm Friedemann and Anna Magdalena Bach's inheritance) and acquired by the St. Thomas School in 1750. BWV 128 was separated from the remainder for unknown reasons around 1800; see *BC* A 76.

15. See *BC* A 9a–b (BWV 91) and A 137a–b (BWV 8).

16. Quoted from Carl Philipp Emanuel's autobiography in *Carl Burney's der Musik Doctors Tagebuch seiner Musikalischen Reisen*, part III (Hamburg, 1773), p. 201.

17. *BD* II, p. 486. The wording's lack of precise details actually suggests that the transaction had been planned for some time, and might even have been arranged by Bach himself.

18. Anna Magdalena Bach's performing parts of the chorale cantatas, acquired in 1750 by the St. Thomas School and today housed in the Leipzig Bach Archive, comprise the bulk of the listing in Table 4-3, sections 1 and 2. Missing apparently from the very beginning, due most likely to the turmoil after the composer's death, are the parts of cantatas no. 135, 113, 180, 115, and 111; parts of BWV 80 seem to have been kept separately.

Chapter 5: Proclaiming the State of the Art in Keyboard Music

1. The Italian version was used by Domenico Scarlatti for his *Essercizi per gravicembalo* (London, 1738), and also by Telemann for his solos and trios under the heading *Essercizii musici* (Hamburg, 1739–40).

2. Graupner's titles: (1) *Partien auf das Clavier, bestehend in Allemanden, Couranten, Sarabanden, Menuetten, Giguen etc.*; (2) *Monatliche Clavier-Früchte, bestehend in Praeludien, Allemanden, Couranten, Sarabanden, Menuetten, Giguen etc., meistentheils vor Anfänger.*

3. *BD* II, no. 214.

4. *BD* II, no. 224.

5. For details, see Wolff 1973, Butler 1980.

6. The chamber cantata "Armida abbandonata," HWV 105, and the so-called *Brockes Passion* HWV 48 (Beißwenger 1992, pp. 289–94).

7. Talle 2003[b], pp. 64–69.

8. *The Notebooks of Anna Magdalena Bach, 1722 and 1725*, ed. C. Wolff (Leipzig: C. F. Peters, 2019), preface and critical report.

9. The Corrente and Tempo di Gavotta movements in their album versions of 1725 were borrowed and slightly revised from originals in the G-major Sonata for harpsichord and violin, BWV 1019.

10. Wolff 1991[a], pp. 220–22.

11. Christoph Willibald Gluck arranged the opening section of the giga for the orchestral score of the aria "Perché, se tanti siete" from the opera *Antigono* (1756), reusing it in the arias "S'a estinguer non bastate" from *Telemaco* (1765) and "J t'implore et je tremble," *Iphigénie en Tauride* (1779).

12. *NBR*, p. 403.

13. *BD* II, no. 276.

14. Sigmund Gottlieb Staden, *Der VII Tugenden, Planeten, Töne oder Stimmen Aufzug in kunstzierliche Melodeien gesetzet* (Nuremberg, 1645).

15. Mattheson 1739, p. 130.

16. Reported by J. G. Walther (*BD* II, no. 323); no copy of the single edition of Partita 6 survives.

17. Mattheson 1713 presents an extended discussion in the chapter "Von der Musicalischen Thone Eigenschafft und Würckung in Ausdrückung der Affecten" (On the musical keys and their effect on the expression of the affects), pp. 231–52.

18. *BD* II, no. 249.

19. *BD* II, no. 309; Talle 2017, p. 117.

20. NBA V/2, KB (W. Emery, 1981), p. 14.

21. *Das beschützte Orchestre* (Hamburg, 1717), p. 129.

22. Walther 1732, article "Stylus": "Der Italiänische Styl ist scharff, bunt, und ausdruckend; der Frantzösische hergegen natürlich, fliessend, zärtlich, etc."

23. NBA V/11, KB (K. Heller, 1997), p. 25f.

24. Wolff 2000, pp. 169–74.

25. Beißwenger 1992, pp. 279, 350f.

26. Beißwenger 1992, pp. 226f., 284f., 287f.

27. The prelude and fugue, both in E-flat major, function as bookends of the collection. Separated from each other in the original edition of 1739, they were catalogued under a single number in the BWV.

28. *BD* II, no. 455.

29. *BD* II, no. 434.

30. Butler 1980 and Butler 1990.

31. Reported by Forkel 1802 (*NBR*, p. 440).

32. *BD* III, no. 767, p. 221. From about 1738, Bach set out counterpoint studies for his son Wilhelm Friedemann that deal specifically with the church modes; see NBA-Supplement (P. Wollny, 2011), p. 83.

33. *Clavier-Übung*, part I = 73 pages of music; part II = 27 pages; part IV = 32 pages.

34. German original: "wenn wir heimfahrn aus diesem Elende, Kyrieleis."

35. *NBR*, no. 343.

36. *NBR*, no. 333.

37. *NBR*, no. 343.

38. *NBR*, no. 342.

39. *NBR*, p. 464f. In November 1741 (Kalendarium, p. 81), Bach is known to have visited with Keyserlinck, and may have presented him on this occasion with a copy of the newest keyboard opus.

40. While both ciaccona (chaconne) and passacaglia (passecaille) move in ternary meter, the ostinato bass of the ciaccona begins on the downbeat, whereas the passacaglia starts with a pickup. Bach apparently grew up with this distinction, which was clearly made in Buxtehude's ostinato variations for organ, BuxWV 159–161, the Passacaglia in D minor, and the two Ciacconas in E and C minor, all three included in the Andreas Bach Book (see above, page 72).

41. Robert Schumann in fact used one of the melody's characteristic motifs in mm. 9–12 of the last movement of his *Papillons*, op. 2, of 1831. The first line of the tune is shared (deliberately, it appears) with the 1690 chorale melody "Was Gott tut, das ist wohlgetan" (What God does is well done), frequently set by Bach.

42. NBA V/2, KB (C. Wolff, 1981), p. 98.

Chapter 6: A Grand Liturgical Messiah Cycle

1. Some excerpts from the only surviving fragmentary source were published by Arnold Schering in vol. 2 of *Musikgeschichte Leipzigs, 1650 bis 1723* (Leipzig, 1926), pp. 25–33.

2. First pointed out by Friedrich Smend (1926).

3. *Das Privilegirte Ordentl. und Vermehrte Dreßdnische Gesang-Buch* (Dresden and Leipzig, 1725), with numerous reprints through the 1750s; appendix: *Tägliche Kirchen-Andachten* (prayers from the Dresden palace church by the court preacher Matthias Hoe von Hoenegg), p. 47: "Herr, unser Herrscher, dessen Nahme herrlich ist in allen Landen!"

4. *Der für die Sünde der Welt gemarterte und sterbende Jesus aus den IV. Evangelisten in gebundener Rede vorgestellet* (Hamburg, 1711).

5. Text and melody in the *Passionale melicum* by Martin Jan (Görlitz, 1663); contained in a four-part setting in the chorale book edited by Gottfried Vopelius (Leipzig, 1682), where it precedes the liturgical *St. Matthew Passion* by Johann Walter.

6. Transmitted in the collection of four-part chorales, ed. C. P. E. Bach, vol. 2 (Birnstiel: Berlin, 1769).

7. On the influence of Postel, see Smend 1926, and Dürr 1988, p. 60f.

8. Strophe 4 of the hymn "Du großer Schmerzensmann" (see note 5 above) projects the very same image when it states "Dein Kampf ist unser Sieg, dein Tod ist unser Leben" (Your fight is our victory, your death is our life).

9. The various changes and revisions made to the work are reflected in the extant original performing materials used for the final performance under Bach's direction in 1749, D-B: Mus. ms. P 28 (score) and Mus. ms. St 111 (parts). The first twenty pages of the score (P 28) are a fair copy in Bach's hand and contain the revisions made in around 1738 (facsimile in NBA II/4, supplement); the continuation of the score stems from 1748–49 and is in the hand of Bach's assistant, Johann Nathanael Bammler, with few minor entries by the composer.

10. *Erbauliche Gedancken auf den Grünen Donnerstag und Charfreytag über den Leiden-den JESUM, in einem ORATORIO entworfen von Picandern*, 1725.

11. BC I/3 (D 5), p. 1082.

12. See Axmacher 1984 and Marquard 2017.

13. Picander's *Ernst-Schertzhaffte und Satyrische Gedichte*, part II (Leipzig, 1729), p. 203.

14. Such chorale interpolations were a favorite device of Bach's, used in many cantata movements.

15. D-LEb: Peters Ms. R 18.

16. Cf. the four-part chorales from the manuscript collection of Bach's pupil Johann Ludwig Dietel, 1734/35 (D-LEb: Ms. R 18).

17. Bach fit "Oratorium" into the heading of the *Christmas Oratorio* at a later point, making it correspond to the other two (with corresponding subtitles for the individual feast days "Pars I [II, III, etc.] Oratorii").

18. *BD* IX, p. 223.

19. "Die Kirchenstücke, welche man insgemein Oratorien, das ist Bethstücke nennet, pflegen auch den Cantaten darin ähnlich zu seyn, daß sie Arien and Recitative enthalten. Sie führen auch insgemein verschiedene Personen redend ein, damit die Abwechslung verschiedener Singstimmen statt haben möge. Hier muß nun der Dichter entweder biblischen Personen, aus den Evangelien, oder andern Texten, ja Jesum, und Gott selbst; oder doch allegorische Personen, die sich auf die Religion gründen; als Glaube, Liebe, Hoffnung, die christliche Kirche, geistliche Braut, Sulamith, die Tochter Zion, oder die gläubige Seele, u.d.m. redend einführen: damit alles der Absicht und dem Orte gemäß herauskomme" (p. 728).

20. "Oratorium . . . eine geistliche Opera, oder musicalische Vorstellung einer geistlichen Historie in den Capellen oder Cammern gewisser großer Herrn, aus Gesprächen, Soli, Duo und Trio, Ritornellen, starcken Chören etc. bestehend. Die musicalische Composition muß reich an allen seyn, was nur die Kunst sinnreiches und gesuchtes aufzubringen vermag" (451f.).

21. *NBR*, no. 98.

22. *NBR*, no. 100.

23. Performance schedule 1734–35:

> December 25, Part I—Morning: St. Nicholas's; afternoon: St. Thomas's
> December 26, Part II—Morning: St. Thomas's; afternoon: St. Nicholas's
> December 27, Part III—Morning (only): St. Nicholas's
> January 1, Part IV—Morning: St. Thomas's; afternoon: St. Nicholas's
> January 2, Part V—Morning (only): St. Nicholas's
> January 6, Part VI—Morning: St. Thomas's; afternoon: St. Nicholas's

The specific sequence of holidays, that is, New Year's Day appearing before the Sunday after Christmas, repeated during Bach's lifetime in 1739/40, 1744/45, and 1745/46.

24. The liturgical schedule of lessons for the six feast days (First Day of Christmas, Luke 2:1–14; Second Day of Christmas, Luke 2:15–20; Third Day of Christmas, John 1:1–14; New Year's Day, Luke 1:21; Sunday after Christmas, Matthew 2:13–23; Epiphany, Matthew 2:1–12) differs significantly from Bach's selection of biblical texts for the Christmas Oratorio.

25. The paper was used up by midsummer 1735, which suggests that the interruption of the oratorio project most likely occurred earlier that year, perhaps during Lent.

26. Wollny 2016, pp. 83–91.

27. The other two cantatas for Easter Sunday, BWV 4 and BWV 31, are of pre-Leipzig origin. Leipzig performances of BWV 4 can be established for 1724 and 1725, in both instances as a second cantata (after the sermon). BWV 31 was performed in 1724 and 1731; in 1726 Bach presented the Easter cantata "Denn du wirst meine Seele nicht in der Hölle lassen" by his cousin Johann Ludwig Bach, BWV Anh. III/15.

28. Only the instrumental parts of 1725 are extant; the 1725 score was discarded after Bach made the fair copy in 1738.

29. Bugenhagen's *Evangelien-Harmonie* was included in the appendix of the principal Leipzig hymnals.

30. Performed with new text under the headline "Frohes Volk, vergnügte Sachsen" (Happy folk, contented Saxons, BWV 1158), for the name day of Elector Friedrich August II of Saxony on August 3, 1733.

31. The hand of Bach's second youngest son, Johann Christoph Friedrich, shows up in the performing parts of the *Christmas Oratorio*, which point to a performance in 1749. I am grateful to Peter Wollny for this information.

32. In his official pledge document, dated May 5, 1723, Bach agreed under point 7 "to arrange the music that it shall not last too long, and shall be of such a nature as not to make an operatic impression, but rather incite the listeners to devotion" (*NBR*, p. 103).

33. *NBR*, p. 161.

Chapter 7: In Critical Survey and Review Mode

1. The inauguration of the renovated school took place on June 5, 1732, with a performance of the cantata "Froher Tag, verlangte Stunden," BWV 1162.

2. *CPEB-CW: Clavier-Werke Verzeichnis* (facsimile, ed. C. Wolff, 2014), introduction.

3. Limited essentially to four keyboard pieces (BWV 535.1, BWV 739, BWV 764, and BWV 1121) and six vocal works (BWV 71, BWV 131, BWV 199, BWV 524, BWV 1127, and 1164); to the latter group may be added BWV 106 and BWV 150, autograph scores of which are lost but which were available in the 1750s to Leipzig copyists; see BC I/4, B 18, and B 24.

4. *NBR*, p. 200 (no. 24).

5. *NBR*, no. 303, p. 288.

6. *NBR*, no. 344; see Wolff 2000, "Epilogue: Bach and the Idea of 'Musical Perfection.'"

7. A double leaf, probably accidentally left inside and later bound into the manuscript.

8. D-B: Mus. ms. Bach P 271, pp. 57–110.

9. Wolff 2000, pp. 449–51.

10. Also referred to as Anon. Vr, copying for Bach 1742–50, and later for C. P. E. Bach in Berlin.

11. US-NYpm: Lehman deposit.

12. The autographs of BWV 541 and BWV 566 (both now lost) were also marked "Christel"; see NBA IV/5–6, KB (D. Kilian, 1978), p. 223f.

13. D-B: Am. B. 60, plus the six organ sonatas (D-B: Am. B. 51a); see Koska 2017, p. 156.

14. D-B: Mus. ms. Bach P 402 and Mus. ms. Bach P 229.

15. Stauffer 2015, pp. 177–92.

16. Schulze 2008 argues that the edition of the *Six Chorales* might have been a project initiated and undertaken by Schübler, with the composer's permission but not his active participation.

17. The heading of BWV 646 refers to two hymns using the same melody, whereas BWV 650 oddly (perhaps for lack of space on the page?) does not include the title of "Lobe den Herren, den mächtigen König der Ehren" from the cantata BWV 137.

18. D-B: Mus. ms. Bach P 234.

19. A possible reason for discontinuing work on BWV 1059 in m. 9 might have been related to questions about just how to redefine the role of the single oboe (doubling violin I in the ritornello) vis-à-vis the harpsichord.

20. The notation of BWV 1058 also begins with a new paper signature (using the same paper as before).

21. Disregarding the Concerto in C major, BWV 1061, for two harpsichords (originally without string accompaniment) and the Concerto in A minor, BWV 1065, an arrangement of Vivaldi's concerto for four violins, strings, and continuo, op. 3, no. 10.

22. NBA VII/4, KB (W. Breig, 2001), pp. 89, 111, 133, and 160.

23. BG 17, p. xiv.

24. NBA VII/7 (W. Fischer, 1970), pp. 3–30.

25. See NBA VII/4, KB (W. Breig, 2001), pp. 86, 132, 158, and 206.

26. Wolff 2008 and Wolff 2016.

27. NBR, p. 117; Wolff 2008, p. 106f.

28. See also the clever adaptation of violin figuration in the Bach-Vivaldi concerto BWV 593.

29. Copies of individual concertos were made by J. F. Agricola (BWV 1052–1053), J. C. Nichelmann (BWV 1053), J. C. Altnickol (BWV 1054).

30. His name appears, for instance, on the list of subscribers to Telemann's *Nouveaux Quatuors* (Paris, 1738); *BD* II, p. 328.

31. Details regarding the order of service are provided by Stockigt 2018.

32. The presentation was arranged with the assistance of Bach's friend Jan Dismas Zelenka, director of church music at the Dresden court, and the set of parts was prepared entirely within the Bach household by family members and private students; see *BC* I/4: E 2 (p. 1186).

33. The Dresden appointment was delayed until December 1736 because of Bach's competing post as titular capellmeister at the Weißenfels court, a title that expired in June 1736 with the death of Duke Christian of Saxe-Weißenfels.

34. Two liturgical melodies: the German Agnus Dei hymn "Christe, du Lamm Gottes," and the Litany, both being vocal parts in the early version; in the later Mass version, the Agnus Dei melody is played by horns and oboes in unison.

35. D-B: Mus. ms. Bach P 430.

36. GB-Lbl: Add. MS 35021; the incomplete source lacks BWV 873–874 and BWV 881, with parts of the manuscripts written by Anna Magdalena.

37. NBA V/6.2, KB (A. Dürr, 1996), p. 201f.

38. For details, see NBA V/6.2, KB (A. Dürr, 1996), pp. 70–73.

Chapter 8: Instrumental and Vocal Polyphony at Its Peak

1. Walther 1708, p. 47.

2. For details, see Wolff 2004.

3. See the edition in "Beiträge zur Generalbass-, und Satzlehre, Kontrapunktstudien . . ." in the NBA Supplement (P. Wollny, 2011), pp. 41–62.

4. NBR, no. 220 (incl. facsimile); see Schieckel 1982.

5. NBR, p. 305.

6. NBR, p. 300.

7. *NBR*, p. 398.
8. *NBR*, p. 305.
9. *NBR*, p. 342.
10. For details, see Wolff 1991[a], Chapter 20 ("The Compositional History of the Art of Fugue"), based on a paper read in 1979 at a Leipzig Bach conference (published 1983).
11. For a discussion of this movement, see Wolff 1991[a], Chapter 12.
12. BWV 1076 = BWV 1087/13; BWV 1077 = BWV 1087/11. The canons BWV 1076 and 1077 were listed separately in the *Bach-Werke-Verzeichnis* (1950) long before the canon series BWV 1087 became known in 1975.
13. NBA V/2, KB (C. Wolff, 1981), p. 109f., and Wolff 1991[a], Chapter 13.
14. *NBR*, p. 307.
15. *NBR*, no. 245.
16. At the Potsdam event, Bach had declined (no doubt wisely) to improvise a six-part fugue on the royal theme and instead played a fugue on a subject of his own choice.
17. Wolff 1991[a], Chapter 18.
18. These are manuscript additions in the dedication exemplar of the *Musical Offering* (D-B: Am. B 73); NBA VIII/1 (C. Wolff, 1976), p. 59.
19. *NBR*, no. 360.
20. *BD* III, p. 519.
21. *BD* III, p. 113.
22. Table 8-5 differs in a few details from the contents of the original edition of 1751, which contains a number of errors as a result of the confusion surrounding the publication, which at the time of the composer's death was still a work in progress. The differences are as follows:

> 1. After Contrapunctus inversus 13[b]: "Contrapunctus a 4" (not numbered). This is an uncorrected version of Contrapunctus 10 and an erroneous addition.
> 2. After the group of four canons: "Fuga a 2 clav." This arrangement of Contrapunctus 13 for two keyboards, with an additional fourth part not mirrored, is also an erroneous addition.
> 3. The augmentation canon appears misplaced at the beginning of the group of four canons. The projected page turns for the canons indicate that the first canon in fact belongs at the end of the group.
> 4. After the "Fuga a 3 Soggetti" (the unfinished quadruple fugue), C. P. E. Bach, editor of the edition, added the organ chorale "Wenn wir in höchsten Nöten sein" (BWV 668) in order to "compensate" for the incomplete state of the work.

See also NBA VII/1/KB (K. Hofmann, 1995); and Wolff 1991[a], Chapters 19–21.
23. Marpurg recalled his Leipzig visit in writings of 1750 (*BD* III, no. 632) and 1759 (*BD* III, no. 701, p. 144f.).
24. The close neighboring relationship of the double and triple fugues X and XI was also lost.
25. Wolff 2000, p. 435, diagram.
26. *NBR*, p. 304.
27. He owned the original plates of the engraved music.
28. *NBR*, p. 375.

29. Blanken 2018.
30. *NBR*, no. 281.
31. *NV 1790*, p. 72.
32. *NBR*, no. 364.
33. Table 8-6 presents the Mass exactly as it appears in the autograph score (D-B: Mus. ms. P 180), which represents a continuation of the Kyrie-Gloria score Bach had composed in 1733. BWV[3] reflects the compositional history of the work:

    > BWV 232.1 = Sanctus D major of 1724
    > BWV 232.2 = Missa (Kyrie-Gloria) of 1733
    > BWV 232.3 = Credo in G major (early version) of c. 1740
    > BWV 232.4 = B-*minor Mass* in its complete form of 1748–49, including a new fair copy of BWV 232.1.

34. Walther 1732, p. 459.
35. The two voices of the duet relate to the doctrine of the dual nature of Jesus Christ (fully God and fully human), a core tenet of early Christian belief as transmitted by the Nicene Creed of 325. For the same reason, the text passages "Domine Deus" (no. 8) and "Et in unum" (no. 15) are set as duets as well.
36. Bach performed an arrangement of Pergolesi's *Stabat Mater* around 1746/47. Regarding the relationship between the *Stabat Mater* and the "Et incarnatus est" movement (no. 16), see Wolff 2009, pp. 86–89.
37. He had composed three single Sanctus works during the first two Leipzig years: C major, BWV 237 (37 measures long), D major, BWV 238 (48 mm.), and D major, BWV 232.3 (168 mm.).
38. The Lutheran liturgy changed the Sanctus text of the *Missale romanum* to the Latin biblical text.
39. Wolff 2009, pp. 119–21.
40. *NBR*, p. 371.
41. Wolff 2009, pp. 35–40, regarding Leipzig performances of sacred works in Latin in the 1740s and under Thomascantor Gottlob Harrer after 1750.

Epilogue: "Praxis cum theoria"

1. Jackson 2005; on Bach and the Bose family, see Neumann 1970.
2. *BD* II, p. 346 (slightly rephrased): "eine musikalische Übung, in welcher man theils eigene, theils fremde Gedanken richtig, deutlich, ordentlich, zusammenhängend, rührend, aber nicht ohne gelehrtes Nachsinnen ausdrücken soll."
3. *NBR*, p. 305.
4. For details, see Wolff 2000, pp. 169–74.
5. *NBR*, p. 176—a statement made in the context of the 1736 dispute with the rector of the St. Thomas School over the appointment of choir prefects and their qualifications. The prefect assigned to the First Choir, unlike the prefect for the Second Choir, had to be able to conduct works by Bach.
6. *BD* II, no. 452 (Abraham Kriegel: *Nützliche Nachrichten von denen Bemühungen derer Gelehrten und andern Begebenheiten*, Leipzig, 1739).

7. *NBR*, no. 328 (Gesner's Latin Quintilian commentary of 1738).

8. *NBR*, no. 405, p. 412.

9. He collaborated with Bach for the first time in 1727, on the Funeral Ode, BWV 198.

10. *BD* II, no. 309.

11. See Wolff 2000, "Epilogue: Bach and the Idea of 'Musical Perfection.'"

BIBLIOGRAPHY

Library Sigla

As assigned by RISM (Répertoire International des Sources Musicales): www.rism.info.

Bach digital (www.bach-digial.de) provides an extensive digital library of manuscript and printed sources of J. S. Bach's works. Location of sources is indicated by RISM library sigla.

A-Wn	Österreichische Nationalbibliothek, Musiksammlung, Wien
D-B	Staatsbibliothek zu Berlin, Preußischer Kulturbesitz, Musikabteilung
D-Bhm	Universität der Künste, Berlin
D-Bsa	Sing-Akademie zu Berlin, Notenarchiv (on deposit at D-B)
D-DS	Universitäts- und Landesbibliothek, Musikabteilung, Darmstadt
D-F	Universitätsbibliothek J. C. Senckenberg, Abteilung Musik und Theater, Frankfurt am Main
D-LEb	Bach-Archiv, Leipzig
D-LEm	Leipziger Stadtbibliothek, Musikbibliothek, Leipzig
D-Dl	Sächsische Landesbibliothek, Staats- und Universitätsbibliothek, Dresden
D-WFk	Evangelische Stadtkirche St. Marien, Kantoreiarchiv, Weißenfels
F-Pn	Bibliothèque nationale de France, Départment de la Musique, Paris
GB-Lbl	The British Library, London
US-NHub	Yale University, Beinecke Rare Book and Manuscript Library, New Haven, CT
US-NYpm	The Morgan Library and Museum, New York, NY

Bibliographic Abbreviations

AmZ	*Allgemeine musikalische Zeitung.* Leipzig, 1798–1848.
BC	Hans-Joachim Schulze and Christoph Wolff. *Bach Compendium. Analytisch-bibliographisches Repertorium der Werke Johann Sebastian Bachs. Vokalwerke*, parts I–IV. Leipzig and Frankfurt, 1986–1989.
BD	*Bach-Dokumente.* Leipzig and Kassel, 1963.
	Vol. I (1963): *Schriftstücke von der Hand Johann Sebastian Bachs*, ed. Werner Neumann and Hans-Joachim Schulze.
	Vol. II (1969): *Fremdschriftliche und gedruckte Dokumente zur Lebensgeschichte Johann Sebastian Bachs 1685–1750*, ed. Werner Neumann and Hans-Joachim Schulze.
	Vol. III (1972): *Dokumente zum Nachwirken Johann Sebastian Bachs 1750–1800*, ed. Hans-Joachim Schulze.
	Vol. VII (2008): J. N. Forkel, *Ueber Johann Sebastian Bachs Leben, Kunst und Kunstwerke* (Leipzig, 1802): Edition, Quellen, Materialien, ed.

Christoph Wolff, unter Mitarbeit von Michael Maul.
Vol. IX (2017): *Bach—Eine Lebensgeschichte in Bildern / A Life in Pictures*, ed. Christoph Wolff.

BG   *Johann Sebastian Bachs Werke*, issued by the Bach-Gesellschaft. Leipzig, 1851–99.

BJ   *Bach-Jahrbuch* (Leipzig and Berlin), ed. Arnold Schering (1904–39); Max Schneider (1940–52); Alfred Dürr and Werner Neumann (1953–74); Hans-Joachim Schulze and Christoph Wolff (1975–2004); Peter Wollny (2005–).

BP   *Bach Perspectives*. Urbana and Chicago, IL, 1995–.

BWV   Wolfgang Schmieder. *Thematisch-systematisches Verzeichnis der musikalischen Werke Johann Sebastian Bachs: Bach-Werke-Verzeichnis*. Leipzig, 1950.

BWV²   ——Revised and enlarged edition. Wiesbaden, 1990.

BWV³   Updated and expanded new edition, issued under the auspices of the Bach-Archiv Leipzig, ed. Christine Blanken, Christoph Wolff, and Peter Wollny. Wiesbaden, forthcoming.

BuxWV   *Thematisch-systematisches Verzeichnis der musikalischen Werke von Dietrich Buxtehude—Buxtehude-Werke-Verzeichnis*, ed. Georg Karstädt, 2nd edition. Wiesbaden, 1985.

CPEB-CW   *Carl Philipp Emanuel Bach: The Complete Works*. The Packard Humanities Institute, Los Altos, CA, 2004–.

HWV   Bernd Baselt, *Thematisch-systematisches Verzeichnis der Werke Georg Friedrich Händels—Händel-Handbuch*, vols. 1–3. Kassel and Leipzig, 1978–86.

Kalendarium *Kalendarium zur Lebensgeschichte Johann Sebastian Bachs*, ed. Andreas Glöckner. Leipzig, 2008.

LBB   *Leipziger Beiträge zur Bach-Forschung*. 1993–.

NBA   Johann Sebastian Bach. *Neue Ausgabe sämtlicher Werke. Neue Bach-Ausgabe*. Issued under the auspices of the Johann-Sebastian-Bach-Institut Göttingen and the Bach-Archiv Leipzig. Kassel and Leipzig, 1954–2006.

NBA/KB   *Neue Bach-Ausgabe: Kritischer Bericht* (critical report).

NBA^rev   Selected revised volumes, issued under the auspices of the Bach-Archiv Leipzig. Kassel, 2010–.

NBR   Hans T. David and Arthur Mendel, eds. *The New Bach Reader: A Life of Johann Sebastian Bach in Letters and Documents*, rev. and expanded by Christoph Wolff. New York, 1998.

NV 1790   *Verzeichniß des musikalischen Nachlasses des verstorbenen Capellmeisters Carl Philipp Emanuel Bach*. Hamburg, 1790.

Works Cited

In the endnotes, literature is cited by author (last name only) and year of publication (same-year publications differentiated by letters in square brackets). The bibliographic items listed below are limited to those cited in this book. For further references, see the Online Bach Bibliography: www.bach-bibliographie.de.

Axmacher, Elke. *"Aus Liebe will mein Heyland sterben": Untersuchungen zum Wandel des Passionsverständnisses im frühen 18. Jahrhundert.* Stuttgart, 1984.

Beißwenger, Kirsten. *Johann Sebastian Bachs Notenbibliothek.* Kassel, 1992.

Blanken, Christine. "Christoph Birkmanns Kantatenzyklus 'Gott-geheiligte Sabbaths-Zehnden' von 1728 und die Leipziger Kirchenmusik unter J. S. Bach in den Jahren 1724–1727." *BJ* 101 (2015): 13–74.

——. "Neue Dokumente zur Erbteilung nach dem Tod Johann Sebastian Bachs." *BJ* 104 (2018): 133–54.

Butler, Gregory. "Leipziger Stecher in Bachs Originaldrucken." *BJ* 66 (1980): 9–26.

——. *Bach's Clavier-Übung III. The Making of a Print.* Durham, NC, and London, 1990.

Clark, Stephen L. *The Letters of C. P. E. Bach.* Oxford, 1997.

Dadelsen, Georg. "Zur Entstehung des Bachschen Orgelbüchleins." In *Festschrift Friedrich Blume zum 70. Geburtstag.* Kassel, 1963: 74–79.

Dirksen, Pieter. "Buxtehude und Bach: Neue Perspektiven." *Buxtehude-Studien*, vol. 3 (Bonn, 2019): 59–80.

Dreyfus, Laurence. *Bach and the Patterns of Invention.* Cambridge, MA, 1996.

Dürr, Alfred. "Heinrich Nicolaus Gerber als Schüler Bachs." *BJ* 64 (1978): 7–18.

——. *Die Kantaten von Johann Sebastian Bach.* Kassel, 1985.

——. *Die Johannes-Passion von Johann Sebastian Bach.* Kassel, 1988.

——. *Das Wohltemperierte Klavier.* Kassel, 1998.

Forkel, Johann Nicolaus. *Ueber Johann Sebastian Bachs Leben, Kunst und Kunstwerke.* Leipzig, 1802 (Eng. trans. in NBR, Part VI).

Fux, Johann Joseph. *Gradus ad Parnassum* [Vienna, 1724]. . . *Aus dem Lateinischen in Teutsche übersetzt, mit nöthigen und nützlichen Anmerckungen versehen und heraus gegeben von Lorenz Mizlern.* Leipzig, 1742.

Gerber, Erst Ludwig. *Historisch-Biographisches Lexicon der Tonkünstler.* 2 vols. Leipzig, 1790.

Horn, Wolfgang. *Die Dresdner Hofkirchenmusik. 1720–1745: Studien zu ihren Voraussetzungen und ihrem Repertoire.* Kassel, 1987.

Jackson, Myles W. "Johann Heinrich Winkler und die Elektrizität in Leipzig in der Mitte des 18. Jahrhunderts." In *LBB 7: Musik, Kunst und Wissenschaft im Zeitalter Johann Sebastian Bachs,* ed. Ulrich Leisinger and Christoph Wolff. Hildesheim, 2005: 61–65.

Jungius, Christiane. *Telemanns Frankfurter Kantatenzyklen.* Kassel, 2008.

Koska, Bernd. "Die Berliner Notenkopisten Johann Gottfried Siebe und Johann Nicolaus Schober und ihre Bach-Abschriften." *BJ* 103 (2017): 149–84.

Krummacher, Friedhelm. *Johann Sebastian Bach—Die Kantaten und Passionen.* 2 vols. Kassel, 2018.

Marquard, Reiner. "'Ich will mich in dir versenken': Die Lehre von der unio mystica in der Matthäus-Passion von Johann Sebastian Bach." *BJ* 104 (2017): 155–70.

Mattheson, Johann. *Das Neu-Eröffnete Orchestre,* Hamburg, 1713.

——. *Der vollkommene Capellmeister.* Hamburg, 1739.

Maul, Michael. *"Dero berühmbter Chor." Die Leipziger Thomasschule und ihre Kantoren, 1212–1804.* Leipzig, 2012. (Eng. trans., *Bach's Famous Choir: The Saint Thomas School in Leipzig, 1212–1804.* Woodbridge, 2018.)

Mizler, Lorenz Christoph, see Fux, Johann Joseph.

Neumann, Werner. "Eine Leipziger Bach-Gedenkstätte. Über die Beziehungen der Familien Bach und Bose." *BJ* 56 (1970): 19–31.

Poetzsch, Ute. "Grundlegung und Diversifizierung—die Eisenacher und Frankfurter Jahrgänge 1708–1721." *Die Tonkunst*, 2017/4: 449–55.

Schabalina, Tatjana. "'Texte zur Musik' in Sankt Petersburg. Neue Quellen zur Leipziger Musikgeschichte sowie zur Kompositions- und Aufführungstätigkeit Johann Sebastian Bachs." *BJ* 94 (2008): 33–98.

Schieckel, Harald. "Johann Sebastian Bachs Auflösung eines Kanons von Teodoro Riccio." *BJ* 68 (1982): 125–30.

Schletterer, Hans Michael. *Joh. Friedrich Reichardt: Sein Leben und seine Werke.* 2 vols. Augsburg, 1865.

Schulze, Hans-Joachim. "Melodiezitate und Mehrtextigkeit in der Bauernkantate und in den Goldbergvariationen." *BJ* 62 (1976): 58–72.

——. *Studien zur Bach-Überlieferung in 18. Jahrhundert.* Leipzig, 1984.

——. "*Die sechs Choräle kosten nichts*—Zur Bewertung des Originaldrucks der Schübler-Choräle." BJ 94 (2008): 301–4.

——. "Das *Grosse Concert*, die Freimaurer und Johann Sebastian Bach. Konstellationen im Leipziger Musikleben der 1740er Jahre." *BJ* 104 (2018): 11–42.

Simpfendörfer, Gottfried. "Die Leipziger Pfingstkantate von 1721—ein Werk von Johann Sebastian Bach?" *BJ* 96 (2010): 275–79.

Schweitzer, Albert. *J. S. Bach.* Leipzig, 1908 [Eng. trans., London, 1911].

Smend, Friedrich. "Die Johannes-Passion von Bach: Auf ihren Bau untersucht." *BJ* 1926: 105–28.

Spitta, Philipp. *Johann Sebastian Bach.* 2 vols. Leipzig, 1873 and 1880. (Eng. trans., 3 vols., London, 1884–85.)

Spree, Eberhard. *Die verwitwete Frau Capellmeisterin Bach. Studie über die Verteilung des Nachlasses von Johann Sebastian Bach.* Altenburg, 2019.

Stauffer, George B. "Noch ein 'Handexemplar': Der Fall der Schübler-Choräle." *BJ* 101 (2015): 177–92.

Stinson, Russell. *Bach—the Orgelbüchlein.* New York, 1996.

Stockigt, Janice B. "Liturgical Music for a New Elector: Origins of Bach's 1733 Missa Revisited." In *BP*, vol. 12: *Bach and the Counterpoint of Religion*, ed. Robin A. Leaver. Urbana and Chicago, IL, 2018: 63–83.

Suchalla, Ernst (ed.). *Carl Philipp Emanuel Bach, Briefe und Dokumente: Kritische Gesamtausgabe.* 2 vols. Göttingen, 1994.

Talle, Andrew. "Nürnberg, Darmstadt, Köthen. Neuerkenntnisse zur Bach-Überlieferung in der ersten Hälfte des 18. Jahrhunderts." *BJ* 89 (2003[a]): 143–72.

——. "J. S. Bach's Keyboard Partitas and Their Early Audience." Dissertation, Harvard University, 2003[b].

——. *Beyond Bach: Music and Everyday Life in the Eighteenth Century.* Urbana and Chicago, IL, 2017.

Walther, Johann Gottfried. *Praecepta der Musicalischen Composition* (Weimar, 1708), ed. Peter Benary, Leipzig, 1955.

——. *Musicalisches Lexicon.* Leipzig, 1732.

Wolff, Christoph. *Der stile antico in der Musik Johann Sebastian Bachs. Studien zu Bachs Spätwerk.* Wiesbaden, 1968.

———. "Die Originaldrucke J. S. Bachs. Einführung und Verzeichnis." In *Die Nürnberger Drucke von J. S. und C. P. E. Bach. Katalog der Ausstellung*, ed. Willi Wörthmüller. Nürnberg, 1973: 15–20.

———. *Bach: Essays on His Life and Music*. Cambridge, MA, and London, 1991[a].

———. "'Intricate Kirchen-Stücke' und 'Dresdener Liederchen': Bach und die Instrumentalisierung der Vokalmusik." In *Johann Sebastian Bach und der süddeutsche Raum: Aspekte der Wirkungsgeschichte Bachs. Symposion München 1990*, ed. Hans-Joachim Schulze and Christoph Wolff. Regensburg, 1991[b]: 19–23.

———. *Johann Sebastian Bach: The Learned Musician*. New York, 2000 (updated edition, 2013).

———. "Miscellanea musico-biographica zu Johann Sebastian Bach." In *LBB*, 5: *Bach in Leipzig: Bach und Leipzig. Konferenzbericht Leipzig 2000*. ed. Ulrich Leisinger. Leipzig, 2002: 443–53.

———. "Johann Sebastian Bachs Regeln für den fünfstimmigen Satz." In *BJ* 90 (2004): 100-120.

———. "Sicilianos and Organ Recitals: Observations on J. S. Bach's Concertos." In *BP*, vol. 7: *J. S. Bach's Concerted Ensemble Music: The Concerto*, ed. Gregory Butler. Urbana and Chicago, IL, 2008: 9–114.

———. "Under the Spell of Opera? Johann Sebastian Bach's Oratorio Trilogy." In *BP*, vol. 8: *J. S. Bach and the Oratorio Tradition*, ed. Daniel R. Melamed. Urbana and Chicago, IL, 2011: 1–12.

———. *Johann Sebastian Bach: Messe in H-Moll*. Kassel, 2009; updated 2nd ed., 2014.

———. "Did J. S. Bach Write Organ Concertos? Apropos the Prehistory of Cantata Movements with Obbligato Organ." In *BP*, vol. 10: *Bach and the Organ*, ed. Matthew Dirst. Urbana and Chicago, IL, 2016: 60–75.

Wollny, Peter. "Traditionen des fantastischen Stils in J. S. Bachs Toccaten BWV 910–916. In: *Bach, Lübeck und die norddeutsche Musiktradition*, ed. Wolfgang Sandberger (Kassel, 2002): 245–55.

———. "Neuerkenntnisse zu einigen Kopisten der 1730er Jahre." In *BJ* 102 (2016): 63–114.

Zehnder, Jean-Claude. *Die frühen Werke Johann Sebastian Bachs. Stil, Chronologie, Satztechnik*, 2 vols. Basel, 2009.

ILLUSTRATION CREDITS

Bach-Archiv Leipzig: Frontispiece and Fig. P-1 (Bach-Museum), Figs. 1-1 (DK XIV 2/4), 2-9 (Rara II, 219-B), 4-1 and 4-3 (Rara I, 14), 4-4 (Thomana 38), 4-5 (Thomana 101), 4-6a-c (Thomana 33), 5-5, 5-6 and 5-7 (Rara II, 224-L), 8-1 (Rara II, 108/1-B), 8-7 and 8-8 (14 316b).

Bach-Archiv Leipzig, Depositum Peters: Figs. 5-1 and 5-3 (PM 1402), 5-10, 5-8 and 5-9 (PM 1403), 5-11 and 5-12 (PM 1400), 7-2 (PM 5694), 8-2 (no shelfmark), 8-9 (PM 5696), 8-10 and 8-11 (PM 5695).

Bibliothèque nationale de France, Département de la Musique, Paris: Fig. 8-6 (Ms. 17 669).

British Library, London: Fig. 7-7 (Add. MS. 35021).

Heinrich-Schütz-Haus, Weißenfels: Fig. 8-4 (Depositum D-WFk).

Kunsthalle Hamburg: Fig. 6-4.

Leipziger Stadtbibliothek, Musikbibliothek: Figs. 3-1a and 3-2 (Becker III.8.4).

Österreichische Nationalbibliothek, Musiksammlung, Wien: Fig. P-2 (MS 64. 460).

Staatsbibliothek zu Berlin—Preußischer Kulturbesitz, Musikabteilung: Figs. 2-1, 2-4a-b, 2-5, 2-6, 2-7 and 2-8 (Mus. ms. Bach P 283), 2-2 and 2-10 (Mus. ms. Bach P 415), 2-3, 2-12 and 2-13 (Mus. ms. Bach P 610), 3-3 (Mus. ms. Bach P 803), 3-4 (Mus. ms. Bach P 824), 3-7 (Mus. ms. Bach P 967), 3-8a (D-B: Mus. ms. Bach P 269), 3-8b (Mus. ms. Bach P 289), 3-9 (Am. B. 78), 3-10 and 3-11 (Mus. ms. Bach P 229), 3-12 and 7-1 (Mus. Ms. Bach P 271), 4-2 (N. Mus. Ms. 681), 5-2 (Mus. ms. Bach P 225), 6-1, 6-2, 6-3 and 6-5a-b (Mus. ms. Bach P 28), 6-6 (Mus. ms. Bach P 25), 6-7a (Mus. ms. Bach P 32), 6-7b (Mus. ms. Bach P 34), 6-7c and 6-8 (Mus. ms. Bach P 44), 7-3, 7-4 and 7-5 (Mus. ms. Bach P 234), 8-5 (Mus. ms. Bach P 200), 8-12 (Mus. 1160), 8-13 and 8-14 (Mus. ms. Bach P 180).

Staatsbibliothek zu Berlin—Preußischer Kulturbesitz, Musikabteilung: Depositum Sing-Akademie zu Berlin, Notenarchiv: Fig. 8-3 (SA 3650).

Universitätsbibliothek Johann Christian Senckenberg, Frankfurt/Main: Fig. 3-5 (Mus. Hs. 1538).

Universitäts- und Landesbibliothek, Darmstadt: Fig. 7-6 (Mus. ms. 972).

Württembergische Landesbibliothek, Stuttgart: Fig. 3-1a (Cod. mus. II, fol. 288).

Yale University, Beinecke Library, New Haven, CT: Fig. 2-11 (Music Deposit 31).

Note: Page numbers in *italics* indicate illustrations or music examples. Page numbers followed by *t* indicate tables.

BWV numbers in use prior to BWV³ are placed in parentheses.

Note: Page numbers in italics indicate illustrations or music examples. Page numbers followed by *t* indicate tables.

BWV numbers in use prior to BWV³ are placed in parentheses.

GENERAL INDEX

Note: Page numbers in *italics* indicate illustrations or music examples. Page numbers followed by *t* indicate tables.

Agricola, Johann Friedrich
  as Bach's student, 285, 335
  copies of Bach's works, 320, 360n29
  obituary and evaluation of Bach and his
    works, 8–11, 13–15, 25, 97, 336, 338
  transmission of Bach's counterpoint rules,
    286
Albinoni, Tomaso, 351n10
"all-embracing polyphony" (*Vollstimmigkeit*) in
  Bach's works, 8, 9, 25, 97–98, 338,
  340–41
Alt-Bachisches Archiv. *See* "Old Bach Archive"
Altnickol, Johann Christoph, 256
  as Bach's son-in-law, 281, 340
  copies of Bach's works, 107, *110*, *111*, 254,
    255*t*, 258, 272, 279, 281, 282*t*, 310,
    340, 360n29
Ammerbach, Elias Nicolaus, *Orgel oder Instrument Tabulatur*, 173
André, Johann, 347n10
"Andreas Bach Book," 72, 76, 351n11, 351n15,
  351n17
Anna Amalia, Princess of Prussia, 353n58
Augustus II ("the Strong"), elector of Saxony
  and king of Poland
  cantata for, 329
  death of, 233, 270–71
Augustus III, elector of Saxony and king of
  Poland, 233–34, 244*t*, 270–71,
  359n30

Bach, Anna Magdalena
  Bach's marriage to, 27, 81
  chorale cantatas given to St. Thomas
    School, 23, 151, 355n14, 355nn17–18
  Clavier-Büchleins for, 70, 77, 80–82, 85,
    144, 159–60, *160*, 163–64
  copies made by, *81*, *85*, 88–89, 95, 112, 168,
    258, 281, 282*t*

friendship with Bose's daughter Christiana
  Sybilla, 333
Bach, Carl Philipp Emanuel, 251, 258
  Bach's and Handel's fugues compared by,
    163
  catalog of father's works, 13–15, *14*, *16*,
    17–18, 23–24, 65–66
  as conductor of first performance of
    Symbolum Nicenum from Bach's
    B-minor Mass, 318, 330
  early works discarded by, 19, 250
  on father as violist, 68
  on father's habit of composing without a
    keyboard, 46
  on father's harpsichord and violin sonatas,
    BWV 1014–1016, 107
  on father's insistence on tuning keyboard
    instruments himself, 48
  on father's violin and cello unaccompanied
    solos, 89–90
  galant style embraced by, 280, 309
  items omitted in catalog of father's works,
    15, 106
  keyboard concertos, 264, 269
  Marches and Polonaises nos. 15–18 and 22,
    352n37
  obituary of father, 8–11, 13–15, 17–18, 96,
    289, 314–15, 316, 317, 339
  portrait collection assembled by, 347n9
  posthumous edition of *Art of Fugue*, 310–
    11, 315, 317
  Schmid and, 157
  *Versuch über die wahre Art das Clavier zu
    spielen*, 62, 340
  violin and harpsichord sonatas, 109, 258
Bach, Johann Ambrosius (father), 67–68
Bach, Johann Christian, 78, 351n25
  keyboard sonatas, op. 5, 269
  share of inheritance, 258

Bach, Johann Christoph (1642–1703), 14, 251
Bach, Johann Christoph (1671–1721)
    manuscript anthologies of, 72, 74, 75, 76,
        348n8, 351n16
    Pachelbel as teacher of, 121
Bach, Johann Christoph Friedrich, 107, 359n31
Bach, Johann Elias, 174
Bach, Johann Ernst, 172
Bach, Johann Heinrich, 106–7, 109
Bach, Johann Michael, 14
Bach, Johann Sebastian
    aborted harpsichord duel with Louis
        Marchand, 68
    application for St. Thomas Leipzig
        position, 27–29, 33–34, 62
    Arnstadt post, 67, 69
    arrested by Duke of Weimar, 46
    benchmark works, 20–25, 65, 338–41
    catalog of works prepared by C. P. E. Bach,
        13–15, 14, 16, 17–18, 23–24, 65–66,
        261
    as cellist, 67–68, 89
    childhood musical studies of, 69
    church cantatas' difficulty described by,
        10–11, 336
    compositional method and musical
        thinking, 334–35, 339–40
    conflicts with Leipzig officials, 241, 247,
        285, 362n5
    continuous compositional development as
        shown through opus-style works,
        24–25, 65–66, 75–76, 252, 338–41
    Cöthen post, 27, 46, 67, 83, 87, 90–91, 105,
        116, 118
    court title bestowed on, 167, 271, 285, 325,
        360n33
    culling of musical output, 250–53
    deep religiosity of, 248, 283
    demands on musicians, 10–11, 167, 182–83,
        336–38
    early works discarded by, 250
    elaboration principle in compositional
        method, 287–90
    estate of, 14–15, 18–19, 65–66, 106–7, 151,
        224, 258, 348n2
    experiments with temperament, 44–45
    fascination with canonic technique,
        298
    fugal writing and counterpoint identified
        with, 284–87, 291, 338–40
    funeral of, 348n2

    Fux's pedagogical method disapproved of
        by, 285–86
    handwriting of, 349n7
    improvisations of, 119
    insistence on tuning keyboard instruments
        himself, 48
    instrument collection of, 96
    Italianized name preferred by, 72
    lack of university education, 28
    legacy of, 19, 25, 151, 317, 330–32
    as Leipzig Collegium Musicum musical
        director, 67, 105–6, 116, 153, 233–
        34, 238, 249, 266, 268
    Leipzig compositional output, 249
    Leipzig housing disruptions, 249–50
    Leipzig post, 67, 90, 105–6, 118, 193–95,
        232, 247, 248, 270–72, 285, 331–32
    Leipzig Thomascantor contractual
        obligations, 232
    lost works and manuscripts of, 19, 65–66,
        89, 99, 250, 257–58
    melodies of, 8, 10–11, 336
    membership in Corresponding Society of
        Musical Sciences, 3–4, 7
    Mühlhausen post, 67
    musical experiments of, 86
    musical priorities and trajectory of, 24–25,
        65–67, 86, 98, 103–4, 116, 148–49,
        178, 183, 190–91, 192, 247–48, 252–
        53, 282–83, 285–90, 291, 316–17,
        331–32, 334–41
    music library of, 15, 20, 35, 76–77, 157,
        173–74, 354n6, 354n10
    on nature of music, 6
    obituary of and evaluation of works by
        C. P. E. Bach and Agricola, 3, 8–11,
        13–15, 17–18, 69, 96, 289, 314–15,
        316, 317, 339, 348n5
    as organ and keyboard virtuoso, 27–28,
        49–50, 63, 67, 68–69, 86, 100, 122,
        153–54, 173, 265–66
    as organ examiner, 27
    portrait of, iv, 1–2, 2, 4, 7, 12, 299, 347n3
    possible culling of compositions, 19
    public image of, 7–8
    recitals and concerts of, 68–69, 112,
        265–66
    relationship between transcriptions and
        parody procedures, 290
    reluctance to write about his life and work, 1
    rules on five-part composition, 285–86, 335